RACE IN IRISH LITERATURE
AND CULTURE

Race in Irish Literature and Culture provides an in-depth understanding of intersections between Irish literature, culture, and questions of race, racialization, and racism. Covering a vast historical terrain from the sixteenth century to the present, it spotlights the work of canonical, understudied, and contemporary authors in Ireland, Northern Ireland, and among diasporic Irish communities. By focusing on questions related to Black Irish identities, Irish whiteness, Irish racial sciences, postcolonial solidarities, and decolonial strategies to address racialization, the volume moves beyond the familiar frameworks of British/Irish and Catholic/Protestant binarisms and demonstrates methods for Irish Studies scholars to engage with the question of race from a contemporary perspective.

MALCOLM SEN is Associate Professor in the Department of English at University of Massachusetts Amherst. His research focuses on questions of sovereignty, migration, and race as they emerge in climate change discourse and contemporary culture. He is the editor of *A History of Irish Literature and the Environment* (Cambridge University Press, 2022).

JULIE MCCORMICK WENG is Assistant Professor of English at Texas State University. She coedited *Science, Technology, and Irish Modernism* (2019) and currently serves as Secretary of the American Conference for Irish Studies.

CAMBRIDGE THEMES IN IRISH LITERATURE
AND CULTURE

Series Editor
Ronan McDonald, The University of Melbourne

By putting an idea, topic, or theme at the forefront of each volume, this series opens fresh perspectives on past and present, affording a rich conceptual exploration of the relation between literature, culture, and history.

Titles in the Series

Transnationalism in Irish Literature and Culture
Edited by Cóilín Parsons, Georgetown University

Religion in Irish Literature and Culture
Edited by Willa Murphy, Ulster University, and Christopher Murray, Monash University

The Revival in Irish Literature and Culture
Edited by Gregory Castle, Arizona State University

Technology in Irish Literature and Culture
Edited by Margaret Kelleher, University College Dublin, and James O'Sullivan, University College Cork

RACE IN IRISH LITERATURE AND CULTURE

EDITED BY

MALCOLM SEN

University of Massachusetts Amherst

JULIE McCORMICK WENG

Texas State University

CAMBRIDGE
UNIVERSITY PRESS

Shaftesbury Road, Cambridge CB2 8EA, United Kingdom

One Liberty Plaza, 20th Floor, New York, NY 10006, USA

477 Williamstown Road, Port Melbourne, VIC 3207, Australia

314–321, 3rd Floor, Plot 3, Splendor Forum, Jasola District Centre, New Delhi – 110025, India

103 Penang Road, #05–06/07, Visioncrest Commercial, Singapore 238467

Cambridge University Press is part of Cambridge University Press & Assessment, a department of the University of Cambridge.

We share the University's mission to contribute to society through the pursuit of education, learning and research at the highest international levels of excellence.

www.cambridge.org
Information on this title: www.cambridge.org/9781316513118

DOI: 10.1017/9781009071802

First published 2024

A catalogue record for this publication is available from the British Library

A Cataloging-in-Publication data record for this book is available from the Library of Congress

ISBN 978-1-316-51311-8 Hardback

To children of the Irish, Indian, and Taiwanese diasporas—
Anoushka Róisín O'Callaghan Sen
Afrah Saoirse O'Callaghan Sen
Ashlyn 家安 Weng
Aidan 家瀚 Weng

Contents

List of Figures   *page* ix
List of Contributors   x
Editors' Note   xvi

Introduction: The Racial Imaginaries of Irish Literature
and Culture   1
Malcolm Sen and Julie McCormick Weng

1 "Our Heroic Ancestors": Antiquarian Literature and
   the Discourse of Racial Heritage   25
   Clare O'Halloran

2 Racializing Irish Historical Consciousness   42
   Guy Beiner and Oded Y. Steinberg

3 Race, Minstrelsy, and the Irish Stage: The Origins
   and Afterlives of Dion Boucicault's *The Octoroon*   59
   Patrick Lonergan

4 Race and Irish Women's Novels in the Long
   Nineteenth Century   81
   Matthew L. Reznicek

5 Blackface Minstrelsy, Irish Modernism, and the Histories
   of Irish Whiteness   103
   John Brannigan

6 Joyce's Racial Comedy   121
   Vicki Mahaffey

7 W. B. Yeats, the Irish Free State, and the Rhetoric
   of Race Suicide   143
   Julie McCormick Weng

8   "Ulster's White Negroes": Rhetoric of Race at the Start
    of the Troubles   172
    Simon Prince

9   Learning from Walcott: Heaney's Black and Green Atlantic   190
    Richard Rankin Russell

10 Race, Irishness, and Popular Culture in Australia   205
    Dianne Hall

11 White Nationalism and Irish America: A Cultural
    History Told through Works by James T. Farrell
    and Eugene O'Neill   225
    Peter D. O'Neill

12 Diasporic Afterlives: An Irish–Jewish Archive
    for Ruth Gilligan's *Nine Folds Make a Paper Swan*   242
    Stephen Watt

13 "Dubh": Poets of Color and New Irish Poetry   259
    Ailbhe McDaid

14 Split Selves and Double Consciousness in
    Recent Irish Fiction   281
    Oona Frawley

15 Race, Place, and the Grounds of Irish Geopolitics   302
    Shirley Lau Wong

Select Bibliography   318
Index   348

Figures

3.1   Theatre Royal Playbill   *page* 66
3.2   *Othello*   71
3.3   *The Emperor Jones*   72
3.4   Samuel L. Jackson, Elain Graham, and S. Epatha Merkerson   74
10.1 "Some Misapprehension"   206
10.2 "The Wearing of Green"   211
10.3 "Quite Easy"   214
10.4 "The Child of Nature"   216
13.1 Dagogo Hart's *Uruemu's Home*   267
13.2 Felispeaks's *DUBH*   269

Contributors

GUY BEINER is Sullivan Chair of Irish Studies at Boston College and Professor of Modern History at Ben-Gurion University of the Negev. He specializes in the study of remembering and forgetting in the late modern period. His prize-winning books include *Remembering the Year of the French: Irish Folk History and Social Memory* (Wisconsin University Press, 2007) and *Forgetful Remembrance: Social Forgetting and Vernacular Historiography of a Rebellion in Ulster* (Oxford University Press, 2018), and he is the editor of *Pandemic Re-Awakenings: The Forgotten and Unforgotten "Spanish" Flu of 1918–1919* (Oxford University Press, 2021).

JOHN BRANNIGAN is Professor of English and Head of the School of English, Drama and Film at University College Dublin. He is the author of several books on modern Irish and British literatures, including *Race in Modern Irish Literature and Culture* (Edinburgh University Press, 2009) and *Archipelagic Modernism: Literature in the Irish and British Isles* (Edinburgh University Press, 2014). His most recent publications include an Oxford World's Classics edition of George Orwell's *Down and Out in Paris and London* (Oxford University Press, 2021) and a book chapter on the work of Hannah Berman, published in *Irish Modernisms: Gaps, Conjectures, Possibilities* (Bloomsbury, 2022), edited by Paul Fagan, John Greaney, and Tamara Radak.

OONA FRAWLEY was born in New York to Irish actor parents and is Associate Professor of English at Maynooth University. She is the author of *Irish Pastoral: Nostalgia in Twentieth-Century Irish Literature.* She is the editor of, among other works, the first three volumes of the *Memory Ireland project,* and, with Katherine O'Callaghan, coeditor of the fourth and final volume, *James Joyce and Cultural Memory.* Her most recent book publication is *Women and the Decade of Commemorations* (Indiana University Press, 2021). Her first novel, *Flight,* was published in 2014 by

Tramp Press, and her creative work has appeared most recently in the journal *Banshee*. She has just completed a new book on extractivist narratives in Australian literature.

DIANNE HALL is Professor of History and Deputy Director of the Institute for Sustainable Industries and Liveable Cities at Victoria University, Melbourne, and she has previously worked at the University of Melbourne and Queen's University Belfast. She has written extensively on the Irish diaspora, particularly in Australia. She is the author with Lindsay Proudfoot of *Imperial Spaces: Placing the Irish and Scots in Colonial Australia* (Oxford University Press, 2011) and with Elizabeth Malcolm of *A New History of the Irish in Australia* (Cork University Press, 2019). She is currently researching women and anti-Catholicism in the Irish diaspora as well as gender and violence in Irish history. She is currently one of the editors of the *Australasian Journal of Irish Studies* and is on the executive of the Irish Studies Association of Australia and New Zealand.

PATRICK LONERGAN is Professor of Drama and Theatre Studies at the National University of Ireland, Galway, and a member of the Royal Irish Academy. He has edited or written twelve books on Irish drama and theatre, including *Theatre and Globalization* (Palgrave Macmillan, 2008), which won the United Kingdom's Theatre Book Prize in 2008, *The Theatre and Films of Martin McDonagh* (Methuen Drama, 2012), *Theatre and Social Media* (Springer, 2015), and *Irish Drama and Theatre since 1950* (Bloomsbury, 2019). For Methuen Drama, he is a coeditor of the "Critical Companions" series, which has published new books on such dramatists as Friel, Murphy, Pinter, Beckett, Churchill, Hwang, and Ruhl, and on topics including disability theatre, verse drama, and the British and American stage musical. He has lectured widely on Irish drama and literature internationally, including recently in Princeton, Florence, Florianópolis, Wrocław, and Tokyo. He was the 2019 Burns Visiting Fellow for Irish Studies at Boston College.

VICKI MAHAFFEY is the Clayton and Thelma Kirkpatrick Professor of English at the University of Illinois at Urbana-Champaign. She has previously served in a wide range of institutions, including Pennsylvania State University, Princeton University, Northwestern University, and several others. She also held the chair of Modern Literature in the University of York. She has received several awards, including the Ira Abrams Award for Distinguished Teaching and the Lindback Award for Distinguished Teaching, and a Guggenheim Fellowship. She is a member of the Board of Trustees of the International James Joyce Foundation. Her research agenda spans gender and women's studies, James Joyce studies, modernism, and Irish and British literatures. She is the author of several key texts on Joyce, including *Reauthorizing Joyce* (Cambridge University Press, 1988), *States of Desire: Wilde, Yeats, Joyce, and the Irish Experiment* (Oxford University Press, 1998), and *Modernist Literature: Challenging Fictions* (Wiley-Blackwell, 2007). She is the editor of *Collaborative Dubliners* (Syracuse University Press, 2012) and the coeditor of *The Edinburgh Companion to Irish Modernism* (Edinburgh University Press, 2021) and *Joycean Possibilities: A Margot Norris Legacy* (Anthem Press, 2022).

AILBHE MCDAID is a lecturer in literature in the Department of English Language and Literature at Mary Immaculate College, University of Limerick. Her research interests include migration, conflict, and gender in twentieth- and twenty-first-century Irish writing. Her first book is entitled *The Poetics of Migration in Contemporary Irish Poetry* (Springer, 2017), and she is currently completing her second monograph, *Domestic Disruptions: Women, Literature and Conflict*. Her research has been funded by the Irish Research Council, the British Academy, and the Royal Irish Academy.

CLARE O'HALLORAN lectured in the School of History in University College Cork until her retirement in 2021. She is the author of numerous studies of Irish antiquarianism in the long eighteenth century, including "From Antiquarian Text to Fiction's Subtext: The Extended Afterlife of Spenser's *View of the Present State of Ireland*," in *Spenser Studies: A Renaissance Poetry Annual* Volume 31/32 (2018). Her books include *Partition and the Limits of Irish Nationalism: An Ideology under Stress* (Gill and Macmillan, 1987) and *Golden Ages and Barbarous Nations: Antiquarian Debate and Cultural Politics in Ireland, C. 1750-1800* (Cork University Press, 2004).

PETER D. O'NEILL is Associate Professor in the Department of Comparative Literature and Intercultural Studies at the University of Georgia. He has served as Research Fellow at the university's Willson Center for Humanities and Arts and as Lilly Teaching Fellow. With David Lloyd, he coedited an essay collection, *The Black and Green Atlantic: Crosscurrents of the African and Irish Diasporas* (Palgrave Macmillan, 2009). His monograph, *Famine Irish and the American Racial State* (Routledge,

2017), received an Honorable Mention in 2018 for the Donald Murphy Prize for Distinguished First Books. He has just finished coediting an essay collection, *The Famine Diaspora and Irish-American Women's Writing* (Palgrave Macmillan, 2023). An author of over a dozen other peer-reviewed journal articles and book chapters, he is currently at work on a biography of Irish American famine author Dillon O'Brien.

SIMON PRINCE is Senior Lecturer in Modern History at Canterbury Christ Church University. His research focuses on the start of the Northern Irish Troubles. He has published two books: *Northern Ireland's '68: Civil Rights, Global Revolt and the Origins of the Troubles* (Irish Academic Press, 2007) and *Belfast and Derry in Revolt: A New History of the Start of the Troubles* (Irish Academic Press, 2011). His articles have been published in, among other places, the *Historical Journal*, the *Journal of British Studies*, *Irish Political Studies*, and *Contemporary British History*.

MATTHEW L. REZNICEK is Associate Professor of Medical Humanities at the University of Minnesota; he previously taught at Creighton University in the College of Arts and Sciences and the School of Medicine. He has published widely on nineteenth-century Irish women writers; this includes his first monograph, *The European Metropolis: Paris and Nineteenth-Century Irish Women Novelists* (Clemson University Press, 2017). He is the coeditor of two forthcoming manuscripts, *The Irish Bildungsroman, 1800-Present* (Syracuse University Press) and *The Corpse in Irish Literature* (Liverpool University Press). He currently serves as President of the American Conference for Irish Studies.

RICHARD RANKIN RUSSELL is a native of West Tennessee and currently serves as Professor of English and Graduate Program Director at Baylor University in Texas. He has published nine books on writers from Ireland and Northern Ireland, and his most recent books include a revised and expanded edition of his monograph *Modernity, Community, and Place in Brian Friel's Drama* (Syracuse University Press, 2022) and *James Joyce and Samaritan Hospitality: Postcritical and Postsecular Reading in Dubliners and Ulysses* (Edinburgh University Press, 2022). He is currently putting together an edited volume on Irish writers for *Christianity and Literature* and revising a study of James Joyce and Protestantism.

MALCOLM SEN is Associate Professor at University of Massachusetts Amherst and directs the Environmental Humanities specialization offered by the Department of English. His research focuses on questions of sovereignty, migration, and race as they emerge in climate change discourse. His literary archive spans global anglophone, Indian, and Irish literatures. He is the coeditor of *Postcolonial Studies and Challenges of the New Millennium* (Routledge, 2016). He is the editor of *The History of Irish Literature and the Environment* (Cambridge University Press, 2022). His monograph *Unnatural Disasters: Irish Literature, Climate Change and Sovereignty* is currently under review. His recent articles include "An Ordinary Crisis: Covid-19 and Irish Studies," in *A Handbook of Irish Studies* (Routledge, 2021); "Sovereignty at the Margins: The Oceanic Future of the Subaltern," in *Representing Poverty and Precarity in a Postcolonial World* (Brill, 2022); and "Joyce and Race in the Twenty-First Century," in *The New Joyce Studies: Twenty-First Century Critical Revisions* (Cambridge University Press, 2022).

ODED Y. STEINBERG is Assistant Professor in the Departments of International Relations and European Studies (European Forum) at the Hebrew University of Jerusalem. His publications have explored various aspects of British and central European intellectual, cultural, and diplomatic history. His book *Race, Nation, History: Anglo-German Thought in the Victorian Era* (University of Pennsylvania Press, 2019) examines the way a series of nineteenth-century scholars in England and Germany first constructed and then questioned the periodization of history into ancient, medieval, and modern eras, shaping the way we continue to think about the past and present of Western civilization. The book traces the deep connections between the idea of epochal periodization and concepts of race and nation that were prevalent at the time – especially the role that Germanic or Teutonic tribes were assumed to play in the unfolding of Western history.

STEPHEN WATT is Provost Professor Emeritus of English and former Associate Dean of the School of Art, Architecture + Design at Indiana University, Bloomington. His books include *Bernard Shaw's Fiction, Material Psychology, and Affect: Shaw, Freud, Simmel* (Palgrave, 2018), *"Something Dreadful and Grand": American Literature and the Irish-Jewish Unconscious* (Oxford University Press, 2015), and *Beckett and Contemporary Irish Writing* (Cambridge University Press, 2009). His volume *The Worlds of John Wick: The Year's Work at the Continental Hotel*, coedited with Caitlin G. Watt, was published in 2022 by Indiana University Press.

JULIE MCCORMICK WENG is Assistant Professor of English at Texas State University, where she teaches courses in British and global anglophone literatures. She coedited *Science, Technology, and Irish Modernism* (Syracuse University Press, 2019) with Kathryn Conrad and Cóilín Parsons and has published about Irish modernism in a range of academic journals, as well as in a recent collection, *Ethical Crossroads in Literary Modernism* (Clemson University Press, 2023), edited by Katherine Ebury, Bridget English, and Matthew Fogarty. She currently serves as Secretary of the American Conference for Irish Studies.

SHIRLEY LAU WONG is Assistant Professor of English at the US Naval Academy, where she teaches and researches in twentieth- and twenty-first-century British and global anglophone literatures. She is completing a book entitled *Poetics of the Local: Globalization, Place, and Contemporary Irish Poetry* (SUNY Press, 2023), as well as coediting a special issue on "The Detail, Revisited" (forthcoming from the *Modern Language Quarterly*). Her other work has been published in *The Cambridge Journal of Postcolonial Literary Inquiry*, *The Global South*, and *Interventions*.

Editors' Note

We recognize that discourses and terms related to questions of race, and its sinister cultural cousins, racism and racialization, are historically provisional: "race is a historical contingency, not a state of nature."[1] Perhaps more so than most, the discursive terrain of these politically weighted terms is especially fickle, not least because it is currently (and correctly) undergoing radical evaluation and evolution. We have made stylistic and other choices in the volume to best represent the decolonial and justice-oriented impetuses from which this book stems. These choices are conditioned by our historical moment and will undoubtedly be reappraised in future analyses. We especially hope that this book will play its small part in such ongoing discussions surrounding race, racism, and racialization, which are pivotal concerns in Irish Studies.

Unless represented in quoted sources, we have chosen to eschew the acronym "BAME" (Black, Asian, and minority ethnic), which has come under scrutiny in Ireland and in the United Kingdom in recent years.[2] We have also elected to represent racist epithets that are included in original quotations or titles of works through their first letter followed by a star symbol ("*") for omitted letters. Importantly, we are alert to the vagaries and ramifications of color terms (such as "black" and "white") and terms that might harmlessly signal geographical origins but misrepresent questions of cultural authenticity and more problematically suggest ideologies of racial purity (such as "native" and "indigenous"). We opted to capitalize the "B" in the word "black" as a designation for people of African descent but not the "w" in "white" as a description for people of Euro-American descent. We agree with Kwame Anthony Appiah that "[a] good reason to capitalize the racial designation 'black' … is precisely that black … is not a natural category but a social one – a collective identity – with a particular history."[3] Appiah's rationale might also suggest that we capitalize the "w" in "white," which we have chosen not to do. Here we follow the practice of most media outlets and established custom in contemporary scholarly writing. Aware of the fundamentalist and fascist impulses of recent geo-politics, we agree with the sentiment of *The Columbia Journalism Review*, which notes: "White carries a different set of meanings; capitalizing the word in this context risks following the lead of white supremacists."[4] We also opt for the word "indigenous" over the word "native" given the latter's colonial complicity with racialization and racism.

Notes

1 Nina Jablonski and George Chaplin, "We Need to Unpack the Word 'Race' and Find New Language," *The Conversation*, August 2, 2020, https://theconversation.com/we-need-to-unpack-the-word-race-and-find-new-language-138379.

2 See Alex Mistlin, "So the Term BAME Has Had Its Day. But What Should Replace It?," *The Guardian*, April 8, 2021, www.theguardian.com/commentisfree/2021/apr/08/bame-britain-ethnic-minorities-acronym.

3 Kwame Anthony Appiah, "The Case for Capitalizing the *B* in Black," *The Atlantic*, June 18, 2020, www.theatlantic.com/ideas/archive/2020/06/time-to-capitalize-blackand-white/613159/.

4 Mike Laws, "Why We Capitalize 'Black' (and Not 'White')," *Columbia Journalism Review*, June 16, 2020, www.cjr.org/analysis/capital-b-black-styleguide.php.

Introduction
The Racial Imaginaries of Irish Literature and Culture
Malcolm Sen and Julie McCormick Weng

The Irish are neither negroes nor mongrels nor castaways...[1]

Douglas Hyde

The Color Line

In a speech delivered to an American audience at the University of California in 1906, Douglas Hyde made a striking comparison between Irish people, enslaved Africans, and other dispossessed subjects of empire. Emphatically criticizing the British colonial system of education and its dire effects in Ireland, a country that once took delight in intellectual debate, in the Irish language, and in literature, Hyde raised the possibility that Irish people had become like "negroes or castaways" who were "absolutely ignorant of their own past." Analogies are always tricky, but it is notable that Hyde's rhetoric was only meant to highlight the absurdity of this comparison. The Irish stood apart from enslaved peoples and hapless migrants, as Hyde noted: "On the contrary, they boast perhaps the broadest race heritage in Europe. They are the descendants of a stock to which almost every country in western Europe owes and frankly acknowledges that it owes a debt of lasting gratitude." Hyde claimed that unlike enslaved people, who had forgotten (or were made to forget) their history, the Irish were not "a race of nobodies or of slaves," a "people without a past," or a people conditioned through imperial domination to forget their precolonial heritage. He argued that through a revival of the Irish language, Irish people could access and reclaim their "sacred traditions and national heritage."[2]

Hyde's rhetoric appears to unwittingly, and certainly problematically, replay the very violence of imperial discourse that he set out to critique. The comparison of the Irish with the enslaved and the "castaway" only rang true if the audience did not question the dehumanization of the disenfranchised; an important aspect of this dehumanization relied on the normalization of the claim that such peoples were without culture

I

and history before colonial encounters. Historically, this was, of course, not the first instance of such comparisons between the Irish subject of empire and the African subject of the enslavement trade. More than half a century before Hyde, Thomas Carlyle had infamously compared Britain's Caribbean colonies and plantations to Ireland, calling them a "Negro Ireland" and a "Black Ireland" in his essay, "Occasional Discourse on The Negro Question."[3] Writing to challenge the antislavery movement Carlyle, among other assertions, rationalized the enslavement trade in the same vein that colonization was politically, morally, financially, and culturally normalized in the nineteenth century.

Such comparisons are not simply relegated to the halls of history. Discourses that compared and contrasted Irishness with blackness, such as the ones above, appear in other Irish media and literature. More recent examples of such analogies, not least the memorable dialogue from Roddy Doyle's 1987 novel, *The Commitments*, also speak to the continuation of this theme. In a particularly memorable scene, Jimmy Rabbitte insists that his newly formed band play soul music in an effort to imitate "the workin' man's rhythm." He holds that "music should be abou' where you're from an' the sort o' people yeh come from," asking his bandmates, "are yis proud of" being "workin' class[?]" Quoting James Brown's 1968 hit song, "Say It Loud—I'm Black and I'm Proud," he brings Brown's lyrics into an Irish context, imploring his mates to repeat them as their own.[4] At their confusion, he elaborates further (in lines more succinctly put in the book's film adaptation): "Do you not get it lads? The Irish are the blacks of Europe. And Dubliners are the blacks of Ireland. And the Northside Dubliners are the blacks of Dublin. So say it once, say it loud. I'm black and I'm proud."[5] The imitation is not necessarily to demonstrate solidarity with Black history but to express pride in Irishness amid the despairing economic and social conditions of their North Dublin community. Of course, it is also a form of appropriation intended to draw on the success of Black American artistry in the hope that it might pave a career for their newly formed musical band. *The Commitments* was produced at a time when Ireland was experiencing the aftershocks of a severe recession from the previous decade; by invoking blackness, the analogy reflected the scale of economic stagnation in the country and also produced a mirthful response among the band members because of the anomaly of that comparison.

The examples from Hyde, Carlyle, and Doyle deploy racial comparisons that must be read through their unique contexts. Following Nels Irvin Painter, Malcolm Sen has noted that "Race is 'an idea, not a fact' but it is centrally located in the entangled precarities of the present. As an idea, its deployment in cultural, political, and literary discourse is … contingent on historical context."[6] It is important to historicize, especially in the Irish context, where the question of the racial affiliations or identities associated with Irishness is not a uniform construct but dramatically mutates over a long durée: in Gaelic annals, in antiquarian and orientalist narratives, in colonial treatises, in nationalist discourses, in modernist and postmodernist assessments, and in postcolonial retellings. What comes across profoundly in these various contexts is the fact that race as an idea or an ideology persists transhistorically; the fact that it actively and acutely shapes Irish culture and politics is not in question. The specter of race can be persuasively and intentionally voiced (as in Hyde's comments above), or it may arise in tellingly silent ways. The latter is especially dominant in cultural artefacts.

In his important book, *Race in Modern Irish Literature and Culture*, John Brannigan has deftly paid attention to the tobacco industry's presence in narratives of nationalist triumph and industrial modernity at the time of the signing of the Anglo-Irish Treaty in 1922. Focusing on an advertisement for "Golden Blush" cigarettes on the front page of the *Irish Independent* on January 4, 1922, Brannigan notes:

> In contrast to the well-worn themes of colonial oppression, mass emigration, and economic underdevelopment, the sequential illustrations bring us from the raw materials in plantation fields in Virginia, controlled by the Irish manufacturers, through to the cathedral-like cigarette factory in Dublin, and on to the happy male consumers who symbolise an Irish public, mature and contented with its own modernity.[7]

The illustrations were aligned with the cultural nationalist narratives of the Celtic Revival – the advertisement was "embroidered with a Celtic interlace design" and announced "the arrival of a specifically Irish industrial modernity."[8] What was silent but deeply imbricated with this story was that of colonial and capitalist exploitation of Black labor by the tobacco industry in North America. In the advertisement, Irish people are "invited to identify not with the black plantation workers, who are invisible and seemingly irrelevant, but with the white planter."[9] The analysis highlights the cultural forms and international contours that the concept of race acquires in Irish history. It also poignantly traces how the system of enslavement in North America is embroiled in the conceptualization and actualization of Irish political subjectivity.

Race might be a fictional construct, but its deployment is not restricted to the visual rhetoric of advertisements and the literary; its presence is as potent in the material world as it is in practices, in configuring ideologies and infrastructures. The racial undertones surrounding the birth of the Irish State (outside of the Catholic-Protestant divide and other dominant binaries, as seen below) are also notable in contemporary conceptualizations of Irishness. Sarah L. Townsend has, for example, directed our attention to how the carceral apparatus of the Direct Provision system is braided with quintessential signifiers of Irishness, such as the products of the company Avoca: "The company, which began as a modest producer and purveyor of woven textiles, has transformed itself since the mid-1980s into a retail empire and internationally recognized lifestyle brand."[10] Such branding of Irish-made specialty products has a loyal consumer base in Ireland and the Irish expatriate community. However, Townsend points out that Avoca was not only sold to an American company in 2015 but to the infamous Philadelphia-based Aramark, a corporation known for its interests in incarceration regimes in the U.S.

> In addition to Aramark's reputation for serving low-quality food on a mass scale, the corporation has been criticized for its controversial contracts with prisons and immigrant-detention facilities in the United States and with the widely denounced direct-provision system for asylum seekers in Ireland. Although the business profiles of Aramark and Avoca appear antithetical, the acquisition makes perfect sense from an ideological and branding perspective.[11]

Townsend demonstrates how "the anodyne world of Avoca serves as a smokescreen for the profitable systems of incarceration in which Aramark participates." Avoca "emphasizes the Irish provenance of its goods and the historical role that it has played in the Irish handicrafts tradition," while its flagship location in Avoca Village in County Wicklow "evokes the aura of Irish authenticity that distinguishes the brand from large retail chains."[12] Its ownership by Aramark, therefore, troublingly points to the pernicious racial regimes that hide under seemingly harmless signifiers of Irish culture.

Irishness, and its nostalgic associations with both whiteness and pastoral rurality, have been coopted by Irish America for quite some time. Celtic-themed symbols, the Irish language, and sean-nós songs have periodically found purchase among white nationalists in the U.S., but as ethnomusicologist Sean Williams writes, that usage was "fairly diffuse" until the "public rise of white nationalism" during the 2016 U.S. Presidential election.[13] Just as the recent story of Avoca reveals an underbelly of a violent carceral regime in the U.S. (and its associated violence against people of color), the demonstrably Irish associations with the rise of Trumpian racist nationalism expose a deeply disturbing characteristic of exported Irishness. President Trump famously remarked to the then Taoiseach Leo Varadkar: "We have millions of Irish, and I think I know most of them, because they're my friends."[14] This was not just bluster, however. The curation of a Trumpian Irish coalition was notable for the cooptation of cultural signifiers of Irishness for racist politics. *The New York Times* reported that his campaign had instructed supporters to text the word "SHAMROCK" to join a coalition called Irish Americans for Trump. In the politics of things, the "Trump Luck of the Irish" whiskey glasses (selling for $30 a pair) claimed two Irish stereotypes – luck and alcohol – to bolster a brazen politics of disenfranchisement that would define the second decade of the twenty-first century.[15]

This celebration of Irishness by Trump and his allies, and the peddling of appropriated Irish emblems and other Celtic imagery, was intended to draw the support and solidarity of white Americans and to appeal to those with white nationalist impulses. Such racialized invocations of Irishness (and their accompanying harmful effects) became so prominent in circulation at the time that it prompted Harvard University's Department of Celtic Languages and Literatures to issue the following statement in 2020:

> There is no essential genetic "Celtic" identity, nor is any ethnicity or group of ethnicities entitled to a privileged position within the field. Certain symbols associated with medieval Ireland and loosely identified as "Celtic" have been appropriated by groups asserting the supremacy of persons with white skin. We repudiate this appropriation in the strongest possible terms. We are committed in our teaching and research to dispelling the notion that responsible Celtic studies can in any way privilege or essentialize whiteness.[16]

As Williams adroitly demonstrates, the fact that the Center for Irish Studies at Villanova University released a similar "Anti-Racism Statement," in addition to another from the Celtic Studies Association of North America, speaks to the prevalence of the appropriation and the need felt by Irish cultural institutions and learning centers to distinguish themselves and their work.[17] Laid bare is the fear that their mission to promote the study and engagement of Irish culture was becoming associated with the promotion of racist politics. These public disclaimers underscore the profound implications the whiskey glasses and other examples above have for scholars of Irish Studies. They show that "exploring what it means to be white through the appropriation of Irish elements of culture necessarily places Irish Studies scholars in proximity with those who would use these elements against a perceived Other."[18] What Williams articulates is the very urgency for Irish Studies scholars to offer awareness, understanding, and when necessary, correctives (as in the Harvard announcement), not just in press releases and public statements, but in the classroom and in academic research, to give judicious accounts of the myriad roles that race and racism have played in Irish literature and culture of the past and present; in other words, to come together and represent these themes in a book like this one.

The political moment of the Trump presidency clarified to no small degree the diverse and discordant ways in which racialization narratives determine the political currency of Irishness in the contemporary world. Against this American offshoot of instrumentalized Irishness, it should be noted that Trump's unexpected victory also entailed a swift and critical response by some Irish politicians. In a speech that went viral in November 2016, Senator Aodhán Ó Ríordáin, challenging Trumpian rhetoric against people of color, famously proclaimed that "We were the Muslims, once," and "We were the Mexicans."[19] The question of race and Irishness, it seems, is a challenging one. The Senator's comments show how Ireland's postcolonial solidarities with disenfranchised peoples in the global South, both historically (in the case of Irish and Indian anticolonial struggles) and in contemporary culture, demonstrate an opposing narrative to the cooptation of Irish whiteness by neoliberal fundamentalism.

Despite the caveat of such historicization and contextualization, it requires no stretch of the imagination to note that the cultural fiction underlying the concept of race has transhistorically produced real-world political effects. Although race is an idea, racism is very much a fact. Postcolonial theory has long argued that many of the foundational documents of modern democracies, such as John Locke's theorizations of "political and economic rights to property and commerce were also notoriously employed to justify the slave trade and the ownership of slaves"; similarly, the concept of the European birthplace of political modernity itself was a product of colonial imaginaries.[20] Irish history has an intimate relationship with the growth of the dominant geopolitical framework of governance of our time, the (neo)liberal democracy, and numerous Irish Studies scholars have witnessed and assessed the ways in which Irishness and its allegedly dark, simianized hue served as a counterfoil to colonial constructions of political modernity.[21] However, as is clear from the opening remarks of this book, we are alert to the contemporary reworkings of Irishness in which the politics of color reemerge in contexts that vex the Irishness-blackness binary, in which, just as in history, complexion and color bear a close and dangerous proximity to culture and citizenship. In this landscape, "the hegemony of a white

Irish vantage point," as Anne Mulhall notes, produces the homegrown equivalent of a "global apartheid line."[22]

Mulhall's context is the Direct Provision system used to detain asylum seekers in contemporary Ireland. Its carceral configuration has not only been squarely focused upon by Irish Studies scholars in recent years, but it has also gained international notoriety. The renowned journalist Masha Gessen described it in the following words, "Ireland has created a system that boils the process of seeking asylum down to its essence: waiting." *The New Yorker*'s headline for that article captured the careless cruelty against some of the most vulnerable guests of the land of a thousand welcomes: "Ireland's Strange, Cruel System for Asylum Seekers."[23] The discrepancy between the racialized and oppressed Irish of the nineteenth and twentieth centuries, and the practices and policies of a financialized, neoliberal Ireland, is stark. Ronit Lentin's assessment is noteworthy here:

> ...theorizing Irishness as white privilege has been hampered by legacies of the racialization of Irishness as structured by anti-Irish racism in Ireland and abroad. However, Ireland's new position as topping the Globalization Index, its status symbol as the locus of "cool" culture, and its privileged position within an ever-expanding European Community calls for the understanding of Irishness as white supremacy. Whiteness works best when it remains a hidden part of the normative social order.[24]

Phenotypical questions are never far from political ones. Color, for example, was very much on the minds of Irish voters in 2004, when they overwhelmingly passed the Citizenship Referendum and limited the constitutional right to Irish citizenship of individuals born on the island of Ireland solely to the children of Irish citizens. Empirical studies have shown that the dominant motifs used to curate a "Yes" vote for that referendum relied on terms such as "abuse of Irish citizenship," "asylum abuse," "citizenship loophole," and "maternity tourists," which were directed against people of color.[25]

Almost two decades later, the question of race and skin color has once again been raised in the context of Irish citizenship, but in a wholly different cultural milieu and with a radically different consensus. This story emerges from the arc of recent legislative cornerstones in post-Celtic Tiger Ireland. Landmark decisions, such as the passing of the Marriage Equality Act in 2015 (which grants legal permission for two people to marry without distinction of their gender) and the highly successful overturning of the Eighth Amendment of the Irish Constitution in 2018 (which prohibited abortion, even in cases of incest and rape), define the trend of secularization that has washed over the post-financial-collapse Zeitgeist in contemporary Ireland. The secularization has gone hand-in-hand with an increased awareness of the racist implications of the Citizenship Referendum and the real-world consequences of the avowed politics of color blindness behind which Irish cultural responses to immigration once hid. What is especially hopeful is that the catalytic convergence of land-mark achievements in LGBTQ+ and women's rights may well produce an Ireland that is "intent on bucking the illiberal tide in the West," as *The New York Times* recently put it.[26] There is a significant racial component to this liberalism that simultaneously emerges with Ireland's seculariza-tion. The *Times* article contextualizes its claim among data that reveals the growing public support in Ireland (71%, according to a recent poll) to reinstate birthright citizenship. This support appears highly anomalous at a time when most countries in the global North are instituting more severe restrictions on immigration. If passed, "the proposed law [on birthright citizenship] would grant the right to citizenship to any person who is born in Ireland and subsequently lives in the country for three years, regardless of the parents' citizenship or residency status."[27] There is little doubt that the original citizenship referendum was racialized from the moment it was introduced in the public arena. The growing support to reinstate birthright citizenship marks a radical departure for the Irish State's self-image, which until now has been predominantly white and mostly Catholic.

The present moment is an exceptional vantage point to assess questions related to race in Ireland and among the global Irish diaspora for other reasons too. The second decade of the twenty-first century marks a time when the first generation of children born to Celtic Tiger immigrants are coming of age. This is a unique moment in the history of Ireland, and it is partly because of a growing crescendo of cultural identification by a biracial population *within* Ireland. "We are Irish," claims this new demographic, and it seems plausible that a significant portion of the voting public in Ireland agrees. Irish people, once deemed as the Blacks of Europe, subse-quently attained whiteness in distant parts of the globe. That whiteness, largely unacknowledged within Ireland's shores, had to be reassessed in the context of immigration from African and Asian countries during and after the Celtic Tiger. Currently, it seems that such an acknowledgement has also led to the championing of biracial Irishness, especially among a younger demographic.

This fact alone should not, however, be taken as representative of official policies dictating the lives of Ireland's others, immigrants, refugees, and asylum seekers. Indeed, the detention complex of the Direct Provision sys-tem and the racism being faced by people of color in Ireland run counter to any public support for reinstating birthright citizenship. Author and scholar Emma Dabiri noted the singular challenges of growing up in Ireland as a biracial child: "My race seemed to be the first port of call in everybody's perception of me. Growing up in Ireland was characterised by overt racism, covert racism, isolation, bullying and stigmatisation." Dabiri has passionately spoken about how not being white "became the defining feature of [her] existence."[28] Her manifesto, *What White People Can Do Next: From Allyship to Coalition* (2021), published in the thick of the COVID-19 pandemic, is a testament to the intersectional, global, and critical lenses needed to equitably address issues surrounding race.[29]

While editing this volume, we are also acutely aware that its publication coincides with a contemporary historical moment that is marked by the cascading crises of climate, economy, and politics. The question of race and Irishness cannot be hermetically sealed off from these wider geopolitical concerns. Rob Nixon summarizes the moment thus:

> In society after society rulers have embraced a scaled-back democracy that cultivates exclusion, widening the circles of disenfranchisement. Autocracy and plutocracy blend and fuse. People find themselves both globalized and atomized, abandoned to conditions of compounded vulnerability. Many of those abandoned crave an alternative to government by the few for the few, an alternative to mega-mergers for the wealthy and community fracture for the rest. The successful have effectively seceded, leaving in their wake disguised democracies that are shadows of what democracy should be. Brazil, Hungary, Indonesia, the Philippines, South Africa, Russia, Turkey, the United Kingdom, the United States, and many more are all countries where to varying degrees the divide between democratic and plutocratic rule has become diaphanously thin.[30]

The fragility of neoliberal worldmaking was made especially visible in the pandemic conditions of contemporary history. COVID-19 was the singular catalytic agent whose protracted unfolding brought to public focus the cracks and fissures of a business-as-usual worldview, despite depleting resources, escalating precarities, and an ongoing sixth extinction. Politically, however, the pandemic only provided further ammunition to fascist populist politics, which utilized the climate of fear to widen the "circles of disenfranchisement."[31]

While a resurgence of autocratic rule may not have been mirrored in Irish politics, that fact offers little comfort. For example, the Irish government's response to COVID-19 increased the vulnerability of asylum-seekers and refugees in an already precarious moment in history. As Sen has argued, "ecologies of disease outbreaks" display great intersectional complexity and provide "a sociocultural underpinning to biomedical urgencies."

> A climate of disease allows us to identify symptoms of underlying ones such as systemic racism that virally replicates itself across the global spectrum. Here the Irish example becomes noteworthy. While its responses to COVID-19 demonstrated quick and decisive measures [in the beginning months of the pandemic], the Irish government simultaneously displayed the public dangers of a state of exception in which certain bodies, mostly black, have all been marked for pestilence and death. The Direct Provision system that "houses" asylum seekers and refugees in unhygienically close proximity is the underbelly of a state which has otherwise prided itself on "cocooning" its mostly white vulnerable populations. To be considered vulnerable in COVID times thus becomes a luxurious rung beyond reach for the immigrant; vulnerability, oddly, becomes a sign of social and political mobility.[32]

The state of emergency was racialized; some asylum seekers who could work both lost their jobs and were ineligible for the pandemic unemployment payment in Ireland. The Direct Provision system not only segregated some of the most vulnerable people under the care of the State, but it also actively heightened that vulnerability in moments of crisis. The Irish Network Against Racism's report later clarified that, in addition to such mismanagement, hate speech and racist incidents against minorities in Ireland doubled in 2020 compared to 2019.[33]

No less problematic is the very ironic nature of such violence. Irishness was exported and globalized not only through the British empire but also through the outward migration from the country at the time of the Great Irish Famine of the 1840s and as a result of the economic recession of the 1980s. Irishness was also made mobile, as Paige Reynolds has argued, after the Good Friday Agreement and then again after Ireland's entry into the European Union: "With the 1998 Good Friday/Belfast Agreement, the hard border between Northern Ireland and Ireland was opened; and the eventual ratification of the Nice (2003) and Lisbon Treaties (2009) in the Republic secured the country's place in the expanding European Union (EU) and opened its borders to other member countries."[34] Such mobilities, Reynolds goes on to claim, produce a "kinetic nature of contemporary life in Ireland."[35] This history of transnationality, which underwrites the racialization of the Irish in other parts of the world, as noted by scholars in this collection and elsewhere, behooves an equitable and just response toward the stateless subalterns and the seekers of refuge, most of whom, overwhelmingly, are people of color.

The free movement of people across borders also establishes, or is predicated on, the movement of capital and corporations across nation states. The Celtic Tiger years epitomized such porosities. As Julieann Veronica Ulin has noted: "Since 1991, each intercensal period in Ireland showed net inward migration, which peaked at 48,000 per annum during 2002–2006, facilitated by a system of 'Social Partnership' and the economic boom years of the Celtic Tiger. Ireland offered 'Irish hospitality' as well as 'a clean slate' and 'a new start' to migrants whose 'welcome has run out elsewhere.'"[36] This group included Irish emigrants who had been trapped in the underground economy of the U.S., a large majority of migrant workers from within the European Union (especially Poland), and a new generation of migrant workers from outside the Union (especially from African and South Asian states). However, although the Celtic Tiger is often cited as the precursor of contemporary multicultural Ireland, Robbie McVeigh notes that historically, the dominant binaries of Irish/British and Catholic/Protestant did not mean that there were no other ethnic groups in the island of Ireland. Even before the inception of statehood, Northern Ireland (like the Republic) had, for example, a Jewish and Irish Traveller population. Noting that Irish Studies has failed to connect issues of race in Northern Ireland and those in the Republic, McVeigh further historicizes inward migration and the discourse of race relations in the island of Ireland:

> The 1960s saw the growth of a new people of color population—mostly Chinese and South Asian—as part of a much larger migration to the United Kingdom from colonies and former colonies in the postwar period. This relatively small minority ethnic population—Chinese, South Asian, Traveller, and Jewish—was the subject of the first discussion and activism around racism in the north of Ireland in the 1980s and 1990s.[37]

This longer history of immigration into Ireland was effectively erased during the Celtic Tiger years. Along with it, a reckoning with systemic racism in Ireland well before that moment of economic excesses (against the Traveller community, for example) was equally expunged from the cultural mindset.[38] The production of cultural amnesia had no small part to play in the politics of fear and alarm that fed the passage of the Citizenship Referendum, and in the rising incidents of racism in Ireland. In those years, inward migration into Ireland from distant parts of the globe was made to appear as a historical anomaly in need of correction.[39]

Compared to the first decade of the present century, multiculturalism, racism, migrant workers' rights, and the rights of asylum seekers and refugees, appear at the forefront of Irish cultural consciousness today. Much of that awareness-raising and advocacy work has been carried out by non-governmental organizations: Migrant Rights Centre Ireland (MCRI), the Irish Network Against Racism (INAR), Nasc (the Irish word for "link"), Spirasi, and a host of other organizations, such as those utilizing sports to build multicultural links between immigrants and the Irish people.[40] Simultaneously, it has been heartening to see a growing trend in Irish Studies scholarship to focus attention on questions of Irish whiteness as well as Irish neoliberalism's and the Irish diaspora's racial components. Postcolonial and decolonial thought, critical race theory, feminist, queer, and environmental methods are robustly being utilized by Irish Studies scholars (both within and outside of Ireland) to rethink the place of the wider discipline in the precarity-laden landscape of the twenty-first century.[41] Such activism and scholarship have made significant headway in nudging Irish Studies to confront the color line of Irishness that travels well beyond the pale of established binaries between Irish/British and Catholic/Protestant.

Chapters

This book reorients older assessments and introduces new ones that have often been overlooked in Irish Studies scholarship. While there has been much critical energy dispensed to understand Ireland's unique role in the construction of new forms of imperial governance – the growth of liberalism, wage labor, and free trade, as well as the construction of the "human" as a site of political agency – these questions have not always been seen within the racialized frames that they demand. This volume significantly expands the scope of previous studies and provides a comprehensive analysis of themes related to race, racialization, racism, and Irishness, as they emerge in Irish literary and cultural discourses from the sixteenth century to the present. The volume complements this historical scope by closely scrutinizing the historical and contemporary genealogies that shape understandings of race in Irish literature and culture. It pays attention to major authors and texts, key literary and sociopolitical movements within Ireland, and to the different international and multicultural contexts within which Irishness was and is debated.

The volume begins with two chapters that situate competing theories of race in Irish history, literature, and culture. These theories emerged from a common dilemma faced by Irish populations: tracing their ancestral origins. To discover their origins, however, they needed to agree on what the "Irish race" was and how "race" was produced and passed down over generations. Was race a trait that was intrinsic, acquired through genetic inheritance, or was it the culmination of a community's culture, a feature put on by a people themselves through their beliefs and lifestyles?

The book's first chapter from Clare O'Halloran reveals that since the twelfth century, Irish writers have tended to follow the model set by Gerald of Wales in defining race through "customs and manners." For the Cambro-Norman priest, this meant the "barbaric lifestyle" of the Irish and their "inveterate treachery toward the colonial government" exemplified their race. In the sixteenth century, Edmund Spenser would continue this approach in *View of the Present State of Ireland* (*w. c.* 1596 and p. 1633), explaining Irish racial heritage through characteristics such as Irish dress and "pastoral modes of living." Sir William Petty's *The Political Anatomy of Ireland* (1691), would mark a change in rhetoric by offering a physical assessment, noting the unremarkable variation of appearance between the Irish and their colonizing counterparts. But Petty's approach, which was influenced by his medical training and which would become relevant to emerging racial sciences of the nineteenth century, was an anomaly at the time, and it was eschewed by Irish antiquaries of the eighteenth century who were seeking to understand Irish origins. O'Halloran argues that in their quest for answers a number of both Protestant and Catholic antiquaries in Ireland would follow the methodology of Gerald of Wales and Spenser. Inspired by the Enlightenment period's legacy of religious skepticism, some antiquaries abandoned Christian universalism, which considered a unity of human origins through the biblical figure of Adam, and they sought instead secular explanations of origins and race. Some also pursued Germanic, or "Gothic," linkages as an alternative to increasingly challenged Celtic ones, but over time, these explanations resulted in what O'Halloran calls a "harder-edged" debate that anticipated the nineteenth-century turn to biological discourses of race.

The consequences of turning to biological rather than cultural models of race are discussed in Guy Beiner's and Oded Y. Steinberg's chapter on Irish historiography of the long nineteenth century. Frequently distinguishing the "Irish race" from their "foreign oppressors," Irish historians were motivated to perceive race as an "intrinsic quality, inherited from antiquity." This framework, however, was more nuanced in practice. The poetry of Thomas Davis, for instance, introduced a racial ideology for Young Ireland that was neither "Celtic" nor "Saxon" but "multi-racial, or supra-racial." By making racial identity inclusive of both Irish Catholics and Anglo-Irish Protestants, Davis was following the variety of republicanism modeled by the United Irishmen while also trying to assuage the

Anglo-Irish conflict in the nationalist movement. Irish nationalist history books of the period also deployed the term "race" to contradictory effects, sometimes referencing "genealogical pedigree stemming back to ancestral heroes" and sometimes gesturing to Adamic origins. Beiner and Steinberg argue that these nationalist writers understood that scientific explanations of race were incompatible with Irish history – its stories of "migrations and conquests," its "countless instances of intermixture and amalgamation" – but they nevertheless believed asserting Irish racial difference was important to mark an innate national identity and character. The strategy of claiming an essential Irishness also bolstered transnational connections, for "bonding the fate" of the Irish people with "diasporic communities worldwide."

Beiner's and Steinberg's chapter exhibits a feature of many in this book, a dual motivation to present both a study of the history of racial discourse in Ireland and, at the same time, to assess the tendencies and limitations of existing scholarship on that history. The coauthors argue in the context of their chapter, for instance, that the legacy and appeal of nineteenth-century discourses of racial essentialism in Irish historiography linger today and are evidence of the need to recognize that in Ireland, "historiographical racialization has a history of its own, which needs to be unraveled."

An awareness of an Irish racial historiography that requires consistent reappraisal plays a role in the next two chapters of the book. The contributions from Patrick Lonergan and Matthew L. Reznicek offer comparative studies of race in texts of the nineteenth and early-twentieth centuries, and they show that Irish writers were not just looking within Ireland to develop their understanding of race; they were looking outside of Ireland as well. Lonergan's essay situates Dion Boucicault's melodrama *The Octoroon* (1859) into a history of minstrelsy and blackface performance in Irish theater, and he underscores how the cultural form "fed back into Irish life." While the play is more commonly associated in scholarship with the American setting of the story, the effects of its Irish origins have been understudied. Lonergan contends that the result of making the play "tangential" in Irish history and scholarship signifies a "failure to understand how the Irish theater was informed by the institution of slavery and the broader patterns of racism that accompanied it." Reznicek's chapter reviews representations of race and racism in a variety of Irish women's writings of the nineteenth and early-twentieth centuries. By surveying an extensive number of novels – ranging from Sydney Owenson's *The Missionary: An Indian Tale* (1811), to Katherine Cecil Thurston's *Max* (1910), to Kate O'Brien's *Mary Lavelle* (1936), and more – Reznicek argues that Irish women's fiction has "depended upon racial politics" to define the terms of freedom: "This politics sometimes appears sympathetic and as though it is rooted in affective anti-imperialism, and other times it is a politics of denial and erasure." Some of these varied examples exhibit the damaging effects of what we might consider today to be occasions of benevolent racism. Reznicek argues compellingly for identifying the patterns of racial discrimination behind such depictions but also for recognizing the implications of these patterns for Irish women; that they "challenge the ability of Irish women to achieve independence alongside rather than against the colonized, enslaved, indentured peoples of the nineteenth-century literary landscape."

Reznicek presents a continuity between treatments of racial difference in nineteenth-century Irish fiction and O'Brien's modernist production of the twentieth century. John Brannigan's and Vicki Mahaffey's chapters extend this book's study of Irish modernism to the works of James Joyce and his characterization of Black and/or "dark" peoples. Brannigan asserts that in *Ulysses* (1922), Joyce enjoins blackface minstrelsy with menacing displays of sexual desire and miscegenation that "delineate the boundaries of racial identity" – the cultural construction of "blackness in the process of defining whiteness." These "pastiche" performances for white audiences disregard "authentic or denotative" images of blackness and exemplify Brannigan's overarching point: that white Irish performances of blackface are extensions of cultural and "almost exclusively male" power, making blackface performance "an extension of *male* as well as white privilege in exercising the power to define racial hierarchies." Mahaffey presents an alternative reading of Joyce's subversive depictions of "dark" figures and "darkness." Associating the subject of race with comedy, but "without lessening its seriousness," Joyce analogizes race to sporting competitions in *Dubliners* (1914), contests between groups of "the human race" that are "rigged, because more privileged groups" have financial and other advantages. However, Joyce deliberately spites that story of a predetermined victory. As Mahaffey reveals, he shows through comedy in *Ulysses* that the "darker colored outsider wins," and this result complements his recoding of "darkness" in *Finnegans Wake* (1939) as a "generative and humane" force located "*inside*" the body. This darkness signifies the "divine" and a "capacious embrace of that great unknown."

Brannigan's chapter adds to this discussion of modernist literature a crucial connection to blackface performance in Irish modernist artwork. He notes that Jack B. Yeats's portrayals of blackface minstrel entertainment at times seem aware of a "common humanity and an aggressive appropriative staging of racial difference." A particularly disturbing depiction, however, relates to Yeats's broadside illustration of an Irish mumming scene or wren boy calling. This folk tradition, which extends beyond Ireland, suggests that "blackface minstrelsy did not emerge simply or only from racial conflicts between Black Americans and various white-skinned groups" in the United States, "but perhaps also from the rural European folk cultures in which mumming practices were already deploying forms of blackface masquerade."

Rounding out this book's study of Irish modernism, Julie McCormick Weng's chapter explores the writings of the painter's brother, W. B. Yeats. She argues that Yeats's *On the Boiler* (1939) contains "hallmarks" of his visionary modernist works while contrasting with them in its polemical assertion of Irish racial degeneration. Especially worried about Anglo-Irish Protestant population decline, Yeats alludes to the possibility of their race suicide. This style of "replacement theory" (or racial extinction theory) had become popular in eugenic and pronatalist discourses of the period, including in debates in the Oireachtas about the Censorship of Publications Bill of 1928. The former senator vehemently opposed the Bill's contraception clause (which banned publications that promoted or even casually referenced birth control), in part because he feared it would result in Catholic population growth and thus Protestant replacement in the Free State. Weng writes that *On the Boiler* exhibits his imagined remedy to dwindling Protestant numbers, as he envisions an "applied eugenics paradigm" to reduce birth rates among "lower classes" – coded references to Irish Catholics – through control of their reproductive rights: "Presenting strategies of selective breeding among an Irish elite, alongside restraints on lower-class reproduction, Yeats imagines conditions through which the 'descendancy' could ascend once more."

The next two chapters from Simon Prince and Richard Rankin Russell explore the interdependence of race and politics in the context of Northern Ireland while introducing connections to transnational histories of race and anticolonial struggle. Prince's chapter charts the conflicting racialized rhetoric employed by activists in the early years of the Troubles – for example, in the forging of transatlantic bonds between Northern Irish leftists and Black Power activists, in the contested embrace of "Third Worldism" among some members of the Irish Republican Army (IRA), and finally, in two occasions of Loyalist racism in 1969. These examples reveal a picture of various Northern Irish communities harnessing racial discourses to "imagine their roles within a changing world," and they illustrate the fact of Northern Ireland as a "networked space," with the "movement of people, goods, and ideas" creating "complex, overlapping networks" that associate the local with "the national, the imperial, and the global." This was also a moment, Prince contends, when "decolonization" itself was "in the process of breaking and remaking these webs." Russell's chapter builds on this story of global networks by showing that the paths of influence included reciprocal exchanges between the poets and friends Derek Walcott and Seamus Heaney. These Nobel Prize winners both designed a "poetics of race" in which colonial linguistic histories were a driving force. St. Lucian born Walcott had long admired writers like James Joyce and John Millington Synge who sought linguistic innovations to characterize their "racialized" and colonial subjectivities. Their example helped Walcott identify "racial and cultural hybridity as a foundation of strength" for poetry, which Heaney came to identify as well. Russell argues that both poets composed "song" out of their discomfiting states of hybridity, and Heaney's song was especially inspired by Walcott's, enabling him to establish expressions of Northern Irish experiences that accounted for "woundedness and healing" alongside "history and hope."

The chapters from Dianne Hall and Peter D. O'Neill survey histories of the Irish diaspora in Australian and American contexts, showing that Irish assimilation abroad was fraught with examples of racism *of* and *by* Irish descendants themselves. Hall's study of nineteenth- and twentieth-century Australia elucidates the forms and circulation of racialized Irish stereotypes in visual and print media, literature, and theater. These derogatory representations, including simianized illustrations of Irish people, were popular and correlated with evidence of discrimination against Irish people in areas such as employment. Many Irish Australians, however, would go on to seek differentiation rather than solidarity with other minority groups, emphasizing their "positive" contributions to society at the expense of excluding "Asian and other racialized minorities." O'Neill's chapter maps a similarly fraught trajectory of belonging among Irish Americans, acknowledging that they had endured "vilification" by militant white nationalist groups like the Know-Nothings and the Ku Klux Klan (KKK). They responded over time, however, by developing a form of American patriotism that white nationalists found irresistible. This transformation is registered, O'Neill reveals, in James T. Farrell's *Studs Lonigan* Trilogy (1935), as well as in many plays of Eugene O'Neill's; for instance, *Thirst* (1914), *Moon of the Caribbees* (1917), *The Dreamy Kid* (1918), *The Emperor Jones* (1920), and *All God's Chillun Got Wings* (1924). Farrell's texts capture a "brutal realism" that ties Irish American class mobility to the "racialization processes at work in the United States," and O'Neill's plays rely on racist stereotypes of Black and mixed-race peoples. Both authors therefore contribute to the evolution of making a once "expendable people in the British colonial state" into "valued American citizens, and in many cases, into white nationalists."

Advancing this book's study of diasporic communities, Stephen Watt's chapter turns to the Jewish diaspora in Ireland, a topic that recalls iconic works of Irish literature, from Maria Edgeworth's *Castle Rackrent* (1800) to Joyce's *Ulysses*. Using Paige Reynolds's theory of "afterlives" as a launch point, Watt argues that Ruth Gilligan's novel *Nine Folds Make a Paper Swan* (2016) represents "the afterlife of the Irish-Jewish novel" while containing within it "an Irish-Jewish archive." Gilligan's depictions of emigrant subjectivity, including her study of Jewish identity and racism in Ireland, draw on a canon of Jewish American, British, and Irish texts, creating a "formidable and multifoliate" "*diasporic archive*" that cannot be generalized. Featuring the "complexities of Jews' lives in Ireland," from their first arrival to the island, to their experiences in the twentieth century, and to hardships faced during the economic crises of the twenty-first century, the book makes the case that notions of "home" and "homeland" for Irish Jews "are as complex as they are emotional and transactional."

The next two chapters from Ailbhe McDaid and Oona Frawley mark a thematic shift in the book. They turn to contemporary Irish poetry and fiction and take a closer look at systemic exclusion of writers of color by publishing houses in Ireland. Although the island's racial diversity has increased dramatically over the decades, writers of color living in Ireland have faced barriers to publication. McDaid points to an important survey conducted by Words Ireland in 2021. The survey concluded that across the literary arts "all ethnic groups aside from white Irish were underrepresented." In fact, until 2022, no publisher of Irish poetry had released "a full-length volume by a poet of color based in Ireland." This is astonishing in light of the fact that Ireland boasts a staggering number of small presses and literary magazines, and Irish writers have garnered international attention, evidenced most recently by Anna Burns and Sally Rooney winning the Booker Prize and Costa Award for Best Novel in the *same year*, 2018. Frawley concludes that Irish fiction has tended to reinforce outdated conceptualizations of Irish identity that are "predictably white" and out of step with Ireland's "multiracial, multiethnic present."

Both McDaid and Frawley praise recent measures to make the publishing industry more inclusive and representative of diverse voices in Ireland. These initiatives, as Frawley writes, "all attest to a changing landscape, actively working toward inclusion." At the same time, however, McDaid's research found that Irish writers of color have faced uncomfortable scrutiny by their white Irish colleagues. When brought alongside white Irish writers, they find a peer group that often fetishizes their experiences, or, as poet Chiamaka Enyi-Amadi states, "what it's like being black and a migrant in Ireland" rather than focusing on their accomplishments – the contents of their creative compositions.[42] There is sometimes an added expectation that their literature reflect "pain" rather than "pleasure,"[43] or what poet Mary Jean Chan describes among the British writing community as a picture of herself as either an "'authentically' traumatized" and "suffering Other" or a "perfectly assimilated migrant who is defiant yet empowered."[44]

Out of these contexts, both McDaid's and Frawley's chapters provide analyses of contemporary literature. McDaid's essay explores the emergence of spoken word and performance poetry by Irish poets of color. For example, poet and rap artist Denise Chaila combines spoken word and musical performance to articulate her Irish Zambian heritage. Nigerian Irish artists Dagogo Hart and Felispeaks (Felicia Olusanya) – whose poem "For Our Mothers" was added to the Leaving Certificate curriculum in 2021 for the 2023 exam – collaborated on "See True" (2018), a spoken word theater show. As McDaid writes, through such compilations, the artists "challenge notions of essential Irishness" and are "claiming space within the body of the nation while expressing pride in diverse heritage." Their channels of production also cleverly "circumvent" the "power dynamics and marketplace proscriptions" of publishers. These artists are thus "redefining the contours of Irish literary culture" through "multimedia, multidisciplinary interventions" and are establishing their own "creative networks." However, these networks also limit the distribution of their work, revealing an issue of making it widely accessible and perhaps hampering the ability of these poets to forge more public profiles. Turning to Irish fiction, Frawley's chapter treads the psychological terrains of individuals represented in Donal Ryan's novel *From a Low and Quiet Sea* (2018), Melatu Uche Okorie's short story collection *This Hostel Life* (2018), and Stephen Rea's and Jessica Traynor's edited collection *Correspondences: An Anthology to Call for an End to Direct Provision* (2019). Using W. E. B. Du Bois's concept of "double consciousness," Frawley argues that these texts depict characters of color with a "fragmented" sense of self. Some even exhibit what Frawley describes as a form of "triple consciousness," when layers of "gender and other categories are accounted for." Through Du Bois, Frawley's chapter offers a theory and critical syntax for discussing the intersectional forces through which characters of color mediate their identities and chart their own paths of self-determination.

Concluding this book is a powerful chapter from Shirley Lau Wong that traces the connection between race and place in Irish literature and culture, a connection of vital importance to Ireland's past, present, and future. While studies of place and land in Ireland are "well-trodden" in scholarship, Wong asserts that intersections with race are rarely discussed. Yet from the nineteenth century to today, the rhetoric of soil underwrites "discussions around race, nation, and citizenship" in Ireland. Taking Seamus Heaney's bog poems as a case study, Wong centralizes their common themes of soil, kinship, and race. While the bog poems are often read "against the backdrop of colonialism, decolonization, and partition," Wong prompts readers to ask: "What new insights might be revealed by situating Irish poetry" from Heaney and other poets "within a framework that forefronts race?" Responding to this question in academic research will enable scholars to avoid assuming racism in Ireland is a new, contemporary concern and to "recognize the pervasive racist ideologies that have long percolated Irish cultural and political identity."

Altogether, the chapters of this book are a small step in responding to Wong's important question. They seek to "understand how the contemporary moment emerges from a long lineage of racial ideologies that have underwritten the formation of the Irish State ... and that continue to endure in and shape the present." It is fitting then that many of the chapters in this book, even some that study the distant past, end in the present. These contemporary conclusions demonstrate that discourses of race in Ireland have their own distinct echoes across time, and these echoes may seem to sound at a distance but are shown by the contributors here to be deeply discernible today. Lonergan's chapter, for instance, highlights the revival and reinterpretation of Boucicault's *The Octoroon* (retitling it *An Octoroon*) by the American playwright Branden Jacobs-Jenkins and the way the staging "recalibrated" the themes of the play "for the contemporary era." Weng's chapter connects replacement theories of the past to those of the present, and she warns that even though Yeats's support of scientific racism is "now debunked," theories like the poet's "still attract followers," "influence public policy," and therefore require our persistent scrutiny. Hall's chapter calls for further investigation of Irish Australian experiences alongside those of Indigenous Australians, suggesting that recent films such as *The Nightingale* (2019) present affinities and differences that have yet to be adequately addressed. And O'Neill's chapter showcases through early-twentieth century Irish American fiction and drama a "lineage of the white nationalist movement" in the U.S. that helps to "explain the remarkable prominence of Irish American Catholics in today's increasingly far-right Republican Party." These examples stress the relevance of situating the study of race in Ireland's past alongside ongoing issues today, and they point to the need for scholars of Irish Studies to rigorously and relentlessly revisit these themes in criticism.

Writing in 2004, Steve Garner noted that the theme of race in Irish history "has been approached from one direction," by which he meant "the historical racialisation of the Irish per se."[45] In 2009, Brannigan reasserted Garner's claim and noted that "racial ideologies and racist practices have not only undergirded the Irish state and its defining cultural institutions and policies, often in muted and insidious forms, but have been central to the ways in which official discourses of 'Irishness' have been negotiated and contested in the cultural sphere."[46] At that time, Brannigan further stated that race "remains relatively underexplored as an affective agent in Irish culture" and noted that crucial studies of Irish literature and culture, such as *The Cambridge Companion to Modern Irish Culture* (2005) or *Reinventing Ireland: Culture, Society and the Global Economy* (2002), showed little or no evidence of engaging with this theme.[47] Much has changed since, and this book is part of that conversation but in no way a conclusion to it. We hope that the contributions here prompt future research into the study of race in Irish literature and culture.

Notes

1 Douglas Hyde, "Explains Objects of Gaelic League," *The San Francisco Examiner*, February 15, 1906.
2 Hyde, "Explains Objects of Gaelic League."
3 Thomas Carlyle, "Occasional Discourse on the Negro Question," *Fraser's Magazine for Town and Country* 40, no. 240 (1849): 672. The essay was revised into a pamphlet in 1853 and retitled as "Occasional Discourse on the N***** Question."
4 Roddy Doyle, *The Commitments* (New York: Vintage, 1987), 39, 9.
5 *The Commitments*, directed by Alan Parker, Beacon Pictures, 1991. In this scene in the book, the characters alternate between referring to themselves as "black" and "the n*****s of Ireland" (9).
6 Malcolm Sen, "Joyce and Race in the Twenty-First Century," in *The New Joyce Studies*, ed. Catherine Flynn (Cambridge: Cambridge University Press, 2022), 36. See also, Nells Irvin Painter, *The History of White People* (New York and London: W. W. Norton and Company, 2010), ix.
7 John Brannigan, *Race in Modern Irish Literature and Culture* (Edinburgh: Edinburgh University Press, 2009), 16.
8 Brannigan, *Race in Modern Irish Literature and Culture*, 16.
9 Brannigan, *Race in Modern Irish Literature and Culture*, 16.

10 Sarah L. Townsend, "Direct Provision, Immigrant Detention, and the Wonderful World of Avoca," *Éire-Ireland* 57, no. 3–4 (Fall/Winter 2022): 64.

11 Townshend, "Direct Provision, Immigrant Detention," 64.

12 Townshend, "Direct Provision, Immigrant Detention," 64–65, 66.

13 Sean Williams, "The Magical Whiteness of Being Irish: Language and Song in American White Nationalism," *New Hibernia Review* 25, no. 4 (Winter 2021): 134.

14 Shawn McCreesh, "Donald Trump, Joe Biden and the Vote of the Irish," May 25, 2020, www.nytimes.com/2020/05/25/opinion/trump-biden-irish-americans.html.

15 McCreesh, "Donald Trump."

16 "Diversity and Inclusion," Department of Celtic Languages and Literatures, Harvard University, https://celtic.fas.harvard.edu/diversity-and-inclusion. See also the discussion of the statement in Williams, "*The Magical Whiteness of Being Irish*," 134–35.

17 Williams, "*The Magical Whiteness of Being Irish*," 135–36.

18 Williams, "*The Magical Whiteness of Being Irish*," 136.

19 See Peter McDermott, "Ó Ríordáin Takes an Irish Stand," *The Irish Echo*, November 7, 2017, www.irishecho.com/2017/11/o-riordain-takes-an-irish-stand/.

20 Lisa Lowe, *The Intimacies of Four Continents* (Durham: Duke University Press, 2015), 11. Also see Dipesh Chakrabarty, *Provincializing Europe: Postcolonial Thought and Historical Difference* (Princeton, NJ: Princeton University Press, 2000).

21 For example, L. Perry Curtis, Jr. studies the simianization of the Irish in Victorian political cartoons in *Apes and Angels: The Irishman in Victorian Caricature* (1971).

22 Anne Mulhall, "Arrivals: Inward Migration and Irish Literature," in *Irish Literature in Transition: 1980–2020*, eds. Eric Falci and Paige Reynolds (Cambridge: Cambridge University Press, 2020), 182, 183.

23 Masha Gessen, "Ireland's Strange, Cruel System for Asylum Seekers," *The New Yorker*, June 4, 2019, www.newyorker.com/news/dispatch/irelands-strange-cruel-system-for-asylum-seekers.

24 Ronit Lentin, "Black Bodies and Headless Hookers: Alternative Global Narratives for Twenty-First Century Ireland," *Irish Review* 33 (Spring 2005): 9.

25 Citizenship tourism was actually a very small fraction of this alleged abuse of Irish citizenship laws. See Mark Brennock, "'Citizenship tourists' a tiny group, statistics indicate," *Irish Times*, April 22, 2004, www.irishtimes.com/news/citizenship-tourists-a-tiny-group-statistics-indicate-1.1309031.

26 Ed O'Loughlin, "In Ireland, Bid to Restore Birthright Citizenship Gains Ground," *The New York Times*, November 24, 2018, www.nytimes.com/2018/11/24/world/europe/ireland-birthright-citizenship.html.

27 O'Loughlin, "In Ireland."

28 Emma Dabiri, "I'm Irish but I'm not white. Why is that still a problem as we celebrate the Easter Rising?," *The Guardian*, March 29, 2016, www.theguardian.com/commentisfree/2016/mar/29/irish-white-easter-rising-ireland-racism.

29 See Emma Dabiri, *What White People Can Do Next: From Allyship to Coalition* (Harper Perennial: London and New York, 2021).

30 Rob Nixon, "The Less Selfish Gene: Forest Altruism, Neoliberalism, and the Tree of Life," *Environmental Humanities* 13, no. 2 (2021): 352.

31 Nixon, "The Less Selfish Gene," 352.

32 The Skellig Accommodation Centre especially demonstrated this. See Malcolm Sen, "An Ordinary Crisis: SARS-CoV-2 and Irish Studies," in *Routledge International Handbook of Irish Studies*, eds. Renée Fox, Mike Cronin, and Brian Ó Conchubhair (London: Routledge, 2021), 471–84, 476.

33 Lucy Michael, "Reports of Racism in Ireland," *Irish Network against Racism*, 2020, https://inar.ie/wp-content/uploads/2021/03/2020_iReport-Reports-of-Racism-in-Ireland.pdf.

34 Paige Reynolds, "Introduction," in *The New Irish Studies*, ed. Paige Reynolds (Cambridge: Cambridge University Press, 2020), 4.

35 Reynolds, "Introduction," 4.

36 Julieann Veronica Ulin, "Introduction: Ireland's New Strangers," in *Race and Immigration in the New Ireland*, ed. Julieann V. Ulin (Notre Dame, IN: University of Notre Dame Press, 2016), 3.

37 Robbie McVeigh, "Racism in the Six Counties," in *Race and Immigration in the New Ireland*, ed. Julieann V. Ulin (Notre Dame, IN: University of Notre Dame Press, 2016), 78.

38 See Mary Burke, "Irish Travellers, the Environment, and Literature," in *History of Irish Literature and the Environment*, ed. Malcolm Sen (Cambridge: Cambridge University Press, 2022), 206–26. Also see Bryan Fanning, *Racism and Social Change in the Republic of Ireland* (Manchester: Manchester University Press, 2002), 112–51.

39 Ironically, the Irish free market depended on migrant labor. On the role of immigrants and Irish economy, see Kieran Allen, "Neo-liberalism and Immigration," in *Immigration and Social Change in the Republic of Ireland*, ed. Bryan Fanning (Manchester: Manchester University Press, 2007), 84–98.

40 See Ronit Lentin, "(M)other Ireland: Migrant Women Subverting the Racial State?," in *Race and Immigration in the New Ireland*, ed. Julieann V. Ulin (Notre Dame, IN: University of Notre Dame Press, 2016), 51–74. Also see Mike Cronin, "Integration through Sport," in *Race and Immigration in the New Ireland*, ed. Julieann V. Ulin (Notre Dame, IN: University of Notre Dame Press, 2016), 157–74.

41 See, for example, Mary Burke, *Race, Politics, and Irish America: A Gothic History* (Oxford: Oxford University Press, 2023).

42 Chiamaka Enyi-Amadi and Emma Penney, "Are We Doing Diversity Justice?: A Critical Exchange," *Irish University Review* 50 no. 1 (2020): 113.

43 "Are We Doing Diversity Justice? Part 2: Panel Discussion," www.youtube .com/watch?v=ErLU6lXjSIU.

44 Mary Jean Chan, "'Journeying is Hard': Difficulty, Race and Poetics in Sarah Howe's Loop of Jade," *Journal of British and Irish Innovative Poetry* 12 no. 1 (2020): 25.

45 Steve Garner, *Racism in the Irish Experience* (London: Pluto, 2004): 244.

46 Brannigan, *Race in Modern Irish Literature and Culture*, 5.

47 Brannigan, *Race in Modern Irish Literature and Culture*, 6. Also, see *The Cambridge Companion to Modern Irish Culture*, eds. Joe Cleary and Claire Connolly (Cambridge: Cambridge University Press, 2005); and *Reinventing Ireland: Culture, Society and the Global Economy*, eds. Peadar Kirby, Luke Gibbons, and Mike Cronin (London: Pluto, 2002).

CHAPTER I

"Our Heroic Ancestors"
Antiquarian Literature and the Discourse of Racial Heritage

Clare O'Halloran

The early modern period did not want for works meditating on what was wrong with the indigenous Irish.[1] Written in 1671–72 (though published posthumously in 1691), Sir William Petty's *The Political Anatomy of Ireland* dissected Ireland and its people with a view to suggesting measures that would improve their lot. Since the first English conquest in the twelfth century, colonists and commentators had followed in the footsteps of Gerald of Wales in anatomizing the indigenous Irish people. Such accounts emphasized their alleged unchanging barbaric lifestyle and inveterate treachery toward the colonial government; only their full subjugation, the argument went, would ensure their admittance into the civilized world. With Petty's *Political Anatomy*, however, there is a development that is of note for this study of changing ideas about race. While granting that the Irish of his day subscribed to a superstitious religion that was "rather a custom than a dogma amongst them" and that their lifestyle was characterized by an idleness traditionally associated with the state of barbarism, Petty denied that they were marked out by any physical characteristics: "For their shape, stature, colour, and complexion, I see nothing in them inferior to any other people."[2] This would seem to suggest a physical dimension to previous colonial discourse, and one that is far more associated with the biological racism that developed in the nineteenth century, which focused on physiological indicators of racial distinction and established hierarchies based on them.

In fact, Petty's musings about the physical characteristics of the Irish are not representative of the debates of his day and may stem more from his medical training than from any established point of dispute. The antiquarian writings of the eighteenth century that are the focus of this chapter eschewed direct consideration of the physical features of the Irish, confining their attention to their customs and manners, a topic that had been established by Gerald of Wales and then extended by Edmund Spenser in the late sixteenth century in his *View of the Present State of*

Ireland (written *c.* 1596 and published in 1633) to include their clothing and pastoral modes of living.[3]

A central area of concern in all antiquarian research was origins; in this case, to establish where the Irish had come from. Everywhere in Europe, the various answers to such a question were shaped by a Christian universalism that posited unity rather than diversity in the origins and history of mankind, tracing all humanity back to Adam. A steadily growing Enlightenment skepticism about orthodox Christianity made it even more important to defend revealed religion in all its detail against what one Church of Ireland bishop called "Atheistical Men."[4] Thus, enquiries into the history of the origins of a people, as first retailed in medieval texts, continued to be situated within a biblical framework up until the nineteenth century. Religious skepticism, however, was working in a subterranean way and was to bubble up in the final decades of the eighteenth century, paving the way for a discourse of race that either overtly, or more frequently covertly, abandoned loyalty to scriptural frameworks. This process, from scriptural orthodoxy to a more secular concept of origins and race, can be mapped onto the antiquarian writings that are the focus of this chapter. Language origins provided a crucial layer of such antiquarian research; it was in this century that Irish was identified as belonging to the Celtic family of languages. This, in turn, allowed Irish ethnicity to be tied more firmly to the Celts but happened just at the time when Celticism began to be challenged as the dominant lens through which Northern European ancient history and languages should be understood.[5] There was a growing drive to foreground the Germanic, often called Gothic, inheritance instead. In Ireland, this Gothicist movement became evident at the end of the century, and, merging with skepticism about the Mosaic account of origins, produced a harder-edged, more racializing origins debate that foreshadowed the emergence of nineteenth-century biological racial discourse.

As Colin Kidd points out in *The Forging of Races: Race and Scripture in the Protestant Atlantic World*, "race" is a cultural concept with "no real substance in nature or in sciences." Its meaning therefore changes over time and space, "from one society to the next, and within the same society from one era to the next."[6] In eighteenth-century Irish antiquarian texts, the word was used synonymously with "nation" and "people," as it had been in earlier centuries; it was just another collective term. This understanding was derived from the Bible, where the Greek term *genos* was rendered as "race," but also variously as "nation," "generation," "genus," "family," and so on.[7] This biblical influence is key, as in the early modern period, scripture, and specifically the Old Testament Book of Genesis, was the starting point for any investigation of the origins of not just races but also linguistic groups, ethnicities, and nations of the world.[8]

In the case of the origin myth of the Irish, the Gaelic medieval foundational text was based on an embellished form of the biblical template. Known popularly in English as the *Book of Invasions, Leabhar Gabhála Érinn* (henceforth *LGÉ*) recounted the peopling of Ireland from even before the Noachian Flood by a series of different peoples, finishing with the arrival of the Gael. Consisting of a number of separate and much earlier manuscript narratives, filled with what John Carey terms "a heterogeneous body of legends and speculations regarding the ancient history of the country," these were integrated by monks in the mid-eleventh century to form one text harmonized with scripture. The influence of classical and early medieval sources, such as Orosius and Isidore, can also be clearly seen, however, in some of the detail of the narrative.[9]

According to *LGÉ*, the successive waves of invaders who moved into Ireland were, like the rest of the peoples of Europe, descended from Noah's son Japhet, but, uniquely, they were united by a common origin in Scythia, that area roughly between the Caspian and Black Seas. The Scythians were reputed by the classical sources to be a martial and nomadic people; some, like Herodotus, contrasted them with the civilized, city-dwelling Greeks, while others praised their simple, hardy lifestyle and portrayed them as noble savages.[10] The latter view may have been influential on the creators of *LGÉ* in their choice of the Scythians as founding ancestors, possibly reinforced by the visual and aural similarities between "Scythia" and "Scotia," the Roman name for Ireland. The consecutive waves of peoples from Scythia who were said to have landed in Ireland – Partholonians, Nemedians, Fir Bolg, and Tuath Dé Danann – mainly gained their hold by military conquest. But they were followed by the most glorious of the invading peoples, the Gael, named for their eponymous ancestor Gaedheal Glas, whose forefathers had also originated in Scythia, but who had journeyed to Egypt and married the pharoah's daughter.

This strand of the origin myth is where the monkish hand seems most evident, as the experiences of Gaedheal Glas and his people are made to parallel those of the Children of Israel. Like the latter, the Gael are expelled from Egypt and forced to embark on a long journey involving a return to Scythia, a passage through the Mediterranean, pausing in Greece (thereby showing a connection to another of the great civilizations), and finally landing in Spain. After spending some time in Spain, Gaedheal's descendants, now led by Míl (whence the name Milesians), send an advance party to Ireland, which some of their number have spied from the top of a tower in the northwest of Spain. After various vicissitudes, the Milesian forces launch an expedition to Ireland, overwhelm the incumbent people, the Tuath Dé Danann, and set in place a great polity that was said to still hold sway as *LGÉ* was being put together.[11] Thus, in the Irish version of their origins, the Gael are a chosen people who have journeyed from afar to reach the promised land of Ireland, where they have established a monarchy and laws – all the trappings, in other words, of a great civilization, which is further reinforced by their early embrace of Christianity and of Christian learning.

The continuing attraction of this myth well into the early modern period is signaled by the creation of a new recension of *LGÉ* in 1631 by the Irish Franciscan scholars of Louvain and Donegal, headed by Micheál Ó Cléirigh. This ensured that it was circulated (in manuscript) and read by new generations, those who had endured the renewed trauma of recent colonization and warfare of the late sixteenth and early seventeenth centuries. As Bernadette Comerford states, *LGÉ* "was deemed by seventeenth-century historians to form the essential framework of any account of the earliest phase of Irish history."[12] This is evident in the first narrative history in modern Irish, *Foras Feasa ar Éirinn* (henceforth *FFÉ*), which translates as "Compendium of Wisdom about Ireland." Written around 1633 by Geoffrey Keating, a Counter-Reformation cleric, this work aimed to provide a shared history and identity for all the Catholics of Ireland, whether "native" Irish or (like himself) of Old English descent, that is, from the first English colonization in the late twelfth century. Drawing from a wide range of Gaelic sources over the course of the work, Keating nevertheless chose to base the pre-Christian part of his narrative wholly on *LGÉ* and its framework of successive waves of incoming inhabitants since the time of the Flood. This allowed him to integrate his own people into the Irish origin myth, so that the arrival in 1169 of the ancestors of the Old English community could be portrayed as the culmination of the historic process of the settlement of the island. According to Keating, it had been a Christian conquest, one sanctioned by the papacy and achieved by moderation and benevolence toward the indigenous inhabitants and their language and culture, which, over time, the colonists had embraced.[13]

The implicit but very deliberate contrast here was with the Tudor and Stuart colonization process which, in its twin aims of Reformation and Anglicization, involved the enforced uprooting of the religion and language of the indigenous inhabitants. Keating dubbed this form of colonization a pagan conquest, and thus wholly lacking in legitimacy. *FFÉ*, in terms of the focus on this chapter, is significant in two linked ways. In the first place, by opening up the "invasion" framework of *LGÉ* to include the arrival of the English in 1169, it created an origin myth and identity for his own ethnic community, and second, it established a nomenclature that recognized the complicated makeup of the inhabitants of the island. There were the *Sean-Ghaill* (literally, "old foreigners" but rendered as "Old English"), their long inhabitation of the island underlined by his branding the *arriviste* Tudor and Stuart colonists *Nua-Ghaill* (New English); but he created an entirely new category marked by a neologism, *Éireannaigh* (Irish), meaning the Catholics of Ireland, Old English as well as *Gael* (indigenous Irish). Thus, religion was to be the principal badge of identity; the small minority of Old English that had embraced Protestantism did not qualify as *Éireannaigh*.[14] The biblical template of *LGÉ* was important for Keating in his attempt to forge a legitimate bi-ethnic Catholic origin legend in this era of Counter-Reformation. The Old English were being attached to the "Chosen People" narrative of the medieval Gaelic tradition by virtue of the alleged assimilative thrust of their policy and behavior as colonists historically, and, more recently, of their heroic adherence to the "one true religion" in the face of an abrasive and Protestant colonialism.

FFÉ circulated widely in manuscript, including English translations, throughout the rest of the seventeenth century and beyond.[15] It first appeared in print, in an English translation, in 1723. This was a lavish production, intended for a wealthy readership and particularly targeting the descendants of the great Gaelic and Old English landowners, most of whom retained only a fraction of their holdings after the previous century of war, expropriation, and plantation. The translation, in characteristic eighteenth-century fashion, took liberties with the original, chiefly in an effort to update it to take account of the new political realities some ninety years after its composition. Thus, to appeal widely, the translation mitigated as far as possible the Catholic tenor of the original by amending that term to "Christian" wherever possible, thereby not seeming to exclude Gaelic and Old English families that had converted to Protestantism in the intervening century. In addition, the Old English, as a distinct ethnic group, were made invisible in the English text by the simple expedient of changing, for example, Keating's *na husaile do Shean-Ghallaibh and do Ghaedhealaibh* (the nobility and gentry of the Old English and the Irish) to "the Irish nobility and gentry."[16] In doing this, the translator was also reflecting the decline in the fortunes of the Old English as a separate ethnic group in the aftermath of the Williamite wars, 1689–91, when Irish Catholics found themselves on the losing side. In the aftermath, the defeated were known simply as the Irish, and religion became the sole badge of identity, largely occluding the original ethnic diversity of the Catholic community.

This translation of Keating's *FFÉ* is also significant because it became the medium for the dissemination, among the non-Irish-speaking educated elite, of the origin myth retailed in *LGÉ*. It therefore brought into focus again the extent to which that narrative conformed to the Old Testament version of ancient history and of the peopling of the earth. This was still of acute relevance to scholars, since, as Kidd has shown, even in late early modern Europe, antiquarian research into origins was closely intertwined with theological imperatives. As Kidd puts it, the emphasis in such investigations "was not upon divisions between races, but on race as an accidental, epiphenomenal mask concealing the unitary Adamic origins of a single, extended human family."[17] Faced with a small but increasingly vocal strain of Enlightenment skepticism about revealed religion, it became vital to promote a version of the past that adhered to monogenist orthodoxy based on the account in Genesis of the antediluvian peopling of the world. Taking their cue from the neighboring island, Protestant writers in Ireland made it a particular focus. Thus, we find the Church of Ireland bishop of Down and Connor, Francis Hutchinson (1660–1739), championing the traditional narrative, as retailed in the translation of Keating's *FFÉ*, of the origins of the Irish, in spite of his hostility to their religion.[18] His eye was on the wider picture, as he explained in *A Defence of the Antient Historians* (1734):

> If we by neglecting to keep up the Credit of those Historians, by which only we can prove the new-peopling of our several Nations after the Flood, and let Atheistical Men banter us out of the Belief of the Creation; we know not how low we may sink into Brutality and Wickedness.[19]

A similar preoccupation lay behind Charles Vallancey's *Vindication of the Ancient History of Ireland* (1786), which treated *FFÉ* as a redaction of the entire medieval Gaelic historiographical tradition and posed a radically new interpretation of its narrative of the peopling of Ireland. The account of Irish origins derived from *LGÉ* had, Vallancey claimed, been entirely misinterpreted, owing to the failure of early scholars to see that "the early periods of this History, related not to Ireland, but to those parts of Asia their Ancestors came from." He alone had discovered that the pagan deities of the Irish, to be found in Keating's *FFÉ*, provided proof of their Asian origin:

> Their history informs us that they mixed and embodied with the Chaldeans or Dadanites, consequently that Colony introduced their own mode of

worship: The Brahmans of India are supposed by Mons. Bailly to have been originally of Chaldaea: The Tibetans are asserted, by Father Georgius who lived amongst them many years, to have been originally Scythians, and to have adopted the Chaldaean deities. These assertions are verified in great measure by the Irish History.[20]

Vallancey's work has been subject to criticism and indeed scorn since its first publication, but, notwithstanding the undoubted wrongheadedness of all he produced, in recent decades, the serious agenda behind his increasingly eccentric theories and publications has been recognized.[21]

An English officer in the army engineer corps, Charles Vallancey (1725–1812) was posted to Ireland around 1750 on cartographic duties, eventually attaining the rank of general and chief surveyor in Ireland.[22] He had trained at the Royal Military Academy at Woolwich in the 1740s in the company of many who were posted to the army of the East India Company (henceforth EIC).[23] Throughout his career in Ireland, Vallancey kept in touch with soldiers of the EIC who, like him in Ireland, developed interests in the history and literature of the subject populations of the subcontinent.[24] Vallancey's particular hero, however, was Sir William Jones (1746–94), historian and philologist, and judge of the Supreme Court in Bengal, whose work on Persian literature and history was influential and may explain why Vallancey became mesmerized by the similarities between the Gaelic name for the island, *Eirinn*, and "Iran," another name for Persia.[25] Jones himself maintained in 1792 as "an absolute certainty" that "the whole race of man proceeded from Iran … whence they migrated at first in three great colonies; and that those three branches grew from a common stock, which had been miraculously preserved in a general convulsion and inundation of this globe."[26] The reference to "inundation" here pinpoints a major objective of the scholarship of the EIC, of which Jones was the outstanding exemplar. This was to enlist the history, literature, and languages of Asia to defend the status of scripture as the authoritative source on the creation and peopling of the world. Thus, Vallancey's focus on the pagan deities of the Irish as providing the key to the nature of pagan worship in India and Tibet had the same defensive objective but with the added bonus of connecting the cultures of the empire's oldest and newest colonies and harnessing them both in support of religious orthodoxy in the mother country.

The biblical dimensions of the origin myth were also important for Catholic antiquaries, though for different reasons. Determined to promote *LGÉ* as the authentic narrative of the exotic, and exalted, origins of their ancestors, they emphasized the connections it made between their ancestors and the Children of Israel. Thus, for Charles O'Conor, in *Dissertations on the Antient History of Ireland* (1753), this element of the traditional narrative accounted for the survival in pre-Christian Ireland of the religion of the Old Testament; "the antient Iberians of Ireland," he claimed, having a "Theology, grafted upon the Religion of Nature, and partly, deduced from the clearest Fountains of the old Patriarchal Worship." A chosen people, "the Blessing promised, in Holy Writ, to the Posterity of Japheth was extended, in a peculiar Manner, to that Branch of it, which inhabited this Western Country."[27] The agenda here had nothing to do with religious orthodoxy but rather was the age-old one of combatting derogatory representations in colonial writings of the Irish as barbarous semi-pagans.

While important aspects of the debate around origins were shaped by ideas and concepts inherited from the Middle Ages, new developments in philology at the turn of the eighteenth century introduced another framework to the discourse. Since the Renaissance, European philologists and antiquaries had been fascinated by the Celts and understood them to have inhabited much of the continent in ancient times.[28] Ireland, however, stood outside the Celtic paradigm, as its language was not recognized as belonging to the accepted classification of European languages and their interrelations. It was the Welsh philologist Edward Lhuyd who, in 1707, established that Gaelic belonged to the same family of Celtic languages as Welsh, Breton, Cornish, and Manx, thereby admitting it into the matrix of European languages.[29]

As a consequence, some eighteenth-century Irish antiquaries began to write of their ancestors as "Scythocelts," combining the older *LGÉ* tradition of a Scythian origin with the findings of the new philological scholarship.[30] Lhuyd further contributed to an increasing emphasis on the Irish language as a source of pride and identity by estimating it to be the oldest of the Celtic languages.[31] This tied in with earlier claims about the uniquely ancient status of Irish to be found in *LGÉ*, which recounts that the Scythian ancestor of the Irish, Fénius Farsa, was one of the seventy-two leaders who built the Tower of Babel. Following the destruction of the tower, and the fragmentation of one universal language into seventy-two, so the narrative goes, Fénius Farsa (in some recensions of the text, however, it is his son Nél or grandson Gaedheal Glas) created Gaelic out of the best elements of those languages.[32] Versions of this linguistic patriotism based on the biblical story of Babel can be found in national histories in many parts of Europe through the Middle Ages and beyond.[33]

After Lhuyd, Irish antiquaries did not have to rely on medieval historiographical tradition alone to argue for their glorious origins; Gaelic could be harnessed to provide support for those claims. As Anthony Raymond, a Church of Ireland clergyman with interests in both the contemporary Irish language (as a tool of proselytism) and its philology, put it in 1725: "the Affinity of Languages, where it is not forced or strained, is look'd [*sic*] upon to be a certain Method to discover from whence any Nation derives its Original." His conclusion, based on a comparison of versions of the Lord's Prayer in Irish and a number of different languages, including Welsh and Breton, was emphatic: "It must therefore be allowed as a certain Truth, that Ireland was peopled by those *Celtae*, or *Scythoceltae*, who in the Dispute of Antiquity with the *AEgyptians*, were allowed to be the most ancient People."[34]

For O'Conor, in the late 1740s, the Irish were descended "from the most humane and knowing Nation of all the Celts," and their ancestors, "the ancient Spaniards," were "certainly the most martial and free, the most humanized by Letters, and the most conversant with the Egyptians, Phoenicians, Persians and Grecians." It was beyond dispute, he maintained, that the Irish language "comes nearest the original Language of the Posterity of Japeth [*sic*]."[35] O'Conor's contribution to the development of the origin legend, beyond that laid down in *LGÉ* and elaborated by Keating, was to introduce the idea that these Iberian Celts (or Milesians) were literate, playing here on the claimed connections with other Mediterranean peoples who were reputed to have had the art of writing long before the Greeks and Romans. Thus, O'Conor's version goes, the founding ancestors of the Irish established in Ireland a literate and learned civilization in the remotest part of western Europe: "a People who should be the rudest, as they were the remotest, inhabitants of the old World ... never, even in the infancy and most confused State of their Government, sunk into ignorance or Barbarity."[36] O'Conor, like Keating before him, was writing history to repudiate the colonial slur of the Irish as barbarians in need of a civilizing English influence and was manipulating the new philological scholarship to do so.

Linguistic speculations also lay at the heart of Charles Vallancey's works, beginning with his *Essay on the Antiquity of the Irish Language* (1772), which claimed that Gaelic was the long-lost Phoenician, or Punic, language, brought to the island by "several colonies from Africa." This was based on what he asserted was the strong "affinity of the Language, Worship and Manners of the Carthaginians [a synonym for Phoenician] with those of the ancient Irish."[37] As we have already seen, Vallancey kept a close eye on the colonial scholarship emanating from India, and he was confirmed (to his own satisfaction at least) in the rightness of his theories by Sir William

Jones's suggestion, in 1786, of a common origin for the classical languages of India, the Near East, and Europe.[38] As the years passed, Vallancey's speculations about the origins of the Irish and their language diverged so sharply from the main body of Irish antiquarian scholarship that he cut a lonely and indeed largely discredited figure in his old age.[39]

The tendency of Irish antiquaries to adopt the term Celtic for their ancestors was boosted by the publication and popularity of the Ossian poems in the 1760s. These loose English versions of Scots Gallic poetry and folkloric material by James Macpherson were greeted with acclaim in most of Europe as the work of Ossian, a third-century blind bard, in commemoration and celebration of his father, Fingal, the king of Morven in the Scottish Highlands, and his Celtic warrior tribe. The response in Ireland was more guarded, as the material was easily identified as pertaining to recognizably Irish figures and the stories were versions of those circulating since the Middle Ages in Ireland, and which had spread to Scotland, along with the Gaelic language, from the time of significant Irish settlement in western Scotland in 500 CE. The poems were branded in Ireland as theft and Macpherson a traducer for his undoubted twisting, in the poems and the explanatory material surrounding them, of both the mythic and historically accurate elements of Hiberno-Scottish interconnections. There was nonetheless an awareness of the opportunity the Ossian vogue presented for Irish antiquaries to promote their own history and literature in Britain and more widely.[40]

Chief among these was Sylvester O'Halloran, a Catholic medical doctor with some Irish language and literature learning and a passion for the history and reputation of his country. The appearance of the Ossian poems triggered his first foray into print: an article and open letter to Macpherson, in a bid to reclaim the poems for Ireland, and referring to himself in so doing as a "Milesian."[41] Unlike Charles O'Conor, who had little interest in the material at issue, seeing it as merely the degraded folk tales of the poor, and Macpherson as having perpetrated a fraud, O'Halloran was enthused by the poems, despite what he took to be Macpherson's wholesale theft. In letters to O'Conor, he argued that they were based on "real originals," full of "romantically beautifull [sic]" descriptions, "the thoughts and similes drawn from Nature, and the sentiments so noble, and so Correspondent to that [sic] of our antient [sic] Heroes."[42]

As Macpherson came under increasing scrutiny over his claims to have been merely the collector and translator of poems that had been handed down unchanged since the third century, a move began in Ireland to produce English translations of the Irish poetry about Fionn Mac Cumhal and other heroes of the Finn and Red Branch tale cycles, and to include the

Gaelic originals, which Macpherson had been unable or unwilling to do. Charlotte Brooke's *Reliques of Irish Poetry* (1789) was a largely collaborative project, involving O'Halloran mainly, but also Charles Vallancey and Charles O'Conor, in the collection, translation, and interpretation of this hitherto undervalued material. Brooke, from a settler background in Cavan, may have learned Irish from a servant in that still Irish-speaking part of the country.[43] The editor of the critical edition points out that Brooke's translations are often only loosely based on the originals, and sometimes omitted passages and added embellishments that catered to the eighteenth-century taste for refined sentiments and language in their ancient poetry.[44]

But if Macpherson was the central, if unspoken, target of the work, it was also designed to present Irish literature as superior to that of England. The original poems were expressed, according to Brooke, in a language "distinguished by a force of expression, a sublime dignity, and rapid energy" that was impossible to render convincingly in English, when "One compound epithet must often be translated by two lines of English verse," and consequently "much of the beauty is necessarily lost."[45] O'Halloran's role in the volume was to shape its reception in the way he had first experienced Macpherson's Ossian poems, as an expression of the heroic greatness of the ancient Irish. "Ireland abounded in heroes of the most shining intrepidity," he claimed, "insomuch that they were all over Europe, by way of eminence, called the Heroes of the Western Isle."[46] Significantly, the ethnic identity of these heroes was firmly Celtic: this was the poetry of "the ancient Celtae."[47] The Irish had, thus, by the end of the eighteenth century brought themselves into the mainstream of European historical and literary historical culture, albeit while maintaining the unique purity of their heritage, just as *LGÉ* had laid down in the eleventh century.

Macpherson's Ossian had a concomitant impact on cultural politics in England, where its emphasis on the literary treasures of a Celtic Scotland was rightly seen as a politicized comment on the alleged comparative poverty of the Anglo-Saxon literary heritage. One immediate result was the three-volume *Reliques of English Poetry* (1765) by Thomas Percy (1729–1811), which aimed to show this criticism to be patently untrue, but also to argue that the antecedents of English medieval verse composition and its minstrel creators were the *skalds*, the Scandinavian court poets, rather than the Celtic bardic tradition, now so associated with Ossian. Percy's overall objective was to provide an unambiguously Germanic literary antecedence for English literature that would distinguish it from the peripheral Celtic regions of the British state and establish its cultural superiority as befitting the dominant power in the two islands.[48]

In a seminal work published in 1770, *Northern Antiquities*, Percy demonstrated the fallacy of the long-standing linking together of Celts and Germans as "the descendants of one single race." Rather, the Celts were the ancestors of "the Gauls, Britons and Irish," whereas the Germans, Belgians, Saxons, and Scandinavians were derived from the "Gothic or Teutonic" people. As "*ab origine* two distinct people [*sic*]," they differed considerably "in their manners, customs, religion and laws." Most important for Percy was the contrast in their institutions and laws, the "Gothic tribes" having a "plan of liberty" which they "planted wherever they formed settlements," which meant that while most Celts "were little better than in a state of slavery ... the meanest German was independent and free." Such disparities in history, culture, and lifestyle were also reflected in their physical attributes and appearance, such that they "differed sufficiently in their PERSONS";[49] the capital letters here making up in emphasis for a certain reticence about how such differences were manifest. Here, Percy was drawing, albeit tentatively, on "emerging ideas about biological race and ancestry, descent and identity" and fusing them with existing discourses and ideas about Gothic liberties.[50]

This message of Gothic superiority had a particular resonance in Ireland, to where Percy moved in 1782 when he was appointed Church of Ireland Bishop of Dromore. At this time, there was a marked enthusiasm among the Protestant ruling elite for Irish antiquities. Publications such as Joseph Cooper Walker's *Historical Memoirs of the Irish Bards* (1786) and Brooke's *Reliques of Irish Poetry* (which had borrowed its title from Percy) attested to the continuing vogue for Ossianic and Celticist themes, and overall for a more favorable view among an elite readership of the Gaelic language and its literary remains than had hitherto existed.[51] However, a revanchist undercurrent was gathering force, promoted by a political crisis in the south of the country, where agrarian unrest by the poor was flagged as an attempted pogrom against the minority Church of Ireland community.[52] In this febrile atmosphere, Percy's Gothicizing influence found a receptive follower in Edward Ledwich, a Church of Ireland clergyman who was exercised at what he perceived to be the dangerous cultural politics represented by the Celticist enthusiasm among sections of the elite. In *Antiquities of Ireland* (1790), he followed the precept of "the ingenious and learned Doctor Percy," that "where two people essentially differ in language there are ever found attached to each striking characteristic variations in their modes of thinking, and frequently in their modes of life."[53] Ledwich's mission was to dethrone the Celts as the most important of the ancestors of the Irish, notwithstanding the fact that their language continued as the lingua franca of the vast majority of the people.

A measure of the updated agenda he followed is that he professed no interest in interrogating the medieval tradition of *LGÉ*, which he dismissed as "idle Tales concerning Noah's grand-daughter, of Partholanus and Milesius, and their arrival here in very remote times."[54] His object, rather, was to rewrite early Irish history as "the History of the Goths in Ireland," quoting directly here from the second of his models, the Scottish historian John Pinkerton, whose *Enquiry into the History of Scotland* (1789) was written to replace Macpherson's Celticist narrative of Scottish history with one foregrounding the legacy of the Picts, here figured as Gothic. As an inveterate controversialist, Pinkerton also challenged the standard Mosaic version of the origins of humankind, expressing skepticism that "the many races of men of quite different forms and attributes" could be descended from "one parent." To underline this, he listed a series of what have become familiar racial stereotypes, including "the large-limbed dusky Turk ... the large, blue-eyed German; the squat Dutch; the florid Hibernian," whom he contrasted with, among others, "the curl-pated black Ethiop," to cast ridicule on the received biblical account of the peopling of the world by the sons of Noah.[55]

As clergymen, neither Ledwich nor Percy were in a position to make such a forthright attack on the doctrine of monogenesis contained in scripture, but the absence of any reference to that doctrine in their work is telling. Their silence on the question suggests the inexorable process by which it was being overtaken by a secular and racialized understanding of ancient history. In the case of Ledwich, there is perhaps a sharper edge to his depiction of the Celtic Irish in his contribution to a 1791 work, *The Antiquities of Ireland by Francis Grose*, which he was asked to finish when the English antiquary Grose died suddenly. While Ledwich allowed that the Celts were "the primaeval possessors of Ireland" who "arrived here in an age far beyond the reach of history or conjecture," they were, in his schema, soon overwhelmed by "Scythians, Goths or Teutons, for so the same people were variously named" who, in turn, landed "in ages long antecedent to the light of letters." Thus, in Ledwich's version of Irish origins, the Celts did not enjoy a long and unfettered possession of the island. Faced with the arrival of this "swarm" of martial Gothic "barbarians," the Celts, "a timid and unwarlike race ... wandered over the country without infringing the bounds, or exciting the jealousy of their neighbours."[56] In the second edition of his own *Antiquities of Ireland* (1804), Ledwich incorporated the text he had written for the Grose volume, but also expanded on this characterization of the relative status of the Celts and Scythians, claiming that the Celts were "to the Scythians, who succeeded them, what the savages of America are to the Europeans."[57]

Parallels between Ireland and America had long been made in colonial writing, and the Irish as primitive nomadic pastoralists was a familiar trope since Gerald of Wales, deployed in justification of colonization as the harbinger of civilization. But there are indications that Ledwich saw the incivility of the indigenous Irish as a contemporary and immutable fact. In a letter to another Protestant antiquary, Joseph Cooper Walker, an enthusiastic Celticist and author of *Historical Memoirs of the Irish Bards*, Ledwich criticized him for the tendency to lament the government policy of Anglicization as it had affected Gaelic culture, especially poetry and song. This, Ledwich laid down, was carrying antiquarianism to "a very dangerous excess," further reminding Walker that "it is historically true that [the English], under providence, humanized the Irish, who otherwise at this day would be perfect barbars," and finishing with the telling comment, "even as it is they are but half civilized."[58]

In his brilliant series of essays *States of Mind* (1983), Oliver MacDonagh claimed that "modern Irish historiography was born in 1790 with the publication of the Revd Edward Ledwich's *Antiquities of Ireland*," by which he meant that Ledwich's work signaled that "the Irish past had become an additional arena for current Irish political conflict."[59] The past, however, had always been in the political arena, and the question of origins was a topic of vital import, just as much to the compilers of *LGÉ*, and its later defenders, as to colonial writers, with their contrasting and combative narratives. Where Ledwich does represent a new development is in his role as Irish herald of the overtly racialized historiographical discourse of the nineteenth century, which produced the popular *Punch* cartoon of the violent simianized Irish peasant. We might conclude, therefore, that Petty's casual-seeming musings on the physical appearance of the indigenous Irish, with which this chapter began, experienced a different reception a hundred years after their first publication. While the writings in between lacked a clear racial dimension, they had prepared the ground for its surfacing in the early nineteenth century, aided by the erosion of Christian universalism and gradual fashioning of the typologies of the Gothic-Celtic divide.

Notes

1 The quotation in the title is from Charlotte Brooke, *Reliques of Irish Poetry* (1789), ed. Lesa Ní Mhunghaile (Dublin: Irish Manuscripts Commission, 2009), viii.
2 William Petty, *Tracts Chiefly Relating to Ireland* (Dublin: Boulter Grierson, 1769), 365, 366.

3 Gerald of Wales, *The History and Topography of Ireland* (1185), trans. John O'Meara (London: Penguin, 1982); Edmund Spenser, *A View of the State of Ireland*, from the first printed edition (1633), eds. Andrew Hadfield and Willy Maley (Oxford: Blackwell, 1997).

4 Francis Hutchinson, *A Defence of the Antient Historians, with a Particular Application of It to the History of Ireland and Great Britain, and other Northern Nations* (Dublin: John Smith and William Bruce, 1734), x.

5 Ian B. Stewart, "The Mother Tongue: Historical Study of the Celts and Their Languages(s) in Eighteenth-Century Britain and Ireland," *Past and Present* 243 (May 2019): 85–86.

6 Colin Kidd, *The Forging of Races: Race and Scripture in the Protestant Atlantic World* (Cambridge: Cambridge University Press, 2006), 13.

7 John Kenyon Davies, "Genos," in *The Oxford Classical Dictionary* (Oxford: Oxford University Press, 2012), www-oxfordreference-com.ucc.idm.oclc.org/view/10.1093/acref/9780199545568.001.0001/acref-9780199545568-e-2818.

8 Kidd, *Forging of Races*, 20–21.

9 John Carey, *The Irish National Origin-Legend: Synthetic Pseudohistory* (Cambridge: Department of Anglo-Saxon, Norse and Celtic, University of Cambridge, 1994), 1, 3, 22, 9. Note that the spelling of the name of the text in Irish varies considerably in the secondary sources.

10 Gordon Lindsay Campbell, *Strange Creatures: Anthropology in Antiquity* (London: Duckworth, 2006), 92–111.

11 For the most modern edition, see "The Book of Invasions (First Recension)," trans. John Carey, in *The Celtic Heroic Age: Literary Sources for Ancient Celtic Europe and Early Ireland & Wales*, ed. J. T. Koch in collaboration with John Carey, 4th ed. (Aberystwyth: Celtic Studies Publications, 2005), 226–71.

12 Bernadette Cunningham, "The Louvain Achievement 1: The Annals of the Four Masters," in *The Irish Franciscans, 1534–1990*, eds. Edel Bhreathnach, Joseph MacMahon, and John McCafferty (Dublin: Four Courts Press, 2009), 180.

13 Geoffrey Keating, *Foras Feasa ar Éirinn: The History of Ireland*, eds. and trans. David Comyn and P. S. Dineen, 4 vols. (London: The Irish Texts Society, 1902–14), 1:35–36. See also Brendan Bradshaw, "Geoffrey Keating: Apologist for Irish Ireland," in *Representing Ireland: Literature and the Origins of the Conflict, 1534–1660*, eds. Brendan Bradshaw, Andrew Hadfield, and Willy Maley (Cambridge: Cambridge University Press, 1993), 183, 185.

14 Bernadette Cunningham, *The World of Geoffrey Keating: History, Myth and Religion in Seventeenth-Century Ireland* (Dublin: Four Courts Press, 2000), 109–10.

15 Cunningham, *World of Geoffrey Keating*, 173–225.

16 Cf. Keating, *Foras Feasa ar Éirinn*, 1:4, with Geoffrey Keating, *The General History of Ireland*, trans. Dermo'd O'Connor (London: B. Creake, 1723), i.

17 Kidd, *Forging of Races*, 26.

18 Andrew Sneddon, "Hutchinson, Francis," *Dictionary of Irish Biography*, accessed February 5, 2021, www.dib.ie/biography/hutchinson-francis-a4177.

19 Hutchinson, *A Defence of the Antient Historians*, x.

20 Charles Vallancey, *A Vindication of the Ancient History of Ireland* (Dublin: Luke White, 1786), 50, 156–57.

21 The most recent contribution with a good bibliography is Bernd Roling, "Phoenician Ireland: Charles Vallancey (1725–1812) and the Oriental Roots of Celtic Culture," in *The Quest for an Appropriate Past in Literature, Art and Architecture*, eds. Karl A. E. Enenkel and Konrad Adriaan Ottenheym (Leiden: Brill, 2018), 750–70.

22 Monica Nevin, "Vallancey, Charles," *Dictionary of Irish Biography*, accessed February 10, 2021, www.dib.ie/biography/vallancey-charles-a8781.

23 Norman Vance, "Vallancey, Charles (c. 1726–1812), Antiquary and Military Surveyor," *Oxford Dictionary of National Biography*, accessed April 14, 2021, www-oxforddnb-com.ucc.idm.oclc.org/view/10.1093/ref:odnb/9780198614128 .001.0001/odnb-9780198614128-e-28051.

24 On this, see Clare O'Halloran, *Golden Ages and Barbarous Nations: Antiquarian Debate and Cultural Politics in Ireland, c.1750–1800* (Cork: Cork University Press, 2004), 48–51.

25 Vallancey, *Vindication of the Ancient History*, 49.

26 William Jones, "Ninth Anniversary Discourse on the Origin and Families of Nations," February 23, 1792, in Jones, *Works*, 6 vols. (London: n.p., 1799), 1:137.

27 Charles O'Conor, *Dissertations on the Antient History of Ireland* (Dublin: n.p., 1753), v–vi, 31.

28 Stewart, "Mother Tongue," 79–82.

29 Joep Th. Leerssen, *Mere Irish and Fíor-Ghael: Studies in the Idea of Irish Nationality, Its Development and Literary Expression Prior to the Nineteenth Century*, rev. ed. (Cork: Cork University Press, 1996), 289–93; Stewart, "Mother Tongue," 90–93.

30 See, for example, O'Conor, *Dissertations on the Antient History*, 11, 31; Anthony Raymond, *A Short Preliminary Discourse to the History of Ireland. To be published by Anthony Raymond, D.D. and sometime Fellow of Trinity College near Dublin* (London: n.p., 1725), 8–9.

31 Stewart, "Mother Tongue," 92.

32 Cf. "The Book of Invasions (First Recension)," trans. John Carey, 228–29; with *Lebor Gabála Érenn: The Book of the Taking of Ireland*, ed. R. A. S. Macalister, 5 vols. (Dublin: Irish Text Society, 1938–56), 1:147.

33 Colin Kidd, *British Identities before Nationalism: Ethnicity and Nationhood in the Atlantic World 1600–1800* (Cambridge: Cambridge University Press, 1999), 31.

34 Raymond, *Short Preliminary Discourse*, 6, 8–9.

35 O'Conor, *Dissertations on the Antient History*, v, 11, 37.

36 O'Conor, *Dissertations on the Antient History*, 32.

37 Charles Vallancey, *An Essay on the Antiquity of the Irish Language. Being a Collation of the Irish with the Punic Language* (Dublin: S. Powell, 1772), vii.

38 Stewart, "Mother Tongue," 73–74.

39 O'Halloran, *Golden Ages*, 180–82.

40 Clare O'Halloran, "Irish Re-creations of the Gaelic Past: The Challenge of Macpherson's Ossian," *Past and Present* 124 (1989), 69–95.

41 Miso-Dolos [Sylvester O'Halloran], "The Poems of Ossine, the Son of Fionne Mac Comhal, Reclaimed by a Milesian," *Dublin Magazine* (January 1763): 21–23.

42 Sylvester O'Halloran to Charles O'Conor, March 12–17, 1765; March 1, 1765, ed. J. B. Lyons, *North Munster Antiquarian Journal* 8 (1961): 172, 170.

43 Lesa Ní Mhunghaile, "Introduction," in Brooke, *Reliques of Irish Poetry*, xxv–xxvi.

44 Ní Mhunghaile, "Part II. New Translations and Commentaries," in Brooke, *Reliques of Irish Poetry*, 77, 79–80.

45 Brooke, *Reliques of Irish Poetry*, vi.

46 Sylvester O'Halloran, "An Introductory Discourse to the Poem of Conloch," in Brooke, *Reliques of Irish Poetry*, 6.

47 Brooke, *Reliques of Irish Poetry*, 137–38, 142.

48 Robert Rix, "Thomas Percy's Antiquarian Alternative to Ossian," *Journal of Folklore Research* 46, no. 2 (May–August 2009): 197–98, 201–02.

49 Thomas Percy, *Northern Antiquities: or a Description of the Manners, Customs, Religion and Laws of the Ancient Danes, and other Northern Nations*, 2 vols. (London: n.p., 1770), I:iv, xii–xiii.

50 Helen Young, "Thomas Percy's Racialisation of the European Middle Ages," *Literature Compass* 16, no. 9–10 (September–October 2019): 2.

51 See O'Halloran, *Golden Ages*, 113–24, 165–75.

52 O'Halloran, *Golden Ages*, 159–60.

53 Edward Ledwich, *Antiquities of Ireland* (Dublin, n.p., 1790), 307–08.

54 Ledwich, *Antiquities of Ireland*, i. (Quoting John Pinkerton, *An Enquiry into the History of Scotland Preceding the Reign of Malcolm III, or the Year 1056, including the Authentic History of That Period*, 2 vols. [London: John Nichols, 1789], II:35.)

55 John Pinkerton, *Ancient Scottish Poems, never before in Print*, 2 vols (London and Edinburgh, n.p., 1786), I:xxv–xxvi.

56 Francis Grose and Edward Ledwich, *The Antiquities of Ireland by Francis Grose Esqr. F.A.S*, 2 vols. (London: n.p., 1791–94), I: ii, iv, ix, ii, xvii.

57 Edward Ledwich, *Antiquities of Ireland*, 2nd ed. (Dublin: John Jones, 1804), 13.

58 Edward Ledwich to Joseph Cooper Walker, April 17, 1787, March 1787. Correspondence of Joseph Cooper Walker. Ms. 1461(2), fols. 225, 202. Manuscripts and Archives, Trinity College Dublin.

59 Oliver MacDonagh, *States of Mind: A Study of Anglo-Irish Conflict 1780–1980* (London: George Allen & Unwin, 1983), 1.

CHAPTER 2

Racializing Irish Historical Consciousness

Guy Beiner and Oded Y. Steinberg

Part of the appeal of Irish nationalist history writing, as it formulated and took root over the long nineteenth century, was its distinction between an "Irish race" and its foreign oppressors, a conflict that heralded the struggle for independence and promised the fulfillment of a manifest destiny. Race was perceived as an intrinsic quality, inherited from antiquity, and this essentialism gave a false impression of unchanging continuity, when in practice conceptualizations of race were subject to changes. Historiographical racialization has a history of its own, which needs to be unraveled.

Ignorant of local language and customs, representations of the Gaelic inhabitants in writings that bolstered the Elizabethan reconquest of Ireland recycled deprecating tropes that drew on descriptions of the twelfth-century conquest by the Cambro-Norman cleric Giraldus Cambrensis, whose *Topographia Hiberniae* (1186–87) and *Expugnatio Hibernica* (1189) depicted a "wild and inhospitable people" who "live like beasts."[1] Seeking to justify the violence entailed in the brutal subjugation of the populace, early modern authors – such as Edmund Spenser in his *View of the Present State of Ireland* (1633) – employed prejudiced stereotypes of inbred inferiority and savagery, echoing patronizing encounters with alterity in the New World.[2] In turn, defiant responses to Tudor and Stuart colonization by Irish writers reaffirmed the contrast rooted in late-medieval bardic poetry between the indigenous Irish (*Gael*) and the foreigner (*Gall*).[3]

This dichotomy compounded multi-layered conflicts that were grounded in differences of religion – Catholics pitted against Protestants; economics – dispossessed tenants contesting their subjugation to "planters"; politics – old aristocratic bloodlines seeking to reclaim a status lost to new elites; and what would be considered today as ethnicity – a self-perceived indigenous population resisting English (*Sassanach*) intrusion. The essentialization of Gaelic Irishness, which implied an unadulterated lineage that could be traced back through pseudo-histories to a Milesian quasi-race lost in the mists of primordial time, overlooked a complex history of regional divisions, migrations, and commingling, and unreflectively subsumed into itself the Nordic heritage of more than two centuries of Viking invasions.

Moreover, polar oppositions glossed over the construction of a broad Irish Catholic identity, forged out of resistance to being supplanted by New English Protestant settlers, that brought together the local Gaelic-Irish population and the Old English residents of the towns and the Pale (who, by and large, rejected the reformation). This gradual amalgamation brought to fruition late-medieval processes of cultural assimilation by which the descendants of Anglo-Normans were said to have become *Hiberniores Ipsis Hibernis* ("more Irish than the Irish themselves" – a cliché coined in the late-eighteenth century). At the same time, the Protestants who settled in Ireland were of various mixed pedigrees, with a distinct concentration of Lowland Scottish Presbyterians in the northern province of Ulster (Ulster-Scots). Homogeneity and purity of origin were clearly imagined notions.

After the defeat of James II at the hands of William III of Orange in the so-called "Glorious Revolution" of 1688–89, and the subsequent introduction of discriminatory Penal Laws, sustained Irish Catholic discontent was vented over the following century in the popular culture of vernacular Jacobite poetry, which reified crude differentiations. These subversive literary texts decried the usurpation of "pure Gaels" (*Gaoidheal nglan*) by Protestant heretics (*eircigh*), often depicted in biological – rather than confessional – terms as the progeny of Luther and Calvin, and prophesied a turning of the tables that would culminate in the expulsion (if not the extermination) of the outsiders.[4] In the late-eighteenth century, under the influence of the United Irishmen, Jacobitism would give way to Jacobinism with its more inclusive republican aspiration – as phrased by Theobald Wolfe Tone – "to substitute the common name of Irishman in place of the denominations of Protestant, Catholic, and Dissenter."[5] Yet pluralistic ideologies that hailed inclusive constructions of Irishness were undermined by the perseverance of sectarian animosities, which were considered atavistic and innate.

Antiquarians passionately debated fanciful theories of august origins, arguing whether the Irish were the venerable heirs of an ancient civilization or descended from barbarians whose redemption required external intervention.[6] The epic poems of the Ossian cycle, published by the controversial Scottish writer James Macpherson, romantically idealized the literary remains of an ancient Gaelic civilization in the Highlands, much to the chagrin of Irish scholars – such as Charles O'Conor of Belanagare – who contended that the source material originated in early Irish manuscripts and launched in response their own Celtic revival.[7] Mocking the scholarship of Irish antiquarians, the Scottish historian John Pinkerton anticipated nineteenth-century conceptions of race when he described the Celts as an inferior race "incapable of industry and civilization" and argued that, in contrast to the propensity for progress of the Germanic people of Britain, the "Wild Irish" Gaels – being of Celtic origins, were inherently savage, and "of savages there can be no history."[8]

The enlightenment introduced "a hodgepodge of biological, climatic and stadialist interpretations of racial and cultural difference."[9] In *An History of the Earth and Animated Nature* (1779, reissued in twenty editions), the Anglo-Irish author Oliver Goldsmith combined early racial classifications – found in *Systema naturae* (1735) by the Swedish naturalist Carl Linnaeus and *Histoire naturelle, générale et particulière* (1749–88) by the French naturalist Comte de Buffon – to identify "six distinct varieties in the human." The German physician Johann Friedrich Blumenbach effectively inaugurated the study of physical anthropology in *De generis humani varietate native* (1775), when he compared human skulls to identify four races that had "degenerated" from an original "Caucasian" race (while maintaining that they were not necessarily inferior in their capabilities). For such scholars, who adhered to a biblical belief in monogenesis, whereby all humans emerged from a common origin and varied over time, race was mutable.[10]

By contrast, the English physician Charles White advocated polygenesis, presenting in *An Account of the Regular Gradation in Man* (1799) a fixed racial physical hierarchy in which white people were superior to "Negros." The inhabitants of Ireland, although they "live in rude and smoky huts," could apparently be judged by the quality of their hair – which, according to White, "exhibits a graduation in the same line as the other marks of distinction" – and accordingly "placed in the highest rank of civilization."[11] If physiological attributes, and in particular skin color, were the primary distinguishing feature of race in eighteenth-century Britain and its empire, an equally influential paradigm can be found in the four-stages theory of stadialism developed in the Scottish Enlightenment. This model placed commercially developed England at the pinnacle of progress and considered the Irish to be backward, a condition that the Act of Union was supposed to amend.[12]

The creation of the United Kingdom of Great Britain and Ireland in the aftermath of the failed United Irish Rebellion of 1798 did not ultimately merge the peoples of the two isles into a uniform British citizenry, with the exception of those who chose to identify as unionists. By associating Irish nationalism with the *bête noire* of Catholicism, Daniel O'Connell's campaign for Catholic Emancipation – which resulted in the Roman Catholic Relief Act of 1829 – and his less successful campaign for the Repeal of the Act of Union played into deep-seated sentiments of anti-popery. Exacerbated by xenophobia against Irish migrants in Britain, prejudice against Irish Catholics was rife in mid-Victorian popular culture.[13] Over the nineteenth century, representations of Catholic Irishness increasingly assumed racial underpinnings.[14] This was mirrored in the vogue for Gothic fiction and its visual impact on caricatures in which Irishmen assumed monstrous forms.[15]

The English historical establishment was besotted with the inherited virtues of Anglo-Saxonism. Believing that in antiquity "distinctions of race were not of that odious and fantastic character which they have borne in modern times," Thomas Arnold proclaimed in his inaugural lecture as Regius Professor of Modern History at Oxford (1841) that "our English race is the German race" and that Normans and Saxons "both alike belong to the Teutonic or German stock."[16] Subsequent holders of the chair, including William Stubbs and Edward Augustus Freeman, as well as the Regius Professor of Modern History at Cambridge, Charles Kingsley, alongside authors of such popular works as *A Short History of the English People* (1874) by John Richard Green, promulgated the narrative that an Anglo-Saxon invasion of the fifth century had vanquished the autochthonic Celtic Britons and banished those who remained to the peripheral areas of Ireland, Wales, and the Scottish Highlands. In this national origin myth, "the politically mature and emotionally stable, virile, and enlightened Saxon yeoman emerged as an heroic archetype immeasurably superior in all respects to the clannish, primitive, excitable, and feminine Celt."[17] These racial distinctions were reinforced by mid-Victorian ethnology.[18] Yet, writers who insisted on the inferiority of a Celtic Irish race, tinged with its association with Catholicism, were obliged to acknowledge that over the course of history, racial categories had become blurred. James Anthony Froude (another holder of the Oxford Regius chair) put the blame for the Anglo-Irish conflict on the "inveterate turbulence of the Irish race" but was reminded by his critics that he himself had conceded: "we lay the fault on the intractability of the race; but the modern Irishman is of no race, so blended now is the blood of Celt and Dane, Saxon and Norman, Scot and Frenchman."[19]

Irish nationalists responded to Anglo-Saxonism by extolling the virtues of their origins. The locations of O'Connell's "monster meetings" were carefully chosen symbolic sites that evoked deep historical memories attached to such places as Tara (the ancient seat of Irish High Kings) and

Clontarf (the battleground where the Gaelic king Brian Boru defeated the foreign "Danes" in 1014). Schooled in O'Connellite political agitation, the members of Young Ireland were enamored by the romantic notion of restoring a venerable Celtic race to its former greatness. Thomas Davis, their leading light, used the pseudonym "The Celt" (which suited his mixed Welsh and Irish background) and was interested (albeit critically) in the antiquarian writings of William Wilde, whose juxtaposition of the ethnological examination of skulls found at archaeological burial sites with early historical and folkloric records has been aptly described as "a bridge between the impressionistic Celticist theories of earlier writers" and "the emerging Victorian spirit of scientific analysis and classification."[20] The pages of the *Nation*, the flagship organ of Irish romantic nationalism, and the extremely popular songbook *The Spirit of the Nation* (first published in 1844 and reissued in multiple editions) were replete with descriptions of noble-patriotic Celts facing villainous Saxons. Yet the republican ideals of Young Ireland, which in the vein of the United Irishmen aspired to bring together the traditions of the Green and the Orange, could not sustain the political implications of racial exclusivity.[21]

Davis opened his poem "Celts and Saxons" – which was "written in reply to some very beautiful verses printed in the *Evening Mail*, deprecating and defying the assumed hostility of the Irish Celts to the Irish Saxons" – by recapping time-old animosities:

> We hate the Saxon and the Dane,
> We hate the Norman men
> We curs'd their greed for blood and gain,
> We curse them now again.

But the poem then advocates the imperative of overcoming historical differences:

> Yet start not, Irish born man,
> If you're to Ireland true,
> We heed not blood, nor creed, nor clan
> We have no curse for you.[22]

In Young Ireland's ideology, as formulated by Davis, "the elements of Irish nationality ... must contain and represent the races of Ireland. It must not be Celtic, it must not be Saxon – it must be Irish."[23] Hence, Irishness was conceived as a multi-racial, or supra-racial, category.

The leaders of Young Ireland were inspired by the lectures *On Heroes, Hero-Worship, and The Heroic in History* (1840) of Thomas Carlyle, even though the influential essayist was an adherent of Anglo-Saxonism and an opponent to the repeal of the Union. After visiting Ireland during the Great Famine in the accompaniment of the Young Irelander Charles Gavin Duffy, Carlyle placed the responsibility for the disaster he had witnessed on the inbred primitiveness of the inhabitants:

> The Celt of Connemara, and other repealing finest peasantry, are white and not black; but it is not the colour of the skin that determines the savagery of a man.... Fruitless futile insurrection, continual sanguinary broils and riot that make his dwelling-place a horror to mankind, mark his progress generation after generation; and if no beneficient hand will chain him into wholesome *slavery*, and, with whip on back or otherwise, try to tame him and get some work out of him, Nature herself, intent to have her work tilled, has no resource but to exterminate him.[24]

This blatant justification of servitude for people deemed incapable of self-advancement and on the verge of extinction was echoed in Carlyle's notorious essay "Occasional Discourse on the Negro Question" (1849), which referred to the West Indies as a "Black Ireland" (and was curiously attributed to a fictional "Absconded Reporter" with the mock Irish name of Phelim M'Quirk).[25]

Indeed, "viewed through the cloudy lens of age-old stereotyping of the wild Irish, the Famine appeared to be an obvious instance of self-liquidating savagery."[26] Condescending attitudes of moralism-providentialism dismissed the humanitarian catastrophe of the Great Famine as an opportunity for sweeping reforms, asserting that it was not just a "social state" that needed to be remedied but, as put by the *Times*, "a race is to be changed."[27] Moreover, rebelliousness was construed as "a racially determined character flaw of the Irish."[28] Irish insurgents were depicted with simian features, whether in the illustrations of George Cruikshank for William Hamilton Maxwell's popular *History of the Irish Rebellion in 1798; with Memoirs of the Union, and Emmett's Insurrection in 1803* (originally published in 1845 and reissued in multiple editions) or in the caricatures of the satirical magazine *Punch* depicting Young Ireland's abortive rebellion in 1848 and the Fenian uprising of 1867.[29] Reports in the British press of endemic poverty and recurrent unrest, manifested in rebellions and agrarian agitation, castigated the Irish "Paddy" as different, not only in terms of religion and class, but also "seemed to confirm the notion that Irish Celts were a subrace or people with habits antithetically opposed to English norms of thought and behavior."[30]

Following the turmoil of the revolutions of 1848, racial conceptualizations were phrased in hardened scholarly terms, evident in debates that crossed between ethnology and anthropology.[31] Referring to "physiological laws" in his lectures on *The Races of Man* (originally published in 1850 as "A Fragment" and reissued in an expanded edition in 1862), the controversial Scottish anatomist Robert Knox justified the outcome of the Famine. Knox claimed that "700 years of absolute possession has not advanced by a single step the amalgamation of the Irish Celt with the Saxon-English," since the "races of men still remain distinct," and were inevitably "unaltered and unalterable." According to Knox, the "civilized man cannot sink lower than at Derrynane" (the ancestral home of Daniel O'Connell in county Kerry) or Skiberreen (a town in county Cork associated with the devastation of the Famine), and the "Celtic race of Ireland," being inherently incapable of progress, "must be forced from the soil."[32]

Knox's book elicited responses from Irish ethnologists (including private correspondence from Wilde). Though "totally opposed to his theological opinions, and also to his theory of natural antipathies between races," the Dublin doctor George Ellis wrote a tract on *Irish Ethnology Socially and Politically Considered* (1852) in which he accepted the premise of racial distinctiveness, whereby

> the two great races inhabiting the British Islands, the Saxon and the Celtic, have always exhibited, and continue at this day to exhibit, in as distinct and vivid colours as ever, notwithstanding some hundred years of partial intercommunication, the most strikingly opposed mental characteristics.[33]

Yet Ellis insisted that the Celtic race "is not to be considered and treated as an inferior race" and, as a unionist, maintained that "the *proximity* of a Saxon people has a *prejudicial* effect on the progress of a Celtic, until a close union takes place between them."[34] The nationalist Belfast doctor John M'Elheran, a former student of Knox, wrote a vehement letter to the *Times,* protesting against the "infidel, material theory of race," and in a separate publication, insisted that "the Celtic is the highest type of mankind," whereas "English at large are the most brutified race in Europe."[35] Irish ethnologists essentially accepted the racial categories, but objected to the implications of prejudice.

Although Knox could be considered a marginal figure, his views on racial disparity permeated into mainstream anthropology through his self-ascribed "disciple," the speech therapist James Hunt, who became the inaugural president of the Anthropological Society in 1863.[36] John Beddoe, a founder of the Ethnological Society, president of the Anthropological Society, and later president of the Royal Anthropological Institute of Great Britain and Ireland, convened sessions in which papers were presented on the racial elements of the Irish Celt. In *The Races of Britain* (1885), Beddoe used measurements of fairness of hair and eye color, alongside typology of bone features, to present an "Index of Nigrescence" in which Irish Celts were a distinct race, to the extent that "the great Irish immigration of late years is not at present, ethnologically, very important; for the Irish are amongst us, but not of us, and generally intermarry among themselves."[37]

The belief in separation of unequal races – originally put forward in *Essai sur l'inégalité des races humaines* (1853–55) by the French aristocrat Arthur de Gobineau, for whom racial conflicts propelled history and "mixture of races" resulted in degeneration – was mediated into English political discourse by the cultural commentator Walter Bagehot in *Physics and Politics* (1872).[38] Furthermore, stretched interpretations of Charles Darwin's chapter "On the Races of Man" in *The Descent of Man, and Selection in Relation to Sex* (1871), embellished by Social Darwinists and the adherents of the eugenics movement launched by Francis Galton, paved the way for scientific racism.[39] Yet, this development was less noticeable in Ireland, where Darwinism – introduced in John Tyndall's celebrated Belfast "Address to the British Association for the Advancement of Science" (1874) and promoted rigorously by "Darwin's bulldog" Thomas Henry Huxley – encountered local opposition on nationalist and religious grounds (both from Protestants and Catholics).[40]

Irish nationalist history books published in the mid-late nineteenth century and reissued in multiple editions were littered with references to race. However, uses of the term in such popular works as Martin Haverty's accessible school textbook *The History of Ireland, Ancient and Modern* (originally published 1860) or Francis Mary Cusack's *The Illustrated History of Ireland from the Earliest Period* (1868) were fluid. In its most elementary sense, "race" could signify genealogical pedigree stemming back to ancestral heroes (as in the "race of Conall," "race of Niall," or "race of Heremon" – the mythological first monarch of Ireland); at its broadest, it alluded to all of humanity (the "human race") and its common biblical origin (the "race of Adam"). It facilitated a meta-narrative by labeling recurring waves of migration from mythological times (Firbolgs, Tuatha Dé Danann, and Milesians) through to early history (Scots, Norsemen-Danes), and ultimately separating the English from the Irish. Racial categories were employed liberally to demarcate the power oppositions of colonialism, as put by Cusack: "antipathy of Celt to Saxon is not so much an antipathy of race or person, as the natural enmity which the oppressed entertains towards the oppressor."[41]

The militant Young Ireland exile John Mitchel complained that "English writers were diligent in pointing out and illustrating the difference of 'race' between Celt and Saxon; which proved to their own satisfaction that the former were born to be ruled by the latter."[42] Rather than rejecting racial categories that were evidently constructed for polemical purposes, in *The History of Ireland, from the Treaty of Limerick to the Present Time* – a standard account of recent history – Mitchel joined other nationalist writers in calling attention to the plight of the "Celtic race" in consequence of the Famine.[43] Reviewing the many migrations and conquests, and acknowledging countless instances of intermixture and amalgamation, nationalist writers were aware that the contemporary scientific conceptualizations of race did not fit Irish history. Nevertheless, they willfully bought into the belief that

> there is something in the Irish climate and surroundings which, even within a generation, exercises a powerful influence in bringing the descendants of all foreigners to a type possessing much in common and with characteristics unlike any other people.[44]

Though plainly ahistorical, the notion of a distinct "Irish race" proved to be useful as a marker for innate national uniqueness.

Taken to be a fundamental categorization of humankind, race signified deep roots that determined collective character. As noted by George Mosse, nationalist thinking believed that "the roots determine the firmness of the tree."[45] But for Irish historians, race had added value that went beyond the nation. Association by race with a distinguished ancient civilization contradicted anti-Home Rule rhetoric, which frequently harnessed the imperialist justification of subjugating so-called primitive societies by comparing the Irish to peoples considered to have no history of note, such as the "Hottentot" of the Cape of Africa who was branded as the archetype of racial inferiority.[46] Affronted by the condescension and prejudice of Anglo-Saxonism, writers such as the Irish American priest Fr. C. J. Herlihy felt it "perfectly natural therefore that we should laud the virtues and perfections of the Celts and demonstrate how far superior they are in almost every respect to the Anglo-Saxons."[47]

Race also enhanced nationalism with a transnational dimension, inextricably bonding the fate of the inhabitants of Ireland with Irish diasporic communities worldwide.[48] *The Story of Ireland* (first published in 1867) – an extremely popular historical narrative "written for the youth of Ireland" by the nationalist politician Alexander Martin Sullivan and designed to show that "Irish disaffection" was the outcome of a long-standing "unhappy war between England and the Irish race" – countered post-Famine humiliation from how "the English press gloated over the anticipated extirpation of the Irish race" with a sense of pride in the worldwide solidarity shown in response to the execution of the "Manchester Martyrs," when "the whole Irish race sorrowed," or the support that Charles Stewart Parnell received in the United States, where "the people of Irish race rallied around him."[49] Irish heritage could be celebrated abroad through such biographical compendiums as *Irish Celts: A Cyclopedia of Race History* (1884), which proposed that

> It is in the lives of her children, scattered throughout the entire earth either by zeal or necessity, for a thousand years, more, perhaps, than in the history of its island home, that we must seek the glory and the achievements of a gallant race.[50]

The resonance of race for nineteenth-century Irish history writing was both temporal and spatial.[51]

The Irish Revival at the *fin de siècle* was influenced by the lectures of Professor of Poetry at Oxford Matthew Arnold *On the Study of Celtic Literature* (1867), which in turn were inspired by the Franco-Breton scholar Ernest Renan's *La Poésie des races celtiques* (1854). Infatuated by the poetic creativity he seemed to find in literatures associated with the Celtic race, Renan considered Ireland to be particular as "the only country in Europe where the native can produce the titles of his descent, and designate with certainty, even in the darkness of prehistoric ages, the race from which he has sprung."[52] Arnold believed that his father Thomas had erred in his insistence on the separation of Saxons from Celts, and maintained instead that "commingling" would suffuse English culture with the sentiments of "Celtic genius," while "the Celt, undisciplinable, anarchical, and turbulent by nature" could benefit from "Anglo-Saxon temperament," which was "disciplinable and steadily obedient."[53] This reappraisal of Anglo-Saxonism stimulated the endorsement of Celtic mythology as ancient Irish history, evident in the burst of literature from Standish O'Grady's two-volume *History of Ireland* (1878 and 1880) through to T. W. Rolleston's *Myths & Legends of the Celtic Race* (1911).

While intended to appeal to both nationalists and unionists, the manifesto of the revival, as formulated by Douglas Hyde in "The Necessity for de-Anglicising Ireland" (1892), effectively inverted Arnold's thesis by calling in racial terms for cultural separation:

> In a word, we must strive to cultivate everything that is most racial, most smacking of the soil, most Gaelic, most Irish, because in spite of the little admixture of Saxon blood in the north-east corner, this island *is* and will *ever* remain Celtic at the core, far more Celtic than most people imagine.... On racial lines, then, we shall best develop, following the bent of our own natures.[54]

Ratcheting up national exclusiveness, the language of race turned its back on the multi-cultural legacies of a history of commingling, even though it was adopted by Anglo-Irish Protestants who were the product of such fusions, which in itself was a cause of resentment in the "Irish Ireland" polemics of the journal the *Leader*, edited by D.P. Moran.[55] Around the same time, Ernest Renan, in his far-seeing Sorbonne lecture, "Qu'est-ce qu'une nation?" (1882), had come to the conclusion that "The truth is that there is no pure race; and that making politics depend upon ethnographical analysis, is allowing it to be borne upon a chimaera." Realizing that national distinctions are a product of "the aggregate of humanity," Renan observed that "discussions upon race are interminable, because the word 'race' is taken by the philological historians and by physiological anthropologists in two totally different senses." He contended that "human history is essentially different from zoology. Race is not everything ... and we have no right to go about the world feeling the heads of people, then taking them by the throat, and saying, 'You are of our blood; you belong to us!,'" and cautioned with prescience: "this ethnographical politics is not even safe. You exploit it today on other people; some day you may see it turned against yourselves."[56]

In her popular histories, the nationalist writer Alice Stopford Green – widow of John Richard Green, a popularizer of Anglo-Saxonism – often referred to racial distinctions, yet concluded that "an Irish nation of a double race will not fear to look back on Irish history."[57] Race was configured as the driving force behind Irish history in *The Story of the Irish Race* (1921), written by the nationalist Seumas MacManus during the War of Independence and later updated with a brief survey of subsequent events, which concluded with the conviction that race would continue to be at the fore and that "many a long and glorious Irish day shall yet have come and gone" before a final chapter could be written.[58] At the Irish Race Congress, convened in Paris in 1922 with the participation of delegates from around the world, the Professor of Early Irish History at University College Dublin and nationalist politician Eoin MacNeill delivered a lecture on Irish history to which Éamon de Valera, who schemed to co-opt this forum into an oppositional body to the newly established Irish Free State, responded that "the knowledge of Irish history is particularly valuable to the members of our race throughout the world."[59] As head of government from 1932, de Valera would validate the scientific notion of an Irish race by offering state support to the anthropometric fieldwork of the American physical anthropologist Earnest Albert Hooton, director of the Harvard Irish Mission (1932–36).[60]

By then, however, Irish history had moved on. Signaling a new direction for the professionalization of the discipline, in the first issue of the journal *Irish Historical Studies*, the founding co-editor Theodore William Moody – soon to be appointed Erasmus Smith Professor of Modern History at Trinity College Dublin – reviewed I. J. Herring's secondary school textbook *History of Ireland* (1937) and noted that "it is depressing to find the word 'race' used in its loose, popular sense."[61] Following the espousal of scientific racism in Nazi ideology, the term quickly fell out of fashion and seldom appeared in historical writing, which by the 1980s – during the revisionist controversy – grappled with "varieties of Irishness" and dismissed "racialist" terminology in the analysis of anti-Irish stereotypes.[62]

Although race appears to have been expunged from the vocabulary of Irish historiography and recent conceptualizations of Irishness have embraced multiculturalism, at some level, the appeal of racial essentialism crafted over the long nineteenth century has not entirely vanished. Its lingering presence can be detected, for example, in the continued popularity of *A History of Ireland: From Earliest Times to 1922* by Erasmus Smith and subsequent Lecky Professor of History at Trinity College Dublin, Edmund Curtis, a book which has rarely been out of print since its first publication in 1936, making it "a study of history and an historical document." A twenty-first-century edition still retains the numerous references to race throughout the volume, concluding that the Anglo-Irish – "in many ways a very Irish stock" – lived for centuries alongside "a race of innate Catholic and Celtic temperament." This antiquated categorization is rendered palatable by adding the more rational argument that unionist opposition to nationalism "has been based more on political grounds than on religious or racial prejudice."[63] No longer acceptable in its explicit form, and generally substituted with the more agreeable concept of "ethnicity," it may be that racialization has been sublimated into a popular historical subconsciousness, allowing long-held beliefs of inherent distinctiveness to persevere.

Notes

1 F. X. Martin, "Gerald of Wales, Norman Reporter on Ireland," *Studies* 58, no. 231 (1969): 279–92; John Gillingham, *The English in the Twelfth Century: Imperialism, National Identity, and Political Values* (Woodbridge and Rochester, NY: Boydell Press, 2000), 145–60.
2 Nicholas P. Canny, *Making Ireland British, 1580–1650* (Oxford: Oxford University Press, 2001), 42–55; Patricia Palmer, *Language and Conquest in Early Modern Ireland: English Renaissance Literature and Elizabethan Imperial Expansion* (Cambridge: Cambridge University Press, 2004), 40–107.

3 Joseph Th. Leerssen, *Mere Irish & Fíor-Ghael: Studies in the Idea of Irish Nationality, Its Development, and Literary Expression Prior to the Nineteenth Century*, rev. ed. (Cork: Cork University Press, 1996, 1986), 177–216.

4 The *locus classicus* for Irish Jacobite poetry is Breandán Ó Buachalla, *Aisling Ghéar: Na Stíobhartaigh agus an tAos Léinn, 1603–1788* (Dublin: An Clóchomhar Tta, 1996). See also Vincent Morley, "Irish Jacobitism, 1691–1790," in *The Cambridge History of Ireland*, ed. James Kelly (Cambridge: Cambridge University Press, 2018), 3:23–47.

5 Theobald Wolfe Tone, *Memoirs of Theobald Wolfe Tone*, ed. William Theobald Wolfe Tone (London: Henry Colburn, 1827), 1:64.

6 Joseph Th. Leerssen, *Remembrance and Imagination: Patterns in the Historical and Literary Representation of Ireland in the Nineteenth Century* (Cork: Cork University Press, 1996), 68–73; Clare O'Halloran, *Golden Ages and Barbarous Nations: Antiquarian Debate and Cultural Politics in Ireland, c.1750–1800* (Cork: Cork University Press, 2004), 13–70.

7 Micheal Mac Craith, "'We Know All These Poems': The Irish Response to Ossian," in *The Reception of Ossian in Europe*, ed. Howard Gaskill (London: Thoemmes Continuum, 2004), 91–108; Thomas M. Curley, *Samuel Johnson, the Ossian Fraud and the Celtic Revival in Great Britain and Ireland* (Cambridge: Cambridge University Press, 2009), 123–55.

8 John Pinkerton, *A Dissertation on the Origin and Progress of the Scythians or Goths: Being an Introduction to the Ancient and Modern History of Europe* (London: John Nichols, 1787), 27, 69; John Pinkerton, *An Enquiry into the History of Scotland Preceding the Reign of Malcolm III, or the Year 1056, including the Authentic History of That Period* (London: John Nichols, 1789), 2:1–51. See also Silvia Sebastiani, *The Scottish Enlightenment: Race, Gender, and the Limits of Progress* (New York: Palgrave Macmillan, 2013), 165; Colin Kidd, "Gaelic Antiquity and National Identity in Enlightenment Ireland and Scotland," *English Historical Review* 109, no. 434 (1994): 1207.

9 Colin Kidd, *British Identities before Nationalism: Ethnicity and Nationhood in the Atlantic World, 1600–1800* (Cambridge: Cambridge University Press, 1999), 24.

10 Ivan Hannaford, *Race: The History of an Idea in the West* (Washington, D.C. and Baltimore, MD: Woodrow Wilson Center Press and Johns Hopkins University Press, 1996), 187–234; Thomas Hudson, "From 'Nation' to 'Race': The Origin of Racial Classification in Eighteenth-Century Thought," *Eighteenth Century Studies* 29, no. 3 (1996): 247–64; Bruce Baum, *The Rise and Fall of the Caucasian Race: A Political History of Racial Identity* (New York: New York University Press, 2006), 59–94.

11 Charles White, *An Account of the Regular Gradation in Man and in Different Animals and Vegetables* (London: Printed for C. Dilly, 1799), 91–2.

12 Roxann Wheeler, *The Complexion of Race: Categories of Difference in Eighteenth-Century British Culture* (Philadelphia: University of Pennsylvania Press, 2000), 176–233; Kevin Whelan, "Writing Ireland: Reading England," in *Ireland in the Nineteenth Century: Regional Identity*, eds. Leon Litvack and Glenn Hooper (Dublin: Four Courts Press, 2000), 185–98.

13 D. G. Paz, "Anti-Catholicism, Anti-Irish Stereotyping, and Anti-Celtic Racism in Mid-Victorian Working-Class Periodicals," *Albion* 18, no. 4 (1986): 601–16.

14 Jim Mac Laughlin, "'Pestilence on Their Backs, Famine in Their Stomachs': The Racial Construction of Irishness and the Irish in Victorian Britain," in *Ireland and Cultural Theory: The Mechanics of Authenticity*, eds. Colin Graham and Richard Kirkland (Houndmills and New York: Macmillan and St. Martin's Press, 1999), 50–76.

15 Luke Gibbons, *Gaelic Gothic: Race, Colonization, and Irish Culture* (Galway: Arlen House, 2004).

16 Thomas Arnold, "Preface to the Third Volume of the Edition of Thucydides," in *The Miscellaneous Works of Thomas Arnold*, ed. Arthur Penrhyn Stanley (London: B. Fellowes, 1845), 393; Thomas Arnold, *Introductory Lectures on Modern History*, 2nd ed. (London: B. Fellowes, 1843), 26; see also Reginald Horsman, "Origins of Racial Anglo-Saxonism in Great Britain Before 1850," *Journal of the History of Ideas* 37, no. 3 (1976): 401–2.

17 L. Perry Curtis, Jr., *Anglo-Saxons and Celts: A Study of Anti-Irish Prejudice in Victorian England* (Bridgeport, Conn.: Conference on British Studies at the University of Bridgeport, 1968), 74–89. See also Hugh A. MacDougall, *Racial Myth in English History: Trojans, Teutons, and Anglo-Saxons* (Hanover, NH: University Press of New England, 1982), 96–102; Oded Y. Steinberg, *Race, Nation, History: Anglo-German Thought in the Victorian Era* (Philadelphia: University of Pennsylvania Press, 2019), 27–30, 124. See also Peter Mandler, "'Race' and 'Nation' in Mid-Victorian Thought," in *History, Religion, and Culture: British Intellectual History, 1750–1950*, eds. Stefan Collini, Richard Whatmore, and B. W. Young (Cambridge: Cambridge University Press, 2000), 224–44.

18 George W. Stocking, Jr., *Victorian Anthropology* (New York: Free Press, 1987), 62–3.

19 James Anthony Froude, *The English in Ireland in the Eighteenth Century* (New York: Scribner, Armstrong, and Co., 1873), 2: 19, 127; Ciaran Brady, *James Anthony Froude: An Intellectual Biography of a Victorian Prophet* (Oxford: Oxford University Press, 2013), 266.

20 Thomas Davis, "Ethnology of the Irish Race," in *Literary and Historical Essays by Thomas Davis*, ed. Charles Gavin Duffy (Dublin: James Duffy, 1846), 80–88; Sean Ryder, "Son and Parents: Speranza and Sir William Wilde," in *Oscar Wilde in Context*, eds. Kerry Powell and Peter Raby (Cambridge: Cambridge University Press, 2013), 10.

21 James Quinn, *Young Ireland and the Writing of Irish History* (Dublin: University College Dublin Press, 2015), 75–6; Julie M. Dugger, "Black Ireland's Race: Thomas Carlyle and the Young Ireland Movement," *Victorian Studies* 48, no. 3 (2006): 461–85.

22 *The Spirit of the Nation: Ballads and Songs by the Writers of "The Nation,"* (Dublin: James Duffy, 1845), 191–93; originally published in *Nation*, April 13, 1844, 425.

23 Thomas Davis, "Ballad Poetry of Ireland," in *Literary and Historical Essays*, 222; originally published as a review of Charles Gavan Duffy, *The Ballad Poetry of Ireland* (Dublin: James Duffy, 1845) in *Nation*, August 2, 1845, 698.

24 Thomas Carlyle, *On the Repeal of the Union* (London: Leadenhall Press, 1889), 48–50 (written in the spring of 1848).

25 Anon. [Thomas Carlyle], "Occasional Discourse on the Negro Question," *Fraser's Magazine for Town and Country* 40, no. 240 (December 1849): 670–79. See also Dugger, "Black Ireland's Race"; John Morrow, "Thomas Carlyle, 'Young Ireland' and the 'Condition of Ireland Question?,'" *The Historical Journal* 51, no. 3 (2008): 643–67.

26 Patrick Brantlinger, *Dark Vanishings: Discourse on the Extinction of Primitive Races, 1800–1930* (Ithaca: Cornell University Press, 2003), 100.

27 *Times*, October 9, 1846, 4.

28 Patrick Brantlinger, *Taming Cannibals: Race and the Victorians* (Ithaca: Cornell University Press, 2011), 138–42.

29 L. Perry Curtis, Jr., *Apes and Angels: The Irishman in Victorian Caricature* (Washington, D.C.: Smithsonian Institution Press, [1971] 1997), 23–57.

30 Curtis, Jr., *Apes and Angels*, 21; see also Michael de Nie, *The Eternal Paddy: Irish Identity and the British Press, 1798–1882* (Madison: University of Wisconsin Press, 2004), 5–13.

31 Adam Kuper, "Civilization, Culture, and Race: Anthropology in the Nineteenth Century," in *The Cambridge History of Modern European Thought*, eds. Peter E. Gordon and Warren Breckman (Cambridge: Cambridge University Press, 2019), 1:400–1.

32 Robert Knox, *The Races of Men: A Philosophical Enquiry into the Influence of Race over the Destinies of Nations* (London: H. Renshaw, 1862), 2:323, 18, 53, 592, 69, 316, 318, 324–5, 379.

33 George Ellis, *Irish Ethnology Socially and Politically Considered: Embracing a General Outline of the Celtic and Saxon Races, with Practical Inferences* (Dublin: Hodges and Smith, 1852), 6, 12.

34 Ellis, *Irish Ethnology Socially and Politically Considered*, 80, 153.

35 John M'Elheran, "Irish Impudence," *Times*, October 7, 1852, 5; John M'Elheran, *The Condition of Women and Children Among the Celtic, Gothic, and Other Nations* (Boston: Patrick Donahoe, 1858), 60, 225. See also Robert J. C. Young, *The Idea of English Ethnicity* (Malden, MA: Blackwell, 2008), 112–19.

36 Anon. [James Hunt], "Knox on the Celtic Race," *The Anthropological Review* 6, no. 21 (1868): 175–91. See also Terry Jay Ellingson, *The Myth of the Noble Savage* (Berkeley: University of California Press, 2001), 248–62; Ronald Rainger, "Race, Politics, and Science: The Anthropological Society of London in the 1860s," *Victorian Studies* 22, no. 1 (1978): 51–70; Evelleen Richards, "The 'Moral Anatomy' of Robert Knox: The Interplay between Biological and Social Thought in Victorian Scientific Naturalism," *Journal of the History of Biology* 22, no. 3 (1989): 373–436.

37 John Beddoe, *The Races of Britain: A Contribution to the Anthropology of Western Europe* (Bristol and London: J. W. Arrowsmith and Trubner, 1885), 138. See also the protocol of the discussion at a meeting of the *Anthropological Society* on July 14, 1870 on papers read by Henry Hudson "On the Irish Celt," G. H. Kinahan "On the Race Elements of the Irish People," and John Beddoe

"On the Kelts of Ireland," in *Journal of the Anthropological Society of London* 8 (1870): clxxviii–clxxxiv.

38 Edward Beasley, *The Victorian Reinvention of Race: New Racisms and the Problem of Grouping in the Human Sciences* (London: Routledge, 2010), 81–96.

39 Christine Bolt, *Victorian Attitudes to Race* (London: Routledge and K. Paul, 1971), 1–28; Nancy Stepan, *The Idea of Race in Science: Great Britain, 1800–1960* (Hamden, CT: Archon Books, 1982), 47–82; Beasley, *The Victorian Reinvention of Race*, 97–111.

40 Greta Jones, "Nation and Religion: The Debate About Darwinism in Ireland," in *The Reception of Charles Darwin in Europe*, eds. Eve-Marie Engels and Thomas F. Glick (London and New York: Continuum, 2008), 1:66–78; see also Paul B. Rich, "Social Darwinism, Anthropology and English Perspectives of the Irish, 1867–1900," *History of European Ideas* 19, no. 4–6 (July 1994): 777–85.

41 Francis Mary Cusack, *The Illustrated History of Ireland from the Earliest Period* (London: Longmans and Co., 1868), 343.

42 John Mitchel, *The Last Conquest of Ireland (Perhaps)* (Glasgow: R. & T. Washbourne, 1876), 207.

43 John Mitchel, *The History of Ireland, from the Treaty of Limerick to the Present Time* (New York: D. J. Sadlier & Co., 1868), 597–600. See also Isaac Butt, *Land Tenure in Ireland: A Plea for the Celtic Race*, 3rd ed. (Dublin and London: John Falconer & Longmans, Green, Reader, and Dyer, 1866).

44 Thomas Addis Emmet, *Ireland Under English Rule; or, a Plea for the Plaintiff* (New York and London: G. P. Putnam's Sons, 1903), 1:x.

45 George L. Mosse, *Toward the Final Solution: A History of European Racism* (Madison, WI: University of Wisconsin Press, [1978] 1985), 47.

46 Bruce Nelson, *Irish Nationalists and the Making of the Irish Race* (Princeton, NJ: Princeton University Press, 2012), 6. Cf. Nicholas Hudson, "'Hottentots' and the Evolution of European Racism," *Journal of European Studies* 34, no. 4 (2004): 308–32.

47 C. J. Herlihy, *The Celt above the Saxon; or, a Comparative Sketch of the Irish and English People in War*, 2nd ed. (Boston, MA: Angel Guardian Press, 1904), viii.

48 See Cian T. McMahon, *The Global Dimensions of Irish Identity: Race, Nation, and the Popular Press, 1840–1880* (Chapel Hill, NC: University of North Carolina Press, 2015).

49 A. M. Sullivan, *The Story of Ireland; a Narrative of Irish History, from the Earliest Ages to the Insurrection of 1867* (Providence: H. McElroy, 1883), 560, 564, 575, 592, 628.

50 James O'Brien, *Irish Celts: A Cyclopedia of Race History* (Detroit: L.F. Kilroy & Company, 1884), introduction.

51 Luke Gibbons, "Race against Time: Racial Discourse and Irish History," *Oxford Literary Review* 13, no. 1 (1991): 95–117.

52 Ernest Renan, *The Poetry of the Celtic Races, and Other Essays* translated, introduced, and annotated by William G. Hutchison (London: Walter Scott Publishing Co., 1896), 5.

53 Matthew Arnold, *On the Study of Celtic Literature* (London: Smith, Elder and Co., 1867), 16–17, 109. See also Brantlinger, *Taming Cannibals*, 143–50, 154; Joep Th. Leerssen, "Englishness, Ethnicity and Matthew Arnold," *European Journal of English Studies*, 10, no. 1 (2006): 63–79.

54 Douglas Hyde, "The Necessity for de-Anglicising Ireland," in *The Revival of Irish Literature: Addresses by Sir Charles Gavin Duffy, George Sigerson, and Dr. Douglas Hyde* (London: T. Fisher Unwin, 1894), 159.

55 Nelson, *Irish Nationalists*, 46–7.

56 Ernest Renan, "What is a Nation," in *The Poetry of the Celtic Races, and Other Essays*, translated, introduced, and annotated by William G. Hutchison (London: Walter Scott Publishing Co., 1896), 72–5; for the original see Ernest Renan, *Qu'est-ce qu'une nation? Conférence faite en Sorbonne, le 11 Mars 1882* (Paris: Calmann Lévy, 1882), 16–18.

57 Alice Stopford Green, *Irish Nationality* (New York and London: Henry Holt and William & Norgate, 1911), 253.

58 Seumas MacManus, *The Story of the Irish Race: A Popular History of Ireland* (New York: Devin-Adair, [1921] 1977), 723; see also John Brannigan, *Race in Modern Irish Literature and Culture* (Edinburgh: Edinburgh University Press, 2009), 31–4.

59 *Imtheachta Aonaighe na n-Gaedheal ib-Páris, Eanair, 1922: Proceedings of the Irish Race Congress in Paris, January, 1922* (London: Cahill, 1922), 46; see also Brannigan, *Race in Modern Irish Literature and Culture*, 35–48.

60 Mairéad Carew, *The Quest for the Irish Celt: The Harvard Archaeological Mission to Ireland, 1932–1936* (Newbridge, Co. Kildare: Irish Academic Press, 2018).

61 *Irish Historical Studies* 1, no. 1 (1938): 92.

62 R. F. Foster, *Modern Ireland, 1600–1972* (London: Penguin Books, 1989), 363–4.

63 Edmund Curtis, *A History of Ireland: From Earliest Times to 1922* (London and New York: Routledge, [1936] 2002), xi, 343.

CHAPTER 3

Race, Minstrelsy, and the Irish Stage
The Origins and Afterlives of Dion Boucicault's The Octoroon

Patrick Lonergan

Dion Boucicault's 1859 melodrama *The Octoroon* has always proven resistant to categorization. Set in Louisiana and premiered in New York on the eve of the American Civil War, it was written by an Anglo-Irish playwright who had learned about melodrama in France and was presented as a star vehicle for his Edinburgh-born wife, Agnes Robertson. In its attempt to offer a critique of slavery that is also an idealization of Southern gentility, it was an intervention into American politics that aimed to offend as few Americans as possible – but it was also popular internationally: its use of well-worn melodramatic tropes concerning mortgages and the marriage market meant that audiences throughout the Anglophone world found its plot as compelling as its politics.

The Octoroon also had an important presence in the Irish theater. Although less popular than the plays that Boucicault directly set in Ireland, it *was* performed regularly in theaters across the island from the 1860s to the 1920s. It fell out of fashion not because of its themes but simply because large-scale spectacular melodramas lost out in the competition with cinema that had intensified from the 1920s onward.[1] And rather than being seen as different from such work as *The Colleen Bawn* (1860), *Arrah-na-Pogue* (1864), or *The Shaughraun* (1874), *The Octoroon* was praised in Ireland for its similarity to other Boucicault plays, especially in its use of spectacular scenes such as a slave auction and the burning of a steamboat. The Irish audiences of the late nineteenth century did not see *The Octoroon* as anomalous: they had been watching plays about American slavery (some written by Irish authors) for decades, and Boucicault's presentation of racial stereotypes both assumed and underscored their familiarity with blackface minstrelsy, a practice which had been common on the Irish stage since at least the 1830s.

My aim in this chapter is to show that *The Octoroon* must be situated and understood within the context of Irish culture, which is not to deny its importance for other national traditions, but rather to demonstrate that

Irish theater history must account for the importance of minstrelsy and other forms of blackface performance from the eighteenth to the twenty-first century. Although scholars have begun to understand how minstrelsy played a role in the construction of nineteenth-century Irish American identity, we remain insufficiently aware of how those cultural dynamics fed back into Irish life: Joseph Roach has compellingly argued that Boucicault is an exemplary "circum-Atlantic playwright" – yet to date there has been insufficient consideration of how that dynamic might have operated on the Irish and British sides of the ocean.[2] With the exception of important work by Douglas Riach, John Brannigan, Kathleen Gough, and Charlotte McIvor, relatively little scholarship has been conducted about how blackface was performed in Ireland itself: how it was used to construct Irish identity, how it fed into the broader theatrical culture, how it informed attitudes toward slavery and colonialism, whether it promoted racism in the theater or the broader society, and how Irish immigrants to America brought their memories of minstrelsy and other blackface performances with them.[3]

The Octoroon, I suggest, can be seen as operating at the apex of an Irish tradition of blackface performance that needs to be understood better. It is a play that brought to fruition much of what had come before, and its production influenced much of what followed on the Irish stage. The fact that it is now seen as tangential to the Irish tradition – that its themes and techniques are seen as irrelevant – represents a failure to understand how the Irish theater was informed by the institution of slavery and the broader patterns of racism that accompanied it.

Race on the Irish Stage before 1860

The Octoroon has been claimed by many national literatures but is fully at home in none of them. It has several times been anthologized in collections of American drama, but in most cases, its inclusion has been questioned and qualified, often by the anthologists themselves.[4] Its importance for American culture has been evident in many other ways: it was filmed three times in the early silent movie era (in 1903, 1909, and 1913) and had a short, well-received Broadway run in 1961, where it was billed by its producers as "an American classic."[5] It has also been an important presence on Australian stages. One of the first films made in that country was a silent version of the play, indicating its ongoing popularity there in the early twentieth century.[6] *The Octoroon* has also occasionally been revived in Britain: for example, BBC radio performed it in 2013, in an adaptation written and directed by Mark Ravenhill, and it has also been anthologized in collections of British literature. Further, as discussed in more detail below, it has been the subject of renewed interest since 2014, when the American playwright Branden Jacobs-Jenkins developed an adaptation of it, retitling it *An Octoroon*.

The original play has not been ignored in Ireland or within Irish theater studies, but it is usually seen as having limited importance. In her ground-breaking 2012 book *Dion Boucicault: Irish Identity on Stage*, Deirdre McFeely provides information about *The Octoroon* but does so mainly to position it as a stepping stone to *The Colleen Bawn*.[7] Scott Boltwood makes a similar argument in an article published in 2001, suggesting that those two plays display "a marked evolution in Boucicault's conception of racial difference and miscegenation": that what is explicit about race in *The Octoroon* can be seen implicitly in *The Colleen Bawn* and other Irish plays.[8]

Other scholars interpret Boucicault's treatment of race in *The Octoroon* as subtly emblematic of his Irish identity. His biographer Richard Fawkes offers the suggestion that "as a member of a subjugated nation, Boucicault keenly felt the indignity of slavery, of one race being beholden to another" – but he makes that observation in passing, and does not elaborate on how the link might be evident in the play.[9] Similarly, Elizabeth Butler Cullingford proposes that Boucicault's creation of Wahnotee, an Indigenous American character whom he played himself, was founded on a sense of cross-racial identification: "As the red man in full warpaint avenges the murder of the black man by stabbing the white oppressor, Irish members of the audience might see in this racialized moral pantomime a displaced image of their own revolt against the colonizer," she proposes.[10] But again that observation is made in passing, as part of a longer chapter that is about other themes.

In these and similar examples, Boucicault's treatment of race and his use of practices associated with minstrelsy are viewed as relevant only when they contextualize explicitly Irish themes or characteristics. That statement is not intended as a negative criticism: those scholars are simply exploring aspects of the play that are not directly relevant to the present argument. But it seems important to call attention to the indefinite status of *The Octoroon*, which has launched debates in Irish, American, Australian, and English theater criticism without fully being integrated into any of them.

It might be argued that this problem of identification arises because Boucicault had designed the play to travel internationally – that, just as his *Poor of New York* (1857) could become *The Poor of Liverpool*, *The Poor of Chicago*, or the poor of any other city that Boucicault's company happened to be visiting, so was *The Octoroon* seen as a work that would be of interest both within and beyond America. It has often been observed that in writing his play, Boucicault was capitalizing on the success of the stage adaptations of *Uncle Tom's Cabin* that had appeared in the 1850s. But Stowe's novel and its subsequent theatrical versions were often more popular in the British empire and in Europe than they were in America (as Boucicault himself was probably aware).[11] When he brought *The Octoroon* to London, Boucicault infamously changed its ending in response to audience demand, concluding it with a marriage rather than the suicide of the eponymous heroine that American audiences had found so moving (and which also avoided the risk of provoking those American audiences by suggesting that a "mixed marriage" might constitute a happy ending for the play). That decision demonstrates that audiences in Britain and the U.S. had different attitudes to slavery, of course.[12] But we should not lose sight of the fact that most other features of the play were warmly received in the UK, partly because Boucicault was making use of tropes and performance practices that had been present on the Irish and British stages for many decades – some of which he would have encountered as a young man growing up between England and Ireland himself.

The familiarity of those features of the play is important for understanding its Irish reception. *The Octoroon* was certainly not the first Irish drama to feature actors in blackface and to address the theme of slavery in the Americas. That status is likely to belong to William Macready's *The Irishman in London* – subtitled *the Happy African* – which first appeared in London in 1792 and was revived there many times until the 1840s. It was also popular in New York and is thought to have influenced the practice of blackface performance in the U.S. (particularly after minstrelsy began to emerge in the 1820s) through its portrayal of Cubba, the female servant who is referred to in the subtitle and who was always played by a white woman wearing make-up. It premiered at the Theatre Royal in Dublin in 1792, reappearing in Dublin and Belfast at least once every year until 1830, and it continued to be produced intermittently until shortly after the Famine.[13]

Macready's play intermixes Stage Irish conventions with racist stereotypes related to the slave trade, establishing a pattern of comparative representation that would persist for decades and which remains occasionally detectable in the present. In a finale that contrasts interestingly with *The Octoroon's* presentation of the relationship between its hero George Peyton and Zoe, the eponymous octoroon, Macready has Cubba and a stage Irish servant called Murtagh Delaney declare their love for each other – while (again like George and Zoe) acknowledging that their racial differences make it difficult for them to express that love.

CUBBA: Me love a you dearly – but me no want you love me – dat be very wrong – Your face white, me poor negro – me only tell you make me easy, den me pray you be happy.

MURTAGH: [...] I wish she was not sooty – Who knows – may be the journey will bleach her. Troth it's a shame your mistress never found out that fellow, that advertises to whiten ladies [sic] hands and faces, the limping Jew, he'd make you fair as a daisy...

CUBBA: No matter, my colour, if me do right – Good black face be happier den bad white.

MURTAGH: Troth and I believe she may be the daughter of a king, for she has the mind of a prince – If her face was but as white as her heart, she'd be a wife for a pope.[14]

The final act of *The Octoroon* would recast these sentiments as tragedy rather than farce.[15]

Far from falling out of fashion, *The Irishman in London* became even more popular after the 1807 abolition of the slave trade in the United Kingdom, an era when plays about slavery became more common, including in Dublin and Belfast. Most of those plays were imported from London to Ireland, but some premiered there too. For example, in 1819, the year before Boucicault was born, Edward Fitzsimons's *Anzico and Coanza* (or *Gratitude and Freedom*) was performed in the Crowe Street Theatre in Dublin. A comic opera with music by John Stevenson, it was based loosely on Maria Edgeworth's short story "The Grateful Negro" (1804), which concerns a slave revolt in the West Indies. It was never revived, though Fitzsimons suggested that its failure was due to the machinations of his political rivals rather than any deficiencies in the play itself.[16] Contrastingly, another musical play, Thomas Morton's *The Slave* (sometimes referred to as *Gambia*, after its main character) came to Belfast in 1822, six years after its Covent Garden premiere; it became a mainstay in the Irish repertoire until the 1840s.[17]

During the same period, Sheridan's *Pizarro* was also frequently performed. It was published in Dublin in 1799 (the year of its London premiere) and was staged in Belfast (in 1817), Drogheda (in 1836), and Dublin (at least five times in the 1820s alone).[18] Although it is not directly concerned with slavery, its exploration of the Spanish conquest of Peru was often received in the context of that era's debates about imperialism and abolition.[19] The play also provided one of the prominent heroic roles of its era in Rolla, the Peruvian commander – a part that was played in its premiere by John Philip Kemble, and later by Edmund Kean, William Charles Macready (whose father had written *The Irishman in London*), and other important figures.

Significantly, *Pizarro* was also staged in Killarney in 1831, when the part of Rolla was played by Ira Aldridge, the Black American actor (then billed under the name "the African Roscius") who would later become famous throughout Europe for his Shakespearean performances. A reporter for the *Tralee Mercury* wrote about Aldridge ecstatically: the "Peruvian leader, in all the different situations in which his noble and fearless spirit is displayed, was represented by that gentleman [Aldridge] with an excellence and a fidelity which, though by him usually exhibited, was hailed by the most rapturous and enthusiastic applause."[20] During that same tour of towns in Munster, Aldridge also performed in a stage adaptation of Aphra Behn's *Oroonoko* (perhaps using the 1688 stage script that had been written by the Dublin-born dramatist Thomas Southerne). It is very likely that at his final performance in Kerry – a benefit night for himself, attended by the Earl and Countess of Kenmare – he would have given a speech against slavery, as was his usual practice until its abolition in the British empire after the Reform Act of 1832.

Aldridge also performed in Dublin in 1831, where his visit was again well received – though for causes somewhat different from those evident in Kerry. That performance in Ireland's capital is remembered now for Aldridge's acting of Shakespearean roles, but the records show that he also received praise for his performance of minstrel songs: indeed, one Irish newspaper claimed that his rendition of "Possum up a Gum Tree" was more popular than his Othello.[21] It might seem surprising that Dublin audiences were already familiar with those songs: "Jump Jim Crow" (which Aldridge also performed) had been premiered by a minstrel called Daddy Rice in New York only in 1828, and it was not published until the mid-1830s. Yet Dublin audiences seemed to have known it by the time Aldridge performed there (press reports of the time refer to audiences specifically calling for him to sing that song). That example tells us much about the speed of trans-Atlantic cultural transfer during this period.

One explanation for Irish knowledge of such songs might be that many of the people involved in minstrelsy were Irish immigrants to the United States. The role of Irish Americans in developing minstrelsy has been explored in some detail by Eric Lott, David R. Roediger, and Noel Ignatiev, among others – and while those scholars have different preoccupations and employ different methodologies, their consensus is that the popular stage was a "place where Irish- and Afro-Americans came together" (as Ignatiev states) but also that "blackface provided [Irish immigrants] a means of displaced self-expression … [which was] another strain of white ventriloquism through black art," as has been argued by Lott.[22] That apparent contradiction between community and appropriation explains the title of Lott's book about minstrelsy, which he sees as an act of both "love and theft" – an expression of empathy that could also be an expression of hatred. More recently, Michèle Mendelssohn has outlined how the association of Irish Americans with minstrelsy informed the reception of Oscar Wilde's lecture tour to the United States in the early 1880s – an analysis that could readily be applied to other Irish figures (though presumably with different findings), Boucicault among them.[23]

Certainly, there is work to be done on how minstrelsy informed both the art and reception of many Irish writers: from the 1830s, minstrelsy was very popular in Ireland, and there is extensive source material available for exploration. Daddy Rice himself came to the country in 1836. In 1844, the Virginia Minstrels followed him, performing at Dublin's Theatre Royal only a year after they had presented what Jennifer Mooney claims was "the first stand-alone blackface minstrel show" in the United States, appearing at the Bowery Theatre in New York in 1843.[24] As shown on the playbill for one of their performances (see Figure 3.1), they were presented in Dublin alongside a stage Irish comedy called *The Irish Ambassador* by James Kenney – a combination that again reveals how white enactments of Black identity often coincided with Stage Irish performances. That pattern would continue and indeed would inform the reception of Boucicault's work within and beyond Ireland from the 1860s onward.

The link between the Stage Irishman and minstrelsy would prove apparent in other ways. During a speech in Limerick in November 1845, Frederick Douglass criticized an actor called Bateman who had performed a Jim Crow routine there. As Fionnghuala Sweeney emphasizes, far from sympathizing with Douglass's complaints, the local newspaper (*The Limerick Reporter*) defended Bateman as a "clever actor whose representation of a particular negro character … is no more to be considered as a description of negros generally than the representation of … any of the Irish buffoons [on stage should] be viewed as types of the Irish character" – in other words, minstrelsy could be justified by the history of Stage Irishry.[25] Yet at that same Limerick meeting, Douglass had criticized attempts to create an equivalence between Irish and Black American suffering, displaying particular hostility to the suggestion that the Irish were enslaved too: "there was nothing like slavery on the soil on which he now stood. Negro-slavery consisted not in taking away another man's property but in making property of him, and in

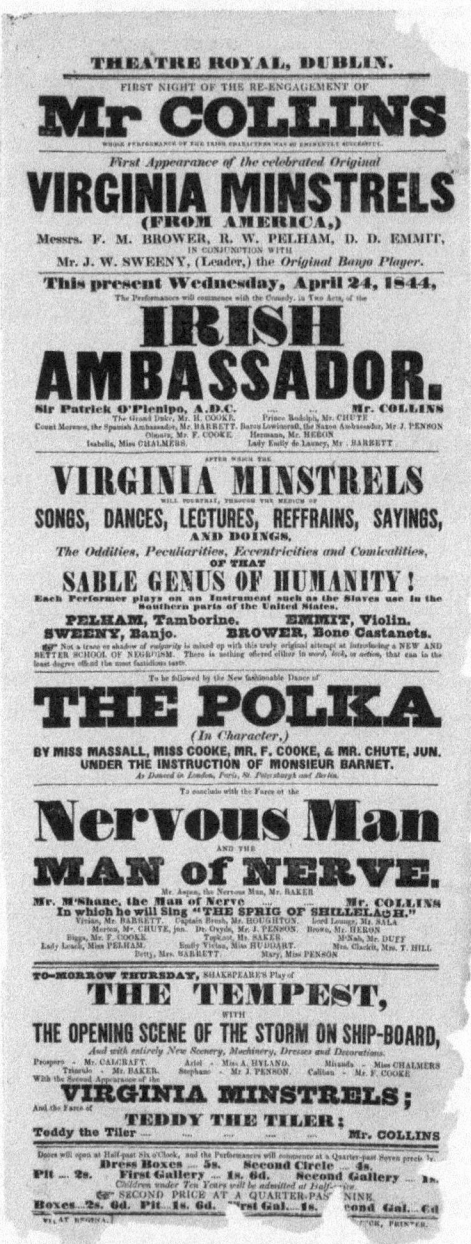

Figure 3.1   Theatre Royal Playbill
Credit: (MS Thr 1848, box 19. Harvard Theatre Collection, Harvard University).

destroying his identity," he said.[26] That false equivalence between oppression against the Irish in America and against Black Americans would prove persistent, especially after the Irish Famine – and it provides interesting context for the related linking of Stage Irish characters with stereotypical representations of Black Americans.

Furthermore, the evidence abundantly displays that Irish audiences usually saw Black American characters not as equals but inferiors: their responses to minstrelsy reveal attitudes that range from the implicitly superior to the nakedly racist. For example, the playbill for the Virginia Minstrels mentioned above takes pains to reassure audiences that "not a trace or shadow of vulgarity is mixed up with this truly original attempt at introducing a NEW AND BETTER SCHOOL OF NEGROISM. There is nothing offered in *word, look* or *action* that can in the least degree offend the most fastidious taste." Noticeably, no such reassurance is considered necessary for any other element of the program: not the Stage Irish play, not the polka, not *The Tempest*. Newspaper advertisements for minstrel shows continued to carry these kinds of statements until the 1880s, betraying an apparent assumption that Black American culture needed to be rendered respectable – a prejudice that would also be evident when Jazz was introduced to Ireland in the 1920s.[27]

The gradual arrival of Black troupes to the Irish stage brought many of those attitudes fully into the open. In 1851, the "Southern Troupe of Sable Harmonists" became one of the first groups of Black American singers to visit Ireland – and, demonstrating that Irish audiences were growing somewhat weary with blackface minstrelsy, the group's managers advertised their players' ability to "faithfully portray the peculiarities of the Ethiopian Race, which cannot be delineated by any of their imitators, who use cork to black."[28] Yet, as Riach points out, the group appear to have sung minstrel songs as part of their act – a decision that earned some criticism from *The Freeman's Journal*, which saw them as "ever aping the fashions of the white men" (yes: a company of Black American performers were criticized for copying white men because they sang minstrel songs). The report went on to praise the "practical company of real n*****s with genuine wooly heads and skins of sable that could not be washed white," who collectively exemplified not what the "bondaged darkies were like, but what they really were."[29] That use of the past tense is quite revealing, considering that it was written some fourteen years before American slavery was abolished – demonstrating how the nostalgic tone of minstrel songs often worked to deflect criticism of the institution of slavery. It should also be conceded that the author of these remarks thought that he was giving the company a rave review.

The extent to which Boucicault would have been aware of the individual performances mentioned here is difficult to determine, though it is impossible that he was unaware of the general trends. It is surely relevant, however, that one of his first professional acting jobs, when he was still going by the name Lee Moreton, was as the Stage Irish servant in a Brighton production of *The Irishman in London*, showing that the resemblances between that play and *The Octoroon* are more than coincidental.[30] But perhaps of greater importance in the present context is the fact that the Irish reception and circulation of *The Octoroon* happened in a theatrical culture that would have viewed Boucicault's themes, characters, and performance practices as already familiar. That in turn explains the reception of the play and its theatrical afterlives in Ireland.

The Octoroon and Its Legacies

The first recorded production of *The Octoroon* in Ireland was in 1862 in Belfast, and thereafter it appeared regularly, often in a double bill with *The Colleen Bawn* (the plays were frequently performed together until the 1880s) – a combination that again demonstrates the link between blackface and the Stage Irishman, while underlining the validity of McFeely's and Boltwood's ideas about the relationship between those two plays. *The Octoroon* then became part of the professional and amateur repertoire in Ireland for more than a century, its impact reverberating during the Revival period and beyond.

In its first Irish performances, *The Octoroon* was often compared to other plays about American slavery. *Uncle Tom's Cabin* had first appeared on stage in Dublin only a year after the novel's publication, in an 1853 adaptation called *Slave Hunt*, which was performed in blackface by white actors.[31] But it was presented several times under its own name thereafter, notably in 1878 in a famous Jarrett & Palmer production that was praised by the *Irish Times* for its decision to cast what that newspaper called "real live N*****s."[32] Also occasionally revived was *The White Slave*, a stage adaptation of Richard Heldreth's 1836 novel of the same name – a book that called for the abolition of slavery by exploiting fears of the possibility that white people could inadvertently be placed in bondage, much as Boucicault would later do by casting his wife in the role of Zoe. "Here at the south," says one of Heldreth's characters, "we reckon all slaves as 'n*****s,' whatever their color. Just catch a stray Irish or German girl, and sell her, – a thing sometimes done, – and she turns a n***** at once, and makes just as good a slave as if there were African blood in her veins."[33] In an era when the migration of young Irish women to the United States was increasing, that line must have had particular force, and the stage version of the play remained in circulation in Ireland until at least 1887.[34] Also occasionally produced was *Dred*, another adaptation of a Harriet Beecher Stowe novel; indeed, an 1882 Belfast performance of that play also featured scenes from *The Octoroon* and *Uncle Tom's Cabin*.[35]

But *The Octoroon* was the most popular of such works. Its auction scene was sometimes performed alone as part of an evening's bill of entertainment, and there were frequent amateur productions of the whole play. One of those amateur versions featured a young Sean O'Casey, who explains in his *Autobiographies* that he acted the part of the villain Jacob McCloskey at the Mechanics Institute, the site of what would later become the Abbey Theatre.[36] And there are records of performances of it being staged in locations as diverse as Ballina (1893), Sligo (1895), and Waterford (1908).[37]

The opening of the Abbey in 1904 precipitated a period of decline in Boucicault's reputation in Ireland, partly because of its founders' famous determination to show that their nation was not the "home of buffoonery and easy sentiment."[38] And in keeping with patterns in the United States, visiting minstrel troupes gradually performed less frequently in the UK and Ireland, being replaced instead by a number of Black American companies. Indeed, in 1904 – the *annus mirabilis* of the Revival – Irish audiences were introduced to the cakewalk when *In Dahomey* toured to Dublin, being staged there only a year after it had become the first musical written and performed by Black Americans on Broadway.[39]

Yet *The Octoroon* continued to be performed, appearing in Dublin in both 1912 and 1924.[40] The latter production was staged only a few months after the premiere of *Juno and the Paycock* (1924), another tragicomic melodrama that placed themes of gender and commodification at its center, illustrating how O'Casey learned much from Boucicault – something that he frequently acknowledged later in his life but felt compelled to keep "firm silence" about during his Abbey years.[41] The proximity of the two productions also illustrates how the reception of plays such as *Juno* would have been informed by Irish audiences' continued awareness of Boucicault's work.

The last recorded appearance of the play in Ireland is an amateur production in 1968 in Waterford where, it seems reasonable to assume, the Black and Indigenous American characters must have been played by white Irish performers in make-up.[42] Yet traces of minstrelsy persisted in Irish performance culture throughout the twentieth century, appearing in Irish pantomime as late as the 1970s – while Lyons Tea, an Irish brand, advertised itself with TV, radio, and newspaper ads that featured the "Lyons Minstrels" until 1996, when their final campaign showed their minstrels riverdancing (yet another demonstration of the overlap between minstrelsy and Stage Irishry). It is perhaps for this reason that Enda Walsh's 2006 play *The Walworth Farce* concludes with a scene in which a white Irish character uses shoe polish to blacken his face. Walsh's play is an excavation of Irish popular performance histories and thus refuses to ignore the centrality of minstrelsy to that tradition.[43]

Irish blackface performances remained relatively common in the twentieth century outside of the conventions of minstrelsy, notably in productions of *Othello*. That play was first performed in Ireland in 1662 in the newly opened Smock Alley Theatre. We do not know who played the lead role on that occasion, but the next recorded production, in 1692, had the white British actor Robert Wilks in the title role. Thereafter, the play was performed more than 400 times in Dublin alone between 1700 and 1904, where the lead was taken by George Farquhar, Thomas Sheridan, Spranger Barry, and hundreds of other white actors, mostly from Ireland and England.[44] The play's popularity declined in the twentieth century, but the role continued to be performed by white actors in blackface: Micheál Mac Liammóir (who was Iago in the celebrated Orson Welles movie adaptation) played Othello at the Gaiety, and his brother-in-law Anew McMaster often played the same character as he toured provincial Ireland from the 1920s to the 1960s, briefly being accompanied by a young Harold Pinter as Iago.[45] As can be seen from his promotional material, McMaster saw the role as an opportunity to promote himself (Figure 3.2), Othello's otherness giving him permission to display his body in a way that would not have been considered acceptable under other circumstances.

Similar forms of exoticization – even eroticization – were evident at the Abbey when Eugene O'Neill's *The Emperor Jones* was performed twice in January 1927, initially under the auspices of the Dublin Drama League and then by the Abbey company itself. The title role was played by the Ulster dramatist Rutherford Mayne, who was widely praised. Other Black characters were performed by members of the (all white) Abbey company: for example, May Craig, who had played Mrs. Gogan in the premiere of O'Casey's *The Plough and the Stars* in 1926, played a slave in the O'Neill play, using make-up to darken the appearance of her skin. The Abbey archive shows that the designer Dorothy Travers-Smith had prepared a stunning array of images for each scene (similar to the practice of storyboarding now used in many Hollywood movies). While allowing for the necessarily abstract style of the drawings, it is notable that the Black

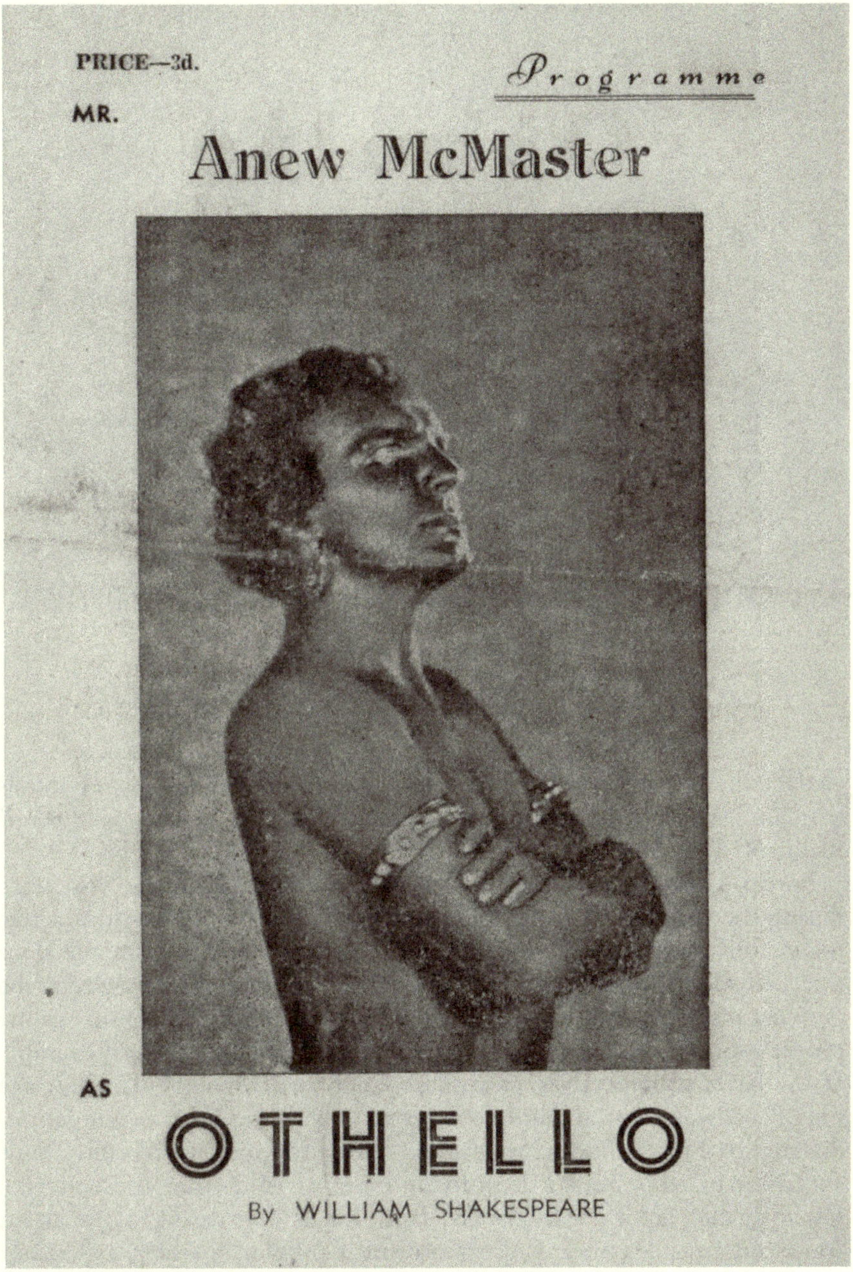

Figure 3.2   *Othello*
Credit: Gate Theatre Digital Archive, University of Galway. GADM_00002108, 2.

Figure 3.3   *The Emperor Jones*
Credit: Abbey Theatre Digital Archive at the University
of Galway. 3117_SM_0001, 5. Courtesy of the Abbey Theatre Archive.

characters are undifferentiated from each other, presented more as symbols than individuals, in a style that seems redolent of Gaugin's pictures of islanders in the South Pacific (see Figure 3.3).

Such pictures demonstrate that the use of blackface on the Irish stage during the twentieth century was often indicative not so much of active malice but perhaps of willful amnesia about Ireland's role in the slave trade. In addition, from mid-century onward, we should acknowledge the growing insularity that allowed Irish society to believe that racism against people of color was a problem experienced elsewhere. A good example of the latter tendency was an Irish production of *Finian's Rainbow*, the 1947 Broadway musical that later became a successful Fred Astaire movie, directed by Francis Ford Coppola and released in 1968. Ostensibly about an Irishman who steals a leprechaun's pot of gold from the end of a rainbow, the play is a thinly veiled (and, for its day, daring) satire about American attitudes toward race, featuring a subplot in which a viciously prejudiced Senator discovers one day that his skin has magically transformed from white to black. It concludes with the American townspeople coming together to share in the financial success of a Black American character's business – suggesting that equality, while desirable, could only be found somewhere "over the rainbow." It is a whimsical play, and often a very funny one, but its seriousness of intent is unmistakable.

Finian's Rainbow was twice produced at the Gaiety in Dublin, in 1957 and 1963, with Jimmy O'Dea in the lead role alongside Maureen Potter and Milo O'Shea. As indicated by production materials in the Dublin City Archive, most of the Black American characters appear to have been played by white actors in blackface.[46] But what is more notable is that both the pre-publicity and the critical reception of the play ignore its treatment of racism: it is almost as if that element were entirely illegible or invisible. This contrasts with the evidence of Irish audiences' awareness of racial discrimination a hundred years previously, when *The Octoroon* was first being performed.

The growing diversity of Ireland's population from the late 1990s led to a decline in the use of blackface and to a growing number of plays that sought to retrieve the histories of Irish racism and anti-racism from the eighteenth and nineteenth centuries. Frederick Douglass became the subject of *The Cambria* (2005), a play by Donal O'Kelly that deploys the melodramatic conventions of dramas like *The Octoroon* to draw a parallel between Douglass and contemporary asylum seekers. Similarly, but less subtly, the Abbey celebrated the centenary of the premiere of *The Playboy of the Western World* in 2007 by presenting a revised version of John Millington Synge's play, co-written by Roddy Doyle and Bisi Adigun, in which Christy Mahon becomes a Nigerian refugee who arrives at a pub in Dublin. And the practice of Black American companies visiting Ireland would gradually resume (having vanished for much of the twentieth century): in 1982, for example, the New York-based Negro Ensemble Company appeared at the Dublin Theatre Festival, with a young Samuel L. Jackson in their cast (see Figure 3.4).[47] Alongside these developments in the theater, there has been a growing body of sophisticated scholarly work tracking the importance of race and interculturalism in contemporary Irish theater, by Charlotte McIvor, Jason King, Matthew Spangler, and others.

Yet the practice of "blacking-up" has persisted into the twenty-first century. The Ulster rugby player Paddy Jackson (later to become the defendant in an infamous rape trial) was strongly criticized when a photograph of him made up as an "Ethiopian slave" was published in 2014; and in 2020, the auditor of the Musical Society of University College Dublin was forced to publicly apologize for its history of casting white actors as Black and Asian characters.[48] Meanwhile, school and amateur productions

Figure 3.4   Samuel L. Jackson, Elain Graham, and S. Epatha Merkerson; Negro
Ensemble Company, Dublin 1982
Credit: Gate Theatre Digital Archive at University of Galway, 1414_PH_0001, p2.

of musicals such as *Hairspray* (2002) or the operetta *The Mikado* (1885) continued to cast white Irish actors in non-white roles – a practice that became the subject of criticism in 2020 as the #BlackLivesMatter movement gained impetus in Ireland.

By then, *The Octoroon* had vanished from the Irish repertoire, but it returned to international notice in 2014 when Branden Jacobs-Jenkins's *An Octoroon* premiered in New York and then began to be revived internationally (an earlier version, directed by Gavin Quinn of the Irish theater company Pan Pan, had fallen apart rather spectacularly in 2010).[49] The prologue of the 2014 version brings Boucicault himself on stage, placing him in dialogue with an avatar of Jacobs-Jenkins, the latter introducing himself to his audience as a "black playwright" – placing the term in quotation marks in order to undermine it.[50] BJJ (as he is called in the script) explains that his decision to adapt Boucicault's play arose from a therapist's suggestion to "re-connect with things you. have ... positive feelings for." When the Boucicault character arrives on stage, the two men shout "fuck you" to each other repeatedly until BJJ exits in frustration. Boucicault becomes "more belligerent," then greets the audience with the words "hey sluts." "Feck," he says, "I'm drunk."[51] The character then puts redface make-up on – as Boucicault himself would have done in order to play Wahnotee – and complains that he's no longer famous:

> Time is like ... so fecked up. You know? Why, you ask? Well, first of all, I'm apparently not famous anymore, which sucks. You don't even know who I am. You got the fecking playwright sitting here – a fecking world-class famous fecking playwright – Right in your face. Dion fecking Boucicault.[52]

Anyone familiar with Irish theater will identify an irony here: Boucicault has been recast as a Stage Irishman. And not, we should say, as a Stage Irishman similar to one of his own creations: Conn the Shaughraun and Myles na Gopaleen may have drank but they were rarely drunk, they may have fought but they were not belligerent – and they never used the word "feck." It is necessary to be cautious when identifying intentionality in a play that seeks to unsettle audiences' understanding of authorship, but it seems likely that Jacobs-Jenkins's aim is not to re-create the historical figure of Boucicault but to evoke contemporary stereotypes associated with Irishness, such as those found in the plays of Martin McDonagh. The Boucicault who appears in *An Octoroon* is therefore at once white *and* racially marked; he is implicated in the histories of blackface performance *and* he exemplifies the histories of Stage Irish performances. To some, those positions might seem incompatible if not contradictory, but Jacobs-Jenkins is using Irishness to demonstrate that (on stage if not in society) identities are always contextual, always comparative, and always in flux – something that, it might be argued, Boucicault's original melodrama also proposed. Hence, the association of the Stage Irish stereotypes with representations of American slavery is being revived and recalibrated for the contemporary era.

The overall impact of Jacobs-Jenkins's version of *The Octoroon* is not just to locate the play in history, but to show its influence *through* history: to demonstrate that the practice of representing slavery as a form of entertainment in 1859 is a seed that bears fruit in the Jim Crow era a century later. This explains the adaptation's huge impact since 2014. It has been staged to acclaim across the United States, feeding into discussions that have been inspired by the #BlackLivesMatter movement, while earning praise for its inventive approach to theatrical stagecraft. It has also enjoyed successful runs in Canada, Australia, and Britain, where again its production generated debate about slavery, colonialism, and racism.

Those associations became particularly visible during the Irish premiere of *An Octoroon* in April 2022 at the Abbey Theatre. As one of the first productions to be programmed by Caitriona McLaughlin and Mark O'Brien (who had taken over as directors of the theater in mid-2021), the Abbey's *An Octoroon* was an important statement of intent. In its marketing material, the theater emphasized that, as an adaptation of a "flawed Irish classic," it was appropriate to stage the play in "Boucicault's hometown" of Dublin – which means, in other words, that the production was in keeping with the Abbey's remit of staging works from the national repertoire.[53] But it was also pointing ways forward. Its English director, Anthony Simpson Pike, became the first person of color to direct a play for the Abbey mainstage – and its cast included an emerging generation of young Black Irish actors, including Patrick Martins, Loré Adewusi, and Jeanne Nicole Ní Ainle.

As McLaughlin explained in her show program note, "On becoming Artistic Director of the Abbey Theatre *An Octoroon* was one of the first plays to make it onto the list for my first year's programme," stating that this choice was necessitated by the rapid transformation of Ireland since the turn of the century. "At a time when we examine concerns about diversity, equality, sustainability, and planetary survival, should we prioritise national identity and what it means to be Irish?" she asked, arguing that *An Octoroon* provides an opportunity to consider "how well we in Ireland … develop support for a new wave of Irish peoples with mixed heritage and a multiplicity of lived experiences." She concluded by stating that "we're deeply proud to be producing it and bringing this company of artists and creatives together to mark a cultural shift in the Irish artistic landscape."[54]

The act of staging the play at the national theater was thus intended to be symbolically important – but the production itself proved a consequential intervention into Irish life. Perhaps most powerfully, Jacobs-Jenkins's "sensation scene" – in which he calls for the projection of a photograph of the lynching of Thomas Shipp and Abram Smith in Indiana in 1930, was reimagined for Irish contexts. It might be possible for a contemporary Irish audience to regard that photograph as irrelevant to their own history (notwithstanding the Irish origins of the word "lynch"), but Simpson Pike and set designer Sabine Dargent projected the photo onto mirrored screens that also allowed the audience to see themselves and the photograph simultaneously. By forcing the audience to consider their own role as audience/spectators in a scene of racist violence, the production required the Abbey audience to *see* its own history more clearly. That stage technique literally held a mirror up to the audience, but the act of provoking self-recognition – and self-evaluation – ran through the entire production. The staging of the *An Octoroon* thus represents a potential turning point: a moment when the histories outlined in this chapter were recognized and reintegrated into the contemporary tradition. It will be for scholars and theater-makers alike to ensure that this moment of recognition is more than merely fleeting.

Conclusions

This discussion of *The Octoroon* and its afterlives is intended to demonstrate the need for new approaches to literary and cultural criticism within Irish theater and its historiography. The tendency in scholarship has generally been to see Irish drama in terms of its history of resistance to oppression – rightly so, given the aims of the Revival. But it is also necessary to consider how Irish theater has contributed to the oppression of others, and to chart the extent to which racist performance practices have informed the composition and reception of Irish plays for several centuries. How much might that cultural history have informed the understanding of race in Ireland? Did those attitudes impinge upon Irish Catholic missions in Africa and Asia in the nineteenth and twentieth centuries? Do they inform how communities think about immigration and direct provision in the present?

We know that minstrel shows, stage adaptations of *Uncle Tom's Cabin*, and *The Octoroon* itself all traveled from America to Ireland – but Irish immigrants to the United States brought those performances back with them in the form of memories, attitudes, and prejudices. How then might we map and model the circum-Atlantic transfer of culture between Ireland and the U.S.? Those questions have been asked before – but when it comes to Irish theater, our answers remain fragmentary, incomplete. There is work to be done in retrieving those histories, but perhaps there is also a need to investigate our methods of criticism, to ask what else we have considered tangential, inessential, and irrelevant – and how we came to mistakenly see *The Octoroon* as tangential in the first place.

Notes

1 Lance Pettitt, *Screening Ireland* (Manchester: Manchester University Press, 2000), 32.

2 Joseph Roach, *Cities of the Dead: Circum-Atlantic Performance* (New York: Columbia University Press, 1996), 183.

3 Kathleen Gough, *Kinship and Performance in the Black and Green Atlantic* (New York: Routledge, 2014): 45–50; Charlotte McIvor, *Performing Intercultural Ireland* (Basingstoke: Palgrave, 2016): 129–50; John Brannigan, "'Ireland, and Black!': Minstrelsy, Racism, And Black Cultural Production In 1970s Ireland," *Textual Practice* 22, no. 2 (2008): 229–248.

4 Roach, *Cities of the Dead*, 183.

5 Kevin Rockett, "Dion Boucicault, Staging, and Early Cinema," *Princeton University Library Chronicle* 68, no. 1–2, (2007): 33–59, 54; "*The Octoroon*," Playbill, accessed October 18, 2019, www.playbill.com/production/the-octoroon-phoenix-theatre-vault-0000013106.

6 Lisa Merrill and Theresa Saxon, "Replaying and Rediscovering The Octoroon," *Theatre Journal* 69, no. 2 (2017): 127–152; Karen Young, *Performing the Unstageable: Success, Imagination, Failure* (London: Bloomsbury, 2020), 104.

7 Deirdre McFeely, *Dion Boucicault: Irish Identity on Stage* (Cambridge: Cambridge University Press, 2012): 9–12.

8 Scott Boltwood, "'The Ineffaceable Curse of Cain': Race, Miscegenation, and the Victorian Staging of Irishness," *Victorian Literature and Culture* 29, no. 2 (2001): 383–96, 386.

9 Richard Fawkes, *Dion Boucicault* (London: Quartet, 2011), 109.

10 Elizabeth Butler Cullingford, *Ireland's Others: Ethnicity and Gender in Irish Literature and Popular Culture* (Cork: Cork University Press, 2001), 174.

11 Heike Paul, "Cultural Mobility Between Boston and Berlin: How Germans Have Read and Reread Narratives of American Slavery," in *Cultural Mobility: A Manifesto*, ed. Stephen Greenblatt (Cambridge University Press, 2009): 122–71.

12 Roach, *Cities of the Dead*, 218.

13 *Freeman's Journal*, July 14, 1792, 1.

14 William Macready, *The Irishman in London – or the Happy African: A Farce* (London: Longman, 1799): 32.

15 See Dion Boucicault, *Selected Plays*, ed. Andrew Parkin (Gerrards Cross: Colin Smythe, 1987), 163.

16 See Peter Kavanagh, *The Irish Theatre* (Tralee: The Kerryman, 1946), 415.

17 *Belfast Newsletter*, December 6, 1822, 2.

18 *Freeman's Journal*, July 13, 1799, 1; *Belfast Newsletter*, March 7, 1817, 3; *Drogheda Argus and Leinster Journal*, June 11, 1836, 2.

19 For a detailed discussion of this link, see Heather McPherson, "Caricature, Cultural Politics, and the Stage: The Case of Pizarro," *Huntington Library Quarterly* 70, no. 4 (2007): 620 and John Loftis, "Whig Oratory on Stage: Sheridan's Pizarro," *Eighteenth-Century Studies* 8, no. 4 (1975): 454–72.

20 *Tralee Mercury*, October 4, 1834, 3.

21 See Bernth Lindfors, *Ira Aldridge: The Vagabond Years, 1833–1852* (Rochester: University of Rochester Press, 2011), 24, 72, 192, 212; Douglas C. Riach, "Blacks and Blackface on the Irish Stage, 1830–60," *Journal of American Studies* 7, no. 3 (December 1973): 239.

22 Eric Lott, *Love & Theft: Blackface Minstrelsy and the American Working Class* (Oxford: Oxford University Press, 2013), 95; Noel Ignatiev, *How the Irish Became White* (London: Routledge, 1995), 48.

23 Michèle Mendelssohn, *Making Oscar Wilde* (Oxford: Oxford University Press, 2019).

24 Jennifer Mooney, *Irish Stereotypes in Vaudeville, 1865–1905* (London: Springer, 2015), 32.

25 Fionnghuala Sweeney, "'Mask in Motion': Dialect Spaces and Class Representations in Frederick Douglass' Atlantic Rhetoric," in *Monuments of the Black Atlantic: Slavery and Memory*, ed. Joanne M. Braxton and Maria I. Diedrich (Münster: Transaction Publishers, 2004), 29; quoting *Limerick Reporter*, November 11, 1845. Some sources describe Bateman as an Irishman whereas others claim he was a visiting American.

26 Christine Kinealy, ed. *Frederick Douglass and Ireland* (London: Routledge, 2018), 231.

27 Damian Evans, "'These Off-beat "Crazy Kids and Gals": Jazz in Ireland, 1918–1960," *Journal of the Society for Musicology in Ireland* (2019): 3–30.

28 *Freeman's Journal*, January 1, 1852, 1.

29 Riach, 234.

30 The University of Kent Boucicault Collection shows he played the role in 1838. UKC/POS/BOUC/THE CHER:0648671.

31 *Freeman's Journal*, March 29, 1853, 3.

32 "*Uncle Tom's Cabin*, Theatre Royal," *Irish Times*, December 10, 1878.

33 Richard Hildreth, *The White Slave*. Electronic Edition, 337, https://docsouth .unc.edu/neh/hildreth/hildreth.html.

34 *Irish Times*, November 28, 1887, 7.

35 *Belfast Newsletter*, June 3, 1882, 1.

36 Sean O'Casey, *Autobiographies Volume 1* (London: Macmillan, 1963), 298–99.

37 *Western People*, December 2, 1893, 3; *Sligo Champion*, September 14, 1895, 5; *Evening Herald*, May 2, 1908.

38 Augusta Gregory, *Our Irish Theatre* (Buckinghamshire: Colin Smythe, 1972), 11.

39 The production was also performed for seven months in London, being staged at Buckingham palace before King Edward VII. See Jeffrey P. Green, "'In Dahomey' in London in 1903," *The Black Perspective in Music* 11, no. 1 (1983): 23–40.

40 *Irish Independent*, October 14, 1924, 8.

41 Sean O'Casey, *Autobiographies Volume 2* (London: Macmillan, 1968), 105.

42 *Munster Express*, October 18, 1968, 18.

43 Enda Walsh, *The Walworth Farce* (London: Nick Hern, 2006).

44 *Shakespeare's Plays in Dublin 1660–1904*, database, www.nuigalway.ie/drama/ shakespeare/.

45 Harold Pinter, "Mac," in *Various Voices – Prose, Poetry, Politics, 1978–2005* (London: Faber, 2005).

46 *Finian's Rainbow* at the Gaiety Theatre, Dublin City Archive, ITA/251/04/171.

47 The production was of Samm-Art Williams's *Home*, and it premiered at the Gate on September 27, 1982.

48 John Mulgrew, "Paddy Jackson Dressed as Slave," *Belfast Telegraph*, July 11, 2014, www.belfasttelegraph.co.uk/news/northern-ireland/ulster-rugby-players-wear-black-make-up-in-ethiopian-photo-paddy-jackson-dressed-as-slave-30424197 .html. For UCD's Musical Society, see http://collegetribune.ie/ucd-musical-society-apologises-for-use-of-black-brown-face/.

49 Sara Keating, "Ireland's Wildest Playwright," *Irish Times*, July 20, 2010, www .irishtimes.com/culture/stage/ireland-s-wildest-playwright-1.624084.

50 Branden Jacobs-Jenkins, *An Octoroon* (New York: Dramatists Play Service, 2015), 7.

51 Jacobs-Jenkins, *An Octoroon*, 8, 14.

52 Jacobs-Jenkins, *An Octoroon*, 14.

53 Abbey Theatre, *An Octoroon*, online listing, accessed April 23, 2022, www .abbeytheatre.ie/whats-on/an-octoroon/.

54 Caitriona McLoughlin, "Artistic Director's Note," *An Octoroon* show program (Dublin: Abbey Theatre, 2022), 2.

CHAPTER 4

Race and Irish Women's Novels in the Long Nineteenth Century

Matthew L. Reznicek

From Sydney Owenson to Kate O'Brien, from the Act of Union to Ireland's independence and its joining the European Economic Community, the way in which Irish women's fiction has defined freedom has depended upon a racial politics. This politics sometimes appears sympathetic and as though it is rooted in affective anti-imperialism, and other times it is a politics of denial and erasure. Representations of race are intimately bound to the struggle for freedom and autonomy, which are made more complex by focusing on novels written by women. The representations of race in Irish women's literature challenge the ability of Irish women to achieve independence alongside rather than against the colonized, enslaved, indentured peoples of the nineteenth-century literary landscape. This is typical of the way in which liberal humanism, according to Lisa Lowe, employs the "economy of affirmation and forgetting" to define freedom in particular terms.[1] If studies of Irish women's literature are to contend fully with the history of race, we must be attuned to these politics even, or especially, if the narratives of self-fulfillment and independence become the objects of critique because of the way they reveal the limitations of such narratives. To borrow from O'Brien's *Mary Lavelle* (1936), the inclusion of race in our assessment of Irish women's writing must begin with the revelation that "there were truths that were indefensible, truths that changed and broke things, that exacted injustice and pain and savagery, truths that were sins and cruelties – but yet were true and had a value there was no use in defending."[2] Race must be a part of the true narrative of Irish women's writing, even if it changes and breaks things.

Empire of Liberty: Personal and National Liberation and the Limits of Race

As Clíona Ó Gallchoir and Heather Ingman note in the introduction to *A History of Modern Irish Women's Literature* (2018), Irish women's writing post-1801 "created a body of work that explored the links between female influence, national identity and political involvement and in the process gave women a public voice."[3] The tension, as Ó Gallchoir and Ingman demonstrate, between the "static image of the woman as an icon of national identity" and "the representation of lived female experience" is central to dominant understandings of Irish women's writing.[4] Some writers like Charlotte Brooke, Elizabeth Sheridan, and Sydney Owenson "aligned themselves as women with the fate of Ireland as a nation."[5] Others were more clearly tied to the British empire, "as travellers and settlers in the colonies and social reformers and as members of the increasingly displaced Protestant Ascendancy."[6] The complexity, then, of discussing a singular trend or thread in Irish women's literature is fraught with counterexamples and exceptions. Despite this, it is fair to say that we can read their literature from 1800 to the mid-twentieth century as revealing an archive of liberalism, or at the very least a search and struggle to achieve some of the key elements promised by liberalism. Lowe helpfully defines the term "liberalism" as a "project that includes at once both the universal promises of rights, emancipation, wage labor, and free trade, as well as the global divisions and asymmetries on which the liberal tradition depends, and according to which such liberties are reserved for some and wholly denied to others."[7] We have largely understood Irish women's literature to reveal the project of liberalism through "the narration of political emancipation through citizenship in the state, the promise of economic freedom in the development of wage labor and exchange markets, and the conferring of civilization to human persons educated in aesthetic and national culture ... through universal concepts of reason and community."[8] The work of scholars like Lisa Lowe, Felicity A. Nussbaum, Laura Doyle, Saidiya V. Hartman, and Ashley L. Cohen, however, challenges the universality of this narrative.[9] Instead, as Lowe writes, the narrative of liberalism reveals "the modern distinction between definitions of the human and those to whom such definitions do not extend"; furthermore, this disjuncture between the purported universality and the categorization of those to whom it does not extend "is the condition of possibility for Western liberalism."[10] Taking Lowe's claim that this racial distinction is the "condition of possibility" for the narrative of progress, self-determination, and freedom that undergirds our understanding of Irish women's literature means we must interrogate the ways in which such texts establish and uphold these distinctions.

It is telling that, for Lowe and Cohen, the end of the eighteenth century and beginning of the nineteenth century are pivotal in a reconceptualization of liberalism and its relationship to race, slavery, economics, and empire. In the wake of the American Revolution, the British empire engaged "in a process of ideological reinvention. If the American Patriots were hypocritical enough to complain about English despotism when all the while practicing chattel slavery, then Britain would take the moral high ground by building a new, post-American empire of liberty."[11] David Brion Davis has called this "the emergence of the second empire," which "might depend on the millions of involuntary laborers, but it was, by definition, a 'free world.'"[12] Responding to Davis, Cohen insists that "it is vitally important that we resist an overly facile construction of freedom's geography that would have us pit East Indian freedom against West Indian slavery."[13] In particular, Cohen draws our attention to the urgency with which these distinctions were drawn during the 1790s and early 1800s as a direct response to the foreign threat of the French and Haitian revolutions and the United Irishmen uprising of 1798.[14] Redrawing the geography of the British empire along the lines of freedom, especially at the moment when Ireland is formally integrated wholly into the United Kingdom of Great Britain and Ireland, underscores the need to interrogate Irish literature from this period in terms of its participation in the elision of colonial slavery, racism, and the limits in the definition of the human.

Unsurprisingly, these tensions and contradictions within liberalism and the geography of freedom shape Irish women's writing even as they articulate and negotiate the boundaries of the nation within the newly constituted geography of the United Kingdom. In order to trace the long history of liberalism and race within Irish women's writing, I will begin with Sydney Owenson, the author whose *The Wild Irish Girl* (1806) is often attributed as establishing the "basic plot" for the genre of the National Tale.[15] Examining the way in which Owenson attempts to include Ireland and Irishness within the limits of liberalism's narrative calls attention to the contradictory ways she connects Ireland's experience with the colonized peoples of South America in her novel *Florence Macarthy: An Irish Tale* (1818). Similarly, her earlier and obviously orientalist novel *The Missionary: An Indian Tale* (1811) attempts to critique the imperial encounter in India, but ultimately maintains racial hierarchies through its representation of progress and the category of the human. In this, Owenson's fiction not only seeks to insert Ireland into a geography of freedom, but also builds a narrative of the "capacity for liberty" that is inherently tied to the racial politics I am attempting to trace.[16] After Owenson, I turn to *fin-de-siècle* writer Katherine Cecil Thurston and her Paris-based novel *Max* (1910) in order to show the way that color and race become the key components for self-determination, even or especially in a metropolitan landscape defined by commodification and consumption. Lastly, I study the writings of

Kate O'Brien to explore the way that Irish women's fiction in the early years of the Republic continues to insist on independence by opposing the self-determination of Black and indigenous peoples. In both *Without My Cloak* (1931) and *Mary Lavelle* (1936), O'Brien connects the ability for self-determination to the occupation of formerly colonized spaces, emptied of their colonized populations. Taken together, these novels provide an historical and literary framework for understanding the complex relationship between Irish women's literary struggle for self-articulation, self-determination, and the racial politics and contradictions that enable the achievement of liberalism's promise.

Ireland and the Imperial Intimacies: Sydney Owenson, Colonial Encounters, and Citizenship

In her definitive study, Katie Trumpener notes a significant shift in the development of the Romantic National Tale as it moves from "the unchanging national world toward the dislocations of the historical novel."[17] The genre "becomes the birthplace of a new literary schizophrenia" as it struggles to reconcile unresolved tensions between its tendency to recognize "cultural distinctiveness," while also "believ[ing] in the possibility of transcultural unions."[18] What makes these tensions so unresolvable is a development within the genre that Trumpener associates with Charles Maturin's *The Milesian Chief* (1812), but which I argue can also be seen in Owenson's *The Missionary*. For Trumpener, the narrative development that enhances the National Tale's schizophrenia is its "meditation on a history of cultural oppression [that] makes rapprochement and reconciliation increasingly inconceivable," upsetting the previously well-established pattern in which national differences are resolved through a marriage that mirrors and enacts a political Act of Union. Based on its recognition of "cultural oppression" that negates "rapprochement and reconciliation," I argue that the National Tale broadly and Owenson's novels explicitly draw their "schizophrenia" from a struggle with Lisa Lowe's "economy of affirmation and forgetting" that is at once "a narrative of freedom overcoming enslavement" but also "denies colonial slavery, erases the seizure of lands from native peoples, displaces migrations and connections across continents and internalizes these processes in a national struggle of history and consciousness."[19] This struggle within the national consciousness reveals the attempts to contend with the unresolvable tensions produced by the achievement of freedom and self-determination for certain people.

In *The Wild Irish Girl*, we most clearly see Owenson attempt to attack "the tradition of imperial description" of Ireland as barbaric and backward, while "constructing an alternative picture" by "embrac[ing] all aspects of the national culture with even a remote resemblance to Mediterranean cultural prototypes, for such similarities provide a particularly powerful means of establishing cultural legitimacy."[20] Banished to the country as a form of punishment, the English protagonist of *The Wild Irish Girl*, Horatio M – (alias Horatio Mortimer), expects to encounter "the barbarity of the Irish," which he associates with images of "an *Esquimaux* group circling round the fire which was to dress a dinner, or broil an enemy."[21] In an expansive footnote, Owenson draws on a parallel between British representations of Ireland and Spanish representations of indigenous peoples of Latin America by connecting the resistance of "MONTEZUMA or ATALIBA ... his countrymen" and their "woes" to the way in which English histories have represented "the name, *Irishman*, ... with the horrid epithet of *cruel*."[22] This English association of Ireland with indigenous peoples from North and South America is notable because it "relegates" the Irish "to geographical and temporal spaces that are constituted as backward, uncivilized, and unfree."[23] On one hand, this strategy reflects an obvious effort to develop an intimacy between Irishness and "foreigners, outsiders, [and] alleged inferiors."[24] This can be interpreted as an early instance of what Leela Gandhi has described as an "elected affinity" between embodiments of the putative West and the putative non-West.[25] For Gandhi, such acts of "solidarity" and "forms of dissent" contradict and disrupt the "project of division, partition, and separation" that defines colonialism.[26] In this framework, Owenson's election to associate Ireland with the Aztecs and the Eskimos of the Americas reveals the "overlapping territories" and "intertwined histories" of colonial encounter.[27] By insisting on the way in which these two experiences reflect similar processes of colonial violence, *The Wild Irish Girl* could be seen as disrupting the division between "the human" who is "freed" by liberal forms and the "other subjects" who "are placed at a distance from 'the human.'"[28]

However, the politics of reconciliation, which are central to the early iteration of the National Tale, fundamentally reinforce the processes of forgetting that are indispensable to maintaining the distinctions between "the human" and the "other subjects." As Julia Anne Miller has demonstrated, the novel's protagonist and embodiment of Ireland does not speak within the last ten pages of the novel, which itself ends "in the voice of the colonial father."[29] While Miller calls attention to Glorvina's "aphasia," it is equally important to note that the novel's socio-political stability,

bringing Ireland into union with Britain, is achieved through "insepa-
rably blend[ing]" and "for ever bur[ying]" of national and religious differences.[30] The rights of citizenship and of political belonging are only
achieved through forgetting colonial violence. Importantly, the Earl of
M – describes this forgetting, burial, and blending as "be[ing] wished
by every liberal mind, by every benevolent heart."[31] The achievement of
social and political stability, of political belonging, depends upon the very
"economy of affirmation and forgetting" that creates and reinforces the
distinctions and differences liberalism uses to afford some populations and
to deny others. Having convinced Henry M – of the humanity of the
Irish, *The Wild Irish Girl* sees Ireland welcomed into the privileged empire
of freedom, so long as it forgets, suppresses, and denies its connections to
Montezuma and the Eskimos.

Similarly, Owenson's *Florence Macarthy* is Owenson's clearest engagement with an Irish politics of transracial sympathy, drawing on the early
nineteenth-century Latin American anti-imperial struggles against Spain.
The freedom offered to the Latin Americans, however, mirrors the type
of "economic dependence" that reflects the ways the free market was
"employed in the expansion of empire."[32] As Jessie Reeder notes, the "competing discourses of 'solidarity ... and domination'" that shape British
attitudes toward Latin America are "not sincere or real but merely a 'justification,' a kind of feint or gambit that serves the goals of imperialism."[33]
In this framework, Owenson's seeming celebration of Latin American liberation in *Florence Macarthy* reveals an instantiation of the racial processes
by which modern liberalism was used in the expansion of empire.

The protagonist of *Florence Macarthy*, General Walter de Montenay
Fitzwalter "of South America, that brave Guerilla chief, whose life and
fortune have been devoted to South American independence," not only
engages this early nineteenth-century obsession with the anti-imperial
wars of South America but makes concrete parallels between such independence and the position of Ireland through an apparent transracial sympathy.[34] The Commodore frames his involvement in Latin American wars
through universal sympathy that transcends race, drawing on the ideas of
suffering and injustice. "I *am* an Irishman," he explains, "and have long
been *an exile*, but not from religious proscription, (for my family were of
the *master cast*), but by circumstances connected with the political state
of the country, through that demoralization which the misrule of centuries has impressed upon all branches of its population."[35] Fitzwalter's
admission that his family came from the Anglo-Irish "*master cast*" mirrors the Irish Volunteers and United Irishmen who transcended sectarian

divisions to produce national sympathy. But Fitzwalter then insists that this national sympathy ought to extend outward, "hav[ing] early claimed alliance with all who suffer, whatever might be the region they inhabited."[36] His alliance with "all who suffer" depends upon the fact that he is "unfettered by the distinctions of clime, country, or kindred."[37] The "distinctions" of climate, country, and kindred all function as a coded understanding for eighteenth- and early nineteenth-century understandings of race. Wheeler notes climate is "[t]he linchpin to understanding most eighteenth-century pronouncements about the body's appearance," suggesting that "some environments were better than others for enabling humans to fulfill their potential."[38] Fitzwalter's disregard for "the distinctions of clime" suggests these claims of sympathy transcend the distinctions of race.

Fitzwalter clearly invokes the narrative of progress and freedom that is central to the reconfiguration of race and geography in the wake of the American Revolution. He insists that "the spirit of freedom ... belongs to humanity: it springs from the laws of nature, and is inevitable; it is borne along by the spirit of the age and the progress of illumination, and it must finally succeed."[39] But in almost the same breath, we see the rhetorical efforts to distance certain peoples from the category of "humanity," denying them participation in this narrative of progress. Conway Crawley declares "For my part, I don't know ... what *parsons* mean about *giving liberty and independence* to an unformed race like South Americans ... creatures destined by nature to work like moles in the mines."[40] Crawley continues, "We have all read the solemn declaration of the CONSULADO, or board of trade, in Mexico, that the Indians are a race of monkies, filled with vice and ignorance; and they have extended their remarks, I believe pretty justly, to the creoles, or degenerate descendants of the first Spanish settlers."[41] What is noteworthy about this racist denial that the indigenous peoples of South America and North America are human is that it is justified by "the board of trade." This reinforces Reeder's argument that the "British informal empire" in Latin America and elsewhere required "a difficult conceptual paradox – that Latin America might be both a signal example of self-rule and a dependent territory of the British Empire."[42] It also significantly reveals the power of Lowe's claim that economics became a mode of extending despotic rule. Drawing on Mill's *Considerations on Representative Government* (1861), Lowe sees nineteenth-century definitions of liberty "distinguishing those 'incapable of self-government' from those with the capacity for liberty."[43] Ultimately, the power of the board of trade to make this distinction means that nineteenth-century "free trade" has become "the new form of imperial sovereignty," still capable of determining who is human enough to deserve liberty.[44]

The tension between "imperial sovereignty" and the capacity for self-government is most fully articulated in Owenson's earlier orientalist novel *The Missionary: An Indian Tale*. In this novel, Owenson quite clearly critiques the seventeenth-century Spanish and Portuguese colonial governments in Goa for their "tyranny of fanaticism," which produces the outbreak of bloody rebellion at the end of the novel.[45] Despite its strident critique of colonialism, *The Missionary*'s evocation of "the tragedy of Westernization" reinforces the limits of liberalism's processes of "bec[oming] *human* through citizenship."[46] The novel repeatedly defines the *sine qua non* of self-government and, thus, citizenship through reason and an opposition to fervent passions; simultaneously, the novel consistently associates India, the Brahmin faith, and especially Luxima with ungovernable passion. The novel's violent denouement reveals liberalism's inability or refusal to extend citizenship and humanity to certain peoples perceived as irrational, even though it also characterizes the Spanish and Portuguese as suffering from their own "bigoted vigilance of an inhuman zeal."[47] The novel's contradictory critique of Indian irrationality and European fervor ultimately reinforces a distinction between the governable and the ungovernable that adheres to eighteenth- and nineteenth-century racial divisions.

From the outset, Hilarion, the Portuguese missionary, conceives of his mission to India in terms of "the enterprise of Alexander," specifically reflecting on "those particular spots, where Alexander fought, where Alexander conquered."[48] The language of militaristic conquest is wedded to the economic conquest of India through Hilarion's travels up the Indus River, whose "course became a guide to the spirit of fearless enterprise … which have been so intimately connected with the interests of Europe, which have so materially contributed to the wealth and luxury of modern states."[49] In this conjunction, Owenson's novel yokes together a residual form of imperialism through militaristic conquest with the emergent "form of imperial sovereignty expressed by nineteenth-century 'free trade' in India and China."[50] Central to this emergent economic form of sovereignty is the concatenation of "liberal notions of education, trade, and government [that] grew out of the conditions of colonial encounter."[51] Taken together, an education program of self-control that produces "the moral and civic subjectivity of the 'competent agent' within deliberative participatory democracy" was necessary for the "form of administration that would 'preserve the peace,' not only in Britain, but also throughout the English-speaking Commonwealth, and in the Asian and African colonies."[52] The repeated emphasis on the suppression of superstition as well as ungovernable passions, fervors, and prejudices throughout *The Missionary* emphasize the need for the development of a better "form of administration."

That the novel applies this critique of ungovernable passion and prejudice equally to the Portuguese/Spanish colonial government and indigenous Indian social structures reveals what Lowe might characterize as "a rhetorical elision."[53] Despite Hilarion's repeated warnings about Luxima's passions and fervor, which extend allegorically to the entire Indian nation, the singular representation of Brahmin society undermines such an equivalency. Indeed, the narrator characterizes the only representation of a Brahmin religious ceremony in terms of "orderly succession, without appearing to feel or excite enthusiasm."[54] And yet, the Brahmins and other Indians are described as "victims of that dreadful fear" and "held in thraldom" by "prejudices so dark and old."[55] The inherent representation of Indian society as governed by passions and prejudices relegates them to the category of being "'unfit' for representative government," even if the Portuguese and Spanish are themselves also "'unfit' for representative government."[56]

While *The Missionary* might critique the Portuguese and the Spanish themselves as being unfit for colonial rule, the fact that the novel largely retains the distinction between a governable and ungovernable categorization based on the ability to subdue one's passions means it maintains the dominant structure of liberal governance in which freedom is only awarded to certain groups.[57] To borrow from Ashley L. Cohen, *The Missionary* "miss[es] an opportunity for a more radical relearning of the meaning of freedom," one that recognizes "*continuities* between chattel slavery and so-called free labor."[58] These "forms of coercion [that] lay at the heart of the new freedom" are made manifest in the death of Owenson's Indian priestess, Luxima.[59] The novel ends with Luxima rushing to Hilarion as the flames from the Inquisition prepare to consume him in a transnational performance of suttee. Hilarion, seeking to protect her from his own death, breaks his bonds and a Spanish soldier "aimed a dagger at his heart; its point was received in the bosom of the Indian; – she shrieked, – and called upon 'Brahma!'"[60] This image of colonial violence causes the surrounding Indians to "f[a]ll with fury on the Christians" with their "religious enthusiasm kindling their human passions."[61] The final image, then, is one that marks India not only as ungovernable, but also as incapable of self-governance and undeserving of freedom.

Ireland and the Empire of White Nations:
Katherine Cecil Thurston's *Max*

Thurston's New Woman novel *Max* in many ways typifies the *fin de siècle* genre with its challenging of gender norms, its complication of the marriage plot, as well as its engagement with the scramble for African and other colonial territories. As scholars have demonstrated, the "inter-relationships between feminist fiction and empire-building in this era of high imperialism" are essential to understanding femininity at the *fin de siècle*.[62] Often set in colonial landscapes like South Africa, India, or the Canadian wilderness, New Woman and New Girl fictions narrate the survival of the white British woman in colonial landscapes that are threatening because of indigenous peoples. Though "minimal," inter-actions with indigenous inhabitants "provide further opportunity for the demonstration of bravery," showcasing the valor of Britishness and also reinforcing the threat posed by the indigenous population.[63] New Woman fiction stages a competition between the survival and indepen-dence of white women and the Black and indigenous bodies within colo-nial territories.

Instead of representing far-flung colonies, Thurston's *Max* subtly employs a similar competition in Paris. By focusing on race in Thurston's thoroughly metropolitan and European novel, we are reminded that race is not something that can or should be consigned to the periphery. *Max* reminds us of the long presence of Black and indigenous peoples in Europe, insisting that race remain a central element in our study of Irish and European literature. Although the French presence in North Africa dates back to the reign of Charles X and the French presence in Senegal dates back to the seventeenth century, Black colonial migrants first settled in large numbers in Paris in the early twentieth century.[64] Thurston's novel largely predates a significant presence of Black Parisians, but *fin-de-siècle* constructions of race mirrored "conquest and 'pacification'" so the French remained "at the pinnacle" of the racial and evolutionary hier-archy.[65] Particularly important for the representation of race in *Max* is the claim that *fin-de-siècle* Paris utilized race as a way of "experienc[ing] difference as exoticism," which enabled the public to "define and redefine self and others."[66] Instead of Owenson's transracial solidarity, race in *fin-de-siècle* literature reinforces boundaries between the white self and the Black other.

Maintaining boundaries between self and other is fundamental to identity in *Max*. This novel traces the struggles of a Russian princess for freedom from a violent second marriage; she arrives in Paris not merely disguised as a young man, but identifying publicly as a young man. Essential to his success is the preservation of this binary between self and other; he insists that he must "strangle the evil spirit" of his feminine self.[67] An Irishman named Blake introduces the Russian to the Bohemian culture of Montmartre, promising to help him navigate his way to artistic fame, before falling in love with a painting of Max as her feminine self. This painting sets off the novel's denouement, in which Max must choose between his aesthetic dreams and her romantic affections for Blake. The rigidity between self and other that shapes Max/ine's struggle for identity and autonomy replicates the broader *fin-de-siècle* distinction between a white self and an exoticized, Black other. The novel most clearly draws this racial distinction in the two competing spaces of Bohemian culture and of official aesthetic culture, framing the competition between the protagonist's freedom and the presence of Black bodies. In order to achieve his aesthetic independence, Max rejects two key representations of blackness, highlighting the need to dissociate Irishness from any non-white identity.

The key scene in which race intrudes takes place at the Rat Mort, a club in Montmartre. Max is immediately struck by the "barbaric music" of the "Ztigane," a form of music associated with European gypsies.[68] The characterization of this lively music as "barbaric" throws into bass relief the "light Parisian waltz" the orchestra next plays.[69] As noted above, the use of "barbarism" functions as a racial code. It is not surprising that a waltz is seen as distinct from "barbaric" gypsy music, but Thurston juxtaposes this European form with "a negro and a negress – properties of the place, as were the glasses and the table linen – waltzing with the pliant suppleness, the conscious sensuality of their race, and close behind them followed a second couple – a Spaniard, restless and lithe, small of stature and pallid of face, and a young Spanish girl of splendid physique."[70] This representation of the two Black dancers is jarring, not least because of the claim that they are "properties of the place," equivalent to the glasses and the table linens. However, this representation also reflects multiple elements of what Dana S. Hale identifies as the *fin-de-siècle* French attitude toward race. Since the French, like most other European nations at the time, conceived of race as a hierarchy of development that determined an individual's and an ethnic group's "potential for 'civilization,'" or their capacity for freedom, the fact that these Black dancers are treated as "properties" of the Rat Mort reinforces the widely held belief that "sub-Saharan Africans ranked at the bottom of the scale."[71]

The second element of Hale's functions of *fin-de-siècle* race these two dancers reveal is the power of exoticism to reinforce the distinction between self and other. This distinction, based on degrees of civilization and development, reinforces the former claims of a racial hierarchy. In *Max*, this is produced through a complicated experience of fascination and disgust that marks the Black dancers as irretrievably other. When Blake asks him if the scene at the Rat Mort is "amusing," Max responds, "It is – and it is not. Those black creatures are extraordinary. They are repulsive – like figures in a nightmare."[72] The initial question of the scene's amusement calls attention to the commodification of colonized peoples in the Third Republic, where the Exposition Universelle increasingly displayed aspects of France's colonial territories for consumption.[73] In this framework, the Black dancers are nothing more than entertainment for white Parisian audiences; just as they pay for the comfort of the table linens and the quality of the music, the Black dancers are a commodity. But Max's response, calling the dancers "extraordinary," "repulsive," and nightmarish, points to the use of race to construct the identity of the self against the "repulsive" other. Race functions, in *Max*, as a form of "social abjection." Imogen Tyler differentiates "social abjection" from the psychoanalytic form of abjection theorized by Kristeva through an emphasis on the "violent exclusionary forces of sovereign power" that mark certain populations as "unassailably other."[74] Rooted in Ahmed's claim that "disgust is crucial to power relations … disgust at 'that which is below' functions to maintain the power relations between above and below, *through which 'aboveness' and 'belowness' become properties of particular bodies, objects and spaces*."[75] Max's characterization of the Black "creatures" as "repulsive" reinforces Ahmed's power relations: first, by the epithet of "creatures," he denies them the status of human; second, the repulsion he feels articulates an elevation of the self above this other. In order to escape the "grotesque black forms of the negro dancers," Max implores Blake to go, even though "the night is young."[76] The movement away from these "grotesque black forms" reestablishes the distance between the self and other that helps maintain the distinction between self and other, separating Max from that which he finds grotesque and repulsive.

As if to make the repulsion even more palpable, Max's use of "nightmare" and "repulsive" recalls an earlier scene in the novel that explicitly links the African dancers to the subhuman and the Gothic. Blake explicitly invokes this earlier scene when he scoffs at the use of "repulsive." "Repulsive, are they," he asks, "And what about a certain picture we once looked at – when I was swept off the face of the earth for using that same word?... These n*****s aren't a bit more disgusting than the monkey suck-ing the fruit."[77] In the first days of Max's life in Paris, Blake takes him to the Société de Peintres et Sculpteurs Français in the Champ de Mars, where the boy stands "entirely engrossed" before

> ...a picture curiously repulsive, yet curiously binding in its realism of con-ception. It was a large canvas that formed one of a group of five or six stud-ies by a particular artist. The details of the picture scarcely held the mind, for the imagination of the beholder was instantly caught and enchained by the central figure—the figure of a great ape, painted with cruel and extraordinary truth. The animal was squatting upon the ground, devouring a luscious fruit; its small and greedy eyes were alight with gluttony; in its unbridled appetite, its hairy fingers crushed the fruit against its teeth, while the juice dripped from its mouth.
>
> The intimate, undisguised portrayal of greed shocked the susceptibilities, but it was the hideous human attributes patent in the brute that disgusted the imagination. With a terrible cunning of mind and brush the artist had laid bare a vice that civilization cloaks.[78]

The repulsion Max experiences at the sight of the Black dancers, linked to the repulsion Blake felt before the gluttonous ape, "la[ys] bare a vice that civilization cloaks."[79] The politics of disgust, while superficially reinforc-ing the hierarchy of races that shapes the Third Republic, actually reveals the similarities between and the proximity of the animal and the human, the "savage" and the cosmopolitan. This is especially important for an Irish novel, considering the simian representations of the Irish that were used to affix them in a lower position in the racial hierarchy. The anxiety Max experiences when confronted with the human presence of the Black dancers, which is absent before the aestheticized image of the painting, reveals both Michelle Meagher's claim that "objects are rendered disgust-ing or dirty through implicit social agreements" and the need to insist emphatically that the Irish ought not be associated with this revolting image.[80]

For Max, the aesthetic image of disgust maintains enough distance between the self and the other, but, when confronted with the physi-cal presence of the Black body, he must insist on reasserting the division between self and other to maintain his own selfhood. Through the concept of social abjection and disgust, this *fin-de-siècle* novel forcefully reasserts the division between races, rejecting the possibility of a trans-racial sympa-thy. In doing so, Thurston's *Max* identifies Ireland with whiteness through an opposition to an image of the Black body that remains "repulsive" and "unassailably other."[81]

Ireland and Post-imperial Freedom in the Writings
of Kate O'Brien

The liberty discourse and the claim for self-government achieve their full-est articulation in the *Bildungsromane* of Kate O'Brien's twentieth-century career, which begins in an Irish Free State and ends in a Republic pre-paring to join the European Economic Community.[82] O'Brien's novels elevate Irish women to a position of independence, most often in a conti-nental landscape that is characterized by "emptiness, on a wide horizon."[83] The emptiness, far from being isolating, represents the promise of self-determination for her female protagonists. But as both *Mary Lavelle* (1936) and *Without My Cloak* (1931) demonstrate, Irish women's representation of liberation depends upon an erasure of Black and indigenous bodies, despite the alluring promise of cosmopolitanism.

Mary Lavelle, a novel that resulted in O'Brien being barred from Franco's Spain, follows the brief tenure of the eponymous protagonist as she teaches English to the daughters of the Areavaga family in a fictional town set in the Basque Country.[84] The geography of O'Brien's Spain is undoubtedly racialized. As Mentxaka notes, O'Brien's Mary Lavelle is "more in empathy with a Spanish-Castillan identity, within a European framework."[85] Parts of Spain are compatible within a European, or white, framework, while "Moorish Spain" must be "held at arm's length" and "could never have her heart."[86] This geography not only draws on the his-tory of Spain's Reconquista, but also enacts a politics of racial purity that insists Europe must be white in the twentieth century.

Lavelle approaches her conception of Spain by prioritizing "the white-skinned Western Christian in her," establishing a fundamental tension with the Islamic and African influence in the southern parts of Spain.[87] This collapsing of Europe and the West with whiteness and Christianity reflects the consolidation of race and geography. As the train crosses the Douro River on their journey to Madrid, Lavelle "gaze[s] on fold after fold of the fair-haired land. Arab indeed!"[88] This Arab influence that Lavelle is so eager to deny and reject seems to pose a double threat: first, it challenges the purity of the white conception of Europe; second, Lavelle's admission that "she had fallen day by day … a little more and a little more in love with" Spain would mean that she was guilty of falling in love with an impure, Arab and potentially African identity.[89] Indeed, Lavelle makes it explicit when she claims that, "if Arab philosophy and Arab fiddle-faddle art were truly dominant in the peninsula, then … it could never have her heart; she would have made a mistake in her twelve weeks on the northern coast — that was all."[90] The threat, ultimately, is one of miscegenation, of corrupting the white and Christian nature of Europe with a Black, Arab other.

This determined refusal to give her heart to a peninsula influenced by Arab philosophy and Arab art quite clearly maintains the opposition between white and Black that reflects not only the history of the Reconquista, but also long-standing fears about the "incivility and degeneracy" of transracial pairings.[91] As Damon Ieremia Salesa argues about mixed-race marriage in a British and Australasian context, interracial marriages "often marked not a 'good' colonialism but an unusually intensive, potent, and ambitious species. Interracial affective ties and marriage, when effectively combined with law, policy and other forms of statecraft, could prove to be strikingly invasive, expansive and virulent colonial strategies."[92] But O'Brien's Spain is not the colonial theater, nor is it equivalent to a white man marrying a Black or indigenous woman. Instead, it echoes both the excised interracial marriage in the 1810 edition of Maria Edgeworth's *Belinda* (1801) and the specter of Shakespeare's Othello and Desdemona, a relationship to which O'Brien returns in *As Music and Splendour* (1958).[93] The parallel to Othello is particularly striking because of the threat of violence embedded within it. In order to maintain her own claim on autonomy and to avoid the death of Desdemona, O'Brien's protagonist must insist upon racial purity and exclusion. *Mary Lavelle*'s insistence on the "fair-haired" landscape erases the Arab influence from Spain. While Lavelle's autonomy and self-governance depends upon the white and Christian nature of Europe, this very dependence relies upon the erasure of the Moor, whose only trace lies in the "dead, fairy tale city" of Toledo.[94] Doubly consigned to death in the Reconquista and the imaginary realm of the fairy tale, the Moorish and African influence of Spain remains largely erased from *Mary Lavelle*, a relic of nearly 500 years.

This project of erasure becomes central to understanding the representation of race in twentieth-century Irish women's writing. We can see the same erasing of non-white populations in the New York section of her award-winning first novel, *Without My Cloak*. This novel follows the rise of the Considine family from a lowly horse-thief to a family that dominates the social and economic order of Mellick, the fictionalized version of the author's native Limerick. *Without My Cloak* ultimately stages the conflict between Denis Considine and the rest of the family, including his father, who has taken on the mantle of family patriarch. After Denis falls in love with a local woman, "a scullery maid, the bastard of a scullery maid," the Considines conspire to send this woman away to either Australia or New

York, not allowing Denis to know which.[95] But Denis is able to follow her to New York where he spends months searching for her. It is through this representation of 1870s New York that we see most clearly the practice of erasing and eliding Black and indigenous peoples not simply in New York City itself but in the United States more broadly.

O'Brien's New York of the 1870s is overwhelmingly white; in addition to the Irish, Denis meets "two Swedish families," "Jews ... and shrill, ingratiating dagos, and noble-looking Scandinavians who could outdrink every race, and Negroes, with voices like deep bells, and Tammany men with Irish names, who wounded that pride of race in him which he had never till now believed himself to possess."[96] Despite the narrator's claim that Denis "swam among cross-tides of type and race," we never meet anyone in this New York who is not white.[97] This is one of only three times that Black Americans are specifically mentioned; in the other two, they are described as "the melancholy Negroes" and, finally, Denis describes for his father "the Bowery and the waterfront, and the Negro life in New York, and the bohemianism of Greenwich Village" after he has returned to Mellick.[98] That Denis is able to describe this "Negro life" is surprising, considering the paucity of exposure the novel shows him experiencing during his time in New York. Similarly, the use of "melancholy" raises more questions than the novel answers: is this state of melancholy a result of racial oppression in post-Civil War America? Is it, more directly, a result of poverty that arises from such oppression?

This New York section is roughly forty pages in length and its representation of the European immigrant community is relatively thorough, leaving room for a French prostitute, Irish Mass-goers, American Dandies who "played so wistfully at the game of being in Europe and in the 'quartier' that most of them had never seen and would never see," and even a German-Swiss restauranteur whom Christina insists she will marry.[99] So the absence of Black Americans is notable for two key reasons: first, it whitewashes O'Brien's New York during a period known for the Great Migration of Black Americans from the South to the North; second, by erasing these Black Americans, O'Brien effectively enacts what Jodi A. Byrd has termed "the transit of empire." For Byrd, the "transit of empire" is a concept through which the "U.S. empire orients and replicates itself" through "elisions, erasures, [and] enjambments."[100] These elisions and erasures are central to the narrative of liberalism, which "asserts freedom and *forgets* enslavement as the condition of possibility for what constitutes 'the human.'"[101] This means that a willful forgetting of the condition and practice of slavery is central to the liberty discourse that I have been tracing.

While Owenson and Thurston have certainly not erased race in the way that O'Brien's narratives do, they largely ignore the condition of enslavement and indentureship that shaped the politics of race in colonial and imperial power structures. Perhaps it is that O'Brien's novels are products of an independent Ireland that has taken its place "within a 'white' and European framework," but these novels erase race and, in so doing, reinforce the whiteness of the Irish, European, and American identity.[102]

Without My Cloak replicates this erasure of Black Americans for Indigenous Americans across the entire continent when it celebrates "the new alchemy – petroleum," the booming oil industry across the American West.[103] In this celebration, "the name of a young man called John D. Rockefeller fell from American tongues as awesomely as long ago the Trojans may have named their Hector, or the Franks Roland; ... there were hero-worshipping tales of the 'Commodore' and of John Jacob Astor. These people were gods."[104] Rockefeller's Standard Oil Company, Cornelius Vanderbilt's railroad and shipping empires, and Astor's real estate holdings all depended upon and resulted in the displacement of indigenous peoples from the American West and, in the case of Astor, involvement in the Spanish-American War resulted in an increase in American sovereignty over Caribbean and Pacific territories. These consequences of post-Civil War economic development are utterly forgotten because "the talk ... was nearly all of money."[105] Indeed, the celebration of Rockefeller, Vanderbilt, and Astor as "gods" prevents any sustained critique of the racial consequences of their fortunes. The "historical aphasia of the conquest of indigenous peoples" is reproduced in the Whitman-like marveling at "how imagination, loose-reined, might ride in this uncharted land to a new Periclean glory."[106] The image of riding across an uncharted land toward Periclean glory necessarily invokes the concept of Manifest Destiny that shapes American thought and identity around the frontier. For O'Brien, this frontier is one of personal fulfilment, the "wide horizon" that becomes characteristic of her novels; however, it is the wide and uncharted nature that obscures and elides the fact that this horizon was neither empty nor uncharted.

Conclusion

In her famous treatise *A Room of One's Own* (1929), Virginia Woolf notes the "formidable" difficulties for women who are seeking to create a "work of genius," or really anything creative or disruptive.[107] A woman, Woolf insists, "must have money and a room of her own if she is to write."[108]

But interrogating Irish women's writing in terms of its relationship to race means we must not be content with ensuring that the woman writer has access to this money and this room. We must ask from where the money comes. Was it derived from colonial sources or from coerced free labor? We must also ask who has access to the room and who is denied access to that room. These questions do not invalidate the struggle for independence for Irish women; instead, they reveal a more complex narrative and truths, to paraphrase Kate O'Brien, that might change and break things.

Notes

1 Lisa Lowe, *The Intimacies of Four Continents* (Durham: Duke University Press, 2015), 5.
2 Kate O'Brien, *Mary Lavelle* (London: Virago, [1936] 2000), 300.
3 Clíona Ó Gallchoir and Heather Ingman, "Introduction," in *A History of Modern Irish Women's Literature*, eds. Clíona Ó Gallchoir and Heather Ingman (New York: Cambridge University Press, 2018), 1–17, 7.
4 Ó Gallchoir and Ingman, "Introduction," 6.
5 Ó Gallchoir and Ingman, "Introduction," 7.
6 Ó Gallchoir and Ingman, "Introduction," 7.
7 Lowe, *The Intimacies of Four Continents*, 3.
8 Lowe, *The Intimacies of Four Continents*, 3–4. Indeed, I have argued elsewhere for understanding Irish women's literature through a socio-economic framework that unites concepts of citizenship and emancipation through wage labor.
9 See Lowe, *Intimacies of Four Continents*; Laura Doyle, *Freedom's Empire: Race and the Rise of the Novel in Atlantic Modernity, 1640–1940* (Durham: Duke University Press, 2008); Felicity A. Nussbaum, *The Limits of the Human: Fictions of Anomaly, Race, and Gender in the Long Eighteenth Century* (Cambridge: Cambridge University Press, 2003); Saidiya V. Hartman, *Scenes of Subjection: Terror, Slavery, and Self-Making in Nineteenth-Century America* (New York: Oxford University Press, 1997); Ashley L. Cohen, *The Global Indies: British Imperial Culture and the Reshaping of the World, 1756–1815* (New Haven: Yale University Press, 2020).
10 Lowe, *The Intimacies of Four Continents*, 3.
11 Cohen, *The Global Indies*, 145.
12 David Brion Davis, *The Problem of Slavery in the Age of Revolution, 1770–1823* (New York: Oxford University Press, 1999), 62.
13 Cohen, *The Global Indies,* 146.
14 Cohen, *The Global Indies*, 147.
15 Katie Trumpener, *Bardic Nationalism: The Romantic Novel and the British Empire* (Princeton: Princeton University Press, 1997), 141.

16 Laura Doyle has shown the rhetoric of Anglo-Saxonism was used to harness freedom to race, constituting a racialized discourse that elevates the white citizens of the Anglo-Atlantic above other races. The initially subversive "recovery" of Anglo-Saxon roots in the early decades of seventeenth-century England began to construct an idea of liberty and self-determination that belonged exclusively to the inheritors of "England's true and free Anglo-Saxon laws" specifically through their "capacity for liberty." This rooted claims to liberty and freedom within the very essence of Englishness; self-determination belonged exclusively to the Anglo-Saxon race. The English, according to Doyle, were capable of self-governance because of their racial identity, and were constituted as a race because they were capable of self-governance. Doyle, *Freedom's Empire*, 29, 31, 12–13.

17 Trumpener, *Bardic Nationalism*, 142.

18 Trumpener, *Bardic Nationalism*, 146.

19 Lowe, *Intimacies of Four Continents*, 3.

20 Trumpener, *Bardic Nationalism*, 142.

21 Sydney Owenson, *The Wild Irish Girl: A National Tale*, ed. Kathryn Kirkpatrick (New York: Oxford University Press, [1806] 2008), 13.

22 Owenson, *The Wild Irish Girl*, 176.

23 Lowe, *The Intimacies of Four Continents*, 3.

24 Leela Gandhi, *Affective Communities: Anticolonial Thought, Fin-de-Siècle Radicalism, and the Politics of Friendship* (Durham: Duke University Press, 2006), 2.

25 Gandhi, *Affective Communities*, 1.

26 Gandhi, *Affective Communities*, 2–3.

27 Edward Said, *Culture and Imperialism* (New York: Pantheon Books, 1978).

28 Lowe, *The Intimacies of Four Continents*, 3.

29 Julia Anne Miller, "Acts of Union: Family Violence and National Courtship in Maria Edgeworth's The Absentee and Sydney Owenson's The Wild Irish Girl," in *Border Crossings: Irish Women Writers and National Identities*, ed. Kathryn Kirkpatrick (Tuscaloosa: University of Alabama Press, 2000), 27.

30 Owenson, *The Wild Irish Girl*, 250.

31 Owenson, *The Wild Irish Girl*, 250.

32 Jessie Reeder, *The Forms of Informal Empire: Britain, Latin America, and Nineteenth-Century Literature* (Baltimore: Johns Hopkins University Press, 2020), 10; Lowe, *The Intimacies of Four Continents*, 6.

33 Reeder, *Forms of Informal Empire*, 13.

34 Sydney Owenson, *Florence Macarthy: An Irish Tale*, ed. Jenny McAuley (London: Pickering & Chatto, [1818] 2012), 212.

35 Owenson, *Florence Macarthy*, 233.

36 Owenson, *Florence Macarthy*, 233.

37 Owenson, *Florence Macarthy*, 233.

38 Roxann Wheeler, *The Complexion of Race: Categories of Difference in Eighteenth-Century British Culture* (Philadelphia: University of Pennsylvania Press, 2000), 21.

39 Owenson, *Florence Macarthy*, 236.
40 Owenson, *Florence Macarthy*, 236.
41 Owenson, *Florence Macarthy*, 236–37.
42 Reeder, *Forms of Informal Empire*, 3.
43 Lowe, *The Intimacies of Four Continents*, 15.
44 Lowe, *The Intimacies of Four Continents*, 15.
45 Sydney Owenson, *The Missionary: An Indian Tale*, ed. Julia M. Wright (Orchard Park, NY: Broadview Press, [1811] 2002), 243.
46 Trumpener, *Bardic Nationalism*, 146; Lowe, *The Intimacies of Four Continents*, 14.
47 Owenson, *The Missionary*, 248.
48 Owenson, *The Missionary*, 85.
49 Owenson, *The Missionary*, 85.
50 Lowe, *The Intimacies of Four Continents*, 15.
51 Lowe, *The Intimacies of Four Continents*, 106.
52 Lowe, *The Intimacies of Four Continents*, 113.
53 Lowe, *The Intimacies of Four Continents*, 14.
54 Owenson, *The Missionary*, 93.
55 Owenson, *The Missionary*, 94.
56 Lowe, *The Intimacies of Four Continents*, 113.
57 This might function as a critique of Hastings and the East India Company in the wake of Burke's and Sheridan's impeachment in 1786. For more on literary representations of critiques of the East India Company, see Cohen, *The Global Indies*, 148–58.
58 Cohen, *The Global Indies*, 146.
59 Thomas Holt, *The Problem of Freedom: Race, Labor, and Politics in Jamaica and Britain, 1832–1938* (Baltimore: Johns Hopkins University Press, 1992), 6.
60 Owenson, *The Missionary*, 249.
61 Owenson, *The Missionary*, 250.
62 Tina O'Toole, *The Irish New Woman* (Basingstoke: Palgrave, 2013), 43. See also Michelle J. Smith, *Empire in British Girls' Literature: Imperial Girls, 1880–1915* (Basingstoke: Palgrave, 2011) and Susan Cahill, "Where Are the Irish Girls?: Girlhood, Irishness and L.T. Meade," in *Girlhood and the Politics of Place*, eds. Claudia Mitchell and Carrie Rentschler (New York: Berghahn Books, 2016), 212–227.
63 Smith, *Empire in British Girls' Literature and Culture*, 94.
64 Jennifer Anne Boittin, "Black in France: The Language and Politics of Race in the Late Third Republic," *French Politics, Culture & Society* 27, no. 2 (2009): 25.
65 Dana S. Hale, *Races on Display: French Representations of Colonized Peoples, 1886–1940* (Bloomington: Indiana University Press, 2008), 13.
66 Hale, *Races on Display*, 13.
67 Katherine Cecil Thurston, *Max* (London: Harper & Brothers, 1910), 184.
68 Thurston, *Max*, 166.
69 Thurston, *Max*, 166.
70 Thurston, *Max*, 166.
71 Hale, *Races on Display*, 13.

72 Thurston, *Max*, 167.
73 Hale, *Races on Display*, 14.
74 Imogen Tyler, *Revolting Subjects: Social Abjection and Resistance in Neoliberal Britain* (London: Zed Books, 2013), 21; William Cohen, "Introduction: Locating Filth," in *Filth: Dirt, Disgust, and Modern Life*, eds. William Cohen and Ryan Johnson (Minneapolis: University of Minnesota Press, 2005), x.
75 Sara Ahmed, *The Cultural Politics of Emotion* (Edinburgh: Edinburgh University Press, 2004), 88, emphasis added.
76 Thurston, *Max*, 173.
77 Thurston, *Max*, 167.
78 Thurston, *Max*, 49–50.
79 Thurston, *Max*, 50.
80 Michelle Meagher, "Jenny Saville and a Feminist Aesthetics of Disgust," *Hypatia* 18, no. 4 (2003): 32.
81 Cohen, "Introduction," x.
82 Ireland becomes a Republic in 1949 and joins the EEC in 1961; O'Brien's final novel is published in 1958, the year before Seán Lemass becomes Taoiseach.
83 Kate O'Brien, *The Land of Spices* (London: Virago, [1942] 2006), 280.
84 Aintzane Legarreta Mentxaka argues that, "[w]ith the exception of Gerardine Meaney and Wanda Balzano, critics have *ignored* the fact that *Mary Lavelle* is set in the Basque Country, immediately raising questions of 'purity'"; Aintzane Legarreta Mentxaka, *Kate O'Brien and the Fiction of Identity: Sex, Art and Politics in Mary Lavelle and Other Writings* (Jefferson: McFarland & Co., 2011), 137, 134.
85 Mentxaka, *Kate O'Brien and the Fiction of Identity*, 136.
86 O'Brien, *Mary Lavelle*, 187–88.
87 O'Brien, *Mary Lavelle*, 187.
88 O'Brien, *Mary Lavelle*, 188.
89 O'Brien, *Mary Lavelle*, 187.
90 O'Brien, *Mary Lavelle*, 188.
91 Nussbaum, *The Limits of the Human*, 9.
92 Damon Ieremia Salesa, *Racial Crossings: Race, Intermarriage, and the Victorian British Empire* (Oxford: Oxford University Press, 2011), 18.
93 See Kathryn J. Kirkpatrick, "'Gentlemen Have Horrors Upon this Subject': West Indian Suitors in Maria Edgeworth's *Belinda*," *Eighteenth-Century Fiction* 5, no. 4 (1993): 331–48; Lyndon J. Dominique, *Imoinda's Shade: Marriage and the African Woman in Eighteenth-Century British Literature, 159–1808* (Columbus: The Ohio State University Press, 2012), 71–72.
94 O'Brien, *Mary Lavelle*, 227.
95 Kate O'Brien, *Without My Cloak* (London: Virago, [1936] 2001), 366.
96 O'Brien, *Without My Cloak*, 379, 385.
97 O'Brien, *Without My Cloak*, 385.
98 O'Brien, *Without My Cloak*, 394, 429.
99 O'Brien, *Without My Cloak*, 386.

100 Jodi A. Byrd, *The Transit of Empire: Indigenous Critiques of Colonialism* (Minneapolis: University of Minnesota Press, 2011), XIII.
101 Byrd, *Transit of Empire*, XXV, emphasis added.
102 Nelson, *Irish Nationalists*, 148.
103 O'Brien, *Without My Cloak*, 385.
104 O'Brien, *Without My Cloak*, 385.
105 O'Brien, *Without My Cloak*, 385.
106 O'Brien, *Without My Cloak*, 386.
107 Virginia Woolf, *A Room of One's Own*. (New York: Penguin, [1929] 1945), 53–54.
108 Virginia Woolf, *A Room of One's Own*, 6.

CHAPTER 5

Blackface Minstrelsy, Irish Modernism, and the Histories of Irish Whiteness

John Brannigan

"The notion that black people are human beings is a relatively new discovery in the modern West." So wrote Cornel West in his influential "A Genealogy of Modern Racism" (1982), which sought to understand the discursive and structural formation of "white supremacy" and the reasons why "the idea of black equality in beauty, culture and intellectual capacity remains problematic and controversial within prestigious halls of learning and sophisticated intellectual circles."[1] It is instructive to reread these statements, which have been generative of the field of critical race theories, in the context of contemporary debates about the institutional whiteness of Irish culture and society. Anne Mulhall has argued that for "BAME" writers and critics, Irish culture remains hegemonically white, and Irish Studies as an academic community remains "slow to address the overwhelming whiteness of the field," and slow too to turn the lens of critical race scholarship upon its own terms and practices.[2] In a country in which over sixty-four thousand people, overwhelmingly from African and Asian ethnic groups, have been held in dehumanizing conditions under the "Direct Provision" laws governing asylum seekers since 2001, and in which there is strong evidence of a "hierarchical racial order" in the labor market, to the detriment in particular of Black Africans, there can be little doubt that whiteness has been systemically and structurally encoded as the norm in Irish society. As Ebun Joseph suggests, the stark realities of Ireland's "colour-coded hierarchy" are often invisible, both because they are "rarely called into question or publicly challenged," and also because of the complex history of Irish whiteness, which has usually only been highlighted in diasporic contexts.[3]

There is a substantial body of scholarship on how the Irish abroad mobilized whiteness in racially stratified labor markets, especially in the United States. Noel Ignatiev (1995) sought to account for the transformation of "the Catholic Irish" from being "an oppressed race in Ireland" to becoming "part of an oppressing race in America."[4] A few years before

Ignatiev, David R. Roediger had made a similar argument in his history of the role of race in the making of the American working class, *The Wages of Whiteness* (1991), that in the years before the American Civil War, "it was by no means clear that the Irish were white." For Roediger, the attainment of the privileges of whiteness crucially hinged on cultural practices of racial mimicry: white working-class performances of blackface minstrelsy were instruments of racial climbing, enabling the Irish in particular to enact their whiteness through the racial parody of blackness.[5] In greater detail, Eric Lott also argues that "those who 'blacked up' and those who witnessed minstrel shows were often working-class *Irish* men," and that minstrelsy can be seen "as a mediator of northern class, racial and ethnic conflict."[6]

The thesis that the Irish became white through self-consciously white performances of Black racial masquerade has been compelling and productive but has not been without its critics. As David Lloyd observed, the thesis that the Irish *became* white provokes as many questions as it answers. Lloyd asks: "How was it possible that the Irish ever seemed to be non-white?... Did the Irish become white only in the United States?... And as the Irish 'became white' in the United States, what effect did their access to whiteness there have on their positioning within Ireland's colonial relationship with Britain?" These questions are particularly pertinent to the history of blackface minstrelsy in Ireland given the burden of evidence in the historical record of "Irish participation in US and British imperial wars of expansion, race riots, racially exclusive unions, and so forth," which Lloyd argues outweigh the more flaunted evidence of Irish racial affinity with other oppressed peoples.[7] Was the whiteness of the Irish earned only in the subjugation of others outside of Ireland, or was there also an internal process of becoming white in Ireland? The whiteness of the Irish, and specifically the process of *becoming* white, demand more detailed and probing study, not least because the whiteness of the Irish in Ireland has attracted almost no scrutiny, and has been allowed to go unexamined.

It is that role of the Irish in racializing others and in the process maintaining white hegemony, particularly as part of emerging state formations, which I want to place under scrutiny here. The focus of this chapter is on white Irish cultural practices of blackface in Ireland as an expression of cultural power. Such practices were often almost exclusively male, and thus blackface performance should be considered an extension of *male* as well as white privilege in exercising the power to define racial hierarchies. As has often and rightly been argued, blackface is a white cultural form and practice. It is practiced by self-consciously white performers, yet is not ultimately about images of other races, but about the ingenuity, humanity, and sensitivity of the white male performer, who can model for the audience a complexity of emotional responses to dehumanized others, recapitulating the superiority of the invisible white human subject. Here, I aim to examine the role of blackface in white Irish culture, especially around the time of the emergence of independent Irish statehood in the first half of the twentieth century, as a critical context for contemporary practices and ideas of whiteness in Ireland. This examination takes three forms: the first is a speculative history (and it can be no more) of blackface minstrel theater in Ireland; the second is an analysis of representations of blackface acts in Irish modernism (specifically in works by James Joyce and Jack B. Yeats); and the third is a brief consideration of the longer and perhaps ultimately more troubling manifestations of blackface in Irish folk culture.

Blackface Theater in Ireland

Under his pen-name "Outis," Donal O'Sullivan wrote the following in a 1944 review of the Gaiety Theatre's production of *Show Boat* in the *Irish Times*:

> It seems so long since Dublin saw a n***** minstrel show that we are in danger of forgetting what it was like. It had all the atmosphere of a family party, to the intimacies of which the members of the audiences were admitted as privileged guests. The minstrels sat in a semi-circle on the stage, with the solo singers and the banjo men in the middle and the cross-talk comedians at either end – Massa Sambo and Massa Bones.[8]

It may seem somewhat odd that *Show Boat*, which had become famous particularly after the 1936 film starring Paul Robeson, should remind O'Sullivan of "n***** minstrel shows," particularly as the musical raised controversial issues of miscegenation and racial exploitation. The Gaiety production, however, included no Black actors; O'Sullivan expressed pride that this showed what a Dublin theater could achieve, "relying entirely on its own resources," namely a cast of white actors and a good supply of burnt cork, and hence the affinity with minstrel shows. The review, in fact, has little to say about *Show Boat*. Instead, O'Sullivan is drawn nostalgically back to the familial intimacies of blackface minstrel shows by solo performers such as Eugene Stratton, Herbert Campbell, G. H. Elliott, and G. H. Chirgwin, more famously known as "the white-eyed kaffir," and the troupes of minstrel performers who formed the famous semi-circle of blacked-up comedians and musicians. Increasingly after 1922, with the demise of blackface minstrel solo performers, and the strictly political sense in which Dublin was no longer on the "British" circuit of music hall venues, those troupes of minstrel performers were "home-grown."

The history of blackface minstrelsy in Irish theaters has yet to be written, but the outlines of such a history would suggest that many Irish cities and towns were included in the touring calendars of both American and British companies from the beginnings of blackface performances in the 1840s right up to the early twentieth century, when such shows had become less popular. In their heyday, such groups as the Matthews Brothers Christy Minstrels, the Livermore's Court Minstrels, Sam Hague's Minstrels, the Moore and Burgess Minstrels, and the Dixie Minstrels all visited Dublin and toured prominent venues around Ireland. In his essay "Blacks and Blackface on the Irish Stage, 1830–1860," Douglas Riach records the frequency and popularity of blackface acts and also notes the surprising silence of prominent Irish abolitionists about them, arguing that "it is probable that the cause of the Negro in America suffered from the failure of the abolitionists in Ireland to condemn as wholly inaccurate the image of the Negro most often presented on the Irish stage, and carried to America in the minds of countless Irish emigrants."[9] In the period after 1922, however, the demise of the visiting groups and solo acts apparently left a vacuum that was filled by occasional Irish acts, such as the "White Blackbirds," the "Swanee Minstrels," and Dave Davis's minstrels, and impersonators such as Tom Finglass and Morgan Hayes. These Irish blackface acts were associated in particular with the popular music hall and musical theaters in Dublin of the time, such as the Queen's, the Tivoli, the Gaiety, and later the Olympia. The shows included some rising Irish stars of the time, such as Noel Purcell and Wilfred Brambell, in blacked-up comic roles. More broadly, blackface acts enjoyed popularity at local fetes, school fairs, talent shows, and even some feis ceoil. As a writer in the *Irish Independent* recalled in 1928, there was even a stage Irish minstrel troupe modeled upon the Christy minstrels, with a semi-circle performance of Irish solos, duets, and choruses, then jigs and Irish sketches, with the characters dressed in "orthodox Irish style – corduroy vest and knee breeches with brass buttons, a green or green and white rosette displayed on the left breast."[10] The production was based upon blackface minstrel shows but "adapted to strictly Irish needs with singular resourcefulness."

The emergence of Irish radio also provided an unlikely platform for Christy Minstrel entertainments, with 2RN broadcasting a regular Christy Minstrel slot in the late 1920s, for example, by Dorothy Day and company, and with a group calling themselves "The Black Jesters" appearing in the early 1940s on Radio Éireann. The radio shows evidently traded on the existing popularity of, and residual nostalgia for, music hall minstrel shows and may serve to illustrate how blackface performance was as much about vocal as visual parody. As Lott argues, when we hear the impersonation of black speech or song, we are very much in "the presence of blackface's unconscious return."[11] Reviewers of Irish blackface productions repeatedly take the visual cues of blackness for granted, and dwell instead on the vocal registers. O'Sullivan, for example, comments that "No doubt, it is true to say that the n***** minstrel is a mere caricature of the real negro, in the same way as the Stage Irishman and Sir Harry Lauder are caricatures. Still, many of these songs ... express that nostalgic melancholy which is perhaps the negro's most prominent characteristic, as well as his quaint and homely humour."[12] The figure that haunts such a comment upon the meanings of blackface performance, of course, is the absent figure of the "real negro," and it is this absence, whether presumed or actual, which repeatedly marks the parameters of a racial discourse of Irish whiteness.

Michael Pickering argues in his study of blackface minstrelsy in Britain and Ireland that the form was "dependent on its becoming oriented to local cultural features and conventions." The arrangement of the performers into a semi-circular shape, for example, not only enabled rapid improvisation and comic exchange between those on stage, but it also enabled engagement with the audience, inviting the atmosphere of "the family party" to which O'Sullivan alludes in his 1944 review. In Britain, Pickering argues, although blackface minstrelsy undoubtedly owed its origins and early success to the constant traffic of American minstrel troupes, it also took on its own peculiar character: in the late nineteenth century, for example, blackface acts acquired an "air of decency and decorum, ... a unique blend of polite and vulgar cultures," which "meant that actual connections with any lived version of African-American culture became increasingly strained."[13] Instead, the parodic forms of blackness staged in minstrel shows in Britain were mapped onto "an essentialist English national identity ... differentiated from other nationalities by its innately given superiority," a characteristic that found anti-Irish and anti-German songs grafted into the same minstrel shows. Blackface minstrel shows performed in Dublin shared the same cultural and social climate of "decency and decorum": they were often advertised as family shows and were performed in venues such as the Rotunda or Leinster Hall, which signified middle-class respectability. They also formed entertainments at charity events, police benefit shows, and Rotary Club pantomimes. But it is as yet unclear how the same performers who traded on racial slurs of Irish and Black peoples in London and Liverpool revised their acts across the

Irish Sea in Dublin and Cork. English nationalism, after all, was explicitly and inextricably tied at the time to imperialist discourses of racial difference, so that mimicry of Black enslaved peoples could be read for the valency of its caricature of blackness elsewhere. Undoubtedly, elements of such imperial caricatures were popular in Irish culture, and not just with empire loyalists, but what is not clear, largely for lack of detail about the local reorientations of blackface performances, is how middle-class Irish nationalism brought blackface minstrelsy into some kind of cultural and ideological functionality.

Signifiers of Black cultural performance were substantially present in Irish theater. William Fay, for example, who with his brother Frank formed the foundations for the stagecraft that made the Abbey Theatre successful, recalls how his love of theater was kindled by a cousin who was "an expert 'Corner Man'" in Christy Minstrel shows. And prior to establishing the Abbey players, Fay toured Ireland with a troupe of Black actors in a lengthy run of *Uncle Tom's Cabin* (1895), billed, as it was famed, for its display of "Real Negroes, freed Slaves, Mulattoes, Quadroons, Octoroons, and Creoles (male and female)."[14] It is clear from such billing that "entertainment" consists not primarily of dramatic or narrative pleasure but spectacle and, specifically, the spectacle of the racially encoded body. Yet as W. T. Lhamon records in *Raising Cain (1998)*, theatrical shows that displayed "real negroes" proved significantly less durable than blackface acts, which he argues became "the first Atlantic mass culture."[15]

Both Lhamon and Pickering have made the case that racism was not the only reason for the enduring success of blackface performances on both sides of the Atlantic. It was successful principally as a cultural formalization of what Lhamon called "the mutualities of expression," which were developed by the material connections of industrial production, merchant shipping, urbanization, and the movement of slave and migrant labor.[16] Here, we might note that although Dublin, Belfast, Cork, and Galway were intimately connected materially and culturally to that Atlantic network, the notion that blackface performances in Ireland might be understood in terms of mutuality, or amalgamation, is strained by the relative absence of significant communities of Black people.

This is the subtext of a one-act play by Matthew Brennan, entitled *The Young Man from Rathmines*, performed at the Abbey Theatre in 1922, which was revived four times,[17] and remained popular, particularly with amateur companies for some time afterward.[18] The play takes place in a one-room tenement flat in Dominick Street in Northside Dublin, in which Mr. and Mrs. Dowd are preparing for a visitor, the eponymous

young man from Rathmines with whom their daughter, Mary, has corre-
sponded, and to whom she is intended for marriage. Mary has responded
to the young man's newspaper advertisement seeking a "nice, refined girl,"
and his address in middle-class Rathmines convinces the family that Mary
has secured the interest of an eligible young bachelor. The family summar-
ily dismisses the attentions of another young man, Barney, who calls to
take Mary out, as it is clear that he is merely of their own class. As Mary
and her family wait to see the young man, George Jackson, for the first
time, the expectation of wealth and respectability is constantly on their
minds, and Mr. Dowd is compelled to wear an uncomfortably stiff white
collar to convey the impression that the family is itself worthy of the young
man's intentions. The play concludes with the shocking revelation, as he
appears at the door, that the young man is black:

> (*A young man enters and pauses inside the door, bowing and smiling. He is a
> N*****. Mrs Dowd and Mary stare at him in open-mouthed bewilderment.
> Mr Dowd starts back in amazement, and almost tumbles into the fire*).

MRS DOWD: (*in tones of horror*): A black student!
MARY: Oh, Barney, Barney, why did I ever send you away. (*Weeping, she
    rushes into her mother's arms, and buries her face on that lady's bosom*).
MR DOWD: An' it was for a black haythen that I was made put on this.
    (*Wrenches off the collar and dashes it on the ground, then strips off his coat,
    and starts rolling up his shirt sleeves*). Just wait a minit, me buckoo, an'
    I'll give ye such a pair of black eyes that the rest of yer face'll look white.
                                  CURTAIN[19]

The capitalization of the word "N*****" in the stage directions is clearly
intended to signal to the play's white reader, as the performance would
have signaled to the white audience, the affective register of shock that an
encounter with a Black man is expected to invoke in Ireland in 1922. The
shock lies not just, of course, in the register of black skin, but also in the
disparity between the young man's capacity to appear middle class in his
letters, and the sub-class, indeed sub-human, category that black skin signifies visually. There is an additional layer of signification added when we
consider that no Black actor was hired for the part of the young man, and
the part was played by Gabriel Fallon, later director of the Abbey Theatre,
who blacked up for the role. So it could be argued that this final allusion
in the scene to Mr. Dowd's threat to give the young man "such a pair of
black eyes that the rest of yer face'll look white" refers us back to the white
skin behind the masquerade of blackness. But whiteness is, of course, also
signaled as supremacy, humanity, and complexity here. The play is clearly

mocking the social pretensions of the Dowd family, and Mary's final cry of regret that she sent Barney (the good white, working-class boy) away indicates a valorization of working-class authenticity. The black skin of George Jackson, or even more ironically the masquerade of black skin, is the theatrical sign of punishment for the social vice of pretension.

Blackface and Irish Modernism

Vincent Cheng argues that Joyce's allusions to blackface acts highlight the problematic dynamics of such racial performances in "a culture in which the only available experience of 'blackness' is the essentialized otherness of a stereotyped construction."[20] Cheng observes that no distinction is made in the mind of Leopold Bloom between "real blacks (since these were almost never experienced by Irish people)" and blackface minstrels, which draws our attention to theatricalization, in all its forms, as the principal arena in which blackness is made present in Irish society. Bloom thinks about figures of blackness several times in the course of *Ulysses* (1922), but each instance is connected to the others. In "Hades," Bloom passes hoardings advertising theater shows, which include Eugene Stratton, Mrs. Bandmann Palmer, *Leah*, *The Lily of Killarney*, and *Fun on the Bristol*, all shows which were performed in Dublin on June 16, 1904.

> They went past the bleak pulpit of Saint Mark's, under the railway bridge, past the Queen's theatre: in silence. Hoardings: Eugene Stratton. Mrs Bandmann Palmer. Could I go to see *Leah* tonight, I wonder. I said I. Or the *Lily of Killarney*? Elster Grimes Opera Company. Big powerful change. Wet bright bills for next week. *Fun on the Bristol*. Martin Cunningham could work a pass for the Gaiety. Have to stand a drink or two. As broad as it's long. (He's coming in the afternoon. Her songs.)[21]

Stratton was billed for this performance as "The Greatest Coon Delineator of the Age" and was doubled at the Theatre Royal with a musical comedy, *Fun on the Bristol.* All of these productions involved cultural crossings of particular kinds: Stratton was an American actor famed for his solo black-face minstrel repertoire, who was enormously popular in the British Isles; Mrs. Bandmann Palmer, star of *Leah*, was an American actress famed for her stage appearances as Hamlet, without gender masquerade; *Leah the Forsaken* was an American translation of a German-Austrian play about anti-Semitism; *The Lily of Killarney* was the operatic version of Boucicault's *The Colleen Bawn* (1860), the libretto written by Julius Benedict, a German-born English composer of Jewish parentage; and *Fun on the Bristol* was an American musical modeled in part upon the formal shape of blackface minstrel shows, which included "negro melodies," a burlesque of Verdi's *Il Travatore*, an encounter with a Turkish patrol, and a caricature of "Levi, the Jew." It is clear from such a list, which represents the principal portion of what was available as public entertainment in Dublin on this single day, that this is a culture evidently preoccupied with what Lhamon describes as "cross-cultural folk mimicry," with the theatricalization of many forms of cultural difference. It is also clear that what is being described here are the cultural products of transatlantic exchange, as befitting a novel preoccupied with the question of what the sea brings in.

Those transatlantic transactions are also at stake in the figure of blackness that Bloom encounters in the "Cyclops" chapter, just before Bloom's identity comes before the scrutiny of the citizen and his companions.

> ...And another one: *Black Beast Burned in Omaha, Ga.* A lot of Deadwood Dicks in slouch hats and they firing at a Sambo strung up in a tree with his tongue out and a bonfire under him. Gob, they ought to drown him in the sea after and electrocute and crucify him to make sure of their job.
>
> —But what about the fighting navy, says Ned, that keeps our foes at bay?
>
> —I'll tell you what about it, says the citizen. Hell upon earth it is. Read the revelations that's going on in the papers about flogging on the training ships at Portsmouth. A fellow writes that calls himself *Disgusted One*.
>
> So he starts telling us about corporal punishment and about the crew of tars and officers and rearadmirals drawn up in cocked hats and the parson with his protestant bible to witness punishment and a young lad brought out, howling for his ma, and they tie him down on the buttend of a gun.
>
> —A rump and dozen, says the citizen, was what that old ruffian sir John Beresford called it but the modern God's Englishman calls it caning on the breech.
>
> And says John Wyse:
>
> —'Tis a custom more honoured in the breach than in the observance.
>
> Then he was telling us the master at arms comes along with a long cane and he draws out and he flogs the bloody backside off of the poor lad till he yells meila murder.
>
> —That's your glorious British navy, says the citizen, that bosses the earth. The fellows that never will be slaves, with the only hereditary chamber on the face of God's earth and their land in the hands of a dozen gamehogs and cottonball barons. That's the great empire they boast about of drudges and whipped serfs.[22]

Here, the newspaper report of a "black beast" hanged, shot, and burned in Omaha, based upon the lynching of a black man accused of raping a young white woman in 1919, takes the reader momentarily away from a dialogue concerning maritime power.[23] Yet the story of a sailor being tied and flogged on board a navy ship, which follows from the citizen's earlier call for the Irish nation to have its own navy, picks up on the lynching victim in several allusions. Throughout the passage, sailors are called "tars," a historically accurate term that derived from the use of tar to weatherproof sailors' clothes and rigging. Of course, the term also implies the "tar and feather" punishment meted out for disloyalty or dishonor, a ritual and folk practice that itself plays upon the symbolism of blackening and feathering the skin. The sailor also "yells meila murder" during the flogging, a curious expression deviating from the more common "blue murder" or "bloody murder." The spelling of "meila" seems to suggest Old Greek for "dark or black," hence melanin, rather than the Gaelic "míle," meaning a thousand, which is how this word has been glossed by Don Gifford, Terence Patrick Dolan, and R. W. Dent.[24] The navy's role in the history of race slavery is then figured in the allusion to "Rule Britannia," in which the British vow never to be enslaved, is based upon "ruling the waves," the oceanic mastery that was essential to providing slave labor in the cotton plantations upon which much of the wealth and industry of imperial England was built. The punished body of the sailor thus becomes interfused with the lynched Black man in Omaha, and both are emblematic of the Atlantic transversality that Ian Baucom identifies as underpinned by the specters of violent histories of slavery and racism.[25] Within the aesthetics of transversality that marks *Ulysses* as a text, as well as the earlier allusions to Stratton, the blackface performer, and the Black melodies of *Fun on the Bristol*, are here mapped on to their grimly ironic doubles, the burnt, tortured body of the Black lynch victim and the flayed skin of the "Jack Tar" sailor.

These allusions recur in the "Circe" chapter, when Bloom associates "Night-town" with Molly's sexual fantasies about Black men.

BLOOM

(*looks behind.*) She often said she'd like to visit. Slumming. The exotic, you see. Negro servants in livery too if she had money. Othello black brute. Eugene Stratton. Even the bones and cornerman at the Livermore christies. Bohee brothers. Sweep for that matter.
(*Tom and Sam Bohee, coloured coons in white duck suits, scarlet socks, upstarched Sambo chokers and large scarlet asters in their buttonholes, leap out. Each has his banjo slung. Their paler smaller negroid hands jingle the twingtwang wires. Flashing white kaffir eyes and tusks they rattle through a breakdown in clumsy clogs, twinging, singing, back to back, toe heel, heel toe, with smackfatclacking n***** lips.*)[26]

The figure of the hanged "black beast" recurs in the allusion to "Othello black brute," and to the Bohee brothers wearing "Sambo chokers," while the blackface minstrel is figured again in reference to "Eugene Stratton," "the Livermore christies," "the white Kaffir eyes," and even the "Sweep for that matter." As Len Platt argues, "the connection between theatre and race representation is emphatic" in both *Ulysses* and *Finnegans Wake*, with the latter novel even punned as "Funnycoon's Wick."[27] By linking blackface minstrelsy to sexual desire, a desire that is also explicitly tied to images of mastery and brutality, *Ulysses* stages the implication of cultural constructions of blackness in the process of defining Irish whiteness. The figures of miscegenation that pervade the novel delineate the boundaries of racial identity. Blackface showed in pastiche form the enacting of racial differentiation, performing for white audiences the image of a blackness that was never required to appear authentic or denotative, but which was always a slippery figure of desire and violence, a symbolic other that could be made to function within the cultural economy of Irish racial legitimation.

The staging of blackface is also a preoccupation in the work of Jack B. Yeats. Unlike his poet brother, Jack Yeats was drawn toward popular forms of theater entertainment, to the music hall, the circus, and the melodrama, and hence the recurring fascination in his paintings with the clown figure, and what could be argued is a version of the whiteface clown in the blackface performer. In both his sketch of a Liverpool Christy Minstrel show and his painting, *Singing "Way Down Upon the Swanee River"* (1942), Yeats signals the semi-circular form of the blackface minstrel show, emphasizing therefore the conventionality within which both performers and audiences experience the show. The huddled conviviality of the audience in the sketch also indicates the "familial intimacy" that O'Sullivan described in his nostalgic account of the minstrel shows in Ireland. That the blackface performer in the sketch is singing a lament for the Irish emigrant reveals the local, adaptive orientations of the form, in which case the blackface masquerade is no longer keyed to a notional depiction of Black plantation life, nor is it a caricature of a Black man. Yet even if the song signals detachment from the visual cues of racial masquerade, the blackface disguise is not incidental, for it announces the conventions of sentimentality, of melancholy, within which diasporic rootlessness in many different forms can be expressed through the agency of the masquerade, even as it disavows the parity or solidarity of cultures that might seem superficially to be available here. Yeats commented upon his fascination with Christy minstrels in his book, *Sligo* (1930):

> I think the fact that their faces are black is the least ingredient in the goblet. Blue, green or purple would be just as exciting. The main joint in the joinery is that the Minstrels are disguised in a frightening way. Oh, don't

say 'Masks': Oh Masks, such a lot of talk about Masks – everyone knows
about Masks just being about the last thing but three…. Christy Minstrel
faces with the great pink mouths are not Masks, they are the faces of our
brothers, our own faces made all awry.[28]

In both his clown paintings and his blackface paintings, Yeats highlights
the emotional expressiveness of the disguised face, the bare meaningfulness
of the eyes and mouth in the gestural performativity of the masquerade.
This is particularly evident in his *South Pacific* (1937). Yeats's insistence
that the disguise of the Christy minstrels should not be seen in terms of
"Masks," especially as the word is capitalized, seems a direct challenge to
his brother's renowned theory of masks, which derived heavily from his
experience of Japanese Noh theater. Instead, Jack Yeats argues, the Christy
minstrel faces are "the faces of our brothers, our own faces made all awry."
I have written elsewhere about this passage, that "If there is a sense of community with 'our brothers,' it is produced within the confines of a spectacle designed for the consumption of self-consciously white people."[29]
The awryness of the black face remarks both upon its racial difference, but
also upon the slippage of the facial signifier. Lhamon reminds us of the
complexity of the artifice: "Blackface performers worked out ways to flash
white skin beneath a layer of burnt cork, stage the pastiche grammar of a
creole dialect, and recast traditional Irish melodies with fantasy images of
fieldhand fun shadowed by violence and dislocation."[30] Yeats's fascination
with the transatlantic forms of blackface minstrel entertainment seems also
to shed light upon this oscillation between an implied common humanity
and an aggressive and appropriative staging of racial difference, upon the
"awryness" constantly being enacted and negotiated on stage.

Blackface in Irish Folk Culture

Jack Yeats takes us to another, and perhaps even more troubling scene of
the theatricalization of blackness within Irish culture in his broadside illustration, "The Bang-the-Door Boys" (1912). Here, Yeats depicts the scene
of a mumming or wren boy calling, the boys bringing a blessing or a curse
depending on whether or not they received their just demands. In many
parts of Ireland, this was a familiar sight on St. Stephen's Day, and the
ritual had its own conventions of dress and performance. Yeats's illustration is unusual in depicting the children wearing masks, whereas the more
common form of disguise was to blacken the face with soot, burnt cork,
or boot polish. In 1947, the Irish Folklore Commission surveyed the wren
boy and mummer festivities to ascertain what forms the customs took in

different localities, and although there were variations, the most consistent and pervasive form of disguise for the revelers was the "blackened face."

Blackening the face, of course, was a disguise used much more widely than in folk ceremonies or rituals. Newspaper reports of robberies, riots, ambushes, and poaching in the late nineteenth and early twentieth centuries frequently allude to the protagonists blackening their faces in disguise, and the term "blackened faces" also appears with some regularity in the headlines. The disguise, almost as much as the criminal act, it seems, was a sign of social disturbance. It would be wrong to suggest that these acts of disguise are instances of racial masquerade. They are obviously not attempts by robbers or gunmen to feign the appearance of Black people. Yet, as Dale Cockrell argues of blackening disguises in folk culture more generally, there is a resonance between the emergent transatlantic form of blackface minstrelsy that appeared in theaters from the 1840s onward and the roots of blackface disguise in agrarian folk rituals and folk rebellions.[31] Doubtless, both robbers and mummers adopted blackface disguise because of the ease with which soot, boot polish, or charcoal could be obtained and used. Yet, of course, as the newspaper headlines attest, the blackened face retains a symbolic significance that exceeds the intention merely to disguise identity. Cockrell associates it with rituals of social inversion, misrule, and carnival. It "might have first followed from direct contact with dark-skinned Moors," Cockrell argues, "but probably did not," and if the blackface disguise lost its racial associations over time, its concurrent use in everyday criminal acts, seasonal folk rituals, and popular urban theater raises intriguing and perhaps even unanswerable questions about its provenance and affective meanings. Did the blackness of a robber's disguise produce the same open-mouthed reactions among his victims as the appearance of a Black man in Matthew Brennan's *The Young Man from Rathmines*? Was a gunman with a blacked-up face more capable of invoking fear in his victim because of the theatrical associations of blackness and brutality? Was there, as Cockrell suggests, a primeval and elemental association of blackness with death and infertility for white, northern peoples, which found its way into solstitial mumming rites about the triumph of light over darkness, and thus into the fear of blackness? Were these meanings encoded for "high-latitude agrarian societies" in their long, cold experience of darkness, meanings that would return in every encounter with black-skinned peoples?

Cockrell's study is a compelling reminder that blackface minstrelsy did not emerge simply or only from racial conflicts between Black Americans and various white-skinned groups in the fraught labor markets of early nineteenth-century America, but perhaps also from the rural European folk cultures in which mumming practices were already deploying forms of blackface masquerade. These were as common in Ireland as they were in Dorset or Pennsylvania.[32] They deserve our attention because they were an early and persistent form of blackface performance, which, even if they had no discernible racial meanings prior to the nineteenth century, were eventually circulated concurrently with blackface minstrel acts and other forms of racial masquerade. As the folklore commission survey reported of Irish examples of the form in 1947, in some cases only members of the band blacked up, in others only some of the boys calling to doors blacked up, while others wore masks or women's clothing, but in most responses to the survey, the blackening of the face was the most common form of disguise and was used by all or most participants.[33] The survey asked for no comment on the provenance of this convention, nor on its rationale, and any respondent who offered comment indicated that the function of the blackened faces was disguise. In Alan Gailey's seminal study of *Irish Folk Drama*, the pervasive use of blackface is explained as "the oldest and simplest form of disguise which we know."[34] It is presumed to have no racial connotations, nor is it linked to blackface minstrelsy, and importantly, it seems to predate the origins of blackface theater. Yet in the examples Gailey provides of plays performed as part of the revelry, there lurk the racist stereotypes familiar from the stage – the "Darkie," the Turk, and the Witch Doctor – and in some of the plays, all of the characters, including St. Patrick, Prince George, and Cromwell, blackened their faces. Gailey argues that the distribution of mumming practices in Ireland "suggests influence from across the Irish Sea," mainly to seventeenth- and eighteenth-century forms, but with some precedents in medieval folk drama, and he also indicates that from Ireland, England, and Scotland, mumming also migrated across the Atlantic, most notably to Philadelphia and Newfoundland. Like blackface minstrelsy, the use of blackface in folk drama was always adaptive, improvised into local idioms, and yet too part of an Atlantic matrix of circulation and exchange. In both minstrelsy and folk drama, the question of how cultural forms traverse the seas, the question of how those cultural forms become part of local practices of social formation, and part of local economies of desire and aggression have yet to be fully addressed.

The Folklore Commission survey was partly conceived on the understanding that the traditions of mummers and wren boys were in decline, and their rhymes, rituals, and costumes survive today mainly through the commercialized forms available at Halloween. So too, Donal O'Sullivan's writings in the *Irish Times* acknowledged the demise of blackface minstrelsy and associated it with cheap English holiday resorts catering for large industrial populations: "I'm glad," he wrote, "that the Irish ... are able to contemplate their seashore without automatically associating it with buckets and spades and black-faced comedians."[35] This seems to send blackface minstrelsy back across the sea, as if it was always a cheap foreign import. The meaning of that sentiment and the potency of its investment in the protective symbolism of the seashore are illuminated by O'Sullivan's depiction of his own holiday home in the Gaeltacht: "I am writing on the seashore within a stone's throw of the little village that always lies so close to my heart. I have known it intimately, as well as the surrounding countryside, for the greater part of my life and have come to regard it with the affection with which one regards one's second home. As William Allingham says in his poem on Ballyshannon: 'Not a face in all the place but partly seems my own.'"[36] The construction of that sentiment about what constitutes "my own," in an Irish culture heavily mythologized as having been racially homogenous until recently, relies upon a complex investment in the visual and verbal codes of race and racism.

Conclusions

The performance and representation of blackface acts in Irish culture were, and remain, part of what Philomena Essed describes as an "everyday racism," which through "cumulative instantiation" of racist practices and acts exerts power over racialized others.[37] There are several conclusions that I believe can be drawn from this speculative genealogy of Irish blackface performance.

The first is that the popularity of blackface minstrelsy in Ireland before and after independence may be taken as evidence of cultural complicity in the system of privilege that defines whiteness. Apart from the participation of theaters, actors, and audiences in sustaining blackface minstrel acts, whether visiting from Britain and America or based in Ireland, newspaper reviews show no sign of a critical or ironic understanding of blackface.

The second is that although there were no discernible differences in the forms that blackface minstrelsy took in Ireland from elsewhere (and therefore one might say that anti-black racism in Ireland was not distinct from elsewhere), the common perception that there were probably few Black people and no sizeable Black communities in Ireland meant that blackface minstrelsy was a white cultural practice performed to white audiences for whom there was little or no social tension or economic competition with Black peoples. If the dominant explanation of the rise of blackface minstrelsy in the U.S. invokes the context of labor competition and cheek-by-jowl ghettoes defined by competing races and ethnicities, it is more difficult to explain the popularity of blackface minstrelsy in Ireland. It might be implied that the Irish were passive consumers (or indeed active adopters) of the racial ideologies produced in Britain and the U.S., that racist prejudices based on skin color were preexistent in Ireland regardless of historical experience. The latter scenario is particularly concerning because it is dangerously close to seeing race as a transcendent category rather than a reified concept, and it is that process of reification that I believe we should be analyzing and deconstructing.

Third, it is important for us to conceptualize the relationship between nationalist politics and racist culture as a model that might incorporate contradiction and paradox, but which equally might involve continuity. It may be the case that Irish people were persuaded of analogies between their histories and the histories of other oppressed peoples and minor nations, analogies that may well have prompted feelings of solidarity and charity, while at the same time enjoying and participating in cultural practices that reinforced derogatory racial stereotypes and enacted racist distinctions. Perhaps such contradictions are an inevitable product of our multiple, intersecting narratives of identity, but it seems more likely, as Foucault argued of the role of "biological monism" in national state formation, that there is an exploitative relationship between nationalist politics and racist culture, and that narratives of solidarity in the Irish state have readily sought to capitalize upon both the privileges of whiteness and the moral advantages of siding with the oppressed.

Fourth, while I am conscious that the focus above may seem to be going against Richard Dyer's call for studies of white representations of whiteness, rather than "the images of other races in white cultural production," my argument here is that blackface masquerade is a white cultural practice of whiteness.[38] Since whiteness is, as Dyer argues, or at least aspires to be, invisible, un-raced, or simply "human," it has made itself visible only through structures of differentiation, discrimination, and masquerade. The adoption of the blackface masquerade is, thus, a performative enactment of whiteness behind the mask, and therefore a useful object of the critical analysis of the construction of whiteness. That such performances of racial differentiation were enacted within and by a culture that represented itself over and over again as a racially and culturally homogenous nation should alert us to the constitutive anxieties of race and nation, and the ways in which white supremacy in Ireland has been continually, if often elusively, maintained.

Notes

1 Cornel West, "A Genealogy of Modern Racism," in *Race Critical Theories*, eds. Philomena Essed and David Theo Goldberg (Oxford: Blackwell, 2002), 90.

2 Anne Mulhall, "The Ends of Irish Studies? On Whiteness, Academia, and Activism," *Irish University Review* 50, no. 1 (2020): 98, 99, 107. As a collective term for the minoritized experiences of Black, Asian, and minority ethnic groups, "BAME" has been commonly used in the United Kingdom and Ireland, particularly in government, medical, and media reports. The acronym is strongly contested by minority ethnic groups, however, for homogenizing the experiences of different communities.

3 Ebun Joseph, "Whiteness and Racism: Examining the Racial Order in Ireland," *Irish Journal of Sociology* 26, no. 1 (2018): 65, 53, 66.

4 Noel Ignatiev, *How the Irish Became White* (London: Routledge, 1995), 1.

5 David R. Roediger, *The Wages of Whiteness: Race and the Making of the American Working Class* (London: Verso, [1991] 1999), 134, 115–32.

6 Eric Lott, *Love and Theft: Blackface Minstrelsy and the American Working Class* (Oxford: Oxford University Press, 1995), 35.

7 David Lloyd, "Black Irish, Irish Whiteness and Atlantic State Formation," in *The Black and Green Atlantic: Cross-Currents of the African and Irish Diasporas*, eds. Peter D. O'Neill and David Lloyd (Basingstoke: Palgrave, 2009), 3.

8 Outis, [Donal O'Sullivan], "Listen to the Minstrels: 'Show Boat' Shakes Up the Musical Memories," *Irish Times: Times Pictorial*, July 22, 1944, 4.

9 Douglas C. Riach, "Blacks and Blackface on the Irish Stage, 1830–1860," *Journal of American Studies* 7, no. 3 (1973): 241.

10 Kevin Foster, "Irish Minstrels – Why Not?," *Irish Independent*, February 10, 1928, 6.

11 Lott, *Love & Theft*, 5.

12 Outis, [Donal O'Sullivan], "Listen to the Minstrels," 4.

13 Michael Pickering, *Blackface Minstrelsy in Britain* (Aldershot: Ashgate, 2008), 18, 5.

14 W. G. Fay and Catherine Carswell, *The Fays of the Abbey Theatre* (London: Rich and Cowan, 1935), 12, 71–80. See also the advertisement for the Leinster Hall production of *Uncle Tom's Cabin* in the *Freeman's Journal*, April 13, 1895, 4.

15 W. T. Lhamon Jr., *Raising Cain: Blackface Performance from Jim Crow to Hip Hop* (Cambridge, MA: Harvard University Press, 1998), 58.

16 Lhamon Jr., *Raising Cain*, 39.

17 Elizabeth Mannion, "The Dublin Tenement Plays of the Early Abbey Theatre," *New Hibernia Review* 14, no. 2 (Summer 2010): 82.

18 Robert Hogan and Richard Burnham, *The Years of O'Casey, 1921–1926: A Documentary History* (Newark: University of Delaware Press, 1992), 74–6.

19 Matthew Brennan, *The Young Man from Rathmines* (Dublin: Talbot Press, n.d.), 23.

20 Vincent J. Cheng, *Joyce, Race, and Empire* (Cambridge: Cambridge University Press, 1995), 175.

21 James Joyce, *Ulysses* (New York: Vintage, 1986), 6.183–190.

22 Joyce, *Ulysses*, 12.1324–1350.

23 Timothy Weiss, "The 'Black Beast' Headline: The Key to an Allusion in 'Ulysses,'" *James Joyce Quarterly* 19, no. 2 (1982): 183–6. The racial meanings of lynching and tarring, and the increasing social complexity of such acts in early twentieth century America are discussed in J. William Harris, "Etiquette, Lynching, and Racial Boundaries in Southern History: A Mississippi Example," *American Historical Review* 100, no. 2 (1995): 387–410.

24 See Don Gifford, *Ulysses Annotated: Notes for James Joyce's Ulysses* (Berkeley, CA: University of California Press, 1989), 357; Terence Patrick Dolan, *A Dictionary of Hiberno-English* (Dublin: Gill and Macmillan, 2004), 155; and R. W. Dent, *Colloquial Language in Ulysses: A Reference Tool* (Cranbury: Associated University Presses, 1994), 142.

25 Ian Baucom, *Specters of the Atlantic: Finance Capital, Slavery, and the Philosophy of History* (Durham: Duke University Press, 2005), 311.

26 Joyce, *Ulysses*, 14.407–418.

27 Len Platt, *Joyce, Race and Finnegans Wake* (Cambridge: Cambridge University Press, 2007), 137; Joyce, *Finnegans Wake*, 499.13.

28 Jack B. Yeats, *Sligo* (London: Wishart, 1930), 132.

29 John Brannigan, *Race in Modern Irish Literature and Culture* (Edinburgh: Edinburgh University Press, 2009), 129.

30 Lhamon, *Raising Cain*, 42.

31 Dale Cockrell, *Demons of Disorder: Early Blackface Minstrels and their World* (Cambridge: Cambridge University Press, 1997), 30–61.

32 See Alan Gailey, *Irish Folk Drama* (Cork: Mercier Press, 1969).

33 "St Stephen's Day Questionnaire," 1947, Irish Folklore Commission, UCD National Folklore Collection, MSS 1088, 1089, 1090.

34 Gailey, *Irish Folk Drama*, 43.

35 Donal O'Sullivan, *The Spice of Life and Other Essays* (Dublin: Browne and Nolan, 1948), 67–8.

36 O'Sullivan, *The Spice of Life*, 114.

37 Philomena Essed, *Understanding Everyday Racism: An Interdisciplinary Theory* (London: Sage, 1991), 3.

38 Richard Dyer, *White: Essays on Race and Culture* (London: Routledge, 1997), 1.

CHAPTER 6

Joyce's Racial Comedy

Vicki Mahaffey

What could be comic about race, which is possibly the most urgent, hotly contested, and widely misunderstood issue of our time? James Joyce subjected race to comic treatment without lessening its seriousness. Joycean comedy (like "Christian comedy") is produced by broadening one's perspective and deferring judgment about the relative value of different values and cultures. Deferral of judgment precludes prejudice, which literally means premature judgment (*pre* + *judice*). Joyce broadens our perspective on race by pivoting on the meaning of the word. The most common definition is "A group of people, animals, or plants, connected by common descent or origin."[1] This is the sense Joyce draws upon when he calls *Ulysses* the "epic of two races (Israelite-Irish)."[2] The comic pivot is to another meaning, "A contest of speed in running, riding, sailing, or some other activity, between two or more competitors, in combination with related usages that imply forward movement along a course or channel."[3] Joyce's mélange of meanings produces a humorous send-up of racism that simultaneously belittles it: the human race is reframed as a socially conditioned competition between different groups where the channeling of the course serves as a metaphor for social conditioning. The goal is for one group to outflank or overpower all the others, but the contest is rigged, because more privileged groups with more money behind them have an added advantage. Moreover, people bet on the race, which is to say they *pre-judge* (as well as predict) the results. In the story "After the Race" in *Dubliners* (1914), Joyce uses the Gordon Bennett motor derby to exemplify the competition between contestants with different national origins, but in *Ulysses* (1922), he shifts focus to a different race, the Ascot Gold Cup horse race, to feature race as competition between bodies of different colors: gold and black, which connote money and waste, day and night, respectively. Unexpectedly, comically, triumphantly, against most pre-judgments, the darker-colored outsider wins what is symbolically the human race itself. In *Finnegans Wake* (1939), it is the darkness *inside* (rather than outside) the body that is reframed as both generative and humane: the cognitive "darkness" of the vast unknown and the devalued darkness of human waste. Shem the Penman, the semi-autobiographical artist figure, alchemically changes his body's waste into ink, which he uses to write on his white skin, effectively changing – blackening – the skin color with which he was born through his writing.

Joyce depicts social racism as a game gone viral, a contest that is neither fair nor fun, in which humans have either melded with machines (as in an automobile race) or with horses (a centaur race), and large amounts of money are deployed to back the anticipated winners. His treatment anticipates – with a comic twist – what Ta-Nehisi Coates would assert almost a century later, that "race is the child of racism, not the father."[4] Racism, a distortion of perception wrongly believed to be validated by biology or nature, is what turns the game ugly.[5] As Noel Ignatiev points out: "It is not free competition that leads to racial animosity, but its absence. Race becomes a social fact at the moment 'racial' identification begins to impose barriers to free competition among atomized and otherwise interchangeable individuals."[6]

The title of "After the Race" seems to refer to the card game that comes after the motor race (the Gordon Bennett) in Dublin that took place July 2, 1903. The alignment of motor race and card game is significant because both the race and the game depend on an admixture of skill, alertness, resources, and luck that can make the playing field uneven. But the title also refers to something broader – ordinary life in Ireland after the race, which is how Joyce used the phrase in his interview with the French driver Henri Fournier.[7] What happens when the race is over, when the flashy contestants have concluded their expensive contest? Joyce describes the race cars speeding "through this channel of poverty and inaction" through which "the Continent sped its wealth and industry."[8] The title of the story underscores the opportunism of the racers, who use Dublin only as a stage for their prosperity and success, and not as a destination to be explored or appreciated on its own terms.

The "channel" of poverty and inaction through which the cars move underscores one of the lesser used meanings of "race" as a path or a course. It designates a physical place, the Naas Road southwest of Dublin, but it also gestures toward a social structure that pits nations against one another in a contest of skill and speed: especially Germany, France, England, and the United States. When Joyce asked Fournier which nation he feared the most, Fournier replied, "I fear them all – Germans, Americans, and English. They are all to be feared."[9] The Gordon Bennett was a competition between countries, each of which could enter three cars that must have been composed of parts made in that country.[10] At the time Joyce was writing, different nations could be considered races, although the more modern meaning of "race" as a group *without* a nation was also in play, as in Joyce's reference to the Israelites as a race, or the treatment of Catholics as a race.[11]

The racial aspect of Joyce's play with a motorcar race is heightened by his description of the racers as hybrids: of animals, machines, and humans. He describes the experience of the journey as laying "a magical finger on the genuine pulse of life" as "gallantly the *machinery* of *human* nerves strove to answer the bounding courses of the swift blue *animal*."[12] Those who engage in the international social contest are themselves artificial constructs; the human beings striving against each other are part machine and part animal. Although the participants of this race are privileged, their "racial" competition nonetheless serves to dehumanize them in ways that mirror the dehumanization of oppressed racial groups, who are (reductively) conflated with both animals and machines.[13]

The political allegory in "After the Race," which Gillespie and Weir rightly describe as "almost too obvious," in which the Irish lose and the English win, applies only to the card game, not the motorcar race (although as noted above, the card game can be read as an alternative version of the official race, both of which were hosted by a wealthy American: Gordon Bennett – who established four international motor races in his name – and Farley, who owns the yacht on which the men play cards).[14] More interesting than the allegory itself are the seductions that ensure Jimmy will lose: the dazzling allure of prestige and wealth, the expensive dinner and free flow of drinks, the condescension with which Ségouin "allows" him to invest in his motor business: "Ségouin had managed to give the impression that it was by a favour of friendship the mite of Irish money was to be included in the capital of the concern."[15] The "buried" Irish nationalism of Jimmy and his father is revealed as little more than an affectation that can be dissipated by the magic wand of wealth and success.[16] Like national identity, once associated with "race," nationalism is actually negligible in the master "race" to accrue capital. As Gillespie and Weir point out, the national identities of three of the characters – Farley (Irish American), Rivière (French Canadian), and Villona (Hungarian, still aligned with Austria in 1903) – "are hybridized by modern forces of culture and commerce. The basic idea seems to be that capitalism destroys old historical alliances based on culture and forges new alliances based on economic interests."[17]

"After the Race" suggests that even as early as 1903, nations were sub-ordinating national allegiance to enter a newer international contest for money and prestige. To put it more precisely, national alliance had become almost a marketing tool for gathering local support, not unlike the way sports teams today are named after a specific city or state which can be moved for monetary reasons: the Houston Oilers became the Tennessee Titans after Houston declined to invest more money in their recently renovated stadium. The implications of this reading of national rivalries extend to racial divisions today: race as an ontological category does not in fact exist, although social operations depend upon the fantasy that it does.[18] As Ibram X. Kendi explains, "race is a mirage but one that humanity has organized itself around in very real ways," defining race as "A power construct of collected or merged difference that lives socially."[19] What exists (still, as it did in Joyce's time) is racism: a contest of unequal opportunity in which allegations of racial (once national) superiority are used to justify a great disparity in rewards. The Gordon Bennett Cup *seemed* to be about the different levels of skill and engineering native to different countries, but what it obscures is the money and power needed even to enter this race. The contestants included Great Britain, Germany, France, and the USA; Great Britain was defending its title and wanted to host the race, but racing was illegal on English roads, so legislation was passed to hold it in impoverished Ireland, cheered on by groups of the "gratefully oppressed."[20] Racism – understood here as a mask for capitalist ruthlessness that works by creating hierarchies of human value – persists. As Kendi so powerfully insists, "The root problem – from Prince Henry to President Trump – has always been the self-interest of racist power."[21]

Gillespie and Weir accentuate Joyce's dissatisfaction with this tale, his disclosure to his brother Stanislaus that "After the Race" and "A Painful Case" are "the two worst stories in the collection."[22] They concur with Joyce's judgment, but it might be more fruitful to relate Joyce's frustration to the difficulty of achieving his objective, which was to use an actual race to dramatize how racism is glamorized, even by those whose self-worth (here represented by monetary worth) is diminished by it. It is paradoxi-cally easier to appreciate Joyce's searing critique of racism from the per-spective of a century later, when rivalry between groups artificially coded as racial has been decoupled from national identity.

On the front page of the June 16 *Evening Telegraph* are two headlines: "Exciting Scene in Homburg" and "Race Cars in Danger from Burning Petrol." The reference is to what happened after the Gordon Bennett Cup of July 1902: a second competition on June 17, 1904 in Homburg. When the race was run on the following day, France won, Germany came in second, and Henri Fournier (also from France and the man Joyce interviewed for the *Irish Times* a year earlier) took third. But this is not the only race mentioned on the front page of the *Evening Telegraph*: the other is the Ascot Gold Cup, run at 3:00 p.m. on June 16 in England. The *Telegraph* headline reads, "Outsider Wins Gold Cup." The outsider named here is the horse Throwaway, a five-year-old owned by F. Alexander and ridden by William Lane, who won against odds of 20 to 1.[23] Joyce's use of a race to depict racism differs significantly here from his earlier treatment of the Gordon Bennett Cup, in part because it associates the winner with night – or darkness – and the losing favorite with day – or "enlightenment" and by extension whiteness – through the colors of their coats. By substituting a horse race for a motor derby, Joyce no longer makes it a contest between (wealthy) countries. Racing machines have been supplanted by animals, which makes each horse-and-rider unit a closer approximation of a human, with the rider acting as the "head" and the horse as the "body." Colorism has replaced nationality as an invitation to prejudice: one of the two favorites (backed by Lenehan and Boylan in *Ulysses*), "Sceptre," has a name that suggests gold and sovereignty, in contrast to Throwaway, or waste (with its darkly scatological overtones).[24] Moreover, Throwaway is described as a "dark horse" – a horse not expected to win – a term explicitly applied to the novel's hero, Leopold Bloom, whom Joe Hynes dubs "a bloody dark horse himself" in "Cyclops" (*U* 12.1557–58).[25] The contrast between the two horses is quite literally the difference between day and night, or gold (which combines money and lightness of color) and black. Light is privileged as "clear" whereas darkness is obscure, therefore calling for greater discernment.

Joyce's reading of an actual race as an analogue for racial competition is almost obvious, as is his contrast between the "golden" favorite, Sceptre (the overall favorite was Zinfandel, whose name would have made him less convenient as a contrast to the dark horse), and the dark outsider, Throwaway, who unexpectedly won. Bloom's inadvertent comment to Bantam Lyons about being on the verge of throwing his newspaper away – which Lyons understands as a tip to back Throwaway – further links him to the dark horse, and to waste.[26] So far, readers are privy to a comedy of inadvertence, one that has nasty effects: the men in the bar in "Cyclops" erroneously think that Bloom has won a pot of money on Throwaway (Lenehan is convinced Bloom "had a few bob on *Throwaway* and he's gone to gather in the shekels") but will not even stand a round of drinks in the pub.[27] This in turn reinforces their stereotypical view of

Jews as moneyhoarders, a slur that Deasy makes explicit in "Nestor" when he accuses "the jew merchants" as "eat[ing] up" the "vital strength" of England, agents of the country's decay.[28] Halting in "a broad sunbeam," having counted out a gold sovereign and two crowns, two shillings for Stephen (coins mentally dismissed by Stephen as "Symbols ... of beauty and of power ... soiled by greed and misery"), surrounded by framed images of "vanished horses" from former races, Deasy is a half-comic symbol of racism.[29] Associated with the gold of sunlight and coins ("the sun flung spangles, dancing coins" on his shoulders), he collects and basks in golden symbols of power, ignoring his own aging body and the loneliness of his hoarding.[30] Stephen sees Deasy not as threatening but as sad, impotent, and imprisoned by his grievances (the "coughball" of his laughter at his misogynistic and anti-Semitic comments drags "after it a rattling chain of phlegm").[31] Nonetheless, Stephen dismisses Deasy as a version of the "lions couchant on the pillars as he passed out through the gate: toothless terrors" and decides to "help him in his fight."[32] Why? Stephen is surprisingly gentle with Deasy, despite his acute awareness of Deasy's many – often pernicious – misconceptions.

The answer is important, and it helps to explain how *Ulysses* became a comedy rather than a social satire. Joyce is belittling not racists, but racism. Racism is a complex social structure (like sexism); it is woven into the fabric of the status quo, passed down through generations, and intensified by greed and self-interest (hence Deasy's association with gold). The racism so fully expressed through the décor of the old man's study (as well as in his "jokes") has little to do with taking joy in competition, which would be harmless. In essence, races are fun, healthy games. What is destructive is when winners and losers begin to take on meaning as ontological categories that can be attached to other categories such as skin color, sex organs, or nationality, and when winning begins to carry significant monetary rewards and an increase in prestige. The problem is exacerbated by betting, because then the *spectators* stand to become winners as well simply by accurately predicting (or pre-judging) the results. Expectations are generated, favorites are created, and luck replaces effort as the basis of reward. Instead of being deferred, judgment takes place before the contest, and onlookers invest in their "prejudices." These spectators are not "gratefully oppressed"; they are betting on the expected outcomes in the hope of becoming winners themselves. In other words, they are complicit in a racism that has become an institution, a business venture, with very real stakes.

Nothing is to be gained, then, by disparaging Deasy or cheering for Bloom: Deasy is a sad old man nostalgic for a fantasized past with an estranged wife that Myles Crawford dismisses as a tartar.[33] Advocating for Bloom because he is an underdog is equally demeaning; what makes Bloom admirable is not his exclusion from power and privilege, but his capacity to project himself imaginatively into so many different subject positions. The disadvantages of such an exclusion are obvious, but the outsider also has a potential advantage: he has no investment in the social fictions that his compatriots buy into; he can see the artificiality of their constructions of a race. This advantage was also claimed for Black Americans by the great James Baldwin forty years later in *The Fire Next Time* (1963):

> The American Negro has the great advantage of having never believed that collection of myths to which white Americans cling: that their ancestors were all freedom-loving heroes, that they were born in the greatest country the world has ever seen, or that Americans are invincible in battle and wise in peace, that Americans have always dealt honorably with Mexicans and Indians and all other neighbors or inferiors, that American men are the world's most direct and virile, that American women are pure…. And one felt that if one had had that white man's worldly advantages, one would never have become as bewildered and as joyless and as thoughtlessly cruel as he.[34]

One could argue that what Baldwin says of the white man also applies (with variations) to the British: their superiority is a delusion. The Irish might have made better use of the British citizens' worldly advantage.

Like Black Americans, Joyce's "dark" Irish-Hungarian outsider can claim a certain detachment from the dominant social fictions, a detachment that in Joyce's case lays the ground for a comic perspective. Bloom does not engage in a politics of grievance; instead, he offers a larger view, what Coates calls a "cosmic" rather than a "racial" consciousness.[35] The great comic example of this occurs at the end of "Cyclops," when Bloom is arguing with the citizen. The men in the bar have been generating disparaging judgments of Bloom, accusing him of "defrauding widows and orphans," calling him "a perverted jew … from a place in Hungary" that "gave the ideas for Sinn Fein to Arthur Griffith to put in his paper all kinds of jerrymandering, packed juries and swindling the taxes off of the government and appointing consuls all over the world to walk about selling Irish industries."[36] The citizen questions Bloom's manhood ("Do you call that a man?") and Joe Hynes wonders if Bloom has ever had sex with a woman. The citizen escalates his vitriolic anti-Semitism, calling Bloom Ahasuerus, "Cursed by God," and a "thing" that has "contaminate[d] our shores."[37] Then Bloom enters, and the unnamed narrator imagines his "pockets hanging down with gold and silver. Mean bloody scut. Stand us a drink itself.... There's a jew for you! All for number one. Cute as a shithouse rat."[38] Martin Cunningham ushers Bloom and Jack Power and Crofton out as quickly as possible, but the citizen goes to the door and taunts Bloom, bawling, "Three cheers for Israel!" and gets up "on his high horse about the jews and the loafers."[39] This is where Bloom, standing up on the car, attempts to broaden the citizen's perspective:

> Mendelssohn was a jew and Karl Marx and Mercadante and Spinoza. And the Saviour was a jew and his father was a jew. Your God... Your God was a jew. Christ was a jew like me.[40]

Then the citizen, oblivious to the irony of his reaction, threatens to "crucify him so I will."[41] The means of crucifixion is a tin of biscuits that he throws at the departing car – "Did I kill him?" – as Bloom is comically, impossibly assumed into heaven as the prophet Elijah.[42]

It might be helpful to contextualize Joyce's ridicule of racism (murder by biscuitbox as the climax to an orgy of name calling spurred on by envy and spite) with more recent descriptions of race and racism by various American writers of color. James McBride writes that when he was young, "We did not consider ourselves poor or deprived, or depressed, for the rules of the outside world seemed meaningless to us as children." McBride's (white) mother had created a space for her children that was relatively free from the huge and racist world beyond. But "the question of race was like the power of the moon in my house. It's what made the river flow, the ocean swell, and the tide rise, but it was a silent power, intractable, indomitable, indisputable, and thus completely ignorable." Children can ignore the power of race if they are lucky enough to be shielded from it. Even McBride's Black stepfather disregarded it: "race was something he never talked about. To him it was a detail that you stepped over, like a crack in the sidewalk." But that was not an option for McBride's own generation. As a freshman in college, he confidently tells his Black roommate, "racism is a problem that should end just about the time we graduate. Instead it smashed me across the face like a bottle when I walked into the real world."[43]

The option of adopting a larger perspective is no longer enough by the end of the twentieth century because, as Coates points out, "racism is a visceral experience"; it "lands, with great violence, upon the body."[44] Bloom evades the "missile" thrown by the anti-Semitic citizen, but it would only take a little more than twenty years after the publication of *Ulysses* for the violence to land on the bodies of millions of Jews. As Baldwin recounts,

> For the crime of their ancestry, millions of people in the middle of the twentieth century and in the heart of Europe—God's citadel—were sent to

a death so calculated, so hideous, and so prolonged that no age before this enlightened one had been able to imagine it, much less achieve and record it … the fact of the Third Reich alone makes obsolete forever any question of Christian superiority.[45]

Those who have been mocked and terrorized as animals or worthless objects, whether they are the Irish, Jews, or those inaccurately described as "black," can survive only by remembering that they have been put in a tribe that is "on the one hand, invented, and on the other, no less real." To be fictional and real at the same time tends to stunt the imagination while rendering one's body vulnerable to violence that the other has justified in advance. The violence lies in the act and nature of naming: Coates explains, "what divided me from the world was not anything intrinsic to us but the actual injury done by people intent on naming us, intent on believing that what they have named us matters more than anything we could ever actually do."[46] As Joyce had Shem the Penman ask in *Finnegans Wake*, "when is a man not a man?" The answer given by Shem is when he is a Sham.[47] "Sham" is Shem himself ("Shem was a sham and a low sham"), and it points toward another sham that produces shame: the name.[48] "Man" spelled backward is "nam," and "Shem" means "name" in Hebrew. What can a person who has been shamefully "named" do about it? Coates's answer is much the same as Joyce's was a century earlier: "an unceasing interrogation of the stories told to us"; "a constant questioning as ritual, questioning as exploration rather than the search for certainty"; to eschew hate (which "gives identity") by learning the love that "is an act of heroism."[49] Such "heroic" or courageously honest love is the kind that Baldwin earlier exhorted Americans to cultivate:

> Love takes off the masks that we fear we cannot live without and know we cannot live within. I use the word "love" here not merely in the personal sense but as a state of being, or a state of grace—not in the infantile American sense of being made happy but in the tough and universal sense of quest and daring and growth.[50]

This is the love that Bloom, who belongs "to a race that is hated and persecuted," preaches in Barney Kiernan's for which he is derided as a "new apostle to the Gentiles"[51]:

> But it's no use…. Force, hatred, history, all that. That's not life for men and women, insult and hatred. And everybody knows that it's the very opposite of that that is really life… Love. I mean the opposite of hatred.[52]

Love is a notoriously slippery word, often used sentimentally or even to designate its opposite – the desire to control or possess its object – but these writers are pointing to something different: the courage to be honest with oneself and to respect and value the other in an effort to sustain the increasingly difficult task of learning and growing. Love, then, depends upon a constant interrogation of ourselves and the stories we have been taught to believe.

Race may be an artificial construct, but it is one that cannot be ignored. Nella Larsen's Irene Redfield is also "unable to disregard the burden of race." In *Passing,* first published in 1929, Larsen describes Irene as "caught between two allegiances, different, yet the same. Herself. Her race. Race! The thing that bound and suffocated her. Whatever steps she took, or if she took none at all, something would be crushed. A person or the race. [Her friend] Clare, herself, or the race. Or, it might be, all three."[53] In the twenty-first century, Angie Thomas dramatizes the importance of speaking out against hate and the structural discrimination that keeps so many Black people poor and without hope for a better future. In *The Hate U Give* (2017), Thomas's protagonist Starr has a talk with her Daddy about a line from a Tupac rap song: "The Hate you Give Little Infants F----s Everybody."[54] Starr's friend Khalil (killed by a police officer at a traffic stop) explained to her that "it's about what society feeds us as youth and how it comes back and bites them later," although she thinks it does not just apply to youth but to Black people, minorities, and the poor more broadly. When her father asks her what the hate they give is, she asks, "Racism?" but he says the answer must be more specific.[55]

> Lack of opportunities…. Corporate America don't bring jobs to our communities, and they damn sure ain't quick to hire us. Then, shit, even if you do have a high school diploma, so many of the schools in our neighborhoods don't prepare us well enough … the system's still giving hate, and everybody's still getting fucked (168–9).[56]

The problem, Angie's father knows, is broadly systemic, baked in by a long tradition of uneven opportunities.

James Baldwin also lacerates the systemic reach of racism in America, an effect that diminishes white people as well as Black ones, for "*Whoever debases others is debasing himself.*"[57] As Coates would do fifty years later, Baldwin calls for his compatriots in the West to stop placing so much value on color: "Color is not a human or a personal reality; it is a political reality. But this is a distinction so extremely hard to make that the West has not been able to make it yet…. For the sake of one's children, … one must be careful not to take refuge in any delusion – and the value placed on the color of the skin is always and everywhere and forever a delusion."

He calls on "the relatively conscious whites and the relatively conscious blacks" to "end the racial nightmare."[58] Baldwin's reference to race as a nightmare draws our attention back to Stephen's view of history in *Ulysses* as "a nightmare from which I am trying to awake."[59] His nightmare is also implicitly racial, since a mare is a horse, and if she is associated with night, that makes her a black horse. Stephen is aware of the literal meaning of his phrase, as we can see when he asks himself, "What if that nightmare gave you a back kick?"[60]

As a (fictional) construct, then, race lumps many different people with different shades of dark skin into a single reductive (and pejorative) category. Joyce, as an Aristotelian, seems to have seen such evaluative "rankings" of binary categories as rooted in the preference for day over night, or light over darkness (the preference for male over female, Gentile over Jew, is part of the same structure for preferring one "opposite" over another). In the *Metaphysics,* Aristotle lists ten principles, called cognates, identified by members of the Pythagorean school, in which "light," "right," "good," "male," and "one," for example, are paired with their less-desirable opposites: "darkness," "left," "bad," "female," and "plurality."[61] As a formerly Catholic thinker with a formidable knowledge of both theology and heresy, Joyce identified himself with darkness over light, obscurity over clarity, beautifully identifying himself with the vastness of human ignorance over the relatively small achievements of human knowledge and reason. *Ulysses* is a book of the day that champions the power of darkness and, like Stephen, distrusts "aquacities of thought and language," affirming "The incompatibility of aquacity with the erratic originality of genius."[62] Stephen and Bloom are presented as two "dark" men, both in black, who, like the dark horse that wins the Gold Cup, point toward "the obscure soul of the world, a darkness shining in brightness which brightness could not comprehend."[63] I have written elsewhere about the importance and meaning of darkness and its relation to stylistic obscurity in *Ulysses*, and much has also been written on Joyce's refutation of anti-Semitism as hypocritical bigotry in his epic work.[64] What I would like to do now is to bring the use of racial darkness forward into Joyce's "book of the dark," *Finnegans Wake*, by focusing on the excoriation of the semi-autobiographical artist figure, Shem, as a Black man.[65] The denunciation of Shem in I.7 (probably by his twin brother Shaun) includes a twist, showing how Shem uses blackness (which he identifies as "common to allflesh") in his writing: he converts the external or superficial blackness of skin that has been misread as inferiority into something internal – the feces produced within everyone – to make the ink with which he writes. This "recuperation" of darkness is also "comic" in the sense that it exposes the hypocrisy of denigrating darkness when darkness is produced daily by every individual. Stephen thinks in "Proteus," "darkness is in our souls, do you not think?"[66] In *Finnegans Wake*, the darkness of ignorance and sin (everyone has "sinned against the light") is extended to the body and mind not only through intestinal products and ink but also through the stylistic approximation of the darkness of the mind in sleep.[67]

The voice that lacerates Shem in I.7 is often associated with Shem's twin brother Shaun, with good reason, but it is more accurately described as a mix of different voices who have been critical of Joyce's own literary works and life choices. His brother Stanislaus and his contemporary Wyndham Lewis are two such fierce critics, but Joyce supplements their objections with phrases from contemptuous reviews of his books, while adding exaggerated denunciations of his own. The most well-known of these is the reference to *Ulysses* as the "usylessly unreadable Blue Book of Eccles," but the accusations are varied, extreme, and personal as well as professional.[68] Most controversially, they include racist, homophobic, anti-Semitic, and anti-Chinese slurs, which implicitly align Shem with a variety of oppressed groups. Shem's name is not only Irish for James (Shemus, a homonym for "shame us"), and evocative of "shim," defined by the *Oxford English Dictionary* as an effeminate man, but it is also a reference to one of Noah's trio of sons, the one who was thought to be the ancestor of the Semitic peoples. At one point in the episode, Shem is said to have been born "Hamis," or Ham, Shem's brother, the son who was cursed to servitude or slavery for seeing his father naked after he had been drinking, believed to be the progenitor of the African races (Hamis is also Hungarian for "false").[69]

Shem, then, is Shem *and* Ham, the originators of both the Semitic and the Black races, in contrast to Japhet, his twin brother Shaun, from whom the Europeans descended. Shem is cursed, and the invective that is heaped upon him is based not upon his membership in *one* race; it is the hate speech of a favored "son" directed to his brother(s), to whom he is closely related and with whom he races for dominance. Shem is decried as the biblical Cain, cursed for killing his brother Abel, but what we see in the chapter is the "good" brother arguing that because his twin once laid him low, he will kill *him*, and justly: "He points the deathbone and the quick are still."[70]

In addition to being Shem-Ham and Japhet, the brothers are identified as Angel and Devil, painted as white and black, respectively: "Lefty takes the cherubcake while Rights cloves his hoof."[71] What follows is Shem's admission that although he is black in the pejorative sense (associated with dirt, earth, sin, and evil), and although he is offensively described as a "coon," other Black people would never play or sing with him: "Darkies never done tug that coon out to play non-excretory, anti-sexuous, misoxenetic, gassy pure, flesh and blood games, ... same as piccaninnies play all day."[72] This section is uncomfortable to read from a twenty-first-century perspective because of its reliance on racist stereotypes to characterize Black culture.[73] The games from which Shem was excluded are described as innocent and non-sexual, compared to games played by pickaninnies, a word originating in the West Indies to designate "a small black or Aboriginal child" that most dictionaries now identify as an ethnic slur.[74] The games are also likened to "fun" games "we used to play with Dina and old Joe kicking her behind and before and the yellow girl kicking him behind old Joe."[75] This is a reference to a racist minstrel song called "Old Joe, or Somebody in the House with Dinah," which dates from the 1830s or 1840s and originated in London, music attributed to J. H. Cave. It is familiar now as the basis of one verse of "I've been Working on the Railroad." The song became part of a minstrel skit spoken in an exaggerated Black dialect, and its subject is the fear of a man that another man is in the house "making lub wid my Dinah."[76] What this shows is that at least one of the sources for Joyce's understanding of Black cultures included blackface minstrelsy, raising the possibility that Shem is being denigrated as an impersonator of a Black person, a comic stereotype roughly analogous to the "Stage Irishman."

The epithets used to deride Shem are often racial, either directly, when he is described as "Nigerian," "old sooty," and a "black beast," or metaphorically, when he is called a "blackguard" (someone who behaves in a contemptible way; see the reference to his "lowdown blackguardism," and the comment that "it woolies one to think over it").[77] The allegation that "it is looking pretty black against you, we suggest, Sheem avick [Irish 'my boy']"[78] uses black to represent Shem's guilt, a usage that draws our attention to the etymology of the word "denigrate" (what the narrators of the chapter are doing to Shem throughout). It stems from the Latin *denigrare,* to blacken or defame; the eventual association of blackness with dirt and therefore shame is woven into language. Shem is decried as "a nogger among the blankards [Dutch, *blanke,* white men, also slang for bastards] of this dastard century,"[79] and JUSTIUS warns that the KKK are getting riled up against him (the KKK appear as the implied acronym of the Irishmen "Kelly, Kenny, and Keogh" who are described as "up up and in arms").[80] Finally, Shem's alleged "blackness" leads JUSTIUS to identify him with shit when he confesses that "the good brother feels he would need to defecate you."[81]

By the logic that opposite extremes cannot be equally valued, so one must always be preferred, the devalued term is frequently discarded as waste, derided as excrement. An early denunciation of Molly Bloom described her as a *saccum stercoris,* a sack of dung.[82] Critics have often noted the scatological bent of writers from colonized countries; an excremental sensibility is produced by having been used, depleted of valuable resources and then discarded. Various Irish writers – including Jonathan Swift and Samuel Beckett as well as Joyce – respond by paying more careful, even comic attention to waste products.[83] The Irish writer Mary Lavin, in her story "Happiness," goes so far as to champion waste products for their capacity to fertilize and thereby promote growth. What Joyce does in "Shem the Penman" is significantly different, however. He responds to Shaun's desire to defecate his brother Shem by making a move that recalls the one Bloom deploys in the "Cyclops" episode of *Ulysses*: he appeals to something Jesus says in the Sermon on the Mount in Luke 6:41: "And why beholdest thou the mote that is in thy brother's eye, but considerest not the beam that is in thine own eye?" ("Some people, says Bloom, can see the mote in others' eyes but they can't see the beam in their own").[84] In *Finnegans Wake*, the reference explains why the speaker uses Latin to explain how Shem "made synthetic ink and sensitive paper for his own end out of his wit's waste": he replies that he will "cloak" up the answer in "the language of blushfed purpurates [those who are fit to be purpled, or made cardinal]," so that "an Anglican ordinal, not reading his own rude dunsky tunga, may ever behold the brand of scarlet on the brow of her of Babylon and feel not the pink one in his own damned cheek."[85] In other words, the use of Latin protects the hypocrisy of pious readers from recognizing their own deeper implication in the things they condemn.

The Latin passage explains how Shem's (and by extension, Joyce's) writing is derived from the darkness internal to everyone: feces, referred to as the "black beast" and "downcastings." Shem puts his own dung into an urn and then happily and mellifluously urinates on it while chanting a line from the Vulgate, Psalm 44:2; "Finally, from the foul dung mixed ... with the 'sweetness of divine Orion,' and baked and then exposed to the cold, he made himself an indelible ink."[86] Then, in one of the most beautiful passages in *Finnegans Wake*, Shem recuperates the "lead" of darkness (and the "weeping and groaning" associated with it) by alchemically using that ink to produce the "gold" of a radically egalitarian and honest prose. His process explains not only why his work is decried as "obscene" (it proceeds daily "from his unheavenly body"), but it also details his painful effort to use his wasting body together with its wastes to transform the injustices of the world[87]:

> through the bowels of his misery, flashly, faithly, nastily, appropriately, this Esuan Menschavik [refers not only to Esau and a Mensch but also a Russian socialist] and the first till last alchemist wrote over every square inch of the only foolscap available, his own body, till by its corrosive sublimation one continuous present tense integument slowly unfolded all marryvoising moodmoulded cyclewheeling history (thereby, he said, reflecting from his own individual person life unlivable, transaccidentated through the slow fires of consciousness into a dividual chaos, perilous, potent, *common to allflesh*, human only, mortal) but with each word that would not pass away the squidself which he had squirtscreened from the crystalline world waned chagreenold and doriangrayer in its dudhud.[88]

Shem, like Joyce, at great cost to himself, *transforms* his own darkness (common to allflesh), into an ink that allows him to inscribe a "dividual chaos" onto his skin, darkening it. In making himself a "black person" through tattooing himself with ink derived from his body's waste, he succeeds in embracing – with humility and compassion – the sublime diversity of an entire, complex world.

It is misleading, then, to see Joyce as a champion of the underdog, as some critics have suggested, because it implicitly validates the social assumptions that created the disparities in the first place.[89] Instead, Joyce advocates for the comic truth that most of what we think we know is actually error. (*Finnegans Wake* encodes this view of human misprision in its style, made entirely up of apparent misprints.) Misunderstandings are so longstanding and widespread that the only thing left to do is to recognize and celebrate them. As the singer chirps in the "Ballat of Perce-Oreille [earwig, literally 'pierce the ear']," "*Hirp! Hirp! for their Missed Understandings!*"[90] We are all speaking different languages, misunderstanding (and therefore misrepresenting) other cultures. Len Platt argues that in *Finnegans Wake*, "the racial Other becomes a product of popular culture, where race was, as it was largely in the academy, a matter of fabrication and appropriation."[91] In his view, Joyce marks his depictions of Black and East Asian identities as inauthentic by placing them "almost without exception in the world of play-acting and make-believe": "It is not the racial Other that is being laughed at – the 'Oriental' or the 'black' has no real cultural presence here – but rather the cultural insecurities that produce such usages as 'coon' talk and 'pidgin' Chinese."[92]

The first way that race becomes comic is that it does not exist; there is no such thing as racial purity. Widespread adulteration, hybridization, and miscegenation undermine all fantasies of racial identity. Joyce himself makes this argument in one of his earliest essays, "Ireland, Island of Saints and Sages."[93] The second is that the model of the human race as a contest of speed results in grotesque distortions of those competitors not currently winning but who are perceived as a threat. Those representations are not only offensive to those who are so caricatured, they are also ludicrous, so much so that their exaggerations once made them popular as entertainment, as Platt demonstrates. Finally, though, Joyce unveils the discrimination against people of color as an extension of the dislike of all darkness, all that is unknown. In the metaphorical sense, what is unknown or dark lives not only within the body; it is also divine, and Joyce described his project as a capacious embrace of that great unknown. When Shem transmutes his waste into the ink with which he wrote, he does so with humility intertwined with his experience of humiliation. Like W. E. B. Du Bois, Shem has a double consciousness, described in *Finnegans Wake* as "twosome twiminds."[94] His goal is not, as Stephen once proclaimed, to forge the uncreated conscience of his race, but to replace the concept of human society as a ruthless race for dominance fueled by self-interest into something more harmonious, fair-minded, and complex, "a chorale in canon," with "Melodiotiosities in purefusion by the score." *Finnegans Wake* tries to reconceive the concept of the human race, replacing its contest with music, as the children do in the Mime of Mick, Nick, and the Maggies. Music (like the multivocal babbling "nonsense" of *Finnegans Wake* itself) is addressed to the senses rather than the understanding, soliciting the willing participation of all.

> To start with in the beginning, we need hirtly bemark, a community prayer, everyone for himself, and to conclude with as an exodus, we think it well to add, a chorale in canon, good for us all for us all us all all.[95]

Notes

1 "race, n.6," *OED Online*, Oxford University Press.
2 To Carlo Linati, 1920; James Joyce, *Letters*, I, ed. Stuart Gilbert (New York: Viking, 1957), 146.
3 "race, n.1.IV.," *OED Online*, Oxford University Press; see, for example, n.1.II: "a path, channel, or course."
4 Ta-Nehisi Coates, *Between the World and Me* (Melbourne, Australia: Text Publishing, 2015), 7.

5 See Len Platt's excellent account of Joyce's send-up of "scientific racism" in *Joyce, Race and Finnegans Wake* (Cambridge: Cambridge University Press, 2007). Platt details Joyce's reading and note taking on "race history and social classification" during the early years of writing the *Wake* (8–10). Platt stresses the urgency of the historical period of the twenties and thirties when Joyce was writing: "Racial identity had never been more vital, nor the implications of being the 'wrong' race more grave" (9). As he rightly asserts, "Race in Joyce is a construct, the primary purpose of which is understood in terms of the maintenance of social cohesion and consent. Race identity here becomes not a matter of biology but of culture. This recognition means that the racism which typically disguised itself as the rational measurement and management of difference becomes exposed as an ideology, operating at the structural levels of culture and society as knowledge, authority, and power" (4). It is because racism operates at the level of knowledge as well as power that Joyce's emphasis on the vastness of human ignorance is so crucial.

6 Noel Ignatiev, *How the Irish Became White* (London and New York: Routledge, 1995), 114.

7 This more general implication of the title is suggested by its appearance in Joyce's interview with Henri Fournier, the manager of the "Paris-Automobile" company in Paris and the model for Ségouin in the story. (Joyce's interview was published in the *Irish Times* on April 7, 1903, and is reprinted in *Occasional, Critical, and Political Writing,* ed. Kevin Barry [Oxford: Oxford University Press, 2000], 77–79). Joyce asks Fournier if he plans to remain for any time in Ireland and Fournier inquires, "After the race?" He then says no, expressing his regret.

8 James Joyce, *Dubliners,* (London: Penguin, 1992), 35.

9 Joyce, *Occasional, Critical, and Political Writing,* 79.

10 Joyce, *Occasional, Critical, and Political Writing,* 305.

11 See Ignatiev, 42, on eighteenth-century Ireland's treatment of Catholics as a "race" rather than a nation. It is their nationless status that allows the Irish under the Penal Laws to be categorized as a race, like Indigenous and Black Americans. According to Ignatiev, the Act of Union of 1801 "marked a turning point in British colonial policy in Ireland from racial to national oppression, a shift which required sacrificing the Protestant Ascendancy in order to gain the support of the Catholic bourgeoisie" (44).

12 Joyce, *Dubliners,* 38, my emphasis.

13 See L. Perry Curtis, Jr., *Apes and Angels: The Irishman in Victorian Caricature* (Smithsonian Institution Press, [1971] 1996). See also Ignatiev, 40–70.

14 Michael Patrick Gillespie and David Weir, "'After the Race' and the Problem of Belonging," *Collaborative Dubliners,* ed. Vicki Mahaffey (Syracuse: Syracuse University Press, 2012), 115.

15 Joyce, *Dubliners,* 37.

16 Joyce, *Dubliners,* 36, 39. Jimmy's father was a butcher who "had begun life as an advanced Nationalist" but "modified his view early" after he began opening shops in Dublin, becoming a "merchant prince" (36). When at dinner,

"Ségouin shepherded his party into politics," and "Jimmy, under generous influences, felt the buried zeal of his father wake within him," and he rouses the Englishman into hot debate (39). Why do "generous influences" ignite Jimmy's nationalism, when it was the acquisition of wealth that extinguished his father's? Nationalism here is depicted as little more than a rhetorical stance, a pose that money can dissipate or license. More significant are the "generous influences" that render Jimmy incapable of playing the game, much less winning it ("he frequently mistook his cards and the other men had to calculate his I.O.U.'s for him" [41]).

17 Gillespie and Weir, *Collaborative Dubliners*, 117. Contemplating the persistence of inequality despite multiple prolonged challenges, Tressie McMillan Cottom recalls that "racism and sexism and class warfare are resilient and necessary for global capitalism." See *Thick and Other Essays* (New York: The New Press, 2019), 90.

18 Compare the problems encountered by Nazis in categorizing Jews, given the numbers of those who were *mischlinge,* or mixed.

19 Ibram X. Kendi, *How to Be an Antiracist* (New York: One World, 2019), 54, 35. See also Platt's similar assertion from 2007, quoted in above as well.

20 Joyce, *Dubliners*, 35.

21 Kendi, *How to Be an Antiracist*, 42. See also Kendi's account of the history of racist power, especially the first formal definition of "race" in 1606 by Jean Nicot in the *Trésor de la lange française*: "Race ... means descent.... Therefore, it is said that a man, a horse, a dog, or another animal is from a good race or bad race." As Kendi points out, "from the beginning, to make races was to make a racial hierarchy," 40.

22 James Joyce, *Letters*, II, ed. Richard Ellmann (New York: Viking, 1966), 151, 189. Cited in *Collaborative Dubliners*, 109.

23 For a detailed account of the race, its contenders, and references to it throughout *Ulysses*, see Vivien Igoe, "'Spot the Winner': Some of the Horses in *Ulysses*," *Dublin James Joyce Journal* 4 (2011): 72–86.

24 See, for example, the Hebrew Scriptures, especially the book of Esther, for descriptions of a golden sceptre that represents the monarch's authority: Est. 4:11; 5:2; and 8:4: "Then the king held out the golden sceptre towards Esther"; See Valérie Bénéjam, "The Reprocessing of Trash in *Ulysses*: Recycling and (Post)Creation," *Hypermedia Joyce Studies* 5 (2004).

25 In Lenehan's words, Throwaway "hasn't an earthly" (James Joyce, *Ulysses* [New York: Vintage, 1986], 10.518–19); See Vincent J. Cheng, "White Horse, Dark Horse: Joyce's Allhorse of Another Color," *Joyce Studies Annual* 2 (Summer 1991), 101–128; "Dark horses and horses of a different color combine in Joyce to suggest both race (ethnicity and color) and races (horseracing)." Cheng focuses more on the white horse as a symbol of authority and empire, representing the dark horse as the disempowered other, arguing that in *Finnegans Wake*, the dark horse and the white horse are positive and negative versions of the same photograph of a "horse." My own interest is more in the contrast between gold and darkness, because the gold accents coins and

sunlight: it is the sign of both capitalism and enlightenment, accenting the difference between day and night, the privilege that claims transparency and the *via negativa* of humility. See Vicki Mahaffey, "Love, Race, and Exiles: The Bleak Side of *Ulysses*," in *Joyce Studies Annual* (New York: Fordham University Press, 2007), 92–108.

26 Joyce, *Ulysses*, 5.534.

27 Joyce, *Ulysses*, 12.1550–51.

28 Joyce, *Ulysses*, 2.350, 348.

29 Joyce, *Ulysses*, 2.352–3, 354–7; 2.217, 221, 226–8.

30 Joyce, *Ulysses*, 2.448–9.

31 Joyce, *Ulysses*, 2.443–4.

32 Joyce, *Ulysses*, 2.429–30.

33 Joyce, *Ulysses*, 7.532–39.

34 James Baldwin, *The Fire Next Time* (New York: Random-Vintage, 1962), 101–2.

35 As Coates reminds his son, "Remember that you and I are brothers, are the children of trans-Atlantic rape. Remember the broader consciousness that comes with that. Remember that this consciousness can never ultimately be racial; it must be cosmic" (*Between the World and Me*, 128).

36 Joyce, *Ulysses*, Lenehan, 12.1622; Martin Cunningham, 12.1635; John Wyse, 12.1573–7.

37 Joyce, *Ulysses*, 12.1654; 12.1667; 12.1672.

38 Joyce, *Ulysses*, 12.1759–61.

39 Joyce, *Ulysses*, 12.1791, 1798.

40 Joyce, *Ulysses*, 12.1804–9.

41 Joyce, *Ulysses*, 12.1812.

42 Joyce, *Ulysses*, 12.1903.

43 James McBride, *The Color of Water: A Black Man's Tribute to His White Mother* (New York: Riverhead Books, 1996), 95, 94, 125, 204.

44 Coates, *Between the World and Me*, 10.

45 Baldwin, *The Fire Next Time*, 52.

46 Coates, *Between the World and Me*, 55 ("Black blood wasn't black; black *skin* wasn't even black"), 56, 120.

47 Joyce, *Finnegans Wake* (London: Penguin, 1992), 170.5; 170.24.

48 Joyce, *Finnegans Wake*, 170.25.

49 Coates, *Between the World and Me*, 34, 60–61.

50 Baldwin, *The Fire Next Time*, 95.

51 Joyce, *Ulysses*, 12.1467; 12.1489.

52 Joyce, *Ulysses*, 12.1481–5.

53 Nella Larsen, *Passing* (New York: Penguin, [1929] 2018), 101.

54 Angie Thomas, *The Hate U Give* (London: Walker Books, 2017), 166.

55 Thomas, *The Hate U Give*, 167–168.

56 Compare the lyrics of Nina Simone's song, "Backlash Blues" (1967), based on a poem by Langston Hughes.

57 Baldwin, *The Fire Next Time*, 83.

58 Baldwin, *The Fire Next Time*, 104–5.

59 Joyce, *Ulysses*, 2.377.

60 Joyce, *Ulysses*, 2.379.

61 *The Basic Works of Aristotle*, trans. Richard McKeon (New York: Random House, 1941), Section 986a. I discuss this at greater length in *Reauthorizing Joyce* (Cambridge: Cambridge University Press, 1988), 39–44.

62 Joyce, *Ulysses*, 17.240, 247.

63 Joyce, *Ulysses*, 2.159–60, an inversion of John I.5: "And the light shineth in darkness, and the darkness comprehended it not."

64 See, for example, Mahaffey, "Love, Race, and *Exiles*," 92–108, and (on blindness) "Feeling *Ulysses*: An Address to the Cyclopean Reader," by myself and Wendy Truran. In *Ulysses: Philosophical Perspectives*, ed. Philip Kitcher (Oxford: Oxford University Press: 2020), 100–131; see Marilyn Reizbaum, *Joyce's Judaic Other* (Palo Alto: Stanford University Press, 1999); Ira Bruce Nadel, *Joyce and the Jews: Culture and Text* (Iowa City: University of Iowa Press, 1989); and Vicki Mahaffey, "Wunderlich on Joyce: The Case Against Art," *Critical Inquiry* 17 (Summer 1991): 171–91, for a few examples.

65 Two important recent treatments of this are that of Christine Smedley and Len Platt. Although Smedley's essay on I.7 primarily concerns references to the Famine or the Hunger, she also briefly discusses "pointed references to contemporary or emerging genocidal events including the persecution of black Americans, Jews, and Armenians" (124). See "Shem's 'strabismal apologia': The Split Vision of the Famine in I.7," in *Joyce's Allmaziful Plurabilities: Polyvocal Explorations of Finnegans Wake*, eds. Kimberly J. Devlin and Christine Smedley (Gainesville: University Press of Florida, 2015), 114–132. Platt's account is found primarily in the sixth chapter of *Joyce, Race and Finnegans Wake*: "'Hung Chung Egglyfella': staged race in *Ulysses* and the *Wake*," 121–145. It includes an excellent account of Joyce's fascination with the minstrel show.

66 Joyce, *Ulysses*, 3.421.

67 Joyce, *Ulysses*, 2.361, 373.

68 Joyce, *Finnegans Wake*, 179.26–7.

69 Genesis 9:20–27, Joyce, *Finnegans Wake*, 181.36.

70 "cannibal Cain," Joyce, *Finnegans Wake*, 193.32; 193.29. JUSTIUS describes the preferred brother as "Immaculatus, from head to foot, sir, that pure one … a chum of the angelets" (191.13–19), claiming that it was "him you laid low with one hand one fine May morning in the Meddle of your Might, your bosom foe … to find out how his innards worked!" Moreover, "not one did you slay, no, but a continent!" (191.27–33). The implication seems to be that Shem's crime is a type of vivisection, that he took his brother apart for his fiction.

71 Joyce, *Finnegans Wake*, 175.29–30.

72 Joyce, *Finnegans Wake*, 175.30; 175.30–33.

73 Platt's account of this section is essential here. He argues that Joyce is not portraying Black people; he is appropriating the *performance* of Black identity

in popular culture. He reads this section as a crucial justification of Shaun's attack on Shem that relies not only on racializing his brother, but on normalizing that attack through references to how it has been acculturated in "theatrical representations, sports reportage, and children's games" (*Joyce, Race, and Finnegans Wake*, 139).

74 See *Collins Dictionary* and *The Free Dictionary*, for example.

75 Joyce, *Finnegans Wake*, 175.334–6.

76 For a fuller account of the history of this minstrel song, see "Racist Lyrics in Song Sources and Early Versions of the Song 'I've been Working on the Railroad,'" ed. Azizi Powell. It can be found at http://pancocojams.blogspot .com/2018/06/racist-lyrics-in-song-sources-of-and.html, accessed January 7, 2022.

77 Joyce, *Finnegans Wake*, 181.13, 194.5; in Latin, "*animale nigro exonerates*"; 185.18, 180.32–3.

78 Joyce, *Finnegans Wake*, 188.4–5.

79 Joyce, *Finnegans Wake*, 188.13–4.

80 Joyce, *Finnegans Wake*, 193.24.

81 Joyce, *Finnegans Wake*, 193.22–3.

82 "She is the principle of fleshly existence, foul, frank, and consciously obscene … She is a slut, a sloven, and a voracious sexual animal as conceived by one of those medieval minds to whom the female can never be anything but a *saccum stercoris;* she is a frightening venture into the unconsciousness of evil, and certainly, deliberately obscene," in R. M. Adams, *Surface and Symbol: The Consistency of James Joyce's Ulysses* (Oxford: Oxford University Press, 1962), 166–7.

83 See, for example, Zygmunt Bauman, *Wasted Lives* (2003), Gay Hawkins, *The Ethics of Waste* (2005), and John Scanlan, *On Garbage* (2005). For more recent treatments, see Susan Signe Morrison, *The Literature of Waste: Material Ecopoetics and Ethical Matter* (New York: Palgrave Macmillan, 2015), and Peter J. Smith, *Between Two Stools: Scatology and its Representations in English Literature, from Chaucer to Swift* (Manchester: Manchester University Press, 2012).

84 Joyce, *Ulysses*, 12.1237–8.

85 Joyce, *Finnegans Wake*, 185.6–8; 185.9–13.

86 Roland McHugh, *Annotations to Finnegans Wake* (Baltimore: Johns Hopkins University Press, 2016), 185.

87 Joyce, *Finnegans Wake*, 185.29.

88 Joyce, *Finnegans Wake*, 185.34–186.8, my emphasis.

89 Vincent J. Cheng, *Joyce, Race, and Empire* (Cambridge: Cambridge University Press, 1995).

90 Joyce, *Finnegans Wake*, 175.27–8.

91 Platt, *Joyce, Race, and Finnegans Wake*, 121–2.

92 Platt, *Joyce, Race, and Finnegans Wake*, 121, 144.

93 This argument has been taken up and elaborated by many critics, including Platt in *Joyce, Race, and Finnegans Wake*, 7–11; Smedley, "Shem's 'strabismal apologia,'" 114–5; Vicki Mahaffey, "Fantastic Histories: Nomadology and

Female Piracy in *Finnegans Wake*," in *Joyce and the Subject of History*, eds. Mark Wollaeger, Victor Luftig, and Robert Spoo (Ann Arbor: University of Michigan Press, 2006): 157–76.

94 Joyce, *Finnegans Wake*, 188.14.
95 Joyce, *Finnegans Wake*, 222.2–6.

CHAPTER 7

W. B. Yeats, the Irish Free State, and the Rhetoric of Race Suicide

Julie McCormick Weng

On May 14, 2022, an eighteen-year-old gunman opened fire in a Buffalo, New York, supermarket, murdering ten Black Americans. Police investigations revealed that the shooter's actions were motivated by his belief in the "great replacement theory," a conspiracy that white populations are being "replaced" by populations of racial and/or ethnic difference. While such beliefs may seem extremist, statistics demonstrate otherwise. In the wake of the shooting, journalist Steve Rose surveyed the rise of the theory in mainstream western consciousness, reporting that in the United States, Fox News host Tucker Carlson endorsed it on hundreds of occasions and 61 percent of voters supporting Donald Trump believed it.[1] Only two days after the tragedy, Hungary's Prime Minister, Viktor Orbán, gave a televised speech in which he discussed the "suicide" of white Europeans, warning that the "great European population exchange" is "a suicidal attempt to replace the lack of European, Christian children with adults from other civilizations – migrants."[2] The geopolitical spread of these examples proves that when replacement theory becomes propagated as "fact" by heads of state and media personalities, and when it is widely embraced by citizenry, and when it inspires horrific acts of violence, then the ideology must be understood both as a "fringe concern *and* a mainstream one."[3]

The origin of the great replacement theory – also known as "white replacement," "white extinction," and "white genocide" – stretches back to the turn of the twentieth century when it was known by another name, "race suicide." Developed out of nineteenth-century discourses of eugenics, the rhetoric of race suicide was taken up in immigration and pronatalist debates across the globe.[4] At times endorsed by those on the fringe and in the mainstream, the theory always harbored a potential to inspire violence as well as the making of legislative policies that dehumanized and diminished liberties of a racialized other. Theories of race suicide sit at a crossroads where questions about race, scientific authority, and human rights collide, and today, they still play a role in the personal and political recognition of human rights.

Politicians of the young Irish Free State arrived at this crossroads in 1928 as they drafted the Censorship of Publications Bill. The Bill included a clause banning print media on contraception. As members of the Oireachtas debated the merits of the clause, they leveraged fears of race suicide to justify its necessity in the Bill, arguing that it could counteract Irish population decline by helping "to stamp out absolutely the traffic in this knowledge" of birth control.[5] By fostering ignorance of sexual and reproductive health, the hope was to ensure unhampered procreation among the Irish populace, thereby safeguarding the future of the new nation. Retiring from the Seanad just as the debates began, W. B. Yeats contested the Bill in the press. Part of his resistance was rooted in his growing apprehension of Catholic population growth, and he speculated on whether the government's desire to increase birth rates was part of a subversive strategy to supplant the last vestiges of Anglo-Irish Protestant influence and representation in the Free State.

Over the course of the 1930s, Yeats's perspective on Irish reproduction evolved, and his infamous late work, *On the Boiler* (1939), promoted a new replacement theory based on his conception of an upper-class replacement. However, his descriptions of an Irish elite point to an even narrower population under threat: Anglo-Irish Protestants. For generations, Anglo-Irish Protestants and Catholics were construed as two separate races, with Catholics classified as "native Irish, Celts, or Gaels," and they "were regarded, and frequently spoke of themselves, as a 'race,' rather than a nation," distinct from English and Anglo-Irish populations.[6] Due to centuries of systemic discriminatory colonial policies, categories of race and religious identity intersected with class affiliation, with Protestants associated with upper classes and Catholics associated with lower and (later) middle classes. This chapter argues that in *On the Boiler*, Yeats leans into these intersections of race, religion, and class to outline his own replacement theory. Through references to disproportionate reproduction rates between the upper and lower classes, he promotes a eugenic paradigm for the preservation and expansion of the Protestant minority. Presenting strategies of selective breeding among an Irish elite, alongside restraints on lower-class reproduction, Yeats imagines conditions through which the "descendancy" could ascend once more.[7] His discourse of race suicide, like the Free State's, argues for limitations of rights. But whereas the Free State focused its program of "race control" on the passing of the Censorship Act of 1929 and the later banning of contraception in 1935, Yeats envisions a far more authoritarian scheme, one that welcomes state-sponsored violence to subdue those he presumes are unfit to rule and reproduce.[8]

This chapter situates Yeats's theory into a historical moment where racial science was growing in popularity and being exploited for political gain. A substantial body of scholarship has observed resonances of racial science across Yeats's oeuvre, demonstrating that his attraction to eugenics was not a momentary fancy.[9] Paul Scott Stanfield argues that Yeats "found" in eugenics "a scientific diagnosis of modernity that complemented his own intuitive diagnosis," including his view of Irish society and culture.[10] Written toward the end of his life, *On the Boiler* fits into a record of a writer seeking explanations in racial science to account for the current state of Ireland and to cast a vision for its future. Melissa Dinsman and others have argued that Yeats's pursuit of eugenics ran in parallel with his radicalizing politics and turn to fascism.[11] Scholars have sought to understand his "mature politics," often offering what Joseph Valente calls "a posthumous scholarly trial" of the writer, which has resulted in what Mary Carden declared as long ago as 1969, "attack, apology, and defence."[12] My own objective is to understand the relationship of Yeats's eugenics to his development of an Anglo-Irish Protestant replacement theory. His evolving ideas about race and reproduction offer a study of scientific racism that reflects fringe but also mainstream rhetoric that endures today. An investigation of Yeats can contribute to the ongoing, multidisciplinary effort to pinpoint the origins, development, and effects of theories that bring together questions of science, race, reproduction, and rights.

Eugenic Origins of "Race Suicide"

The concept of race suicide emerged from nineteenth-century eugenics, a field of study oriented around the possibilities of human reproduction. Inspired by Charles Darwin's theory of natural selection, Sir Francis Galton (Darwin's half-cousin) coined the term "eugenics" from the Greek for "good in stock, hereditarily endowed with noble qualities," and he composed *Hereditary Genius: An Inquiry Into its Laws and Consequences* (1869), the first book in what would become a formal field of enquiry.[13] Galton's text sought to apply Darwin's analysis of animal adaptation to humans. In its preface, he touted the scientific approach of his work as its defining feature – that his study was the "first to treat the subject in a statistical manner, to arrive at numerical results, and to introduce the 'law of deviation from an average' into discussions of heredity."[14] His aim was what he later called the "cultivation of race," a phrase which denotes strategic interventions of selective breeding to achieve "the survival of the fittest" humans.[15]

But who were the "fittest" humans? Galton's classification relied on racial stratifications of his own design and, following the trend of nineteenth- and twentieth-century thought, it considered "race" as a signifier related to "cultural, religious, national, linguistic, ethnic and geographical groups of human beings."[16] Through such broad and indeterminate parameters, he would affirm the superiority of English, Italian, and Jewish popula- tions, while claiming the opposite of African populations and the French, who had killed off their "abler races" (the nobility) with the "guillotine."[17] Lyndsay Andrew Farrell notes that Galton's work inaugurated a discourse of scientific racism that influenced the work of biostatistician Karl Pearson and others; it became "representative of the eugenics movement" and bol- stered the belief in the "innate superiority of the white races over all other human populations."[18]

In 1901, Edward Alsworth Ross merged eugenics with sociological research, designing a theory of "race suicide" to account for his uncertainty about the survival of white Americans in an age of increased immigration. He argued that white Americans were "wither[ing] away" due to "prolific" childbearing of immigrants "from the Orient," and he promoted restrict- ing their entry into the country.[19]

> For a case like this I can find no words so apt as "race suicide." There is no bloodshed, no violence, no assault of the race that waxes upon the race that wanes. The higher race quietly and unmurmuringly eliminates itself rather than endure individually the bitter competition it has failed to ward off from itself by collective action.[20]

Interweaving concerns of race suicide with questions about national eco- nomics and the effects of urbanization on family sizes, Ross claimed that immigrants produced "numerous progeny," accepted poor standards of living, and worked jobs once held by white Americans.[21] Alternatively, white Americans were wittingly killing themselves through lax immigra- tion policies and attempting to improve their living standards by having less children. In this picture of what Laura L. Lovett calls a "paradox of civilization" – a paradox Yeats would situate in an Irish context decades later – Ross bemoaned that white Americans would become *more civilized* through declining birth rates, meaning more passive and accepting, while "less-civilized" races overtook society.[22]

The stakes of white American degeneration, for Ross, related not only to economics and urban expansion, but also to something more intangible – the virtues of "native" morality itself. Across his works, Ross used the word "native," not only to reference global indigenous populations, but also to indicate white Americans who had assimilated over generations into a distinct cultural community. In his framework, these "pure Americans" were decent, while immigrants of color and those from southern and eastern Europe lacked moral character, and this "very decency of the native [was] a handicap to success and to fecundity."[23] It caused the "higher race" to demurely accept their extinction rather than resist it through immigration control and reproduction. Lovett writes of Ross's conviction that "regulating birthrates was a matter of regulating the social order in the image of a natural order."[24] With the "natural" order of white fertility fractured, social orders too, he predicted, would decline.

Ross's theories were always controversial but were adopted by President Theodore Roosevelt, who communicated concerns of race suicide before the American public and successfully campaigned for Congress to pass legislation restricting immigration. Lovett notes, however, that Roosevelt would "recast" race suicide "as an issue of women's duty to the state," a position that would become important during the Free State's "race suicide" debates as well.[25] What Roosevelt's rhetoric makes explicit is a connection implicit in Ross's work; that any theorized antidote to race suicide relied on the labor of women's bodies and therefore denied their bodily autonomy. It would likewise need to dampen first-wave feminist – or New Woman – ambitions for a woman's right to self-determination, including her right to work outside of the home, receive an education, and participate in public and political life, all liberties that were perceived as impediments to marriage and motherhood. In a prefatory letter to *The Woman Who Toils* (1903), Roosevelt admonished women's "desire for independence." That desire is no substitute "for the fundamental virtues, for the practice of the strong, racial qualities without which there can be no strong races." "Strong races" require "having and bringing up ... many healthy children."[26] Those white women of "good stock" who eschewed motherhood, he purportedly dubbed "race criminals," and even women "physically depleted by multiple births should act like soldiers," Diane B. Paul writes of his view, "and place their reproductive duty first."[27] In his 1905 speech "On American Motherhood," he summarized his definition of proper womanhood, reiterating that a "woman's task" was to ensure "all national happiness and greatness" through birthing children.[28] Through the mass reproduction of their laboring bodies, they would guarantee the survival and prosperity of the nation.

"Race Suicide" Rhetoric in the Oireachtas

Roosevelt brought Ross's theory into mainstream public discourse, but its influence in Ireland may seem surprising, given that Galton's research – and even Darwin's – never took Irish scientific communities by storm.[29] Some scholars also suggest that Ireland offered little to the racial science debates of the nineteenth century due to its colonial status and distance from European intellectual communities.[30] Ciaran O'Neill has countered this claim, amplifying the importance of research at Trinity College Dublin's Anthropometric Lab (1888–99) in influencing Earnest Hooton's Harvard Irish Study. Hooton's research on Irish heredity was endorsed by Éamon de Valera in 1932 (although he would request the censoring of its findings on "Familism and Sex" when he reviewed the results in 1940).[31] Eugenics was also brought into medical and public policy debates by the Belfast Eugenics Society, which formed in 1911. Its president, Charles Frederick D'Arcy, expressed approval of forced sterilizations of "unfit" American women, and revered physician, Sir Christopher Nixon, recommended an alternative policy for Ireland: keeping "feebleminded and defective women in institutions" from the ages of 16 to 45, "that is during the entire procreative period."[32] This history demonstrates Irish eugenicists' interest in strategically managing reproduction. It also evinces that Ireland was never isolated from eugenic networks, with Irish academics advancing the field and with politicians considering the profitability of its discourses.

Scholars dispute whether the Irish Free State's eventual inception fits David Theo Goldberg's model of a "racial state," but racial discourse and even racial science were crucial to the nation-building project.[33] In the decade after independence, Irish politicians turned to replacement rhetoric, expressing concern about the fate of their citizenry and the prospect of being replaced or "overwhelmed by the child-bearing nations."[34] Positioning the reproductive labor of Irish bodies – and especially women's bodies – as a chief concern, they articulated fears of race suicide in the Oireachtas.[35] In a series of debates on the Censorship of Publications Bill of 1928, they sought to address their fears, introducing a contraception clause and calculating its potential effects on Irish birth rates. This clause would extend the State's proposed censorship policy beyond "indecent" works of literature to include a "prohibition of publications advocating contraceptives." By banning "any book or periodical publication" on the "the unnatural prevention of conception or the procurement of abortion or miscarriage," many politicians believed they could reinforce

Irish women's "privileged" responsibility "to increase the population" and prevent the "suicide" of the "Irish race."[36]

However, what led them to believe race suicide was imminent? They raised two rationales. First, they were worried by statistical evidence of population decline in continental Europe, especially in France, a nation they considered to be the "acme of European civilization" and a contrast to "China where infanticide is permitted" but "the population ... has increased."[37] Setting aside Teachta Dála (TD) John Byrne's misrepresentation of Chinese law, he argued that if the population of France – a national model for a Europeanizing Ireland – floundered while China's expanded, then Irish race suicide was inevitable.[38] Byrne's assumption follows Ross's association of "civilized" white populations with low rates of reproduction and "less-civilized" populations of color with high ones. But France was not the only nation on their minds, with Senator James Fitzgerald-Kenney referencing Italy's efforts to increase births and with the McGillycuddy of the Reeks adding a parallel between France's condition and the "decline and fall of the Grecian and the Roman Empires." However, he posited that Irish people have a history of fertility due to the "absence of contraceptive measures," and they "produced a surplus population" that filled "sparsely populated countries like America and Australia."[39] If only they were to freely reproduce, he hypothesized they would do the same in the Free State.

The second rationale raised in the debates was rooted in the suspicion of a British conspiracy to "deliberately" circulate "propaganda of contraceptives for the purpose of reducing population in order to avoid revolution" and the reunification of Ireland.[40] Citing advertisements for "contraceptive literature" in English newspapers as being the primary source of "propaganda," Senator and medical physician Oliver St. John Gogarty claimed there was another passage of communication the Bill inadequately addressed; the practice of "English firms" mailing Irish mothers "literature, explaining and advocating the use of contraceptives" after they announced a child's birth in the newspaper: "Are we going to open every new mother's letters for six or seven weeks after a birth? Else how are we going to see that this literature cannot creep in?" Distress about the dangers of English texts – routinely construed as "propaganda" – meant that banning their importation was viewed as a national imperative, essential for the security of the "nation's welfare," the "nation's life."[41] If their circulation continued, the politicians were certain "decay and deterioration of the State" would follow.[42]

What is most strange about the debates is the politicians' omission of a third rationale that must have influenced their belief in race suicide: the results of the 1926 census. Among the Irish population, data revealed extraordinarily low marriage rates, patterns of late marriages, and greater proportions of unmarried and celibate people than in any other country on record. In addition, 43 percent of Irish-born children had emigrated abroad.[43] The census and emigration data portended trends that, if continued, guaranteed further population decline.

Support of the contraception clause fell along religious lines, with Catholic politicians conveying broad support and Protestant leadership arguing against it. Seán Kennedy writes that this contrast exposed "the religious fissures along which the debate in Ireland was being conducted," and these divisions would play a role in Yeats's reaction to the Bill, influencing his perception of the relationship between race, religion, and reproductive rights.[44] Fitzgerald-Kenney defined "The Catholic view" as the belief that contraception "is against nature and is wrong."[45] The "sanctity of the marriage tie" was also of importance, with Byrne arguing that "birth control or race suicide" "removed" "the marriage tie" and prevented "the production of a better race."[46] Through a paraphrase of Galton's "cultivation of race," he associated contraception with both racial extinction and spiritual decay. Senator Michael Comyn emphasized another angle: the stakes of contraception on Catholics as a racial group. To safeguard "our Gaelic race," "we as Catholics are determined to put" "contraception, race suicide, call it what you will," "down."[47] Over and over again, Catholic politicians equated "contraception" and "race suicide," deploying the terms as synonyms and arguing that eliminating knowledge of birth control was a Catholic commitment and extension of faith.

Anglo-Irish Senator Sir John Keane represented the Protestant position, advocating for the human right to "the liberty of thought and the freedom of choice." While twice wishing Yeats was present to reiterate their shared stance, he argued that this "moral" outlook epitomized "the Protestant method," but "this Bill is a distinct attempt to deprive those who wish to exercise liberty of choice of the right to do so." Keane's reasoning came closest to considering the effects of the Bill on women's "health and vitality," as he backed broader recognition of Irish bodily autonomy. But in his appeal to Catholic legislators, even his proposals began to rely on eugenics: "There are certain women who, for medical reasons, should be prevented from bearing children," and male authority figures like statesmen, doctors, and husbands should determine reproductive rights. Keane's additional ideas on the Free State's role in cases related to those with "undesirable inheritance," "disease," and mental illness replicated eugenic arguments on designating who is "good stock" for "breeding."[48] In a striking contrast,

Keane espoused the opposite of his Catholic colleagues. While they combined Catholic religious convictions with fears of race suicide to argue *for* censorship, Keane aligned Protestant values of free "choice" with eugenic strategies to argue *against* it.

The rhetoric of these politicians demonstrates how normalized eugenic thought had become in European pronatalist discourse. Simply put, eugenic principles propelled their policymaking and their hope, according to John F. O'Hanlon, TD, that measures of "race control" would affect "the future of our race, and ... the mental and physical development of our people."[49] The passing of the Censorship Act of 1929 and the later banning of contraception reveal the Free State's willingness to curb rights to pursue a national racial agenda, and these actions raise questions about the consequences of a state's assertion of "race control." The outcome of the debates proves that warnings of race suicide can inspire legislation that limits a range of rights.

Yeats's Response to the "Race Suicide" Debates

Only just retiring from the Senate, Yeats publicly blasted the Bill, including the contraception clause, and his arguments about reproduction became entangled with matters of Irish religious and class difference. He voiced his grievances in one of the very venues on trial – English newspapers. In an interview with the *Manchester Guardian*, he decries the contraception clause as unpopular with the "educated," but they are not "bold enough" to contest it. Meanwhile, "zealots" view it as an "opportunity" of "establishing the Kingdom of God upon earth" but will make instead an "island of moral cowards."[50] Directed at ardent Catholic supporters of the Bill, Yeats's mocking words did not go unnoticed in the Dáil, with Byrne quoting from the interview directly and then expressing thankfulness that he was "a pupil of some of those zealots," and Ireland "owes to those zealots to whom Senator Yeats has referred a debt of gratitude."[51] In another interview with the *Sunday Times*, Yeats posits that, if passed, the Bill would force artists and "Irish intellect into exile and turn what remains into a bitter, polemical energy"; for even, he suspects, George Bernard Shaw's recent work, *The Intelligent Woman's Guide to Socialism* (1928), will be banned because of "a page or two on contraception."[52]

On September 29, the day after his retirement, Yeats published in *The Spectator* what Donald R. Pearce calls the "substance" of a "speech" he would have given in the Seanad. Calling the Bill an "instrument of tyranny," he asserts the contraception clause may result in overlarge families that "overtake the food supply" or demand sexual abstinence in marriages. The poet's attention to the stakes of the contraception clause amid debates that were also about censorship of the literary arts is striking. Making dramatic allegations of degenerate Irish parental behavior, he writes, "Twenty years ago illegitimacy was almost unknown, infanticide unknown, and now both are common and increasing, and [legislators] think that if they could exclude English newspapers," then "innocence would return."[53] Accusing the politicians of embarking on a fool's errand, he describes a clandestine quest to curate Irish "innocence" through sexual and reproductive ignorance. (Only Keane would echo this idea in the Senate, denouncing the Bill as a misguided "attempt by the State into the region of the hygiene of the mind."[54] Of course, the term "hygiene" is closely enmeshed with theories of eugenics and racial cleansing. Samuel Beckett, too, would touch on this point in his posthumously published essay "Censorship in the Saorstat."[55]) Taking his argument one step further, Yeats hints that the Bill may be a part of an anti-Protestant agenda, with "the Government" disregarding "the Treaty to favour one religion at the expense of another." He worries that the Bill exposes the goal of "Catholic Ireland" to follow in the footsteps of other unnamed nations by endorsing policies aimed at populating the State with "soldiers and cheap labour" – or as the subtext of his claim suggests, a state run from the top down by Catholic workers.[56]

The contents of Yeats's argument reflected the pressing anxieties of the Protestant community, which had undergone a profound population decline. According to census reports, the Protestant population declined by 33.5 percent between 1911 and 1926, with much of that decline having occurred by mid-1922, the year the Free State was established and when almost a third had emigrated.[57] Senia Pašeta writes, "this substantial demographic shift was accompanied by a corresponding collapse in the social, economic and, most importantly, political power" that Protestants assumed during British colonial rule.[58] A decree of the Catholic Church also dwindled the minority's numbers, with the Vatican's 1907 Ne Temere requiring children of mixed marriages to be raised Catholic.[59] As Kennedy writes, this meant that "Protestants in mixed marriages were actively contributing to the decline of their own community."[60] By forfeiting children to the Catholic majority, these Protestants were perceived to be playing a voluntary part in their population's extinction, in their own "race suicide."

Protestant population decline related to another objection Yeats had with the Censorship Bill: that "well-to-do classes," or Protestants, already use contraception, and while "the knowledge is spreading downwards" to the poor, "the Catholic Church forbids it."[61] Here, he reinforces an alignment of Protestants with upper classes and Catholics with lower classes, highlighting that, together, class and religious affiliation affect the knowledge and implementation of birth control and, thus, each population's rate of reproduction. Byrne took issue with Yeats's claim in the Dáil, including the suggestion that "wealthy classes" could travel abroad for contraceptive information "whether there were restrictions or not."[62] But Yeats's appraisal of each denomination's convictions was corroborated by church leadership just after the passing of the Censorship Act. In 1930, the Anglican Communion's Lambeth Conference approved, for the first time, individuals' right to determine their own "moral obligation" to prevent conception.[63] Shortly following, Pope Pius XI released the *Casti connubii*, a papal encyclical proclaiming the use of contraception to be a violation of the sanctity of marriage. Holding great sway among the Free State's Catholic majority, the encyclical would boost support for the 1935 blanket ban on birth control.[64]

Yeats's rebuttals to the Bill reveal his premonition that, if ratified, the Act would intensify disproportionate birth rates between Catholics and Protestants, and therefore their disproportionate representation in positions of influence. He saw the Bill as written in service of Catholic power and population expansion. This belief mirrors warnings he had issued from the Senate floor years earlier, this time in the context of debates on a divorce policy. Arguing that the Free State was becoming "governed by Catholic ideas and by Catholic ideas alone," moving toward a future in which "Catholic laws" would become the norm, he pronounced that "the minority" would have to make "perfectly plain that it does consider it exceedingly oppressive legislation to deprive it of rights which it has held since the 17th century."[65] Citing colonial privileges, he wrestled with the expectation that in postcolonial Ireland, Protestants were accountable to policies that he believed were "oppressive" and favored Catholic interests.

Yeats's Race Philosophy and Replacement Theory

Yeats's frustrations with the Censorship Bill provide context for understanding how and why his ideas about race and reproductive rights radicalized in the 1930s, and they set the stage for his design of a new replacement theory distinct from the Free State's, one that describes an Anglo-Irish race suicide. By rejecting the whole of the Bill in 1928, he had taken a stance that, in effect, argued against notions of race suicide and endorsed rights for *all* Irish people, even though he was especially concerned about the effects of the contraception clause on Protestant numbers. As time passed, however, he became enamored like so many of his generation with fascism, and his ideas became more explicitly antidemocratic and authoritarian in orientation. Still, practical application of such politics was a question he pondered in his writings. Should transformation, or "the source of all initiative," stem from actions of the individual or the state?[66] His opinions wavered, but by the end of the decade, he would sponsor a eugenics program that relied on both the individual and the state. This program would redress not just what he sensed was Anglo-Irish racial degeneration but a decay of culture and the arts.

In 1933, Yeats penned "A Race Philosophy," a prose piece that reads simultaneously like a modernist manifesto and a philosophical proof.[67] In short, demonstrative points, he advances an argument on the relationship between race, politics, and art. The text follows and responds to another, his "Genealogical Tree of Revolution," in which he pits Marxism against fascism.[68] As in *A Vision* (1925, 1937), where contrary forces drive the motions of history, his race philosophy opens with a claim that contrary politics should push against each other. These "antimonies cannot be solved" and are "inadequate because society is the struggle of two forces not transparent to reason—the family and the individual." Neither "Communism" nor "Fascism" can suitably manage the unpredictable nature of humanity.

In the text, people also belong to contrary groups. Praise is reserved for a minority population made up of families with "good taste," "good habits," "inherited wealth, privilege," and "precedence." These families contrast with the rest of society, "Materially and Spiritually uncreative families or individuals." Although "equality of opportunity, equality of rights" should exist to aid "the individual in his struggle," Yeats anticipates justified prohibitions of those rights. From the "struggle to make and preserve" oneself comes "intellectual initiative" – his synonym for ingenuity and artistic production – but "uncreative families or individuals must not be allowed to triumph over the creative." By classifying populations based on intelligence, skills, and accomplishments, Yeats echoes eugenic tenets to assert that social success is a result of superior heredity, and abler creative families "must" rule over inferior uncreative families.

The text vacillates on the question of the state's role in this suppression. For "the business of Government is not to abate either struggle," but to ensure the "triumph" of its superior citizenry. "Government" has the "right" to implement policies that "limit" a family's "gains," but "the successful family" must have certain "power"; for "it must not be forgotten that Race, which has for its flower the family and the individual, is wiser than Government, and that it is the source of all initiative."[69] In this closing line, Yeats resolves that "Race" itself is an expression of biological inheritance and that it should direct transformation.

Notably, Yeats does not deploy the term "race" as a stand-in for nationality or to negotiate terms of citizenship. Years earlier, he had paraphrased Thomas Davis's stance, writing that "nationality" was not "a thing of race or creed" and "every man born here belonged to the nation."[70] This *jus soli* version of citizenship – which would be overthrown by the Citizenship Referendum of 2004, in a time when Irishness began to attain a more multicultural hue – might appear to the contemporary reader to be at odds with other racial connotations of "A Race Philosophy." For example, Daniel G. Williams has distinguished the poet's tendency to separate configurations of race from ethnicity, the latter of which he tied to "cultural inheritance."[71] Yeats's philosophy instead delineates race, racial superiority, and the right to rulership, as determined by heredity, by the quality of one's ancestral genes. Marjorie Howes concludes that Yeats's "thinking is profoundly inimical to practical decision-making; it is the level at which the course of human events is determined by immense and obscure forces," including "racial imperatives," that are "beyond human understanding and control."[72] A curious document, Yeats's "A Race Philosophy" is difficult to pin down, but it brings together concerns of his later years: the relationship of race and heredity to politics and art.

Yeats roots these concerns in an Irish historical context in *On the Boiler*, written in 1938 and published posthumously in 1939. In some ways, the treatise resembles Yeats's most experimental works, bearing hallmarks of the genre-fluid form of modernism he invented, one that blends elements of myth and the occult with history and philosophy. But whereas his eyes never fully look away from the cosmos in texts like *A Vision*, Yeats lowers his gaze in *On the Boiler* to scrutinize the present state of Ireland. Building on his race philosophy, he outlines an applied eugenics paradigm for Ireland. Yet this time, he espouses specific methods of race control enacted by both the individual and the state.

Donald Childs traces Yeats's introduction to eugenics to the turn of the century, but his self-education took a more vigorous turn when he joined the Eugenics Society in 1936 and sought back issues of *The Eugenics Review*.[73] He paired his learning with research in psychometrics, corresponding with Carlos P. Blacker, the secretary of the Eugenics Society, inquiring about intelligence tests. Especially inquisitive about the "intelligence quota of the leisured classes," "people living upon inherited money," he expected the results "to be pretty high."[74] In this letter, Yeats was angling to confirm a hunch (which Blacker was unable to do) that populations such as those born of Anglo-Irish stock, those descended from the Ascendancy, were genetically superior.

His opinion of leisured classes differed from most eugenicists of the period who cited the middle classes to be the "most desirable classes," and many had "mixed or even negative feelings about the landed aristocracy," even if they suspected they were "eugenically superior."[75] Yet Yeats scorned the middle classes, including the Protestant middle class in which he was raised. He believed his middle-class status was part of a centuries-long process of Anglo-Irish degeneration.[76] What his correspondence with Blacker shows is that his admiration of the Anglo-Irish aristocracy was not just about "metaphorical or aesthetic" virtues the population might represent or exemplify in art. "It is equally true," as Howes argues, that his picture of an "ideal aristocracy" was a "material one; his works insist again and again that such virtues flourish most readily under the conditions provided by wealth, privilege and leisure."[77]

The notion that aristocrats were the most able members of a society spurs his formation of a Galtonian approach to eugenics. Galton's model argued for an interdependence between race and social factors. He sought not just to distinguish hierarchies *of* human races but ability *within* races. This approach differed from Ross's theory of race suicide, which emerged primarily out of a prejudice against people of color, "nations and immigrant groups he considered inferior," rather than apprehension about "fecundity among the poor," unsuccessful members of a group.[78] For Galton, however, racial groups had within them subsets of those with higher and lower ability, hence his conclusion that the French had executed their "abler races" during the French Revolution, with the lower classes overthrowing the aristocracy and monarchy. By studying biographies of men in the past, he associated "hereditary genius" with men whose lives revealed evidence of traits and accomplishments constructed by society as admirable. But what should these successful, "superior" subjects do to advance their race? According to Galton, they should practice targeted population growth, to strengthen their race through the reproduction of their "abler" subjects, supplanting those with "inferior" ability over time. He believed selective breeding would ensure a race's future prosperity.[79]

In *On the Boiler*, Yeats extends Galton's model, maintaining that an individual's social success verifies a predetermined hereditary ability, including their worthiness to participate in selective breeding and strategic population growth. While Yeats's direct engagement with Galton's work is uncertain, his wife and collaborator, Georgie Hyde-Lees, owned a copy of *Hereditary Genius*.[80] Yeats also had in his possession Charles John Bond's

1928 Galton Lecture to the London Eugenics Society, an address that praised Galton's methodology. The lecture was inserted into his edition of Raymond Bernard Cattell's *The Flight of Our National Intelligence* (1937), a book Yeats recommended in a footnote in *On the Boiler*.[81] A psychologist considered "more Galtonian than Galton," Cattell also wrote *Psychology and Social Progress: Mankind and Destiny from the Standpoint of a Scientist* (1933), another book Yeats annotated while making connections between Catholicism and "physical degeneration": "In almost all European countries, especially those where Catholicism encourages large families among the poor, there has been" a "decline" in stature, including in height, chest measurement, and weight.[82] In this single footnote, Yeats is intrigued by evidence of working-class Catholic physiological decline. More broadly, his reflections evince his enjoining of religious and class affiliation with a theory of degeneration, a combination that carries consequential Irish hereditary and racial connotations in *On the Boiler*.

In Yeats's eugenic model, affluent classes are genetically engineered with the capacity for "success in life in the main," while those in "poverty" have none of the stuff for success because their inherited "mother-wit" is fixed. Studies of children reveal the importance of nature rather than nurture, he claims: "take a pair of twins and educate one in wealth, the other in poverty, test from time to time: their mother-wit will be the same. Pick a group of slum children," separate half of them into places of privilege, then "re-examine": "there will be little or no difference."[83] However, if individuals are studied by occupation, from the bottom of society upward, Yeats contends "there is not only an increase of mother-wit but of the size of the body and its freedom from constitutional defects." While there are "clever men born among dunces" and "dunces among clever men," these men are "exceptions." "Professional men" possess hereditary advantages that make their bodies larger, heathier, and abler, and "as intelligence and freedom from bodily defect increase wealth increases in exact measure." Importantly, he groups "leisured classes" with professional classes in a footnote here, but – harking back to his correspondence with Blacker – explains he has no statistical evidence of their superiority because they do not submit to scientific study.[84]

Overall, Yeats's analysis assumes the upper classes are intelligent, healthy, and thus wealthy, by biological design. But they are under threat of extinction, he warns, due to disproportionate reproduction rates among the classes: "the families grow smaller as we ascend; among the unemployed they average between four and five, among the professional classes between two and three; among the unemployed there are still families of twelve and thirteen." To Yeats, these disproportionate birth rates will cause all manner of decay and will topple old ranks and orders:

> Since about 1900 the better stocks have not been replacing their numbers, while the stupider and less healthy have been more than replacing theirs. Unless there is a change in the public mind every rank above the lowest must degenerate, and, as inferior men push up into its gaps, degenerate more and more quickly. The results are already visible in the degeneration of literature, newspapers, amusements...[85]

He describes an environment where those at the top of society are having fewer children than those at the bottom; thus, inferior lower classes are gradually "replacing" (his word) upper classes. The effects of such degeneration will stretch far across society, as he envisages a further deterioration of culture and the arts, unless the "better stocks" exponentially increase birth rates.

Yeats's analysis infers a race suicide and replacement of Anglo-Irish populations. His estimation of class difference becomes one of racial difference, with his eugenic diagnoses and theories regarding the benefits of reproducing a certain class of Irish people having recognizable racial indicators. That is to say, Yeats's discourse of class difference, in the context of measuring heredity and reproduction, functions not just as an upper-class replacement theory but as a thinly veiled Anglo-Irish replacement theory, one with sincere investment in producing a plan to preserve and grow Protestant numbers. Although Yeats alludes to both Catholics and Protestants as having their own "inferior men" – and although he names one exceptional Catholic, Kevin O'Higgins (1892–1927), among eight "true Irish people" of the past – his argument, in which class origins coincide with a fixed "mother-wit," presumes a general rule of Catholic inferiority and Anglo-Irish ability.[86] His convictions are at odds with occasions of sympathies in his poetic and prose works toward what Stanfield calls "Catholic authority and ritual"; however, Howes writes of Yeats's certainty that the nation's future required the guidance of an Anglo-Irish elite, that they were "capable of providing Ireland with the cultural continuity, political leadership and artistic integrity that he thought middle-class Catholic Ireland lacked."[87]

Yeats's theory ignores the systemic forces through which class is produced and opportunity for social success bolstered. Such thinking, as Abdul R. JanMohamed notes, follows a "colonialist" pattern of "substituting natural or generic categories for those that are socially or ideologically determined."[88] Spurgeon Thompson builds on this idea, writing that

Yeats's "Anglo-Irish racial anxiety" and belief in a "displaced elite" drove his "colonialist" eugenics, which responded to Ireland's "transition from a colonial to a postcolonial state." Out of "a specific colonialist structure of feeling and reference," Thompson argues that Yeats reinforces a "'garrison mentality,' which racially marks and condemns" those he deems as "irrevocably barbaric" or "'uneducatable.'"[89] Thompson's assertion draws on Seamus Deane's explanation of the "Protestant self-image" as "bound up with the idea of liberty and the image of the garrison," a company of "elite people (sponsored both by Protestantism and by the exclusive Whig idea of liberty as a racial phenomenon)."[90] According to Thompson, this mentality "produces—and is in turn supported by—symptomatic knowledges: elitism, racism, xenophobic 'liberty,' and ... their second cousin, eugenics." He concludes that *On the Boiler* proposes through this mentality a "colonialist racism," a uniquely "racist version of an Irish cultural and political elite."[91]

Thompson's claim is unusual among academic studies of Yeats's eugenics and, quite reasonably, may sound inappropriate to contemporary scholars uneasy with applying terms of "racism" to contexts involving white populations of the past, no matter their reliance on old, alternative models of race or their entanglement with colonial history. The term "racism," however, was born during Yeats's lifetime and encompassed discriminatory "beliefs" about "racial or ethnic groups," including ideologies estimating hereditary values, and these denotations should prompt considering their affinities with his theory.[92] Shirley Lau Wong asserts in this volume that the field of Irish Studies tends to consider race a matter of interest to the twenty-first century and to scholarship on the "new Irish," leaving "racial ideologies" of the past by the wayside and their negotiation in "canonical works of Irish literature" "naturalized" and "unexamined."[93] Following Wong's insight, I argue that if *On the Boiler* is distanced from discourses of race and racism, there is a risk of overlooking or downplaying the origins and stakes of Yeats's theory. His rhetoric of race suicide emerges not just out of benign interest in racial science but out of racial anxieties and prejudices. He formulates a race philosophy that is not merely figurative or abstract but proposes concrete steps to be taken by and against real Irish populations. These actions are intended to suppress the reproductive rights and birth rates of the majority of Irish Catholics.

As Yeats advances his replacement theory, he centralizes Anglo-Irish interests, proposing a series of eugenic solutions that might become a source of Anglo-Irish regeneration. One solution is to enact a *negative eugenics,* restricting reproduction among those with undesirable traits. He calls for the government to "limit" the reproduction of "unintelligent classes." Whereas "A Race Philosophy" somewhat wavered on the benefits of state intervention, *On the Boiler* recommends it. Instead of mistaking "eugenic and ethnic" problems as "economic" and "social problem[s]" to be worked out among the people, a "government" should use its "necessary authority." Allusions to officials of the Catholic Church make it clear these restrictions especially target Catholic populations: "our government" can "send" them to either a "doctor and clinic" or a "monk and confession box."[94] While we can guess that the former option might enforce sterilizations or use of birth control, the assistance Catholic priests would provide is unclear. Knowing their stance on contraception, it is perplexing that Yeats would reference them at all, but this passage exhibits his awareness that his imagined state policy requires cooperation between the government and Catholic Church to curb Catholic birth rates.

In a second proposal, Yeats urges the Irish elite to practice a *positive eugenics* through selective breeding. This practice could help prevent race suicide, enabling the "better stocks" to begin "replacing their numbers." In centuries past, "leisured men … bred cattle instead of men," but that "great task is done."[95] Now the Anglo-Irish must "defend against degeneration by breeding eugenically." In a surprising twist, Yeats recommends this breeding occur not only among the Anglo-Irish themselves but also with selected Catholic "peasants" who, as Childs writes, could enable "the Anglo-Irish stock of the Protestant Ascendancy" to "come to embody and express biologically and culturally an Irishness equal to that of the Celtic and Catholic peasantry."[96] Throughout his career, Yeats had idealized certain impoverished Catholics as being more likely to possess traces of ancient Celtic wisdom that are "rare among the educated classes." He believed Anglo-Irish Protestants had lost their "allied gifts" in their ascension.[97] However, through selective breeding with "the best" Catholics, the Anglo-Irish could possess and bequeath Celtic "gifts" to their progeny; or as Childs states, "the race's psychical genius will be reclaimed by aristocrats with the biological genius to breed with the right peasant."[98]

What Yeats envisions is a theory of crossbreeding, plans to bring two ideal types of individuals together to form a hybrid breed. References to crossbreeding are brief and difficult to apprehend in *On the Boiler* but they promote a theory of racial uplift inspired by evolutionary theories in plant and animal adaptation. Yeats's zoological comparisons are positioned as instructive models in the matter of choosing a mate: "We should count men and women who pick, as it were, the dam or sire of a Derby winner from between the shafts of a cab, among persons of genius, for this genius makes all other kinds possible." Notice his praise of horse breeders with an eye for spotting "genius" in lowly places, identifying the ideal male or female workhorse from which to breed an award-winning racehorse. The breeder's "genius" enables the birth of new "genius" in the next generation. Analogizing classes of horses with humans, Yeats proposes that pairing "opposites," or a superior aristocratic breed with a peasant breed possessing "what he lacks," will "beget a stronger life" through their child of mixed heredity.[99] He assumes the new generation of mixed children will be raised in society, not as working-class Catholics, but as genius aristocrats, members of an elite order, what Howes names a "kindred aristocracy."[100] Already, he is encouraged that some of the "descendants" of the Ministers of the Treaty of Government have "intermarried" and "able stocks have begun to appear … men of talent everywhere are much linked through marriage and descent." They could "constitute our ruling class."[101] Yeats thus nuances his perspective of Catholic reproduction and creates a theory of Irish racial hybridity in which selected Catholics are "not a negligible biological resource."[102] But his sanctioning of Catholic reproduction is based on the service it will provide the Anglo-Irish, with only "the best bred from the best."[103]

Valente links the "authoritarian inclination" of Yeats's eugenics to a wider European fascism that the poet believed was responding to a degeneration crisis.[104] Democracy was problematic because it promised equality and threatened an elite's centralization of power, just as Yeats suspected it was doing in the "new-formed democratic parliaments of India." He felt that maintaining class structures would preserve a nation's hereditary ability, in a manner similar to "the caste system," which he said had "saved Indian intellect." So how should a state wield its hand among the classes? Yeats predicts that a third eugenic strategy will be required, "civil war"; for "human violence" must be "embodied" by the "government," which is made "legitimate" through its "right to take life in defence of its laws and shores." In this war, the "educated classes" must "seize and control" so that the "docile masses may submit." "Prolonged civil war" is not just inevitable but desirable: "The danger is that there will be no war, that the skilled will attempt nothing, that the European civilisation, like those earlier civilisations that saw the triumph of their gangrel stocks, will accept decay."[105] The parallels between Yeats's words and Ross's theory are evident. Just as Ross feared that white Americans would passively accept their "race suicide," Yeats fears the Irish elite – without civil war – will "accept decay" and replacement.

Civil war fought in the vein Yeats describes is akin to a race war or ethnic conflict, with the outcome determining the dominance of a particular group believed to have superior heredity. However, it is also a culture war, a term popular today but with origins in nineteenth-century descriptions of a "political struggle for control of cultural and educational institutions."[106] Yeats's admiration of violence was intertwined with an assumption that it could engender cultural transformation. Writing affectionately of changes brought about by violence, he quotes himself via the voice of Michael Robartes in *A Vision*, "Love war because of its horror, that belief may be changed, civilization renewed."[107] Yeats's position frighteningly echoes words of fascist and Futurist, Filippo Tommaso Marinetti, who had declared years earlier – that "War" was "the Only Hygiene of the World,"[108] but between the two modernists, only Yeats would venerate old institutions and seek the restoration of the bygone aristocratic tradition from which he descended.

Conclusion

It is difficult to gauge the earnestness of Yeats's message in *On the Boiler*. Would the retired statesman have truly endorsed limitations of reproductive rights? Would the poet of "Easter 1916," so "changed utterly" by the rebellion, have approved of civil war?[109] Elizabeth Cullingford doubts that even Yeats was convinced of his own argument.[110] Bernard McKenna and David Bradshaw write compellingly of Yeats's desire to court controversy and his hope to boost sales at the Cuala Press, which was run by his sisters.[111] At the same time, Bradshaw argues that his eugenics was "deadly serious," and W. J. McCormack purports that Georgie Yeats "toned down the violence" of the text before it went to press.[112] Howes writes that he was "comfortable with various violences on a literal as well as a metaphoric level in a way that many contemporary commentators are not."[113] Yeats admitted as much in a letter, describing his plan: to "lay aside the pleasant patter I have built up for years, & seek the brutality, the ill breeding, the barbarism of truth."[114] He knew his convictions would be disruptive, confessing to Maud Gonne in the summer of 1938, "For the first time I am saying what I believe about Irish and European politics. I wonder how many friends I will have left."[115]

No matter the sincerity of Yeats's multipronged theory of eugenics, its origins and effects must be accounted for, especially as his ideas share relevant connections with replacement theories of the present, such as those mentioned at the start of this chapter. Like those theories, we can conclude that Yeats's rhetoric of race suicide did not develop suddenly. His notions emerged out of wider trends in eugenic thought, which had already spilled over into political discourse at the highest levels of government within the Irish Free State. His example demonstrates how replacement theories are embedded in more expansive histories of racial science. Furthermore, Yeats's hierarchy of Irish heredity was entangled with his sense of Anglo-Irish fragility. His example illustrates how replacement theory arises out of insecurities in one's own identity – how one's self-interest and instincts to self-preservation inform an individual's race philosophy and politics. Racial biases underpin Yeats's theory, and indeed other replacement theories, and reckoning with the origins and force of these biases better enables scholars to interrogate the role of race and racism in eugenic theories of the past and their symmetries with those of the present. By studying Yeats's rhetoric closely, we can recognize its dangers and its place in the ongoing and interconnected story of science, race, reproduction, and rights. Although the forms of scientific racism that Galton, Ross, and Yeats espoused are now debunked theories of race, they still attract followers and influence public policy, so we must debunk them again and again.

Notes

1 Steve Rose, "A Deadly Ideology: How the 'Great Replacement Theory' Went Mainstream," *The Guardian*, June 8, 2022, www.theguardian.com/world/2022/jun/08/a-deadly-ideology-how-the-great-replacement-theory-went-mainstream.

2 Flora Garamvolgyi and Julian Borger, "Orbán and US Right to Bond at Cpac in Hungary over 'Great Replacement' Ideology," *The Guardian*, May 18, 2022, www.theguardian.com/world/2022/may/18/cpac-conference-budapest-hungary-viktor-orban-speaker.

3 Rose, "A deadly ideology." For additional examples of replacement theories, including their association with political discourse and acts of violence around the globe, see Andrew Buncombe, "Inside the Data that Debunks the 'Great Replacement' Theory," *Independent*, May 16, 2022, www.independent.co.uk/news/world/americas/buffalo-shooting-great-replacement-theory-b2080389.html.

4 For example, the terminology would gain traction in British- and Irish-educated physician Robert Reid Rentoul's denunciation of interracial reproduction in *Race Culture; or, Race Suicide: (A Plea for the Unborn)* (London: Walter Scott Publishing Company Limited, 1906). Madison Grant promoted eugenics and race suicide to establish a theory Nordic superiority in *The Passing of the Great Race: or The Racial Basis of European History* (New York: Charles Scribner's Sons, 1916). Grant's book would influence

Adolf Hitler and his conviction of a superior Aryan race. Calling the book his "bible" in a fan letter to Grant, Hitler would translate his beliefs into a national program that would support the murder of millions of Jews during the Holocaust; see Stefan Kühl, *Nazi Connection: Eugenics, American Racism, and German National Socialism* (Oxford: Oxford University Press, 1994), 85. More recently, the French author Renaud Camus has promoted replacement theory in writings such as *Le Grand Remplacement* (2011) and *You Will Not Replace Us!* (2018). See also scholarship from Angus McLaren, *Our Own Master Race: Eugenics in Canada, 1885–1945* (Toronto: University of Toronto Press, 2014); Diane B. Paul, John Stenhouse, and Hamish G. Spencer, *Eugenics at the Edges of Empire: New Zealand, Australia, Canada and South Africa* (Cham: Palgrave, 2018); Richard A. Soloway, *Demography and Degeneration: Eugenics and the Declining Birthrate in Twentieth-Century Britain* (Chapel Hill: University of North Carolina Press, 1995); Sandrine Bertaux, "Demographic Knowledge, 'Race Suicide' and the Making of Racial Jews in Interwar Europe," *European Journal of Turkish Studies* 16 (December 2013): https://journals.openedition.org/ejts/4848; Jin-kyung Park, "Interrogating the 'Population Problem' of the Non-Western Empire: Japanese Colonialism, the Korean Peninsula, and the Global Geopolitics of Race," *Interventions: The International Journal of Postcolonial Studies* 19, no. 8 (November 2017): 1112–31; Elisa Camiscioli, "Producing Citizens, Reproducing the 'French Race': Immigration, Demography, and Pronatalism in Early Twentieth-Century France," *Gender & History* 13, no. 3 (November 2001): 593–621.

5 Michael Comyn, *Seanad Éireann Debates*, April 11, 1929, www.oireachtas.ie/en/debates/debate/seanad/1929-04-11/3/.

6 Noel Ignatiev, *How the Irish Became White* (London: Routledge, 1995), 35. See also, for example, J. W. Jackson, "The Race Question in Ireland," *The Anthropological Review* 7, no. 24 (1869): 54–76.

7 Elizabeth Bowen described her generation of the Ascendancy as the "descendancy." Quoted in Patricia Laurence, *Elizabeth Bowen: A Literary Life* (Cham, Switzerland: Palgrave, 2019), 76.

8 John F. O'Hanlon, *Dáil Éireann Debates*, October 19, 1928, www.oireachtas.ie/en/debates/debate/dail/1928-10-19/2/. The Criminal Law Amendment Act of 1935 banned contraception.

9 For example, Donald Childs identifies eugenic thought in a range of Yeats's early plays and late poetry, as well as in his late play *Purgatory* (1938), etc., in *Modernism and Eugenics: Woolf, Eliot, Yeats and the Culture of Degeneration* (Cambridge, Cambridge University Press, 2001).

10 Paul Scott Stanfield, *Yeats and Politics in the 1930s* (Houndmills: Macmillan, 1988), 162.

11 Melissa Dinsman, "Politics, Eugenics, and Yeats's Radio Broadcasts," *International Yeats Studies* 3, no. 1 (2018): 67.

12 Joseph Valente, "Aging Yeats: from Fascism to Disability," in *Irish Literature in Transition, 1880–1940*, ed. Marjorie Elizabeth Howes (Cambridge: Cambridge University Press, 2020), 176; Mary Carden, "The Few and the Many: An

Examination of W. B. Yeats's Politics," *Studies: An Irish Quarterly Review* 58, no. 229 (1969): 51.

13 Francis Galton, *Inquiries into Human Faculty and Its Development* (London: Macmillan, 1883), 24.

14 Francis Galton, *Hereditary Genius: An Inquiry Into its Laws and Consequences* (London: Macmillan, 1869), vi.

15 Francis Galton, *Inquiries into Human Faculty and Its Development*, 24. Herbert Spencer first used the phrase "survival of the fittest" to describe Darwin's theory of natural selection in *Principles of Biology* (London: Williams and Norgate, 1864), 444.

16 Nancy Stepan, *The Idea of Race in Science: Great Britain: 1800–1960* (Houndmills: Macmillan, 1982), xvii.

17 Galton, *Hereditary Genius*, 4, 350. Galton, *Inquiries into Human Faculty and Its Development*, 317. Galton went so far as to propose the "order loving Chinese" immigrate to Africa to "supplant the inferior Negro race" through reproduction ("Africa for the Chinese," *Times*, June 5, 1873).

18 Lyndsay Andrew Farrell, *The Origins and Growth of the English Eugenics Movement 1865–1925* (New York: Garland, 1985), 51.

19 Edward A. Ross, "The Causes of Race Superiority," *The Annals of the American Academy of Political and Social Science*, 18 (July 1901): 88; Edward A. Ross, *The Changing Chinese* (New York: The Century Co., 1920); Edwin E. Slosson, "Leland Stanford Junior University," *The Independent* 66, no. 3148–3160 (January–June 1909): 679. In 1900, Ross delivered a speech in San Francisco against Japanese immigration, which resulted in Jane Stanford's call for his resignation at Stanford University. The speech not only stirred debates about East Asian immigration, with over 800 newspapers applauding his speech, but also campaigns for the protection of free speech among academics, with many Stanford faculty, in addition to the presidents of both Yale and Harvard, offering him words of support. After resigning from Stanford, Ross continued his academic career at the University of Nebraska and the University of Wisconsin–Madison. For a detailed account of Ross's work and influence, see Laura L. Lovett, *Conceiving the Future: Pronatalism, Reproduction, and the Family in the United States, 1890–1938* (Chapel Hill: University of North Carolina Press, 2007), 77–108.

20 Ross, "The Causes of Race Superiority," 88.

21 Ross, "The Causes of Race Superiority," 88; Edward A. Ross, *The Old World in the New: The Significance of Past and Present Immigration to the American People* (New York: The Century Co., 1914), 303.

22 Lovett, *Conceiving the Future*, 85–86.

23 Ross, *The Old World in the New*, 34, 303. In the book, Ross devotes a chapter to Irish Americans, describing them as drunk, reckless, emotional, superstitious, and backward (24–45). Unlike East Asian immigrants, however, he considers the Irish redeemable, claiming they could possibly become, by their "fourth generation," productive members of American society (45).

24 Lovett, *Conceiving the Future*, 79.

25 Lovett, *Conceiving the Future*, 91.

26 Theodore Roosevelt, "Prefatory Letter," in *The Woman Who Toils: Being the Experiences of Two Gentlewomen as Factory Girls*, written by Mrs. John Van Vorst and Marie Van Vorst (New York: Doubleday, 1903), vii–viii.

27 Diane B. Paul, *Controlling Human Heredity: 1865 to the Present* (Atlantic Highlands: Humanities Press, 1995), 102.

28 Theodore Roosevelt, "On American Motherhood" (speech, March 13, 1905), National Center for Public Policy Research, https://nationalcenter.org/ncppr/2001/11/03/theodore-roosevelt-on-motherhood-1905/.

29 Greta Jones, "Nation and Religion: The Debate About Darwinism in Ireland," in *The Reception of Charles Darwin in Europe*, eds. Eve-Marie Engels and Thomas F. Glick (London: Continuum, 2008), 1:66–78.

30 Richard McMahon, *The Races of Europe: Construction of National Identities in the Social Sciences, 1839–1939* (Basingstoke: Palgrave Macmillan, 2016), 270.

31 A member of the Galton Society, Hooton collected data on the "typical Irishman," promoting "hereditary and racial connotations" of Irishness in order to understand "how characteristics descend through a regionalized population" and to "quantify and measure racial difference in a domestic context"; see Ciaran O'Neill, "'Harvard Scientist Seeks Typical Irishman': Measuring the Irish Race, 1888–1936," *Radical History Review* 2022, no. 143 (2022): 93. See also, Anne Byrne and Eoin O'Sullivan, "Arensberg, Kimball and de Valera: A Story of Sex and Censorship," *Irish Journal of Sociology* 27, no. 3 (2019): 227–50; Mairéad Carew, *The Quest for the Irish Celt: The Harvard Archaeological Mission to Ireland, 1932–1936* (Newbridge: Irish Academic Press, 2018).

32 Greta Jones, "Eugenics in Ireland: The Belfast Eugenics Society, 1911–15," *Irish Historical Studies* 28, no. 109 (1992): 87; Christopher Nixon, "Statement of Evidence Given before the Royal Commission on the Feebleminded," *Dublin Journal of Medical Science* cxxiv (1912): 200.

33 David Theo Goldberg, *The Racial State* (Malden, Massachusetts: Blackwell, 2002); John Brannigan, *Race in Modern Irish Literature and Culture* (Edinburgh: Edinburgh University Press, 2009), 21. When the War of Independence began in 1919, the First Dáil Éireann of the proclaimed Irish Republic (1919–1921) composed a "Message to the Free Nations of the World," establishing grounds for recognition as a nation state. The message begins with an exclamation of Irish racial difference: "Naturally, the race, the language, the customs and traditions of Ireland are radically distinct from the English." In the years following, Éamon de Valera would invoke undercurrents of racial science in his address to the Irish Race Congress of 1922, a chaotic event (with guest lectures from W. B. and Jack B. Yeats, among others) intended to mobilize the Irish diaspora into debates over the Anglo-Irish Treaty. He contended that those with "Irish blood" bear a race responsibility to advance Irish culture abroad so that it "may be given to humanity." His purpose was for the diaspora to convince the world that Irish cultural accomplishment was an expression of racial difference and gave Ireland the right to self-determination. See First Dáil, "Message to the Free Nations of the World," January 21, 1919; *Imtheachta Aonaighe na n-Gaedheal ib-Páris, Eanair, 1922: Proceedings of the*

Irish Race Congress in Paris, January, 1922 (London: Cahill, 1922), 46; Ross, *The Old World in the New*, 24–35.

34 Oliver St. John Gogarty, *Seanad Éireann Debates*, April 11, 1929, www .oireachtas.ie/en/debates/debate/seanad/1929-04-11/3/. In *Ulysses* (1922), James Joyce's character, Buck Mulligan, is a caricature of Gogarty.

35 Marjorie Howes writes, "Fears that the Irish were race-suicidal encouraged a cult of maternity, already strong in Ireland's Catholic culture. This cult insisted that women could best embody and safeguard the national character by staying home and becoming mothers, and in this context female emigration, women working outside the home, and resistance to traditional gender roles were all linked as threats to the national being"; in *Yeats's Nations: Gender, Class, and Irishness* (New York: Cambridge University Press, 1996), 137.

36 "Censorship of Publications Act, 1929," *Electronic Irish Statute Book* (Dublin: Office of the Attorney General, Government of Ireland), www .irishstatutebook.ie/eli/1929/act/21/enacted/en/html; www.irishstatutebook.ie/ eli/1929/act/21/section/16/enacted/en/html#sec16; Gogarty, *Seanad Éireann Debates*, April 11, 1929; John Joseph Byrne, *Dáil Éireann Debates*, October 19, 1928, www.oireachtas.ie/en/debates/debate/dail/1928-10-19/2/; Comyn, *Seanad Éireann Debates*, April 11, 1929.

37 Byrne, *Dáil Éireann Debates*, October 19, 1928.

38 Byrne's speech implies a state-sponsored sanctioning of infanticide in China, but no such policy existed, even as female infanticide was a "hidden social practice." His rhetoric draws on popular Western stigmas about infanticide being a Chinese or broader Asian "'abomination'" with little attention given to Western practices, such as Britain's "infanticide panic" of the nineteenth century, which was "fueled largely by concerns about moral disorder on the part of serving women in the lower classes, who were driven by shame or straitened circumstances to kill their illegitimate children"; see Michelle T. King, *Between Birth and Death: Female Infanticide in Nineteenth-Century China* (Stanford: Stanford University Press, 2014), 2–3. According to Tyrene White, in the 1930s and 1940s, China's "official party policy on population growth was pro-natalist" in orientation, like Ireland's, but birth control was legal for married couples (23). White documents legal and social shifts regarding childbearing and reproductive rights and practices in the latter half of the twentieth century in China; see *China's Longest Campaign: Birth Planning in the People's Republic, 1949–2005* (Ithaca: Cornell University Press, 2006).

39 James Fitzgerald-Kenney, *Seanad Éireann Debates*, April 11, 1929, www .oireachtas.ie/en/debates/debate/seanad/1929-04-11/3/; The McGillycuddy of the Reeks (Ross McGillycuddy), *Seanad Éireann Debates*, April 11, 1929, www .oireachtas.ie/en/debates/debate/seanad/1929-04-11/3/.

40 Patrick J. Little, *Dáil Éireann Debates*, October 18, 1928, www.oireachtas.ie/en/ debates/debate/dail/1928-10-18/19/; Comyn, *Seanad Éireann Debates*, April 11, 1929.

41 Gogarty, *Seanad Éireann Debates*, April 11, 1929.

42 William E. Thrift, *Dáil Éireann Debates*, October 18, 1928, www.oireachtas.ie/ en/debates/debate/dail/1928-10-18/19/.

43 Terence Brown, *Ireland: A Social and Cultural History 1922–2002* (London: Harper Perennial, 2004), 9–10; Howes, *Yeats's Nations*, 136, 138, 213. See also John Anthony O'Brien, ed., *The Vanishing Irish: The Enigma of the Modern World* (New York: McGraw, 1953); Timothy Guinnane, *The Vanishing Irish: Households, Migration, and the Rural Economy in Ireland, 1850–1914* (Princeton: Princeton University Press, 1997).

44 Seán Kennedy, "FIRST LOVE: Abortion and Infanticide in Beckett and Yeats," *Samuel Beckett Today/Aujourd'hui* 22 (2010): 81.

45 Fitzgerald-Kenney, *Seanad Éireann Debates*, April 11, 1929.

46 Byrne, *Dáil Éireann Debates*, October 19, 1928.

47 Comyn, *Seanad Éireann Debates*, April 11, 1929; *Seanad Éireann Debates*, April 29, 1929, www.oireachtas.ie/en/debates/debate/seanad/1929-04-25/2/. Comyn's reference to a "Gaelic race" was not unusual, but according to Marianne Elliot, "the term 'Gaelic' is problematic. In strict scholarly terms it refers to the language spoken in Ireland (and Scotland), rather than to a particular race of people"; see *When God Took Sides: Religion and Identity in Ireland: Unfinished History* (Oxford: Oxford University Press, 2009), 22.

48 John Keane, *Seanad Éireann Debates*, April 11, 1929, www.oireachtas.ie/en/debates/debate/seanad/1929-04-11/3/.

49 O'Hanlon, *Dáil Éireann Debates*, October 19, 1928.

50 W. B. Yeats, "Censorship in Ireland: The Free State Bill: Senator W. B. Yeats's Views," interview by Irish Correspondent, *Manchester Guardian*, August 22, 1928.

51 Byrne, *Dáil Éireann Debates*, October 19, 1928.

52 W. B. Yeats, "Mr. Yeats on Irish Censorship: Driving Intellect into Exile: New Bill 'Full of Danger,'" interview by Special Correspondent, *Sunday Times*, October 21, 1928.

53 W. B. Yeats, "The Irish Censorship," Appendix V, in *The Senate Speeches of W. B. Yeats*, ed. Donald R. Pearce (Bloomington: Indiana University Press, 1960), 175, 178, 179.

54 Keane, *Seanad Éireann Debates*, April 11, 1929.

55 Samuel Beckett, "Censorship in the Saorstat," in *Disjecta: Miscellaneous Writings and a Dramatic Fragment*, ed. Ruby Cohn (New York: Gove Press, 1984), 84–88. I have published on Beckett's essay in "'Decorticated' Brains and 'Steriliz[ed]' Minds: Samuel Beckett and Irish Censorship," *Éire-Ireland* 51, no. 3–4 (2016): 188–215.

56 Yeats, "The Irish Censorship," 178.

57 Dennis Kennedy, *The Widening Gulf: Northern Attitudes to the Independent Irish State, 1919–49* (Belfast: The Blackstaff Press, 1988), 151–2.

58 Senia Pašeta, "Censorship and Its Critics in the Irish Free State 1922–1932," *Past & Present* no. 181 (2003): 195.

59 The contents of *Ne Temere* only discussed the validity of mixed marriages, but in practice, Irish priests would not officiate weddings until both bride and groom agreed to raise their children Catholic. See Eoin de Bhaldraithe, "Mixed Marriages and Irish Politics: The Effect of 'Ne Temere,'" *Studies: An Irish Quarterly Review* 77, no. 307 (1988): 284–99.

60 Kennedy, "FIRST LOVE," 82.

61 Yeats, "The Irish Censorship," 178.

62 Byrne, *Dáil Éireann Debates*, October 19, 1928. Despite Yeats not being present at the debate, Byrne mentions him four times; twice as "Senator Yeats" and twice as an "eminent" "critic" and Senator. In the latter instances, Byrne makes clear Yeats's identity by directly referencing the poet's claims in the *Manchester Guardian* and *The Spectator*.

63 Resolution 15, Lambeth Conference of 1930, Anglican Communion, www .anglicancommunion.org/resources/document-library/lambeth-conference/ 1930/resolution-15-the-life-and-witness-of-the-christian-community-marriage? year=1930.

64 The encyclical also addressed questions of gender roles and racial science, affirming a woman's place in the home and condemning forced sterilizations, calling out those who "put eugenics before aims of a higher order" by deciding who is "fit" for marriage and childbearing; Pius XI, *Casti connubii*, December 31, 1930, www.vatican.va/content/pius-xi/en/encyclicals/documents/hf_p-xi_ enc_19301231_casti-connubii.html.

65 W. B. Yeats, *Seanad Éireann Debates*, June 11, 1925, www.oireachtas.ie/en/ debates/debate/seanad/1925-06-11/12/.

66 W. B. Yeats, "A Race Philosophy," Appendix, in *W. B. Yeats: Man and Poet*, ed. A. Norman Jeffares (New York: Palgrave, 1996), 326.

67 Claire V. Nally writes that the text was "copied into his diary after the Blueshirt incident" in "The Political Occult: Revisiting Fascism, Yeats and *A Vision*," in *W. B. Yeats's "A Vision": Explications and Contexts*, ed. Neil Mann, Matthew Gibson, and Claire V. Nally (Clemson: Clemson University Digital Press, 2012), 340.

68 W. B. Yeats, "Genealogical Tree of Revolution," Appendix, in *W. B. Yeats: Man and Poet*, edited A. Norman Jeffares (New York: Palgrave, 1996), 325.

69 Yeats, "A Race Philosophy," 326.

70 From a draft of Yeats's "Tribute to Thomas Davis"; quoted in Elizabeth Cullingford, *Yeats, Ireland and Fascism* (London: Macmillan, 1981), 8.

71 Daniel G. Williams, *Ethnicity and Cultural Authority: From Arnold to Du Bois* (Edinburgh: Edinburgh University Press, 2006), 148.

72 Howes, *Yeats's Nations*, 162–3.

73 Childs, *Modernism and Eugenics*, 170. "In eugenics," Howes writes, Yeats "found an intellectual movement that seemed to gather together and confirm many important aspects of his race philosophy"; in *Yeats's Nations*, 166.

74 Quoted in David Bradshaw, "The Eugenics Movement in the 1930s and the Emergence of On the Boiler," *Yeats Annual* 9 (1992): 199, 209; William H. O'Donnell, ed., *The Collected Works of W.B. Yeats, Vol. V: Later Essays* (New York: Charles Scribner's Sons, 1994), 428.

75 Howes, *Yeats's Nations*, 169.

76 Donald Childs, "Class and Eugenics," in *W. B. Yeats in Context*, ed. David Holdeman and Ben Levitas (Cambridge: Cambridge University Press, 2010), 169, 176.

77 Howes, *Yeats's Nations*, 106–7.

78 Paul, *Controlling Human Heredity*, 102.

79 Galton, *Hereditary Genius*, 4, 1.

80 Georgie Yeats also owned a copy of William McDougall's *National Welfare and National Decay* (1921). See Bradshaw, "The Eugenics Movement," 200.

81 O'Donnell, *The Collected Works*, 429; Charles John Bond, "Causes of Racial Decay: Distribution of Natural Capacity: the Need for a National Stocktaking," *Eugenics Review* 20 (April 1928): 5–19; W. B. Yeats, *On the Boiler*, in *The Collected Works of W.B. Yeats, Vol. V: Later Essays*, ed. William H. O'Donnell (New York: Charles Scribner's Sons, 1994), 429.

82 William H. Tucker, *The Cattell Controversy: Race, Science, and Ideology* (Urbana: University of Illinois Press, 2009), 91; Yeats, *On the Boiler*, 428.

83 Yeats, *On the Boiler*, 428. Yeats's footnote cites a Scottish study of three hundred children, which found some "improvement" among the children, but he undermines this conclusion via Cattell's commentary on the study. Yeats's assertion about twins mirrors Galton's conclusions in *Inquiries into Human Faculty*, 216–243.

84 Yeats, *On the Boiler*, 229, 428.

85 Yeats, *On the Boiler*, 229.

86 Yeats, *On the Boiler*, 242.

87 Stanfield, *Yeats and Politics*, 26; Howes, *Yeats's Nations*, 103.

88 Abdul R. JanMohamed, "The Economy of Manichean Allegory: The Function of Racial Difference in Colonialist Literature," *Critical Inquiry* 12, no. 1 (1985): 67.

89 Spurgeon Thompson, "Yeats and Eugenicism: The Garrison Mentality in a Decolonizing Ireland," in *W. B. Yeats and Postcolonialism*, ed. Deborah Fleming (West Cornwall, Connecticut: Locust Hill Press, 2001): 37, 47, 27. Thompson notes that "Garrison" is a "conflicted term" and not equivalent with the term "Protestant Ascendancy" (39).

90 Seamus Deane, "Heroic Styles: The Tradition of an Idea," in *Ireland's Field Day* (Notre Dame: Notre Dame University Press, 1986), 53–54.

91 Thompson, "Yeats and Eugenicism," 38, 36, 27.

92 Linked to the nineteenth-century term "racialism," the term "racism" was first used at the turn of the twentieth century. It designated "prejudice, antagonism, or discrimination by an individual, institution, or society, against a person or people on the basis of their nationality or" "membership of a particular racial or ethnic group." Racism is also defined as "an ideology" or set of "beliefs that members of a particular racial or ethnic group possess innate characteristics or qualities, or that some racial or ethnic groups are superior to others." See "racism, n.," in *OED Online*, Oxford University Press.

93 Shirley Lau Wong, "Race, Place, and the Grounds of Irish Geopolitics," *Race in Irish Literature and Culture* (Cambridge: Cambridge University Press, 2024), 314.

94 Yeats, *On the Boiler*, 232, 230.

95 Yeats, *On the Boiler*, 235.

96 Childs, "Class and Eugenics," 176.

97 Yeats, *On the Boiler*, 234.

98 Childs, "Class and Eugenics," 174.

99 Yeats, *On the Boiler*, 234. Galton also compared mating between humans to horse breeding; see *Hereditary Genius*, 1.

100 Howes, *Yeats's Nations*, 174.

101 Yeats, *On the Boiler*, 224.

102 Childs, "Class and Eugenics," 174.

103 Yeats, *On the Boiler*, 238.

104 Valente, "Aging Yeats," 178–79. Scholars debate Yeats's relationship with fascism, including its representation in *On the Boiler*. Howes, for instance, writes that his race philosophy and eugenics "were certainly not fascism" in *Yeats's Nations*, 185.

105 Yeats, *On the Boiler*, 238, 241, 231.

106 The term "culture war" comes from the German, "Kulturkampf." Since the nineteenth century, the term has applied to "*(a)* a political struggle for control of cultural and educational institutions *(rare)*; (b) a conflict between groups with different ideals, beliefs, philosophies, etc.; (now) *spec.* (in the United States) an ideological struggle for political and cultural dominance between conservatives and liberals." See "culture war, n.," in *OED Online*, Oxford University Press.

107 Yeats, *On the Boiler*, 231.

108 Filippo Tommaso Marinetti, "War, the only Hygiene of the World," in *Futurism: An Anthology*, ed. Lawrence Rainey, Christine Poggi, and Laura Wittman (New Haven: Yale University Press, 2009), 84–85. Marinetti repeats the phrase in other Futurist writings as well.

109 W. B. Yeats, "Easter 1916," in *The Collected Poems of W. B. Yeats*, ed. Richard J. Finneran (New York: Scribner, 1983), 180–182.

110 Elizabeth Cullingford, *Yeats, Ireland and Fascism* (London: Macmillan 1981), 231, 228.

111 Bernard McKenna, "Yeats, On the Boiler, the Aesthetics of Cultural Disintegration and the Program for Renewal 'of our own rich experience,'" *Journal of Modern Literature* 35, no. 4 (2012): 74, 88; Bradshaw, "The Eugenics Movement," 88.

112 David Bradshaw, "Eugenics: 'They should certainly be killed,'" in *A Concise Companion to Modernism*, ed. David Bradshaw (Malden, MA: Blackwell, 2003): 48; W. J. McCormack, *Blood Kindred: W.B. Yeats: The Life, the Death, the Politics* (London: Pimlico, 2005), 40.

113 Howes, *Yeats's Nations*, 176.

114 Quoted in Richard Ellmann, *Yeats: The Man and the Masks* (New York: Norton, 1948), 278.

115 Quoted in Howes, *Yeats's Nations*, 173.

CHAPTER 8

"Ulster's White Negroes"
Rhetoric of Race at the Start of the Troubles

Simon Prince

On a Saturday afternoon in October 1968, thousands of people sat down in Derry's main square and began to sing "We shall overcome." This sit-down rally had been organized by the Derry Citizens' Action Committee (DCAC) as "the first step in a campaign of non-violent protest." A fortnight earlier, the Unionist government had banned a civil rights march, and the Royal Ulster Constabulary (RUC) had beaten those who had turned out in defiance off the street; now, the police could not stop the civil rights movement taking physical and symbolic ownership of the city center. One of the DCAC leaders, Fionbarra Ó Dochartaigh, explained to "the representatives of the international Press" that the protesters were "the white Negroes of Derry."[1] In the existing scholarship on the start of the Troubles, this phrase is taken as evidence of how activists told the foreign media stories about the movement that aligned it with its American namesake. Two minority groups were suffering from discrimination, people from both had marched to call for their equal rights, and they had met the same violent response from the authorities.[2] But Ó Dochartaigh was drawing parallels with southern Africa, not the southern United States of America. He asked the journalists to let the Prime Minister of the United Kingdom know that the "white Negroes" "demand the same thing here that [he is] demanding for the blacks in Rhodesia."[3] Just eleven months later, it was the UK Representative telling 10 Downing Street that "Ulster was essentially a colonial situation."[4] Transnational connections went south and east as well as west.

This chapter highlights how activists at the start of the Troubles employed various rhetorics of race to imagine their roles within a changing world.[5] Northern Ireland during the "long Sixties" may have been almost entirely white, but it was also a networked space.[6] The movement of people, goods, and ideas across borders tied it into complex, overlapping networks; the local was enmeshed with the national, the imperial, and the global. Decolonization – "an entire spectrum of political, economic, social, and cultural changes" – was in the process of breaking and remaking these webs.[7] Irish migrants in Britain washed up among men and women who had traveled there over the oceans from Asia, Africa, and the Caribbean, as the imperial tide rolled back.[8] Irish soldiers in the British Army fought small wars against Malayan Communists, Kenya's Mau Mau, Greek-Cypriot nationalists, and Arab Marxist-Leninists. Irish participants in British imperial projects either packed up their belongings or tried to belong in an independent country.[9] With the partial retreat of Europe's colonial powers, the Global South became a battlefield in the Cold War between the United States of America and the Soviet Union. The "Third World," as it came to be known, appeared to be where the future of the whole world would be decided. Some on the radical left in North America and Europe saw in the national liberation fronts the energy and potential that Western labor movements and Eastern Communist states had both long ago lost. By forming concrete connections and imagining solidarities with Third World revolutionaries, these individuals and groups were able to construct new ideas, images, and identifications.[10] Black Power activists, for example, styled themselves as urban guerrillas, working to turn the rebellions in the Third World exclaves of the inner cities into a revolution.[11] In the case of Northern Ireland, making local politics out of these global materials proved to be explosive. Less than a year after Derry's first civil rights march, leftists were giving Black Power salutes behind the barricades of "Free Derry." The Unionist government had to call the British Army into the city's streets to end the "Battle of the Bogside": a small war had begun in the United Kingdom itself.[12] Loyalists, who had had their mental maps of the world redrawn, responded to the British intervention by asserting their Britishness. Following riots in the fall of 1969, Loyalist leaders told army officers that people from Belfast's Shankill district deserved to be treated better than "wogs."[13] Imagined solidarities could be reactionary as well as progressive.

Focusing on the fringes of Irish politics, this chapter sketches out some of the complex, contradictory, and ambiguous ways in which rhetorics of race were used. After setting out the impact of American race crises on the United Kingdom, the first section explores the transatlantic linkages between Black Power activists and Northern Irish leftists. The next section analyzes how some in the Irish Republican Army (IRA) embraced Third Worldism as the future of the movement – while others saw it as a betrayal of the past. The chapter's final section examines two related incidents of Loyalist racism from the fall of 1969 in their British imperial and national contexts.

When Dungannon Urban District Council met in May 1963, a crowd of women and children gathered outside to protest its unfair housing policies. One of the picketers carried a placard with the slogan "If Our Religion Is Against Us Ship Us to Little Rock."[14] The Birmingham movement had ended a week before, yet the campaigners chose to reference the struggle to desegregate Little Rock's schools from six years earlier. Birmingham was still an American story, but Little Rock was becoming, as Kennetta Hammond Perry writes, "an iconic transnational topography of race."[15] During the summer of 1958, almost a year after the nine Black American teenagers had been blocked from attending school by national guardsmen, white youths assaulted Black people living in the British cities of Nottingham and London. For perpetrators, victims, journalists, police officers, and politicians, the Little Rock narrative was a means of making sense of what had happened. Figures on the far right of politics warned that mass immigration risked dividing communities along racial lines and bringing about a series of British "Little Rocks." Anti-racist activists blamed the riots on bigots akin to those found in Little Rock – whom most of the British press and public had been condemning for the previous twelve months. The mainstream view of the violence, however, contrasted events rather than compared them. Britain's cities had witnessed neither a clash of cultures nor attacks that revealed how widespread racism was in society, but instead had suffered an upsurge in hooliganism in some deprived districts during a heat wave.[16] Closing off comparisons with the southern United States of America was as much about how Britain was seen abroad as about how Britons saw themselves. Since the end of the Second World War, agents of the British state had constructed a transnational narrative in which a liberal, tolerant country sat at the heart of a multi-racial Commonwealth of equals. Soft power buttressed hard power: British policymakers wanted to tie the newly independent nations of Africa and Asia into strategic partnerships, retain a leadership role in Western Europe, and contain the Soviet Union.[17] England's difficulty was once again Ireland's opportunity. By citing Little Rock, Dungannon's "white negroes" – a phrase used in the local newspaper – were calling on Britain to live up to its self-proclaimed values and address discrimination in its own "Deep South."[18] Five years later, Ó Dochartaigh did a similar thing in Derry. The Prime Minister, he told the international press, did not have the moral authority to demand the Rhodesian government accept the principle of majority rule while people in his own country were being denied their democratic rights.

By 1968, another international race crisis, Black Power, had hit. Again, ideas from the United States of America, the Third World, and urban Britain were pulled together and carried to Northern Ireland. Eamonn McCann, the main organizer of the first Derry civil rights march, met Black Power leaders while active in London's Trotskyist networks.[19] The year before McCann went back to Northern Ireland, he attended the 1967 Congress on the Dialectics of Liberation.[20] The headline act was the former chair of the Student Non-violent Co-ordinating Committee (SNCC), Stokely Carmichael. "Black Power," Carmichael explained to the congress, "means that black people ... see our struggle as closely related to liberation struggles around the world." He went as far as to class Black Americans among the "peoples of the Third World" and the inner cities as "very real colonies." For Carmichael, the urban riots "occurring in the United States" ("and England is not far behind") were "rebellions." Black Power activists were "working to increase the revolutionary consciousness" of the young people clashing with the police in Buffalo, Newark, and many other places during that long, hot summer. "While we disrupt internally and aim for the eye of the octopus," Carmichael continued, "we are hoping that our brothers are disrupting externally to sever the tentacles of the United States." Indeed, the main battles "must be waged from the Third World" because the "proletariat has become the Third World." Still, Carmichael was confident that Black Power had an important part to play and that urban uprisings would ultimately bring "guerrilla warfare" home from the global south.[21] Looking back four decades later at this speech and his subsequent conversations with Carmichael, McCann recalled him being "a big figure to conjure with."[22] Such was the impact of this encounter upon McCann and his circle that two months afterward the newspaper he edited – the *Irish Militant* – began urging its readers to "do what the Afro-Americans are doing."[23]

Carmichael's London visit ended up indirectly shaping McCann's thinking, too. Following the Congress on the Dialectics of Liberation, another participant, the Trinidadian intellectual C. L. R. James, noted in a speech how "Stokely" had "made the slogan Black Power reverberate." For Britain's Black diaspora, Carmichael's narrative connected much more with their experiences than the civil rights one had. James, though, wanted to stress how Black Power had a deeper history as well as a wider geographical reach. It was the latest "banner" "under which men have struggled for liberty and freedom" – "a banner for people with certain political aims, needs and attitudes." As he reminded his listeners, James had played his own part in the long march toward Black equality across the Atlantic when he had helped the Socialist Workers' Party organize Black Americans in the late 1930s. He had convinced Trotsky himself that the "Negroes in fighting for their democratic rights were making an indispensable addition to the struggle for socialism." Carmichael, according to James, was continuing this journey, getting through the steps in his own time. While he was "far away out," Carmichael was not marching on his own. The future of Black Power globally, James concluded, "depend[ed]" too on "what you who are listening to me ... do."[24] This reading of Black Power influenced an article that McCann wrote in the September 1967 issue of the *Irish Militant* on "The Negro Revolution."[25] Making a revolution within the revolution was what the "Afro-Americans" were doing.

Michael Farrell – a contributor to the *Irish Militant* who had known McCann since their student days at Queen's University Belfast – was explicit about how the Catholic minority in Northern Ireland could play the same role as Black Americans were playing in the United States of America. Once more, given Farrell's connection to Trotskyist networks, James was the lodestar. After Farrell came back to Belfast from Britain, he set up the Young Socialist Alliance in the summer of 1968 "to bring ... together" "the younger political activists." He got "in touch with [the] group of the same name in the United States" and received "a lot of literature."[26] Out of all this material, it was the writings of George Breitman, who had been a founding member of the Socialist Workers' Party, that "particularly impressed."[27] In one pamphlet, the veteran Trotskyist set out "How A Minority Can Change Society" by "[forcing] concessions from the ruling class," "[helping] to educate and radicalize," and "[becoming] part of the general movement of the exploited and oppressed to abolish capitalism."[28] Farrell believed that the Catholic minority was capable of liberating their "neo-colonial" society. In places where the minority was the majority, leftists should try to get the "local Catholic population" "to take over and run its own affairs." "Protestant workers" would see that these "socialist councils" "fulfil[ed] class demands rather than creed demands" – and, so Farrell assumed, "want to create councils for themselves or merge with the Catholics in them." "Catholic Power" would give way to "a revolution in Ireland."[29]

Neither Farrell nor McCann were innovative political thinkers, but their political work in Northern Ireland did represent a new approach. As McCann later recalled, he had "a conviction" that "we could possibly sweep over the local, provincial politics" by "introducing the international dimension to it."[30] This conviction was what he brought to the ad-hoc alliance of Republican and Labour left-wingers that had formed in Derry prior to his homecoming. This grouping had helped homeless families squat in empty properties, tried to block evictions, and disrupted council meetings.[31] Under McCann's leadership, the alliance's tactics became even more confrontational. A year earlier, Carmichael had called on white American leftists to "create disturbances ... keep pushing the system ... until they have to hit back [because] once your enemy hits back, then your revolution starts."[32] In September 1968, Derry's radicals told the media they were going to "fight to force the powers-that-be to act": to build "houses for the homeless or a new wing to Crumlin Road Prison."[33] Creating disturbances, however, was proving difficult. Over the summer, at a failed attempt to occupy the council chamber, one of the activists despaired that "there were not people in Derry prepared to fight ... as the blacks in America were fighting."[34] The overwhelming majority of Derry citizens were not doing what the Black Americans were doing. McCann and the alliance looked to bring people into Derry from Ireland and Britain – and a language of race helped promote the confrontation.

"Everyone," McCann acknowledged a few years later, knew that the "one certain way to ensure a head-on clash with the authorities was to organize a non-Unionist march through the city."[35] The radicals tried to stage one in July 1968, but they found that there was not enough support in Derry to defy the police ban. The pretext for that abandoned march had been to mark the centenary of the birth of James Connolly, a revolutionary socialist who had been one of the leaders of the 1916 Easter Rising.[36] When they tried again, in the fall, the alliance framed that planned march as being about civil rights. This cause was one that gained the support of most of the opposition groups in Northern Ireland, leftists and Republicans from across the border, and three British Labour Members of Parliament (MPs). On October 5, 1968, RUC officers in riot gear lined up to stop them from making it to the city center.[37] The head-on clash that McCann wanted did not come about straightaway, however. The leftists pushed the front ranks of the march into the police cordon, yet the two sides quickly backed off, and an improvised meeting followed. A veteran Communist told the crowd that they had made their point and that they should now disperse. According to the testimony he himself gave at his trial, McCann took a different line when it was his turn to address the meeting. He said he was "not advising anyone to rush the police," but nor was he going to "stop anyone."[38] McCann's fellow leftists hurled "Sieg Heil" taunts and a fusillade of missiles at the police. The officer in charge ordered his men to draw their batons and to "clear the mob."[39] One of the radicals later recalled watching the violence that followed: "McCann and I sort of looked at one

another ... and he said: 'God, the revolution has started!'"[40] And this revolution was televised. Footage of RUC officers and water canon knocking
marchers, onlookers, and even shoppers to the floor played on the nightly
news in Ireland, Britain, and beyond.[41]

In Belfast, Farrell and his alliance had been searching for an issue that
would serve as a "bridge to involvement" for students; with civil rights,
they now had it.[42] On October 9, 1968, hundreds of students marched
in solidarity with Derry from Queen's University toward city hall. When
Loyalists and the police blocked their progress, the students reacted by
holding a sit-down protest and by transforming the march into a movement, the People's Democracy. "Student Power," the campus newspaper
announced, "had come to Belfast."[43] Kevin Boyle, a young law professor popular with his students, subsequently admitted that this movement
was manipulated from the start by older activists. Indeed, Farrell was
present at the founding meeting and gradually came to control People's
Democracy.[44] As had happened with other student movements in North
America and Western Europe, People's Democracy turned to Black
Power for inspiration.[45] Boyle produced for the students a "List of Books
on Black Politics," which had on it *SNCC: The New Abolitionists, The
Autobiography of Malcolm X, Look Out, Whitey! Black Power's Gonna' Get
Your Mama, Soul on Ice*, and *The Wretched of the Earth*.[46] Black Power was
shaping thinking; it was also encouraging more confrontational practices.
People's Democracy publications urged students to make "the relations
of domination ... apparent" by "provok[ing]" "the bureaucracy ... into
showing its dictatorial nature" – something which could not be done by
"protest action."[47]

When the Northern Irish Prime Minister promised a package of
reforms in late November 1968 and made a televised appeal for calm a
fortnight later, most students welcomed those moves and voted to pause
their protests. Farrell, however, was now in a position to make sure that
revolt did not give way to reform. The faction around Farrell exploited
participatory democracy and the holidays to secure a small vote in favor
of marching from Belfast to Derry in the New Year. Farrell explicitly took
as his model the SNCC's Selma to Montgomery march in 1965.[48] "Either
the government would face up to the extreme right [and] protect the
march," Farrell wrote afterward, "or it would be exposed as impotent in
the face of sectarian thuggery."[49] The independent inquiry into the start
of the Troubles concluded that Farrell had been seeking "a calculated
martyrdom." He found it at Burntollet Bridge, in the Unionist heartland
where he had grown up, when off-duty special constables ambushed the

marchers. News of this outrage provoked rioting in nearby Derry that was far fiercer than what had happened on October 5, 1968.[50] Revolution once more seemed possible.

During the first half of 1969, further acts of police brutality and Loyalist vigilantism pushed both the Derry movement and People's Democracy away from non-violence and toward self-defense. Black Power offered the leftists a language that they could use to negotiate this shift in direction. The rising tensions climaxed in Northern Ireland's own long, hot summer. On August 12, 1969, RUC officers pursued a gang of youthful rioters into Derry's nationalist neighborhood – and were chased back out again by what a local priest called a "community in revolt."[51] McCann emerged as one of the leaders of the district's defense, liaising with contacts in London over how best to combat the effects of CS gas.[52] After three days of street fighting, with the RUC planning to fall back to its barracks and to defend them with firearms, the Prime Minister of the United Kingdom authorized the use of the British Army. McCann published a "Barricade Bulletin" declaring "Derry is in a state of war" and promising "[we] shall beat the soldiers as we have now beaten the police." Derry, however, would not be another Detroit. The British Army did not try to occupy the district, the rioting died down, and "Free Derry" remained outside the United Kingdom. While conceding that it was "impossible to build a socialist society in one ghetto," McCann demanded free bus rides, fair rents, and equal pay for women.[53] But, for the vast majority of people in "the liberated area," nationalism mattered more than socialism and Ireland more than internationalism. The defining event of "Free Derry" was a "liberation" *Fleadh Cheoil* at which traditional Irish dancing and music were performed by artists from all over the island.[54]

The summer violence made the leading leftists into international media stars. Boyle and two other People's Democracy activists, Eilis McDermott and Bernadette Devlin, toured the United States of America during the fall of 1969. In New York, such was Devlin's popularity among Irish Americans that the Mayor gave her the key to the city. Politicians elsewhere, though, quickly came to realize that the leftists believed, as McDermott put it in an article for a People's Democracy newssheet, the "Black Panthers [had] more to offer to our movement in terms of advice and support than have many of the sentimental Irish-American populations." In Boston, members of the Black Panther Party, not the Democratic Party, gave McDermott an award, making her an "honorary Black Panther sister."[55] These ties deepened with each fresh tour. When McCann visited New York that spring, he handed the key given to Devlin over to the Black Panthers as a "gesture of solidarity." "The more we alienate ... Irish American hypocrites, so much the better."[56] Conflating identification and interest, the leftists did not fully appreciate that there were useful alliances to be made. The rhetoric of race could close off as well as open up political opportunities.

Back in Derry, during the spring of 1970, McCann defended the Black Panthers against the accusation that they were "anti-white": "They are ... insistent of the necessity to seek and accept the support of white groups." His latest political vehicle, the Derry Youth Organization, sought and accepted support from them. McCann screened a Black Panther propaganda film which caused the "little Che Guevaras" in the audience to "roar and cheer."[57] Like Carmichael, McCann was looking to increase the revolutionary consciousness of the teenagers fighting in the streets. British intelligence was impressed by the attempt to "steer" "the youths." But his "efforts" soon came to be resented by the "hard core" and a group of them "beat [him] up" in October 1970.[58] The Provisional IRA – a traditionalist breakaway group – were to have far greater success winning converts. Three months after being attacked, McCann left for London.[59]

In September 1963, Roy Johnston took the boat back to Ireland after years of living in London. Sailing across the Irish Sea, he wrote what he later described as "some notes on how I saw the movement for Irish national unity and liberation." Since his school days, Johnston had been a revolutionary socialist – but he wanted to be independent of Communist politics. While he was at the École Polytechnique in the early 1950s, Johnston had been "aware of Sartre." After moving to London for work, however, he took a greater interest in the Paris intellectuals and "became aware of most of the others."[60] For French thinkers, decolonization was opening up a "third way" that was distinct from both American liberalism and Soviet socialism. The term "the Third World" was first used in 1952 by a Frenchman, economic historian Alfred Sauvy, who concluded that it had, "like the Third Estate, been ignored and despised and it too wants to be something."[61] Revolutionaries from the Global South were cast as the world-historical actors who were to lead the overthrow of the northern old regimes. Johnston had found a model to adopt and adapt to Ireland. As he sat on the ferry sketching out his Irish revolution, the *Monthly Review*'s special issue on Cuba guided his thinking. The American editors of this socialist magazine set out how "12 men" on "the topmost peak in the Sierra Mountains" succeeded in making a revolution.[62] And how they had done it without the Old Left, too. Johnston recalled marveling at the way "a broad-based movement of politicized working people, rural as well as urban, in the country as a whole, had ... upstaged ... a narrow doctrinaire

urban 'workerist' party based on the orthodoxy of the Communist international movement."[63]

In a draft paper that he wrote shortly after his return, Johnston dis-
mantled the boundaries separating Ireland from the Third World to
build a new revolutionary vision for Ireland. "There are two camps today
in the world," he explained, "the rich nations and the poor nations. By
tradition and inclination Ireland is the senior member of the latter."
Johnston had decentered the map of world politics – and had then
re-centered it on an island in the Atlantic. This claim about Ireland's
international standing was not so much outrageous as outdated: during the interwar years, as "the first example of 'successful' rebellion
against the British Empire," the Irish War of Independence offered a
"blueprint" to anti-colonial nationalists in India and elsewhere.[64] With
the postwar wave of decolonization cresting, Johnston hoped to wash
away what was left of imperialism in Ireland. He wanted Irish people
to "throw in our lot with Africa and jointly to achieve independence
from imperialism."[65] The similarities with what Carmichael would be
saying three years later were because both took inspiration from Frantz
Fanon – a French-trained psychiatrist from Martinique who became
a propagandist for the Algerian national liberation struggle. In *The
Wretched of the Earth* (1961), which had a preface from Sartre, Fanon
predicted that "the European model" was heading toward the abyss and
that the oppressed of the Third World were starting a new history of
humanity.[66] For Johnston, Ireland's future was not in the European
Community but in struggle. He arrived back home to find that the new
IRA leadership was receptive to his ideas.

At the start of 1962, the IRA had abandoned a military campaign,
Operation Harvest, due to the success of the security forces and the gunmen's failure to gain support for the cause. The new Chief of Staff, Cathal
Goulding, began looking outside his own ranks to find people with fresh
approaches. As a member of the Wolfe Tone Societies and later as the
IRA's Political Education Officer, Johnston provided them.[67] The notes
that he had sketched out were expanded into a strategy of "economic
resistance." In the April 1965 issue of the *Irish Democrat*, Johnston told
migrants in Britain that Republicans were seeking to lead "a national
social-economic movement of resistance to the economic forces of imperialism." After "a 26-County 'liberated area' government" took power,
it would oversee the capitalist economy until it gave way to "municipal
or co-operative social ownership" and the state until it gave way to "a
federation of people's organizations." A socialist society was a compelling
necessity if the Irish people were to be free. One of the main goals of the

new regime would be the reunification of Ireland. It would pass laws for the whole island, exploit every available means to enforce them north of the border, and appeal for aid from "the anti-imperialist element in the United Nations."[68]

This new departure was not embraced by everyone in the Republican movement. When Johnston invited Kadar Asmal – a South African exile and co-founder of the Irish Anti-Apartheid Movement – to address an IRA meeting, one of the volunteers called their guest "a coon." A variety of resentments with the leadership had latched on to race. The mass immigration of ideas into the movement was dissolving its culture and traditions. As a prominent dissident put it in a July 1969 speech, "one is now expected to be more conversant with the teachings of Chairman Mao than with those of our dead patriots."[69] Anticipating this line of criticism, Goulding had from the start stressed his position's Irish genealogy: Connolly and Liam Mellows were Marxists, Tone was seeking to unite Protestant, Catholic, and Dissenter.[70] Irish nationality was not based on a common ancestry, but on a shared homeland; Goulding's national liberation struggle did not have any Pieds-Noirs to expel from the country. An August 1966 article in the Wolfe Tone Societies newsletter explained that the "Orange masses" would become part of the "movement for independence" once they were "enlighten[ed]" about the "real nature of Britain's imperialist policy."[71] In struggle, the wretched of Ireland would be forged into a single people. Dissident Republicans, however, continued to see a Loyalist as the other rather than a brother.

The dissidents also complained that Goulding was running down the army, but his national liberation movement still had a role for guerrillas. In the words of its Adjutant-General, the IRA "maintain[ed] disciplined armed forces which will always be available to strike."[72] During the first night of the August 1969 violence in Derry, the IRA veteran in charge of the local defense association called for activities around Northern Ireland that would drain police resources.[73] The next day, in west Belfast, IRA men rained down petrol bombs on a RUC barracks and opened fire on a patrol sent out to flank them. On August 14, 1969, fierce fighting between Republicans and Loyalists only ended after the British Army was deployed.[74] A guerrilla war had started. For a moment, their common Third Worldism brought Goulding's IRA, McCann's Derry Labour, and Farrell's People's Democracy together in the National Liberation Front. Throughout the fall of 1969, McCann had small-arms training with other Labour activists in a secret IRA camp across the Irish border.[75] Following a series of clandestine meetings in the spring of 1970, People's Democracy joined the coalition, too. Seven years after Johnston had sketched out his plan, Goulding sent an IRA volunteer to Cuba to get weapons to fight Ireland's war of national liberation.[76]

On the night of October 11/12, 1969, Loyalist gunmen in the Shankill district of Belfast exchanged fire with British soldiers. Thousands of rounds of ammunition were let loose, hundreds were injured, and three people were killed.[77] A fortnight later, senior officers from the Parachute Regiment and representatives from the Shankill Defence Association (SDA) held talks. According to the army's record of the meeting, the SDA leaders were anxious for "an exchange of confidence." The army would have theirs if it came to recognize whose side British soldiers should be on in Northern Ireland. Contrary to the media's framing of the conflict as being about the denial of civil rights, the Loyalists insisted that it was, in fact, "the IRA men and the Communist agitators (PD [People's Democracy]) who ... started the troubles in Ulster." SDA members, they "repeatedly declared," were "loyal ... to the Queen"; many had even served in Her Majesty's armed forces. The officers, though, restated their commitment to upholding the law – which led to "the tone of the meeting" becoming "blunt and aggressive." One man warned that the Shankill would riot if Bernadette Devlin did not get sent to prison, another "walked out" when the Lieutenant Colonel told him that his soldiers would shoot at Loyalists if lives were in danger. "This is unfair," complained someone in the room as the meeting neared its close. "We are not wogs."[78]

This racial slur had been circulating around British imperial space since at least the 1920s. "Wog" is most likely an abbreviation of "golliwog" – a character from turn-of-the-century children's literature that its American-born English creator had based on blackface minstrels. As its probable origins suggest, white Britons first hurled the word at West Africans. Their use of the term soon became promiscuous; it could refer to anyone who was Black as well as anyone who was from Britain's Middle Eastern, Indian, Southeast Asian, or Mediterranean possessions.[79] During a debate on colonial matters in the House of Commons on July 29, 1949, a Labour MP remarked that Winston Churchill "thinks that the 'wogs' start at Calais."[80] The SDA was afraid that the boundaries separating the United Kingdom from its colonies had been redrawn and the Shankill now lay among the latter. In the course of their own service – in Palestine, Malaya, Kenya, Cyprus, or Aden – some of the SDA men may well have called the locals "wogs" to dehumanize them and justify dealing out violence.[81] But this rough treatment was not something those Loyalists ever expected to have inflicted upon them, their families, and their neighbors.

Regardless of whether the United Kingdom won or lost its small wars, the British empire continued to contract. For Britons with racist views, the flow of people had been reversed, with the "wogs" flooding into their country. On the BBC comedy series *Till Death Us Do Part*, which aimed to reflect and challenge popular attitudes, the anti-hero Alf Garnett raged against these migrants. One of his central criticisms was that the Black and Asian newcomers sponged off the welfare state. The "wogs" were taking what was not theirs: medical care and benefit payments were rewards for the collective sacrifice the British people had made in the Second World War.[82] As a real-life Garnett put it in a letter to the Conservative MP Enoch Powell attacking the policy of mass immigration, "the dirtiest traitors on God's earth, for the sake of a rotten, old tradition of a dead empire ... have wrenched our birth-right from us."[83] For the SDA, confusing Loyalists with "wogs" was to make a mistake about history as well as geography: Ulster *had* fought. Throughout the meeting with the paratroopers, speakers stressed that the residents of the Shankill were fully entitled to their benefits. This argument, however, was another one that failed to persuade the British officers. In the report, "working men" had delegitimizing quotation marks put around it and references were made to "the dole" and "welfare cases."[84] At a time when anti-immigration campaigns were applying the colonial rhetoric of racial hierarchies, Loyalists had reason to fear they were sliding down the ladder.

The year before, in April 1968, Powell – who firmly believed that the people of Ulster were part of the British nation – warned that, even in Tory-voting England, the old order was being upset. He had watched "with horror" as American cities burned that month and worried that mass immigration was bringing the "tragic and intractable" problem of racial conflict to Britain. Quoting an "ordinary working man," Powell predicted that "in fifteen or twenty years' time the black man will have the whip hand over the white man."[85] For the SDA, the harbinger of this world turned upside down was Lance Corporal Everton Roach. The Barbardian paratrooper was one of "the 2,000 odd coloured men in the Army." As the British press had revealed at the end of 1968, the government placed "Limits on Coloured Recruits": 3 percent of all enlisted men.[86] Back in 1961, the Army Council had reasoned that the policy was needed because "the reliability of coloured soldiers is not certain," the "recruitment of a large number ... might effect prestige," and "a white soldier ... does not like to serve under [them]."[87] Seven years later, "Senior NCOs in the Guards Division – where "Irishmen from Eire get in quite nicely" – told the Ministry of Defence that "they would walk out" "if they had any coloured men in their Regiment."[88] Roach, therefore, stood out and put white people out. After the night of October 11/12, 1969, the sole Black soldier was the only paratrooper the SDA individually targeted for revenge. The gossip on the Shankill was that Roach had been brutal with his rifle butt; this was likely just a pretext for a racist attack.[89] Loyalists, though, failed in restoring the old racial order. "Every day," the *Daily Mirror* reported in November 1969, "rifle on hip, [Roach] strolls along Shankill-road with a smile, trailing behind him a band of children."[90] What it meant to be British and what it meant to be a Loyalist were both changing. In the years ahead, these changes helped to shape both government policy and Loyalist identifications and alliances.

"There must be an all-out effort to build an effective solidarity movement," argued the *Red Mole* in July 1970: "The great reserves of Irish workers in Britain are ready to be mobilized.... And in mobilizing them we will begin to mobilize their British fellow workers, not to speak of the Black workers."[91] Leftists in North America and continental Europe also claimed solidarity with "Ulster's white negroes" to build transnational networks and local support.[92] Historical contexts, social relations, economic conditions, cultural traditions, and political practices were all glossed. Bernadette Devlin complained that in one American solidarity committee, "the only qualification for being an expert on Northern Ireland was to have been involved in the Californian grape strike."[93] A few Irish activists began to realize that they, too, had been looking at a mirror more than through a window.[94] Transnationalism had its limits; but the poverty of knowledge was what made rhetorics of race such a rich resource. Having the space to imagine other people and places made it possible to have the space to imagine a different Northern Ireland.

Notes

1 *Derry Journal*, October 22, 1968.
2 Gregory Maney, "White Negroes and the Pink IRA: External Mainstream Media Coverage and Civil Rights Contention in Northern Ireland," in *The Troubles in Northern Ireland and Theories of Social Movements*, eds. Lorenzo Bosi and Gianluca De Fazio (Amsterdam: Amsterdam University Press, 2017), 76.
3 *Derry Journal*, October 22, 1968.
4 UK Representative, "Situation Report," September 13, 1969, CJ3/18, London, National Archives of the United Kingdom (hereafter NAUK).
5 Stephen Howe, *Ireland and Empire: Colonial Legacies in Irish History and Culture* (Cambridge: Cambridge University Press, 2000). Howe offers a

broader discussion of how languages of imperialism and colonialism have been used to interpret the Troubles. Jodi Burkett, *Constructing Post-Imperial Britain: Britishness, "Race" and the Radical Left in the 1960s* (Basingstoke: Palgrave, 2013). Burkett explores moderate civil rights groups as part of her wider history of white, middle-class Britain.

6 Government of Northern Ireland, *Census of Population 1961: General Report* (Belfast: HMSO, 1965).

7 Christoph Kalter, *The Discovery of the Third World: Decolonization and the Rise of the New Left in France, c.1950–1976* (Cambridge: Cambridge University Press, 2016), 21.

8 Clair Wills, *Lovers & Strangers: An Immigrant History of Post-war Britain* (London: Penguin, 2017).

9 Helen O'Shea, *Ireland and the End of the British Empire: The Republic and its Role in the Cyprus Emergency* (London: Bloomsbury, 2015), 2–12.

10 Quinn Slobodian, *Foreign Front: Third World Politics in Sixties West Germany* (Durham: Duke University Press, 2012).

11 Stokely Carmichael, *Stokely Speaks: Black Power Back to Pan-Africanism* (New York: Vintage Books, 1971), 77–100.

12 *Derry Journal*, September 5, 1969.

13 "Record of a Meeting of the Shankill Defence Association," November 3, 1969, WO305/4192, NAUK.

14 *Dungannon Observer*, May 18, 1963.

15 Kennetta Hammond Perry, "'Little Rock' in Britain: Jim Crow's Transatlantic Topographies," *Journal of British Studies* 51, no. 1 (January 2012): 158.

16 Wills, *Lovers & Strangers*, 158–173.

17 Perry, "'Little Rock' in Britain," 160–2.

18 *Dungannon Observer*, September 7, 1963.

19 Bob Purdie, *Politics in the Streets: The Origins of the Civil Rights Movement in Northern Ireland* (Belfast: Blackstaff, 1990), 228–9.

20 Transcript of BBC interview with Eamonn McCann, [summer 2008] (personal notes).

21 Carmichael, *Stokely Speaks*, 77–100.

22 Transcript of BBC interview with McCann.

23 *Irish Militant*, October 1967.

24 C. L. R. James, "Black Power" in *The C. L. R. James Reader*, ed. Anna Grimshaw (Oxford: Wiley-Blackwell, 1992), 363–75.

25 *Irish Militant*, September 1967.

26 Transcript of BBC interview with Michael Farrell, [summer 2008] (personal notes).

27 Purdie, *Politics in the Streets*, 230.

28 George Breitman, "How a Minority Can Change Society," *International Socialist Review* 25, no. 2 (Spring 1964): 34–41.

29 Anthony Barnett, "People's Democracy: A Discussion on Strategy," *New Left Review* 1, no. 55 (May-June 1969): 11–17.

30 Transcript of BBC interview with McCann.

31 *Reality,* Anniversary Edition 1968–9, D2560/4/2, Belfast, Public Record Office of Northern Ireland (hereafter PRONI).

32 Seymour Martin Lipset, *Rebellion in the University: A History of Student Activism in America* (London: Routledge, 1972), xxi.

33 *Derry Journal,* September 6, 1968.

34 *Derry Journal,* August 30, 1968.

35 Eamonn McCann, *War and an Irish Town* (London: Pluto Press, 1993), 91.

36 *Derry Journal,* July 23, 1968.

37 Government of Northern Ireland, *Disturbances in Northern Ireland (Cameron Report)* (Belfast: HMSO, 1969), 28; W. Meharg to J. Hill, December 19, 1968, HA32/2/30, PRONI.

38 *Derry Journal,* April 16, 1968.

39 RUC report, October 5, 1968, HA32/2/26, PRONI.

40 Transcript of BBC interview with Dermie McClenaghan, [summer 2008] (personal notes).

41 Rex Cathcart, *The Most Contrary Region: The BBC in Northern Ireland, 1924–84* (Belfast: Blackstaff, 1984), 207–8.

42 *Irish Militant,* October 1967; MI5 memorandum, February 18, 1969, PREM13/2842, NAUK.

43 *Gown,* October 22, 1968.

44 William Van Voris, *Violence in Ulster: An Oral Documentary* (Amherst: University of Massachusetts Press, 1975), 74.

45 Martin Klimke, *The Other Alliance: Student Protest in West Germany and the United States in the Global Sixties* (Princeton: Princeton University Press, 2011), 109.

46 Kevin Boyle, "List of Books on Black Politics," [n.d.], D3297/7, PRONI.

47 *Defamator,* no. 3, D3219/3, PRONI.

48 Kevin Boyle to James Heaney, [n.d.], D3297/1, PRONI.

49 Michael Farrell, *Northern Ireland: The Orange State* (London: Pluto Press, 1975), 249.

50 *Cameron Report,* 47.

51 Arthur Mulvey's evidence to the Scarman Tribunal, September 25, 1969, London, Institute of Advanced Legal Study (hereafter IALS), 62, 67.

52 *Irish Times,* September 5, 1969.

53 *Barricade Bulletin,* September 10, 1969, Belfast, Linen Hall Library Political Collection.

54 *Derry Journal,* September 2, 1969.

55 *Irish Rebel,* November 1969, D3297/2, PRONI; *Free Citizen,* no. 9, D3297/2, PRONI; Eilis McDermott, "Law and Disorder" in *Twenty Years On,* ed. Michael Farrell (Dingle: Brandon, 1988), 152–3.

56 *Derry Journal,* March 10, 1970.

57 *Derry Journal,* April 10, 1970; Margot Gayle Backus, "'Not Quite Philadelphia, Is It?': An Interview with Eamonn McCann," *Éire-Ireland* 36, no. 3–4 (Fall/Winter 2001): 186.

58 Intelligence Summary, August 5–16, 1970, WO305/3356, NAUK; Intelligence Summary, October 14–20, 1970, WO305/3358, NAUK.

59 *Derry Journal*, January 15, 1971.

60 Email from Roy Johnston to the author, April 21, 2006.

61 B. R. Tomlinson, "What was the Third World?" *Journal of Contemporary History* 38, no. 2 (April 2003): 309.

62 Leo Huberman and Paul Sweezy, *Cuba: Anatomy of a Revolution* (New York: Monthly Review Press, 1960), 55.

63 Roy Johnston, *Century of Endeavour: A Biographical and Autobiographical View of the 20th Century in Ireland* (Dublin: Lilliput Press, 2002), 171.

64 Michael Silvestri, "'The Sinn Fein of India': Irish Nationalism and the Policing of Revolutionary Terrorism in Bengal," *Journal of British Studies* 39, no. 4 (October 2000): 455.

65 Roy Johnston, "A Republican Programme for the 1960s," November 1963, Century of Endeavour electronic archive.

66 Frantz Fanon, *The Wretched of the Earth*, trans. Constance Farrington (New York: Grove Press, 1968), 311, 315.

67 Johnston, *Century of Endeavour*, 185.

68 *Irish Democrat*, April 1965.

69 Brian Hanley and Scott Millar, *The Lost Revolution: The Story of the Official IRA and the Workers' Party* (Dublin: Penguin, 2009), 90, 123.

70 Ultán Gillen, "Theobald Wolfe Tone and the Common Name of Irishman in 1960s Ireland," in *Uncertain Futures: Essays about the Irish Past for Roy Foster*, ed. Senia Pašeta (Oxford: Oxford University Press, 2016), 212–2.

71 *Tuairisc*, August 1966.

72 Garda Síochána, "Review of Unlawful and Allied Organisations: December 1, 1964 to November 21, 1966," JUS96/6/495, Dublin, National Archives of Ireland.

73 *Derry Journal*, August 15, 1969.

74 Scarman Inquiry Belfast exhibits, police logs, August 13 and 14, 1969, IALS.

75 McCann, *War and an Irish* Town, 72–73.

76 Intelligence Summary, May 7–13, 1970, and Intelligence Summary, October 15–21, 1970, WO305/3783, NAUK.

77 Intelligence Summary, October 13–19, 1969, WO305/4192, NAUK.

78 "Record of a Meeting of the Shankill Defence Association."

79 Geoffrey Hughes, *An Encyclopedia of Swearing: The Social History of Oaths, Profanity, Foul Language, and Ethnic Slurs in the English-Speaking World* (London: M. E. Sharpe, 2006), 148, 497.

80 George Wigg, Speech to the House of Commons, July 29, 1949. *Parliamentary Debates*, Commons, 5th ser., vol. 467, col. 2845.

81 David French, "Nasty Not Nice: British Counter-insurgency Doctrine and Practice, 1945–1967," *Small Wars & Insurgencies* 23, no. 4–5 (October-December 2012): 744–61.

82 Gavin Schaffer, "Till Death Us Do Part and the BBC: Racial Politics and the British Working Classes 1965–75," *Journal of Contemporary History* 45, no. 2 (April 2010): 454–7.

83 Robert Gildea, *Empires of the Mind: The Colonial Past and the Politics of the Present* (Cambridge: Cambridge University Press, 2019), 127.

84 "Record of a Meeting of the Shankill Defence Association."
85 Camilla Schofield, *Enoch Powell and the Making of Postcolonial Britain* (Cambridge: Cambridge University Press, 2013), 234.
86 "Coloured Recruits," February 3, 1969, DEFE13/640, NAUK.
87 "The Manning of the Situation of the Army," May 16, 1961, DEFE13/640, NAUK.
88 "Coloured Soldiers in the Guards," December 13, 1968, DEFE13/640, NAUK.
89 Army logs, October 16, 1969, WO305/4192, NAUK.
90 John Gilbert, "Hearts, Minds, and Body Building," *Daily Mirror*, November 7, 1969.
91 *Red Mole*, July 1970.
92 *Rising Up Angry*, Spring 1970, D3297/2, PRONI; Poster advertising McCann and Devlin speaking at the Sorbonne on *"la lutte Populaire Irlandaise,"* (fall 1970), D3253/5/14, PRONI.
93 *Observer*, September 7, 1969.
94 Barnett, "People's Democracy," 10–18.

CHAPTER 9

Learning from Walcott
Heaney's Black and Green Atlantic

Richard Rankin Russell

From early in his career, Seamus Heaney read Caribbean poet and playwright Derek Walcott's work; Walcott read Heaney's work deeply as well. The men became friends in the late 1970s and 1980s, and their friendship continued to grow until Heaney's death in 2013, upon which Walcott proclaimed, "he was a great poet and a friend. In fact he was like a brother to me."[1] Walcott was mixed-race (with both Dutch and English grandfathers and grandmothers of African descent) born on British St. Lucia, one of the Windward Islands in the Lesser Antilles, which is now independent but still maintains a hybrid British and French culture. In addition to appreciating the sheer excellence of Walcott's lyrically graceful poetry, Heaney as a young Catholic intellectual living in Northern Ireland during the 1960s, read the Caribbean poet in part because Walcott understood the historical treatment of the Irish, especially Irish Catholics, as "black" in imperial discourse. While Heaney was biologically white, his status as a minority Catholic in Northern Ireland rendered him "black" in the eyes of many Protestants in the province, just as Irish Catholics for many years were treated as "black" in England and America. Noel Ignatiev's study of the subject, *How the Irish Became White* (1995), remains essential reading in this regard. As John Brannigan has shown, however, in his excellent study, *Race in Modern Irish Literature and Culture* (2009), critics should be wary of simply equating the Irish and those marginalized citizens of "Third World" countries, a practice which "became pervasive in Irish culture in the late 1980s and early 1990s."[2] Because "conspicuous evidence of racism in Ireland against Black and Asian immigrants" has made "such claims of analogy and solidarity seem especially strained" – not just in the early twenty-first century, but also in earlier Irish history – scholars should be wary of automatically making comparisons to citizens of countries more recently decolonized and with somewhat different historical situations.[3] And yet, as we will see, Walcott understood how the Irish were themselves racialized and discriminated against, and he recognized a strategy of linguistic inventiveness on the part of earlier Irish writers such as James Joyce to counter charges that suggested Irish literary endeavors were simplistic. In turn, at a crucial moment early in his career and thereafter, Heaney found corroboration for his own poetry's emphasis on mixed-languages and cultures in Walcott's reclamation of Irish writers through his project of recovering and reclaiming Caribbean culture and literature as worthy of exploration and documentation.

In his review of Walcott's 1979 volume of poetry, *The Star-Apple Kingdom*, Heaney noted how Irish writers such as W.B. Yeats and John Millington Synge served as exemplars for the Caribbean poet. Understanding the importance of what has come to be known as the "Black and Green Atlantic," Heaney highlighted the continuing conversation between the islands of Ireland and those in the Caribbean and the Americas. The foundation for that conversation may have been laid by Frederick Douglass's trip to Ireland in 1848, an event explored with great sensitivity not only in historical analyses but also in contemporary Irish literature, such as in Colum McCann's novel *TransAtlantic* (2013). Apart from that momentous event, Irish writing's evocation of folklore and construction of Hiberno-English (an Irish-inflected English that drew on the rhythms of the Irish language), such as in the writings of John Millington Synge, proved of lasting importance not only for Heaney but also for Walcott.[4] In turn, as we will see, Walcott's appropriation of a particular St. Lucian dialect in his poetry and drama appealed to Heaney's sensitive ear and confirmed in him not only a desire to be inspired by what he has called the "guttural muse"[5] but also a recognition of his shared condition as an exile, a position that both poets made into an imaginative home.

Heaney's time at California-Berkeley between 1970 and 1971 led him to realize his need to chart a middle course for a poetics of race between representatives of violent Black nationalism (Angela Davis, Malcolm X) and those hailing from the Protestant community in Northern Ireland who inspired violence against Catholics (Ian Paisley, among others). His development of a specific poetic language attuned to both his Irish cultural and linguistic heritage and his embrace of the great writers of the English literary tradition became an important part of his poetics of race. This chapter will argue that Walcott confirmed in Heaney a desire to register historical atrocities committed across the Atlantic archipelago against members of minority communities and yet to enrich and complicate this position by seeking accommodation, even reconciliation, with the former colonizers by virtue of recognizing their common humanity, in part through their idiomatic language. By tracing Heaney's engagement with Walcott's work across his career, this chapter will articulate the positive contours of their poetic relationship. It contributed to Heaney's ongoing struggle to write poetry and drama that was attentive to the divided cultural situation in Northern Ireland and his effort to chart ways in which literature might not just dwell on the wound of race and resentment but go beyond that struggle and ascend into something like Walcottian song. Heaney found affirmation in what he argued was Walcott's refusal for "himself to be cast as the specimen victim – the voice of his people and thereby a conscience to others rather than to himself," flying by what Heaney termed in his mid-1980s review of Walcott's *Collected Poems 1948–1984*, the "Caribbean equivalents of those nets that the soul of Stephen Dedalus had to fly past in order to be born": "Imperial, colonial; black, white; oral, written; master, slave; British, West Indian; African, European...."[6] In the process, Heaney modeled such a backward- and forward-looking poetics of race for other poets in Ireland and beyond.

In a 1988 roundtable discussion as part of the Writers' Conference at Dun Laoghaire, Ireland, Heaney was asked about his affinities with three other panelists: the Russian-American poet Joseph Brodsky, the Australian poet Les Murray, and Walcott. He replied that while he was "animated by the body of the language" in Walcott's poetry, "I must say that I was eager to read someone going through a cultural-political experience that somehow was enacted in Ireland, and I read these poems in the 1960s."[7] What poems of Walcott's might Heaney have been reading that seemed analogous to Ireland's changes? He almost certainly was reading Walcott's breakthrough volume, *In a Green Night: Poems, 1948–1960*, which was published in 1962.[8] And he gave further insights into how he perceived parallels between Walcott's poetic depictions of St. Lucian life and Irish life in an interview with Dennis O'Driscoll, noting, "From the time I began to read his poems, in the early sixties, I found myself not only admiring the amplitude of the art, but feeling at home with it. I recognized the nature of the conflicts it arose from."[9] Politically, 1962 was a crucial year in two respects in the Caribbean as well. As Laurence A. Breiner has noted: there were "new, draconian immigration laws in Britain and the slow rollout of independence for the Caribbean colonies."[10] Heaney's reading of *In a Green Night* thus occurred exactly during the time of this gathering independence movement.

Crucially, Heaney was not likening the conflict in Northern Ireland, which would not restart until the decade's end, to the martial conflicts that were part of St. Lucia's history of imperialism or new battles for independence. Instead, he articulated his perception that he and Walcott were part of analogous cultural and linguistic battles that had grown out of imperial legacies. For instance, while there were "obvious parallels between the cultural and political situation in St. Lucia in the second half of the twentieth century and the situation in Ireland in the first half," both in Ireland and on Walcott's home island, "the writers were furnished with two languages, the vernacular of the home and the idiom of the school, and the choice between them had political implications." But just as Heaney rejected the linguistic imperialism England had long forced on Ireland, he also rejected Irish nationalist writer Daniel Corkery's "nativist line, saying you weren't a truly Irish writer if you couldn't find the heart of the matter in the crowd attending a Munster hurling final." He then equated this Irish nativist rejection of all things English to the stance of Caribbean poet Edward Kamau Brathwaite, whose breakthrough volume, *Rights of Passage* (1967), was turned "to the voicing of the Afro-English of the Caribbean, tuning his lines to the African drum rather than the iambic metronome." Brilliantly, he observed that Brathwaite's rejection of Shakespeare's iambic meter "was a playing out in a different time and place of the conflict Joyce had designated in Ireland between the 'full stoppers and semi-colonials.'"[11]

Despite his aversion to British imperialism in its linguistic and political forms, Heaney, like Walcott, has always made clear his love of the English literary tradition and the English language itself. His particular South Derry dialect charged and inflected his poetic line, speckling it with Irish loan words, local expressions, and idiomatic angularity. Clearly, Walcott's refusal to abandon his inherited English language and culture proved exemplary to Heaney's emerging poetic voice, just around the time he was trying to publish some poems that would become part of his first volume, *Death of a Naturalist* (1966). Specifically, Heaney argues, "I was interested … in Walcott's refusal to renege on the inherited English strain [of language and literature] and admired him for trying to let the whole problem play out in his work, and pay into it."[12] That "play and pay" aspect of Walcott's poetry forms an important part of this narrative, whereby one mixed-race island poet from the Caribbean influenced another poet from the island of Ireland.

Critics who have written about the relationship between Heaney and Walcott often focus on the mature work of the two men from the late 1970s onward – as indeed, part of this essay will – but certainly, Heaney knew the complex linguistic and cultural matrix of Walcott's poetry from the late 1940s through the 1960s and beyond, well before they actually met in New York in 1980 in the wake of his positive review of *The Star-Apple Kingdom*. Soon after, Walcott objected to A. Alvarez's contention in the

New York Review of Books about Heaney, that "the English literary establishment always reserved a place for one Irish poet and I was currently
flavour of the month."[13] Walcott clearly sensed the tokenism implicit in
Alvarez's attitude toward Heaney, and, probably having experienced similar tokenism before as the "only" Caribbean poet, he spoke out.

Reading Walcott in the early 1960s, Heaney likely would have responded
with relieved recognition to the complex anguish the persona of "A Far
Cry from Africa" felt in that well-known poem – torn as he is between
the English on his tongue and the African dialects of one side of his family. Late in the poem, after deploring both the imperialist attitude toward
"savages, expendable as Jews" and the attacks on "the white child hacked
in bed" by the Kikuyu (one of the dominant tribes in the guerrilla fighting
force for Kenyan independence from 1952–60), the speaker laments that
he is "poisoned with the blood of both" the "gorilla and the superman."[14]
This latter phrase gives us a terse shorthand for racist attitudes toward
Africans and perhaps indigenous attitudes that would caricature all impe-
rialists as Nietzschean *Ubermenschen*, respectively. One of the concluding
plangent questions, "Where shall I turn, divided to the vein?," must have
stunned Heaney with a shock of recognition during his formative years
just out of Queen's University as he negotiated the demands of the formal
English literary tradition and the dialectical music he still carried in the
back of his throat from South County Derry.[15] Here was a slightly older
poet from another world who had cursed the "drunken officer of British
rule" and yet who could not abandon what Walcott's speaker terms "the
English tongue I love."[16]

By the late 1970s, Walcott would choose an epigraph for *The Star-
Apple Kingdom* that signaled his affiliation with mixed-race and hybrid
cultures in a transoceanic context, quoting Greek-Irish writer Lafcadio
Hearn's *Two Years in the French West Indies* (1900): "And you behold
before you a geological dream, a vision of the primeval sea: the appari-
tion of the land as first brought forth, all peak-tossed and fissured and
naked and grim, in the tremendous birth of an archipelago." Walcott
had mused in his Nobel Prize address that "Antillean art is this restoration of our shattered histories, our shards of vocabulary, our archipelago
becoming a synonym for pieces broken off from the original continent."[17] For Walcott, his poetry involved an historical and linguistic
restoration project, patching and reconstructing these "shattered histories" and "shards of vocabulary," one which also offered the Caribbean
poet a chance to start anew like Adam or Robinson Crusoe. He argued
further that "this process of renaming, of finding new metaphors, is

the same process that the poet faces every morning of his working day, making his own tools like Crusoe, assembling nouns from necessity, from Felicity, even renaming himself."[18] This Adamic project surely confirmed in Heaney a similar desire to draw both on his Gaelic and English historical and literary legacies and to fashion himself anew, free from racialized identities that might be foisted upon him by British critics and Protestant bigots in Northern Ireland. A poem from *Wintering Out* (1972) such as "Anahorish" may reflect the Adamic impulse first modeled for Heaney by Walcott to recreate, to name anew: "My 'place of clear water,' / the first hill in the world...."[19]

And yet that archaeological and linguistic restoration project rendered Heaney susceptible to racializing comments and categories, particularly as the conflict in Northern Ireland increased. Indeed, *Wintering Out* explores the resentments toward Catholics in the province in poems such as "Servant Boy" and "The Other Side": the former views a Protestant Big House in Ireland through the eyes of a local Irish serving boy, while the latter reproduces slighting comments made toward Heaney and his siblings by a local Protestant neighbor, who lords it over them. Blake Morrison has pointed out how by the end of the 1960s, a Celticist caricature of Heaney had already been constructed, and I would add to his argument that this caricature contained racialist overtones, partaking as it did in a long British tradition of stereotyping the Irish as "black," primitive, and emotional. For instance, Ian Hamilton's poetry magazine *The Review* caricatured Heaney in 1970 as a "Longhorn Cow, a big, heavy and ungainly stock once widely distributed in England and Ireland."[20] Another, more pernicious enterprise involved attempts to "consolidate him" as the "poet of muddy-booted blackberry-picking," and thus to categorize him as a simple Celt.[21] Morrison argues that by this point "the English public had indeed firmly labeled him as a rustic, word-spinning Celt with an affection for the simple things of the countryside."[22] Moreover, such a racialized identity was soon more publicly visible, especially when Heaney would reflect at Christmastime in 1971 that he and other Catholics along with Black migrants were already being cast anew as unwelcomed minorities by wall slogans such as "Keep Blacks and Fenians out of Ulster."[23] The equation of "Blacks and Fenians" amply makes the point: Catholics were non-natives for many "Ulster Protestants" – dark, dirty, untrustworthy, and lazy. One of the foremost commentators on religious identities in Northern Ireland, Marianne Elliott, states flatly that "This belief – that Roman Catholicism shackled the mind, inducing lack of spirit, indolence, and poverty – can be found at almost every level of Irish Protestant society in every century since the Reformation."[24] The barbarity ascribed by the English, and later, by Northern Irish Protestants as well, went at least as far back as Giraldus Cambrensis's apologia in the twelfth century for the English conquest of Ireland, in which he argued that the native Irish "preferred wandering, 'primitive,' pastoral ways, which he thought made them lazy and lacking in ambition, and all of this was reflected in their 'barbarous' loose dress and long hair. The Irish, he concludes, were 'a filthy people, wallowing in vice.'"[25] One can see why Heaney would have felt the designation of him as a simple, rural Celt was not only condescending, but also racialized, a status given considerable justification, unfortunately, by Lord Thomas Macaulay's popular *History of England* (1849–61), which contemporary Ulster Unionists have quoted. Macaulay argued for the existence of an Anglo-Saxon race, which he fused with popular Protestantism to suggest that Ulster Protestants were superior to the "aboriginal Roman Catholic Irish, who are considerably inferior in civilization."[26] Significantly, Heaney himself said in 1974 that being a Catholic in Northern Ireland is "*almost a racist term*, a label for a set of cultural suppositions," and he felt the full weight of these suppositions around this time.[27]

Heaney felt at the time that "A little goodwill in the Establishment here towards the notion of being Irish would take some of the twists out of the minority." And he recorded the comment of a supposedly "completely unbigoted and humane friend searching for words to cope with his abhorrence of the Provisionals [the new wing of the Irish Republican Army] and hitting on the *mot juste* quite unconsciously: 'These ... these ... Irish.'"[28] He explicitly used versions of the word "race" twice in the prose essays collected under the title "Belfast," noting in Christmas of 1971 that "I am fatigued by a continuous adjudication between agony and injustice, swung at one moment by the long tail of race and resentment, at another by the more acceptable feelings of pity and terror."[29] Given the intensifying pressures of the conflict in Northern Ireland the next year, Heaney would muse that he felt "drawn towards the old vortex of racial and religious instinct," while "at another time you seek the mean of humane love and reason."[30] Heaney's well-known sonnet, "Strange Fruit," with its title derived from the ballad famously sung by Billie Holliday about lynching from his poetry volume, *North* (1975), along with many of the prose poems Heaney would publish in *Stations* that same year, expressed his sense that he was a member of the racialized, "black" tribe of Catholics in Northern Ireland at the time, assailed and threatened by the dominant Protestant British establishment in the province.[31]

Walcott's "A Far Cry from Africa" suggests how he likely identified with a racially hybridized persona who laments he is "divided to the vein," as we have seen. And yet, Walcott's consistent recourse to his racial and cultural hybridity as a foundation of strength for himself and his poetry modeled the constructive position of being "in-between" for Heaney, nine years his junior. Indeed, his epigraph from Hearne (as quoted above) suggested how the wide-arcing archipelago of the Mediterranean, Caribbean, and Atlantic shares a poetic affirmation of a racial admixture as an enabling condition. A similar belief is found in Heaney; as I have written elsewhere, Heaney displays a penchant for putting himself into liminal positions – *between* culture, languages, identities. Indeed, recent criticism has similarly recognized and lauded Heaney's ability and need to strike such stances.[32] Walcott demonstrates a similar ethic. Rei Terada notes that "we should see Walcott's betweenness [in such poems as "A Far Cry from Africa"] as neither a synthesis nor a separation, but a state of being that incorporates difference within itself."[33] Even if he could have felt compromised early in his career by his liminality, Walcott came to see it as a position of strength and balance, from which he could draw on multiple cultures and languages.

What needs further clarification is that Heaney's cultural hybridity has an ineradicable element that can only be understood as racialized, and that this element engages with the dominant English (white) culture and language in enabling ways for his poetry. Through his hybridized identity, modeled in part for him by Walcott, Heaney recognized racial and other injustices. However, he did not succumb to the pathology of victimhood. Rather, he emerged from such engagements with a more holistic sense of himself and of the possibilities of an integrated society enriched by the contributions of those minorities whose voices had been previously occluded.

Walcott recognized this racialized aspect of Heaney's identity. At one point in his essay about a trip from Northern Ireland down to Dublin with Seamus and Marie Heaney, Walcott wrote about the British soldiers they encountered and how they reminded him of French policemen on Martinique and St. Martin:

> Then near the bridge out of Derry, we saw soldiers, two armoured lorries curving around, and fresh pink faces above the camouflage uniforms, containing the history of siege and defence of the old walled city, a sight familiar to Seamus, but shocking to me. As shocking as the white gendarmes with their kepis and shorts that one sees in the French departments of Martinique and St. Martin, a swift sensation of nausea that took some time to pass.[34]

Note how Walcott points out the "fresh pink faces" of the British soldiers and equates them with the French "white gendarmes with their kepis and shorts" in French-influenced islands in the Caribbean. He uses very similar language about the gendarmes on Martinique and the nausea they induced in him in his poem "French Colonial. 'Vers de Société," collected in *The Arkansas Testament* (1987), which he dedicated to Heaney: there, he muses about the "comfortable colonial" atmosphere there, with "tobacco, awnings, Peugeots, pink / gendarmes" who have a "nauseous sense of heritage and order...."[35] In his essay, he recognizes the similarities shared by the pale-faced purveyors of colonial power in both locations, is even nauseated by their presence – and by extension, reads himself and the Heaney as "black" and other. Yet he is calmed by Heaney's comment, "'ah, they're all right,'" and his further musing that "they were lads, and he had two admirable sons their age, Michael and Christopher, who themselves could have been at risk, on whichever side, in whatever lorries."[36] Heaney instantly apprehends the common humanity shared by his sons and the similarly aged British soldiers and assuages Walcott's fears – that he and Heaney and Marie (Heaney's wife), all minorities in their diverse contexts, are at risk of having violence done to them in this moment.

Such contexts have been illuminated by the critical work that has become known as the "Black and Green Atlantic."[37] For instance, in the 2002 collection, *Irish and Postcolonial Writing*, edited by Glenn Hooper and Colin Graham, Steven Matthews articulates some of the challenges and opportunities of this Black and Green relationship. Matthews suggests that "a comparison of writing from parallel situations" in the Caribbean, which encapsulates "the worst atrocities of the European imperial enterprise anywhere," might "cast light upon the racial issues compacted within recent Irish poetry."[38] Tellingly, besides exploring some issues of language, Matthews largely neglects formal concerns and particularly how Irish modernist writers might have modeled these for the formalist Walcott. We do not have to choose – issues of race can be illuminated through the exploration of formal devices.

Walcott, much like Heaney, chooses formalist strategies as part of his complex postcolonial position on race, including particular rhyming patterns and complex dialects. Heaney recognizes Walcott's formalist position through which he addresses the Caribbean's ongoing issues with colonialism in his review of *The Star-Apple Kingdom* when he remarks, "A few years ago, in the turbulent and beautiful essay" ["What the Twilight Says: An Overture"] which prefaced his collection of plays, *Dream on Monkey Mountain*, Walcott wrote out of and about the hunger for a proper form, for an instrument to bleed off the accumulated humors of his peculiar colonial ague."[39] Heaney does not mean form, technically speaking, here, although Walcott can be a formidable formalist. He means instead a particular aesthetic strategy, true to his allegiance to poetry and true to his culture. Heaney had written a similar statement, about his own "hunger for a proper form ... to bleed off the accumulated humors of his peculiar colonial ague" in his 1974 essay, "Feeling into Words," when the province of Northern Ireland exploded into riots in the summer of 1969. As he avers, "I mean that I felt it imperative to discover a field of force in which, without abandoning fidelity to the processes and experience of poetry as I have outlined them, it would be possible to encompass the perspectives of a humane reason and at the same time to grant the religious intensity of the violence its deplorable authenticity and complexity."[40]

Heaney felt Walcott achieved his "proper form" in "The Schooner *Flight*," the long opening poem of *The Star-Apple Kingdom*. He cites the persona-poet Shabine's closing lines from the first section of this remarkable lyric sequence, noting, "He has now found that instrument and wields it with rare confidence"[41]:

> You ever look up from some lonely beach
> and see a far schooner? Well, when I write
> this poem, each phrase go be soaked in salt;
> I go draw and knot every line as tight
> as ropes in this rigging; in simple speech
> my common language go be the wind,
> my pages the sails of the schooner Flight.[42]

Heaney argues about this passage that "the speaker fixes his language in terms that recall Walcott's description of an ideal troupe of actors, 'sinewy, tuned, elate,' and the language works for him as a well-disciplined troupe for the dramatist."[43] Heaney is thinking of and quoting the passage late in "What the Twilight Says," when Walcott – who worked for decades in West Indian theater (and founded the Trinidad Theatre Workshop in 1959), directing, writing, and even acting in plays that generally had more demotic and idiomatic language than did many of his poems – imagines a troupe of actors at the highest point in St. Lucia overlooking the harbor. They seem to embody his search for a living language attuned to both local culture and Africa:

> some turned towards the lush, dark-pocketed valleys of banana with their
> ochre tracks and canted wooden huts, from whose kitchens, at firelight, the
> poetry which they spoke had come, and farther on, the wild, white-lined

Atlantic coast with an Africa that was no longer home, and the dark, oracu-
lar mountain dying into mythology. It was as if, with this sinewy, tuned,
elate company, he was repaying the island an ancestral debt.[44]

Walcott's vagabond company achieves the realization of a language beyond
binary racial and linguistic categories – and embodies and embraces the
archipelagic inheritance of West Indian inhabitants like the imagined
Shabine, whom Heaney terms "a kind of democratic West Indian Ulysses,
his mind full of wind and poetry and women."

Citing the opening lines of the poem now and its demotic language
wielded by the ocean-going Shabine as he prepares to ship out on the
schooner *Flight*, Heaney claims, "when Walcott lets the sea-breeze freshen
in his imagination, the result is a poetry as spacious and heart-lifting as the
sea-weather at the opening of Joyce's *Ulysses*...."[45] Joyce is another major
Irish influence on Walcott, which exemplified for Heaney a trust in that
stylistic modernist master. Heaney, whose depiction of Joyce in the last
and twelfth section of the title poem of his 1984 volume, *Station Island*,
stressed his independence and relish in the English language, pointed out
in his review of Walcott's first collected volume of poetry that "Walcott's
imagination, like Joyce's, works by correspondence and analogy and has
a similar joy in sporting itself between language and cultures."[46] And
Walcott himself termed Joyce "the greatest prose innovator of our time."[47]

And yet Shabine, whose nickname he likens to being called a "red n****,"
is profoundly displaced from his local culture just as Joyce's Leopold Bloom
is and takes refuge in his dual roles as sailor and poet, which are beautifully
intertwined here.[48] Shabine, wallowing in racial ambiguity and uncertainty, rejected by both the dark-skinned inhabitants of African descent
on St. Lucia and the minority white residents, relishes the precision of
tight lines of poetry that he likens to "ropes in this rigging" and draws his
"common language" from "the wind," the pages of his poetry from the
sails of the ship he is on. Walcott has intimated about himself, drawing on
a pejorative term, that he is "the mulatto of style. The traitor. The assimila-
tor."[49] The "mixed" language of "The Schooner *Flight*" – "formal" English
shot through with local patois, as in this passage – suggests that he found
his voice in such poems and linguistically signals his positive reclamation
of his internal cultural and racial hybridity. Heaney further remarks about
"The Schooner *Flight*" that "From the beginning he [Walcott] has never
simplified or sold short. Africa and England beat messages along his blood.
The humanist voices of his education and the voices from his elemental
inarticulate place keep insisting on their full claims, pulling him in two
different directions."[50]

What Heaney's praise of this passage suggests is that Walcott, through Shabine, rejects simplistic racial binaries not attentive to or sensitive to the many mixed-race members of the varied Caribbean population, and perhaps more important, that Shabine's identity lies first in his allegiance to his language and by extension to his poetry – not to categories that any community would assign him to.

Heaney and Walcott have both written extensively about the suppurating foot wound of Philoctetes and Philoctete, respectively, in Heaney's *The Cure at Troy* and Walcott's *Omeros*, and they use this image of the wound to think through how societies divided by race and sectarian histories might recognize their suffering yet rise above it. Uncannily, Walcott's portrayal of the wounded Philoctete was published the same year Heaney's dramatic version of Sophocles' Philoctetes appeared in 1990.[51] There is no question of influence here: Both men had been thinking about this figure for years as a symbol of their divided societies, and by extension, as a figure whose ongoing fascination with his wound may suggest traumatized minority communities' inability at times to look past their marginalization and suffering at the hands of oppressors. Jahan Ramazani has pointed out that while Walcott "continued to castigate West Indian literature for sulking" about the damage inflicted by slavery, in *Omeros*, Walcott devotes a great deal of attention to Philoctete's wound. Ramazani even claims, "Nursed and inspected, magnified and proliferated, the metaphor of the wound forms the vivid nucleus of Walcott's magnum opus."[52]

Walcott's Philoctete dwells in that wound, admits its horror and power, but will not succumb to it and be defined as a victim, even though, as Ramazani argues, "his wound suggests not only affliction but also colonial penetration, evacuation, and forgetting."[53] He lifts himself and his people out of the condition of woundedness by virtue of his vigorous, creative imagination, fed by the beauty of the natural world of his St. Lucia and the supernatural underpinnings of his faith. As the narrator tells us at the end of *Omeros*, "like Philoctete's wound, this language carries its cure, / its radiant affliction; reluctantly now, / like Achilles my craft slips the chain of its anchor...."[54] This is Walcottian song – poetry lifting off and ascending, transcending racial grievances and categories. In this sea-borne song, we hear language with the potential to cure our wounded racial condition. Seamus Heaney long ago heard that song and learned to sing out of the distress of the ethnic identity a bigoted society ascribed to him, recognizing the wounds of history in Northern Ireland. Yet he also privileges the miraculous power of language to lead us into healing and visionary states beyond even the hurt and pain inflicted upon minorities by centuries of racism. Heaney's poetics of race thus features woundedness and healing, history and hope, and finally embraces the transcendent. As Neoptolemus tells Heaney's still-limping Philoctetes, going off to Troy both to be cured and to fight in the Trojan War late in *The Cure at Troy*, "Stop just licking your wounds. Start seeing things."[55]

Notes

1 Star Reporter, "Nobel-winning Poet Seamus Heaney Dies," *St. Lucia Star*, September 2, 2013. https://stluciastar.com/nobel-winning-poet-seamus-heaney-dies/.
2 John Brannigan, *Race in Modern Irish Literature and Culture* (Edinburgh: Edinburgh University Press, 2009), 214.
3 Brannigan, *Race in Modern Irish Literature and Culture*, 215.
4 Synge was a lasting influence on Walcott, from his early play *The Sea at Dauphin* (1954) to *Omeros* and beyond. For a recent insightful assessment of Synge's influence on this early drama of Walcott's, see Stephanie Pocock Boeninger, *Literary Drowning: Postcolonial Memory in Irish and Caribbean Writing* (Syracuse: Syracuse University Press, 2020), 85–95.
5 Seamus Heaney first uses the phrase in "Traditions," from *Wintering Out*: "Our guttural muse / was bullied long ago / by the alliterative tradition..." (31). He also features the phrase as the title of a poem from *Field Work*, which describes the "thick and comforting" voices of a young crowd leaving a disco and a girl's voice that "swarmed and puddled into laughs..." (20). See Heaney, *Wintering Out* (London: Faber and Faber, 1972); *Field Work* (London: Faber and Faber, 1979).
6 Heaney, "An Authentic Poetic Voice that Bridges Time, Cultures," review of *Collected Poems: 1948–1984*, by Derek Walcott, *Boston Globe*, February 9, 1986: A28.
7 Joseph Brodsky, Seamus Heaney, Les Murray, and Derek Walcott, "Poet's Roundtable: 'A Common Language,'" interview by Michael Schmidt, *PN Review* 15, no. 4 (1989): 39.
8 Heaney identifies "lyrics of memorable grace" in poems such as "In a Green Night" and "Coral," and in his sonnet sequence, "Tales of the Islands" – all collected in *In a Green Night: Poems, 1948–1960* (1962); see "The Language of Exile," review of *The Star-Apple Kingdom*, by Derek Walcott, *Parnassus: Poetry in Review* 8, no. 1 (1980): 8.
9 Heaney, *Stepping Stones: Interview with Seamus Heaney*, interview by Dennis O'Driscoll (New York: Farrar, Straus, Giroux, 2008), 342.
10 Laurence A. Breiner, "Postcolonial Caribbean Poetry," in *The Cambridge Companion to Postcolonial Poetry*, ed. Jahan Ramazani (Cambridge: Cambridge University Press, 2017), 19.
11 Heaney, *Stepping Stones*, 342. See Breiner, "Postcolonial Caribbean Poetry," 23–28, for a more nuanced explanation of the different trajectories the two

men's poetry took, drawing in part on the "more contrasting features" of Brathwaite's *The Arrivants* and Walcott's *Another Life* (both published in 1973) [that] "reinforced the handy but unhelpful dichotomy that saw Brathwaite as an 'oral' poet of the deracinated African folk, and Walcott as a 'humanist' poet, writing out of metropolitan tradition" (23).

12 Heaney, *Stepping Stones*, 342–43.

13 Heaney, *Stepping Stones*, 343. Walcott tells his very similar version of the story about meeting Heaney in "The Art of Poetry XXXVII: Derek Walcott," interview by Edward Hirsch, 1985, *Conversations with Walcott*, ed. William Baer (Jackson: University of Mississippi Press, 1996), 119.

14 Walcott, *The Poetry of Derek Walcott: 1948–2013*, selected by Glyn Maxwell (New York: Farrar, Straus, Giroux, 2014), 27.

15 Walcott, *The Poetry of Derek Walcott*, 27. Heaney notes in "Poet's Roundtable" that "I spoke with the South Derry intonation at the back of my throat for a long time; I didn't really talk English properly" (41).

16 Walcott, *The Poetry of Derek Walcott*, 27, 28.

17 Walcott, "The Antilles: Fragments of Epic Memory," *What the Twilight Says: Essays* (New York: Farrar, Straus, Giroux, 1998), 69.

18 Walcott, "The Antilles: Fragments of Epic Memory," 70.

19 Heaney, *Wintering Out*, 16.

20 Blake Morrison, *Seamus Heaney* (London: Methuen, 1982), 35.

21 Morrison, *Seamus Heaney*, 36, quoting Christopher Ricks lamenting Heaney being caricatured as the "poet of muddy-booted blackberry picking."

22 Morrison, *Seamus Heaney*, 36.

23 Heaney, "Belfast," *Preoccupations: Selected Prose 1968–1978* (London: Faber and Faber, 1980), 31.

24 Marianne Elliott, *When God Took Sides: Religion and Identity in Ireland – Unfinished History* (Oxford: Oxford UP, 2009), 183.

25 Quoted in Elliott, *When God Took Sides*, 189.

26 Quoted in Elliott, *When God Took Sides*, 191.

27 Quoted in Neil Corcoran, *The Poetry of Seamus Heaney: A Critical Study* (London: Faber and Faber, 1998), 238; my italics.

28 Heaney, "Belfast," 32.

29 Heaney, "Belfast," 30.

30 Heaney, "Belfast," 34.

31 See my readings of Heaney's sonnet referencing the lynchings of American Black men and of these prose poems dwelling on his racialized identity as Irish Catholic in Richard Rankin Russell, *Seamus Heaney's Regions* (Notre Dame: Notre Dame University Press, 2014), 162–86, 187–211.

32 See, for instance, Irish poet Micheal O'Siadhail's review of Heaney's *100 Poems*, "Somewhere in Between," review of *100 Poems*, by Seamus Heaney, *Commonweal* (December 2019): 51–53.

33 Rei Terada, *Derek Walcott's Poetry: American Mimicry* (Boston: Northeastern University Press, 1992), 9.

34 Walcott, "Heaney in Ireland," *AGENDA* 47, no. 3–4 (2013): 14.

204   RICHARD RANKIN RUSSELL

35 Walcott, *The Arkansas Testament* (New York: Farrar, Straus, Giroux, 1987), 75.
36 Walcott, "Heaney in Ireland," 14.
37 See the partial listing of critical studies treating the Black and Green Atlantic in my essay, "The Black and Green Atlantic: Violence, History, and Memory in Natasha Trethewey's 'South' and Seamus Heaney's 'North,'" *The Southern Literary Journal* 46, no. 2 (Spring 2014): 156–57.
38 Steven Matthews, "Translations: Difference and Identity in Recent Poetry from Ireland and the West Indies," *Irish and Postcolonial Writing: History, Theory, Practice*, eds. Glenn Hooper and Colin Graham (London: Palgrave, 2002), 110.
39 Heaney, "The Language of Exile," 5.
40 Heaney, "Feeling into Words," *Preoccupations: Selected Prose 1968–1978* (London: Faber and Faber, 1980), 56–57.
41 Heaney, "The Language of Exile," 5.
42 Walcott, *The Star-Apple Kingdom* (New York: Farrar, Straus, Giroux, 1979), 5; cited in Heaney, "The Language of Exile," 5.
43 Heaney, "The Language of Exile," 6.
44 Walcott, "What the Twilight Says," *What the Twilight Says: Essays* (New York: Farrar, Straus, Giroux, 1998), 33.
45 Heaney, "The Language of Exile," 6. Walcott admires Joyce greatly for his facility with the English language. Joyce appears in a striking passage from *Omeros* and even by that late date in Walcott's career clearly was still an important exemplar for him.
46 Heaney, "An Authentic Poetic Voice," A28.
47 Walcott, "Reflections Before and After Carnival: An Interview with Derek Walcott," interview by Sharon Ciccarelli, 1977, *Conversations with Derek Walcott*, ed. William Baer (Jackson: University of Mississippi Press, 1996), 48.
48 In "The Schooner *Flight*," Shabine muses that he's "a rusty head sailor with sea-green eyes / that they nickname Shabine, the patois for / any red n*****...." (Walcott, *The Star-Apple Kingdom*, 4).
49 Walcott, "What the Twilight Says," 9.
50 Heaney, "The Language of Exile," 6.
51 See my reading in *Seamus Heaney's Regions*, 289–94, of Philoctetes' obsession with his wound as emblematic of both Protestants and Catholics in Northern Ireland; each group feels outnumbered, besieged, and discriminated against.
52 Jahan Ramazani, *The Hybrid Muse: Postcolonial Poetry in English* (Chicago: University of Chicago Press, 2001), 53.
53 Ramazani, *The Hybrid Muse*, 55.
54 Walcott, *Omeros* (New York: Farrar, Straus, Giroux, 1990), 323.
55 Heaney, *The Cure at Troy: A Version of Sophocles'* Philoctetes (New York: Noonday Press, 1990), 73.

CHAPTER 10

Race, Irishness, and Popular Culture in Australia[*]

Dianne Hall

In April 1899, the popular Australian illustrated magazine, the *Bulletin* published a small cartoon titled: "Some Misapprehension" by Irish Australian artist, Tom Durkin (Figure 10.1). In the image, Durkin juxtaposed Mrs. Muldoon with "King Billy," who is portrayed as a physically stereotyped Aboriginal man. Mrs. Muldoon has simianized features and speaks to "King Billy" with an exaggerated Irish accent. Over the course of their conversation, she shows her ignorance of the common usage of racial terms, being indignant at the suggestion that her son might be considered not as good as a "black wretch" as "King Billy."[1] Over 100 years later, an Irish woman and an Indigenous man were also connected through popular media in the film, *The Nightingale* (2018), set in the Tasmanian convict settlement in 1825. The film depicts the brutal assault and rape of an Irish-speaking convict woman, Clare (Irish actor Aisling Franciosi), and then her journey to take revenge on her British Army attackers, aided by an Indigenous man, Billy (Yolngu actor Baykali Ganambarr).[2] Mrs. Muldoon's interactions with "King Billy" were published on the eve of the Federation of the Australian colonies and in the context of anxiety and debate over inclusion and exclusion in the new nation.[3] *The Nightingale* was released in a very different historical moment, when Australians were grappling with the legacies of colonial racial oppression and violence. The choice by director Jennifer Kent to show colonial racial and sexual violence from the perspective of an Irish convict woman – arguably occupying the lowest rung of nascent white society – allows her to interrogate the heterogeneity of white settlement. It also references the widespread belief among many Australians of Irish descent that their ancestors were less culpable than the English in the racist policies and practices of colonization in Australia's past.

The reality is more complex, as Michael D. Higgins, President of Ireland, acknowledged on an official tour of Australia in 2017.[4] He said: "we must acknowledge that while most Irish emigrants experienced

205

SOME MISAPPREHENSION.

KING BILLY: "*Mine be know your son Mick this long time,*
now—him ———— white man."

MRS. MULDOON: "*To the divil wid you, you black wretch!*
Isn't a white man as good as you any day."

Figure 10.1   "Some Misapprehension"
Tom Durkin, "Some misapprehension" *Bulletin* April 1, 1899, p. 11.

some measure – often a large measure – of prejudice and injustice, there
were some among their number who inflicted injustice too." Indigenous
member of the Australian Federal Parliament, Wiradjuri woman, Linda
Burney, followed up with an interview with the *Irish Times*, stating that
"it must be acknowledged that the Irish were among the colonists who
committed atrocities against Aboriginal people."[5] It is important that the
complexity of the histories of the Irish and Aboriginal people are starting
to be acknowledged so publicly. This chapter studies one element of that
complexity by analyzing how the Irish were depicted in print and performative popular culture from the late nineteenth century when in the
same frame as other racially marginalized groups, particularly Chinese and
Indigenous peoples.

The Irish and the Foundation of Australia

By 1901, the year that the former British colonies formed the federated nation of Australia, approximately 25 percent of the white population were of either Irish birth or descent.[6] This means that Australia had a proportionally higher Irish diasporic population than either of the other two major diasporic destinations – the United Kingdom or the United States of America. The first wave of European arrivals was associated with the convict settlements between 1788 and 1868. The Irish were a significant minority of convicts sent to the newly instituted penal colony and a significant number of the British Army guarding them. The second wave of arrivals from the 1840s were those who chose to migrate to Australia as free settlers, many taking advantage of various government assistance schemes, and attracted by reports of gold, easily acquired land, and employment. While the majority of Irish migrants were Catholic, approximately 20–25 percent were Protestant. These migrants traveled not only the great physical distance between Ireland and New South Wales, but they also moved into a different colonial landscape, one where there was a Catholic minority among the majority Protestant English and Scottish population. These English and Scottish settlers, and fellow convicts and soldiers, brought with them discriminatory practices and a repertoire of racialized stereotypes. The Irish traveling to the Australian colonies at the same time moved to a white settlement forged through the violent dispossession of its Indigenous peoples and eventual exclusion of non-European peoples, acts justified by theories of race and racial hierarchies.[7]

In many ways, Irish Catholics in colonial Australia occupied a liminal position in popular imaginings. For many Protestant British settlers, the colonies represented the opportunity to build a society free of the religious divisions of the old world. To this end, by mid-century, explicit policies of religious freedom meant that newly surveyed towns and cities all had land and support for building churches of all denominations, including Catholic churches. Yet for all the rhetoric of equality and freedom, ideas about racial and religious hierarchies profoundly shaped colonial society. Patrick O'Farrell, writing his influential *Irish in Australia* in the early 1980s, argued that the Irish Catholic founding population, with their resistance to British values, provided a distinctive character to the modern Australian identity that had rarely been recognized.[8] Although O'Farrell's analysis has been critiqued, the importance of such a large percentage of Irish Catholics within the settling population is certainly significant. Although some Irish Catholics were able to improve their class position in colonial Australia, there was also significant discrimination, particularly in employment.[9]

The Irish on Page and Stage

The discrimination against employing Irish people was underpinned by a strong thread of anti-Irish imagery in caricatures and cartoons, puns and jokes in newspapers, plays and novels. Yet, at the same time that this important strand of racialized anti-Irishness pervaded much popular culture, there was a counter narrative valorizing the Irish as rebels; harking back to an Ireland tinged with nostalgia and gleefully laughing at the discomfiture of the English both in Australia and abroad.

Cartoons and caricatures, such as those published in colonial newspapers and journals, depended for their success on a shared understanding of a defined range of images and words to convey complex layers of meaning.[10] In the nineteenth-century English speaking and reading world, physical characteristics were codes for individual moral worth and value. Physical traits became shorthand for moral judgements based on racial and social categories.[11] In caricatures, these physical traits were exaggerated and then repeated, becoming stereotypes that worked as a commonly understood language by being placed against normative and unexamined "natural" standards and found to be deviant. For the humor inherent in each caricature to work, these stereotypes had to be easily recognized but still capable of infinite variation to accommodate shifts of meaning and context over time and place.

The features denoting Irishness in the cartoonist's toolbox, both in Australia and elsewhere in English, included ape-like facial features – hirsute overhanging brow, receding jaw, eyes close together, and low-slung ears.[12] Irish Australian cartoonist Tom Durkin was particularly adept at exaggerating physical characteristics to depict and satirize racial differences, including in depictions of Chinese, First Nations and Jewish peoples as well as the Irish in the cartoons he drew for illustrated newspapers and journals such *Bulletin* and his own publication *Bull Ant* (1900–02).[13] The enduring characteristics of Irishness he used built on the long tradition of the "the Irish joke" or "bull" told at the expense of the violent, ignorant Irish male peasant and the related stereotype of the alternatively cunning or stupid Biddy or Bridget, the Irish domestic servant.[14]

Durkin's own Irish background invites consideration of the artist's ethnicity in his use of racialized stereotypes. His satires of poor Irish settlers like his parents suggests that he tried to distance himself from his family's background. By the time Durkin was an adult, his family were prosperous settlers in the Williamstown region, and he was able to find success as an artist after attending art school. Durkin's position as a respected member of artistic and bohemian Melbourne demonstrates one of the vectors through which Irish Catholics became participants in the advantages of British Australia. If men like Durkin were to be easily recognized as British, then they had to distance themselves from the imagery of the simianized Irish peasant. Respectability and middle-class status through education and commercial success were common ways of achieving this goal. As artists like Durkin exaggerated the racial characteristics of the "joke" Irish, this stereotype of Irishness was even further separated from the reality of middle-class Irish Australian colonists' experience. Durkin and his fellow Irish Australians might have Irish parents, but they did not want to be equated with violent Paddys or ignorant Bridgets.

It was not only cartoons that reinforced racialized stereotypes of the Irish. Other popular genres, such as poems, plays, and other stage performances, also thrived on a stock of Irish stereotypes. Some of these revolved around exaggerated Irish accents and ignorance, such as the immensely popular, "A Bush Christening" by A.J. (Banjo) Patterson. First published in 1893, the comic poem centers around a ten-year-old Irish Australian boy, ignorant of religion, being christened by a passing "praste" who tricked him out of his hiding place and named him after the first thing that came to hand – Maginnis' whisky. The jest was then amplified by the final lines "And Maginnis Magee has been made a J.P.,/And the one thing he hates more than sin is/To be asked by the folk who have heard of the joke/How he came to be christened 'Maginnis'!"[15] Deflating pretensions to respectability, such as that of J.P.'s was another thread running through Australian popular culture.

While Patterson's poem was Australian in content, many of the performances, jokes, plays and stories that relied on caricatures had already had success elsewhere. There was a ready audience for plays that had been successful in London or New York City. Many of the more successful of these featured comic Irish characters, though critics were less enthusiastic. The Melbourne *Weekly Times* in 1872 was tepid in its review of the play "Innisfallen" by London-based Irish playwright Edmund Falconer (Edmond O'Rourke), then playing at the Melbourne Theatre Royal. In particular, the reviewer queried the stock character, as an "honest, good-natured, bull-making peasant, with his modest and lovely sweetheart; ... the Irish gentleman who has got himself into difficulties by meddling too much in rebellions," but he also noticed the actor's poor attempt at an Irish brogue, calling it "counterfeit."[16] Irish characters and Irish-themed plays continued to be popular throughout the latter years of the nineteenth century and into the first decades of the twentieth, with successful tours of nostalgic Irish plays by the international companies of Dion

Boucicault and Allen Doone, for instance, playing to packed audiences throughout Australian cities and towns.[17]

Variety and minstrel shows were popular in colonial and early federation Australia, incorporating songs and sketches loosely organized around a narrative.[18] Many of the songs and themes were similar to performances in the United Kingdom and United States, and the same companies toured throughout the English-speaking world, though usually employing at least some local cast members. These performances relied on easily recognized satirical and caricatured characters, including Black Americans and Jewish, Chinese, and Irish peoples, as well as specifically Australian characters such as the "new chum," "the larrikin," and the "bushman." These characters drew on and reinforced the same set of stereotypes as satirical cartoons and jokes in newspapers and magazines. Stock Irish characters were common in these variety and minstrel acts. The very popular variety show, *Muldoon's Picnic* toured frequently throughout the Australian colonies from 1886. While American-born Frank M. Clark claimed to have been the original writer, and certainly produced it many times over the next couple of decades in Australia, other versions of it were also popular on the American and English stage. *Muldoon's Picnic* was described as the "most comical of Irish Comedies" when it was performed in Brisbane in 1894.[19] Essentially a vehicle for staging songs and variety performances around a very loose narrative theme, its flexible structure meant performers could adapt songs to include local references. Some of these acts merged or combined several racialized stereotypes together in the same character, particularly while performing in blackface, or "corking," a technique imported with the minstrel genre from the United States.

On Australian stages, acts based around local "larrikin" culture were popular. Larrikin was a label given to typically lower class, street-wise, young people, distinguished by their dress and speech as much as by their irreverent mischief making. Many of them had Irish names, indicating Irish ancestry. One popular stage act featured a song named after an inner-city suburb of Sydney, "Woolloomooloo."

> Oh my name is McCarty
> and I am a rorty party
> A larrikin so hearty
> …I'm a perfect daisy
> won't work because I'm lazy.[20]

Singing such a song while in blackface was another step in the performance's parody, where stereotypes were melded with imported American characterizations of Black Americans.[21] As Melissa Bellanta has demonstrated there were multiple links in the press between the perceived lawlessness of the larrikin with "savages," so fusing fellow urban outcasts, often Irish, with blackface portrayals from American minstrelsy furthered the racialized link between lower class Irish and Black Americans.

While general audiences in Australia clearly appreciated the humor of these stereotypes, the Irish Catholic press was not so amused. It condemned such caricatures and was scathing of audience appreciation of "the Irishman at the music hall ... expressing himself in bulls and blunders and tricky excuses."[22] In 1914, when successful Irish American entertainer, Allen Doone was opening one of his popular Irish themed shows, he was interviewed by the Melbourne Catholic newspaper, the *Advocate*, about a cartoon illustrating the notice of his show, "The Wearing of the Green," published in the *Bulletin* the week before. The cartoon, captioned "A snap from the audience," depicted a man and a woman with simian profiles[23] (Figure 10.2). The *Advocate* described it as "most offensive" portraying members of the

Figure 10.2   "The Wearing of Green"
"A snap from the audience" *Bulletin* February 19, 1914, p. 9.

audience "with features of bull-dog and monkeyfied appearance." Doone, agreed saying it was a "malicious and unjust libel on the Irish race."[24] Many descendants of poor Irish Catholic migrants were increasingly confident about their respectability by the turn of the twentieth century, and they wanted to celebrate a positive sense of Irishness, often couched through nostalgic Irish historical narratives. Performers like Doone, whose company successfully staged Irish romantic dramas between 1904 and 1938 in Australia, were particularly sensitive to caricatures linking the Irish to negative racialized stereotypes.[25]

Irish and Others

Other minstrel pieces linked ethnic or racial outsiders such as Italians, Irish, Chinese and Jews together into single characters by use of accents or dress. The 1886 production of *All Black,* written by Australian comic actor Lance Lenton and performed in Sydney, featured a villain with an Italian name who spoke with an Irish accent.[26] In the early decades of the twentieth century, comedian and Anglo-Australian Nat Phillips wrote popular revues in which he starred as bawdy larrikin character "Stiffy" and Jewish Australian comedian Roy Rene (Harry Vander Sluice) played "Mo," usually describing the character as half Irish and half Hebrew.[27] There are few extant descriptions of the various acts this duo performed, but it is probable that Rene used physical Irishisms along with Jewish accents in his characterisation of Mo, juxtaposed to Phillips's racially neutral characterization of Stiffy as an urban trickster. Surviving scripts indicate Mo's physical performances were often supported by songs based on local events such as "Solicitor Charlie Greif has become a member of the Celtic Club." This song was loosely based on reports that high profile Jewish lawyer, Charles Grief, was a member of the Perth Celtic Club in the 1920s.[28] The song imagines a genealogy for "Charlie" singing that he is from the O'Griffin family from Kildare who went to Jerusalem and "joined the Noses."

> Me ancestry's quare I'm both Sheeny and Pat
> and when I'm wild I can argue blue murther
> and when there's a row on I call for me hat
> and I run further and further.[29]

Imagining characters of mixed race or ethnic identities as being somehow unable to control urges based on their supposed racial or ethnic makeup was not uncommon in popular stage shows of the early twentieth century.

Appointments was written by an Australian author (probably Charles Williams) and advertised in 1880 that it featured three characters, a Chinese woman, a Chinese Irishman, and a New York hoodlum.[30] It is clear from the reported audience reactions that the racialized stereotypes performed on stage were well known. After decades of Irish jokes, caricatures in cartoons, and performance of stage Irishness in variety and minstrel shows, it is not surprising to find that regional audiences both understood and were enthralled by an American comic play about a half Irish/half Chinese cook. Between 1914 and 1927, several amateur theater groups in regional Australia presented the short play *Patsy O'Wang* as part of their entertainment evenings.[31] *Patsy O'Wang* was written by American playwright and publisher, Thomas Stewart Denison in 1895 and published in a collection of short plays specifically designed to be performed by amateur groups.[32] The humor was centered on the main character, a cook described as half Chinese and half Irish. When he drinks tea, he is the docile Chinese Chin Sum, speaking in broken English, but he transforms into the wild Irish accented Patsy O'Wang when he drinks whiskey.[33]

Irish Australians, while rejecting racialized stereotypes of themselves as Irish, generally accepted racialized caricatures of Chinese and Indigenous peoples. This was particularly around the time of Federation and the passing of the raft of legislation known collectively as the White Australia Policy.[34] Chinese people were attracted, like so many British, Irish, Europeans, and Americans, by the gold rushes in Victoria and New South Wales from the 1850s. Their numbers were restricted periodically by colonial governments fearful of the perceived destabilizing effects of waves of Asian migrants and determined to preserve the British colonies for "white" settlers. As well as legal restrictions, Chinese people also faced popular discrimination, stereotyping, and racial violence.[35] Many Irish-born and Irish Australians participated in riots and violence directed at Chinese on the goldfields or joined trade unions campaigning for restrictions on Chinese workers.[36] Underlying much of this was the fear that the Chinese would unfairly compete with Irish Australians for jobs and wives. This last was based on the widely reported, although always small, numbers of Irish women who did successfully form families with Chinese men.[37] It is in this context that a series of cartoons, poems, and commentaries was published in the latter years of the nineteenth century that positioned Irish women as racially superior to Chinese. The short-lived Melbourne-based newspaper, *Bull-Ant*, owned, edited, and largely written and illustrated by Tom Durkin, featured a number of these pieces, including a poem about a fictional laundryman Whang Tart's courtship of Irish servant Biddy. Her disdain and rejection were couched within racial hierarchies based on Black American characters from the popular stage.

> What marry you, ye ugly baste?
> Says Biddy in a rage.
> Troth sooner would I all me life
> Live wid Black Joe the page.[38]

A few years later, Durkin contributed one of his biting caricatures to the *Bulletin* (Figure 10.3). In this cartoon, he displayed a menacing Chinese man in the witness box of the court, closest to the viewer, complete with shadowed face, hair in a queue. The magistrate was portrayed as a typi-cal middle-class be-whiskered man, bending from the bench to catch the words of the accused, a man whose facial features had a monkey-like comic effect. The caption set the scene, that this was a case of "Assault on a Chow"

QUITE EASY.
(Local Police-court. Assault on a Chow.)

JAYPEE *(to prisoner)*: " Well, Clancy, ye are a namesake o' mine, but, thank God, ye are no relation. I'd rather be related to the Chinaman."

CLANCY *(winking at policeman)*: " Sure, thin, why don't ye marry him to wan o' yer daughters?"

Figure 10.3   "Quite Easy"
Tom Durkin, "Quite Easy" *Bulletin,* July 25 1896, p. 16.

and that both the accused and the magistrate were surnamed Clancy. The "jaypee" (JP – Justice of the Peace or Magistrate) states that although they share a surname, he "would rather be related to the Chinaman." To which the accused Clancy replies, "Sure thin, why don't ye marry him to wan o' yer daughters?"[39] Like Banjo Patterson's "Bush Christening," this cartoon uses widely understood Irish stereotypes in its humor to undercut the claims to respectability of Irish Australian magistrate, Clancy. It also points to the way Irish Australians were joining in the chorus of voices clamoring for restrictions on "coloured" labor, enthusiastically supporting "white" Australia policies in letters to the editors of Catholic newspapers and voting for Irish Australian politicians who were outspoken in their support for immigration restrictions.[40]

While many cartoons and jokes positioned Irish and Chinese into the same frame, stereotyping them both, this is not the case with Irish and Indigenous peoples. Given the ubiquity of racialized stereotyping of Irish people in the nineteenth and early twentieth centuries and the frequent links in popular culture between Chinese and Irish peoples, it is significant that there are few depictions of them in the same media. Durkin's cartoon "Some Misapprehension" (Figure 10.1) is one of the few. There are frequent depictions that show Indigenous people as dark skinned, barely clothed, and not knowing the boundaries of "civilised" behavior. These depictions occur in a range of cartoons, photographs, and kitsch souvenir items.[41] When identifiably Irish Australians are in the same frame as Indigenous people, it is significant that cartoonists usually showed them in a more neutral palette, similar to the way that Australians of English or Scottish ancestry were portrayed. In "The Child of Nature," Irish Australian artist Frank P. Mahony depicts an irate outback publican, Pat Ryan, shouting at two Indigenous people, who are wild and violent (Figure 10.4). He yells, "Be off now, or Oi'll belt the divil out of yer!" His Irishness is represented by his speech patterns and his name, but not in his physical features. Billy on the other hand, is overtly coded as an Aboriginal man by his physical features, his name, his speech and his violent actions.[42] Mahony's Pat Ryan and his attitude toward Billy is echoed in Irish Australian participation in dispossession and massacres of Aboriginal people as well as the quieter, more common, racism of neglect and discrimination, which were not readily discussed.[43]

Indeed, attempts to treat both Indigenous and Irish cultures together and sympathetically were often greeted with scorn by Irish Australians. In the first decade of the twentieth century, Daisy Bates, a controversial and eccentric Irish woman who had lived for many years in central Australia

THE CHILD OF NATURE.

RYAN : "Go on, you black nigger; go on now !"
BILLY : "Well, you gib it one feller grog more belongin' to tixpence."
RYAN : "Be off now, or Oi'll belt the divil out of yer !"
BILLY (*picking up two rocks and looking at signboard*) : "Well, s'pose you no gib it grog more, by cripes I mash yer plurry licence."

Figure 10.4   "The Child of Nature"
Frank Mahoney, "Child of Nature" *Bulletin* March 25, 1893, p. 11.

with Indigenous peoples, gave a series of lectures in Perth in which she linked them with Irish Catholics in their use of weapons and sense of connectedness with the land.[44] Irish Australians in Perth were swift to condemn her views in letters in newspapers, declaring that Bates had "stooped to insult a large section of the community by comparing the despised blackfellow with the Irish."[45]

The Irish in Film and Television

After the early years of the twentieth century caricatures of the Irish continued, but there has also been a swell of narratives, songs, plays, and films that have celebrated a different version of Irishness – one that is loyal, rebellious, humorous, and happy to criticize the pretensions of the

English. This Irishness has its roots in nineteenth-century songs, convict plays, and ballads as well as Irish migrant connections with Ireland fostered by print media news and information. *Around the Boree Log* by John O'Brien, the pen name of Irish Australian priest Father Patrick Hartigan, included popular poems such as "Little Irish Mother," a carefully crafted nostalgic version of Irishness and motherhood. The same collection also included "Said Hanrahan," which was a playful account of the pessimistic Hanrahan's response to the vagaries of Australian bush life.[46]

Ned Kelly, the young charismatic Irish Australian bushranger who was caught and executed for murder in 1880, held an extraordinary place in Australian imagination even before his death.[47] His quixotic justifications of his actions are preserved in two dictated letters known as the Cameron and the Jerilderie letters.[48] The main thread running through these justifications was the overt discrimination he and his family had suffered at the hands of the police, often Irish themselves, and a sharply honed knowledge of the sufferings of the Irish in Ireland. Kelly's narrative has been entwined within Australian popular culture since he started his career as an outlaw, with ballads, cartoons, stories, films, plays, novels, and tourist attractions telling and retelling his story.[49]

Since the 1970s, some Australians with Irish heritage have connected their family stories with the political situation of the Northern Irish Troubles and, and at the same time, found links with other decolonizing movements, including the struggle for Aboriginal rights in Australia. Aboriginal activists, such as Gary Foley and Patrick Dodson, in the early 1970s also found common cause with Northern Irish republicans over the history of British colonization, with members of an Irish Republican Army (IRA) delegation visiting Aboriginal activists at the site of the tent embassy protests outside the Federal Parliament in 1972.[50] This has led to many Australians of Irish descent seeing Irish settlers and convicts as having relatively benign connections with Indigenous peoples during the colonizing processes, because of the shared oppression of both groups by the British.[51] Various explorations of the themes of the Irish as colonial outsiders holding innate connections with Indigenous people have appeared in plays, novels, film, and television. Two texts by Indigenous writers, Jack Davis' play *Kullark* (1979) and Eric Willmot's novel *Pemulwuy: The Rainbow Warrior* (1987), both set in the colonial period, explore the potential for Irish settlers to have respectful relationships with Indigenous peoples.[52] In *Pemulwuy*, Willmot includes an Irish character, Sean McDonough, who joins Pemulwuy's resistance warriors, showing them British military tactics and sharing Irish resistance strategies.

The television series, *Glitch* (2015–19), centers on events in a rural Australian town when people, who had been dead for many years, start to rise from their graves.[53] One of the storylines involves Paddy Fitzgerald (Irish actor Ned Dennehy), the Irish-born owner of the town's first hotel, who had died in the nineteenth century. Paddy had, what was portrayed as, a romantic extra-marital relationship with an Aboriginal woman, Kalinda (Yolngu actor Leila Gurruwiwi). His white descendants violently disapprove of Paddy's relationship with Kalinda and try to ensure that Paddy and Kalinda's Indigenous grandchildren cannot inherit the substantial estate. Here, the Irish-born nineteenth-century Paddy is shown as empathetic and warm toward Kalinda and their grandchildren, while the contemporary white grandsons are cruel and racist. This is a narrative that many Irish Australians would find familiar and one supported by the historian of Irish Australia, Patrick O'Farrell in in his influential book *The Irish in Australia* (1987), when he wrote that, "Irish Catholics treated the Aborigines as human beings, as equals."[54] As Ann McGrath acknowledges, it is hard to know whether O'Farrell based this assertion on a personal hunch or more direct research, although there are certainly many Indigenous families who acknowledge happy relationships between Irish and Indigenous parents and grandparents.[55]

In 2021, *New Gold Mountain*, a four-part television series, aired on Australian television. This critically acclaimed production shows the mid nineteenth-century gold rush in Australia from the perspective of Chinese miners on Ballarat goldfields.[56] The narrative includes an Irish miner, Patrick Thomas, played by Australian actor Christopher Baker. He is a man with a troubled past grieving the mysterious death of his wife and is shown to be on good terms with an Indigenous tracker, Hattie, played by Aboriginal actor Leonie Whyman. The writers make explicit connection between English exploitation of Indigenous peoples and the Irish when Hattie says to Patrick, "When a white woman dies, the English look first at blacks, Irish, doesn't matter." Significantly Patrick is also one of only two white male characters in the series who shows compassion toward the Chinese miners, refusing to participate in burning down of one of the Chinese buildings in revenge for his wife's death. These television programs exploring the heterogeneity of the white settler groups, especially the category of British, in Australian narratives of its colonial past, are to be welcomed; however, the implicit equivalence between the sufferings of the Irish and those of the Indigenous and Chinese is more problematic.

A recent film exploration of Irish and Indigenous identities and connections in the colonial past is *The Nightingale* (2019). The film centers on the brutalization of Irish convict, Clare, and the systematic violence perpetrated by the British Army against Indigenous people, particularly the guide, Billy.[57] The film makes explicit connections between the experiences of Clare and Billy, as he guides her through the unforgiving Tasmanian landscape so that she can enact her revenge. Initially, she is contemptuous of him, saying, "I am not travelling with a black – do I want to end up in a pot?" Then, as she learns to trust him, she underlines the commonality of their sufferings at the hand of the English white man. At one point she says, "You know what it's like to have a white fella take everything you have." The film underscores their respective differences from the English by the use of language. This is most clear at the end of the movie when Billy sings in his language while Clare sings in Irish. While many critics have praised the unflinching portrayal of gendered and racial colonial violence in the film, along with the careful and layered portrayal of the Indigenous peoples during the Black Wars in colonial Tasmania, they have tended to accept the implicit equivalence between Clare and Billy as both victims of the British colonial system.[58] However, Eualeyai/Kamillaroi lawyer, academic, novelist, and film-maker Larissa Behrendt has critiqued this equivalence, writing in her review, "in the end, there is no way to escape your own complicity when you are part of the colonial system – no matter how powerless you yourself are."[59] Irish Clare, racialized, discriminated against and brutalized by the English colonizers, also played a part in the violent dispossession of the Indigenous peoples of Australia, however unwillingly. It is significant that at the end of the film, Clare, though wounded and brutalized, lived to face another day, however uncertain that day looked, while Billy died from his wounds.

Conclusion

In 2001, when Michael D. Higgins was a member of the Irish parliament, he issued a statement on the centenary of Australian Federation encouraging Australia to protect and respect the rights of Aboriginal people and to seek a treaty with them. This speech caused Australian officials at the time to label his speech "unfriendly" and likely to "damage Irish-Australian relations."[60] In 2017, however, after his speech in Perth, the reaction from the Australian media was more subdued and reporting was limited to Irish and Indigenous media, reflecting both a more confident Indigenous political environment and perhaps a

conservative mainstream political context. His speech was reported admir-
ingly by Indigenous news outlet NTIV News, while Indigenous member of
the Australian federal parliament Linda Burney was quoted as saying the
acknowledgement was "heart warming and enormously honest."[61] The
climate in Australia had shifted so that in 2017 there was some room for
acknowledging the complexities of the role of the Irish in the colonization project in Australia. This shift is starting to be reflected in popular
culture.

Racialized stereotypes of Irishness circulated in Australia in the nineteenth and twentieth centuries, just as they did in the rest of the English-
speaking world. Cartoons of simianized men and stupid servant women
were popular and endlessly reproduced in illustrated papers, underpinning
real discrimination of Irish people and their children. These stereotypes
were also hugely popular on the stage in plays and in variety, musical,
and minstrel shows, giving Australian audiences access to similar characters that were honed in North America and England. The specificities of
Australian racial hierarchies are also woven within popular visual culture,
plays, and film, with linked Chinese and Irish stereotypes being fodder for
racially based humor. Perhaps partly in response, most Irish Australians
were enthusiastic proponents of the early twentieth-century restrictions
on immigration known as the White Australia policies, aimed at prevent-
ing Asian people from entering Australia. In their responses to anti-Irish
stereotypes, Irish Australians at the time demonstrated their distinctive
positive cultural contributions to emerging white Australian identities
and excluded Asian and other racialized minorities. At the same time,
when Irish people were in the same frame as Indigenous peoples initially,
they were visually coded as white and British. This coding reflects that
many Irish settlers were either active or complicit in the dispossession and
oppression of Indigenous peoples.

Many Irish Australians suggest that they are not the same as the those
of English and Scottish descent, and that because their ancestors were also
oppressed by the English, they were not as involved in the violence of the
frontier as other white settlers.[62] This narrative of shared oppression has
been explored in contemporary Australian literature and film when Irish
and Indigenous characters are portrayed as both suffering from British
colonialism in the harsh colonial landscape. Placing First Nations peoples'
suffering and trauma into the historical past is essential and not yet taken
as seriously as it should be in the Australian imagination. However, the
place of the Irish in this suffering is not straightforward and needs to be
considered in all its multilayered complexity.

Notes

* Research for this chapter was partially funded by an Australian Research Council Grant. My thanks to my co-chief investigator on this project, Professor Elizabeth Malcolm, and to Val Noone, Barry McCarron and William Peart.

1 Tom Durkin, "Some Misapprehension," *Bulletin* (Sydney), April 1, 1899. Discussed in Dianne Hall, "'Now him white man': images of the Irish in colonial Australia," *History Australia* 11, no. 2 (2014): 167–95.

2 Jennifer Kent, dir., *The Nightingale* (2018; Transmission Films), released in Australia in 2019.

3 For discussion of this within an international context see Marilyn Lake and Henry Reynolds, *Drawing the Global Colour Line: White Men's Countries and the International Challenge of Racial Equality* (Melbourne: Melbourne University Press, 2008).

4 Michael D. Higgins, "Ireland and Australia – A Deep, Historic and Valuable Contemporary Relationship," speech to Parliament of Western Australia, October 10, 2017, www.president.ie/en/media-library/speeches/speech-at-the-parliament-of-western-australia.

5 Simon Carswell, "Irish played part in atrocities against Aboriginal people – Australian MP," *Irish Times*, October 18, 2017.

6 Patrick O'Farrell, *The Irish in Australia*, 3rd ed. (Sydney: University of New South Wales Press, 2000).

7 Elizabeth Malcolm and Dianne Hall, *A New History of the Irish in Australia* (Sydney: NewSouth, 2018).

8 O'Farrell, *The Irish in Australia*.

9 Richard Broome, *Aboriginal Australians: A History since 1788* (Sydney: Allen and Unwin, 2010) and Malcolm and Hall, *A New History of the Irish in Australia*, 170–93.

10 Richard Scully and Marion Quartly, "Using cartoons as historical evidence," in *Drawing the Line: Using Cartoons as Historical Evidence*, eds. Richard Scully and Marion Quartly (Melbourne: Monash ePress, 2009), 11–26.

11 L. Perry Curtis, Jr., *Apes and Angels: The Irishman in Victorian Caricature* (Washington and London: Smithsonian Institution Press, [1971] 1997), xvii.

12 Curtis, Jr., *Apes and Angels*.

13 For his biography, see Joanna Gilmore, "Showing character," *Portrait Magazine* 54 (2016). www.portrait.gov.au/magazines/54/showing-character.

14 David Hayton, "From Barbarian to Burlesque: English images of the Irish, c. 1660–1750," *Irish Economic and Social History* 15 (1998): 5–31.

15 A. J. Patterson, "A Bush Christening," *Bulletin*, December 16, 1893; frequently anthologized.

16 *Weekly Times* (Melbourne), February 24, 1872, 9.

17 Peter Kuch, "Kilkenny, Melbourne, New York: George Tallis and the Irish Theatrical Diaspora," in *Irish Theater in America: Essays on Irish Theatrical Diaspora*, ed. John Harrington (Syracuse, NY: Syracuse University Press, 2009), 83, for discussion of Boucicault's tour of Melbourne.

18 Richard Waterhouse, *From Minstrel Show to Vaudeville: the Australian Popular Stage, 1788–1914* (Sydney: New South Wales University Press, 1990).

19 *Brisbane Courier*, November 24, 1894, 2; cited in Clay Roden Djubal, "'What Oh Tonight': The Methodology Factor and Pre-1930s Variety Theatre" (PhD diss., University of Queensland, 2005), 315, 410.

20 Cited in Melissa Bellanta, "The Larrikin's Hop: Larrikinism and Late Colonial Popular Theatre," *Australasian Drama Studies* 52 (2008): 138.

21 Bellanta, "The Larrikin's Hop," 135.

22 *Advocate,* March 21, 1885, 10. Article seems to be reprinted from *Irishman*.

23 *Bulletin*, February 19, 1914, 11.

24 *Advocate*, February 28, 1914, 24.

25 Obituary, *Herald* (Melbourne), May 6, 1948, 2.

26 Cited in Djubal, "'What Oh Tonight,'" 262.

27 Djubal, "'What Oh Tonight,'" 64–78.

28 *Mirror* (Perth), June 17, 1922, 2.

29 "Solicitor Charlie Greif has become a member of the Celtic Club," n.d., University of Queensland Archives, Fryer Library UQFL 9 Box 3, https://espace.library.uq.edu.au/view/UQ:135584.

30 Djubal, "'What Oh Tonight,'" 459 and *Lorgnette* (Melbourne), September 25, 1880, 2.

31 Malcolm and Hall, *A New History of the Irish in Australia*, 86–87.

32 Kevin Byrne, "'Simple Devices are Always Best': An Examination of the Amateur Play Publishing Industry in the United States," *The Papers of the Bibliographical Society of America* 108, no. 2 (2014): 217–37.

33 Gregory T. Carter, "'A Shplit Ticket, Half Irish, Half Chinay': Representations of Mixed-Race and Hybridity in the Turn-of-the-Century Theater," *Ethnic Studies Review* 31, no. 1 (2008): 32–54.

34 Charles A. Price, *The Great White Walls are Built: Restrictive Immigration to North America and Australasian, 1836–1888* (Canberra: Australian National University Press, 1974).

35 Kate Bagnall and Sophie Couchman, eds., *Chinese Australians: Politics, Engagement and Resistance* (Leiden: Brill, 2015); John Fitzgerald, *Big White Lie: Chinese Australians in White Australia* (Sydney: University of New South Wales Press, 2007).

36 Barry McCarron, "'Make it too hot for them to stop in the colony': The Irish Stance on the Chinese Question in Australia, 1851–1901," *Australasian Journal of Irish Studies* 20 (2020): 99–124; Malcolm and Hall, *A New History of the Irish in Australia*, 73–103.

37 Pauline Rule, "Challenging Conventions: Irish-Chinese Marriages in Colonial Victoria," in *Irish-Australian Studies: Papers Delivered at the Ninth Irish-Australian Conference, Galway, April 1997*, ed. Fiona Bateman (Sydney: Crossing Press, 2000), 205–16.

38 *The Bull Ant*, June 12, 1890, 5.

39 Tom Durkin, "Assault on a Chow," *Bulletin*, July 25, 1896, 16.

40 Malcolm and Hall, *A New History of the Irish in Australia*, 96–103.

41 Jane Lydon, *The Flash of Recognition: Photography and the Emergence of Indigenous Rights* (Sydney: University of New South Wales Press, 2013); Liz Conor, *Skin Deep: Settler Impressions of Aboriginal Women* (Perth: University of Western Australia Press, 2016).

42 Frank Mahony, "A Child of Nature," *Bulletin,* March 25, 1893, 9.

43 Malcolm and Hall, *A New History of the Irish in Australia,* 57–62.

44 Bob Reece, *Daisy Bates: Grand Dame of the Desert* (Canberra: National Library of Australia, 2007).

45 Malcolm and Hall, *A New History of the Irish in Australia,* 65, and see *West Australian,* February 8, 1910, 6.

46 G. P. Walsh, "Hartigan, Patrick Joseph (1878–1952)," *Australian Dictionary of Biography,* https://adb.anu.edu.au/biography/hartigan-patrick-joseph-6593/text11349; John O'Brien, *Around the Boree Log and Other Verses* (Sydney: Angus & Robertson Limited, 1922).

47 There is a vast array of literature on Ned Kelly; see Ian Jones, *Ned Kelly: A Short Life* (Melbourne: Lothian Books, 1995).

48 Alex McDermott, "Who Said the Kelly Letters? The Question of Authorship and the Nature of Wild Language in the Cameron and Jerilderie Letters," *Australian Historical Studies* 33, no. 118 (2002): 255–72.

49 Stephen Gaunson, "Ned Kelly and the Movies 1906–2003: Representation, Social Banditry and History" (PhD diss., RMIT University, 2010).

50 S. Robinson, "The Aboriginal Embassy: An Account of the Protests of 1972," in *The Aboriginal Tent Embassy: Sovereignty, Black Power, Land Rights and the State,* eds. Gary Foley, Andrew Schaap, and Edwina Howell (Abingdon: Taylor and Frances, 2013), 8.

51 For example see the writings of Irish Australian left wing activist, Bob Gould, "The Fate and Future of Aboriginal Australians," self published, 1999, www.marxists.org/archive/gould/1999/fateandfuture.htm; See also Malcolm and Hall, *A New History of the Irish in Australia,* 70–71, and Ann McGrath, "Shamrock Aborigines: The Irish, the Aboriginal Australians and their children," *Aboriginal History* 34 (2010), 55–84.

52 Jack Davis, *Kullark and The Dreamers* (Sydney: Currency, 1982); Eric Willmot, *Pemulwuy: the Rainbow Warrior* (Sydney: Bantam, 1987); discussed in Edward Watts, "In Your Head You Are Not Defeated: The Irish in Aboriginal Literature," *Journal of Commonwealth Literature* 26, no.1 (1991): 33–48; and Maggie Nolan, "Conceptualising Irish-Aboriginal Writing," *Australian Literary Studies* 36, no. 2 (2021), http://dx.doi.org/10.20314/als.776fd12cac.

53 *Glitch* (2015–2019; Australian Broadcasting Commission [ABC]), television series.

54 O'Farrell, *The Irish in Australia,* 72.

55 O'Farrell frustratingly did not include references to his extensive research in his influential book. He does cite "Aboriginal writer" Faith Bandler in the quoted sentence. Bandler, a well-known advocate for Aboriginal rights, was actually of South Sea Islander heritage; McGrath, "Shamrock Aborigines," 57, 70–73.

56 Corrie Chen, dir., *New Gold Mountain* (2021; Goalpost Productions), television series. Review by Luke Buckmaster, "Lush neo-western takes a new route through gold rush Australia," *The Guardian*, October 13, 2021, www.theguardian.com/tv-and-radio/2021/oct/13/new-gold-mountain-review-lush-neo-western-takes-a-new-route-through-gold-rush-australia.

57 Michelle Arrow and James Findlay, "A Critical Introduction to The Nightingale: Gender, Race and Troubled Histories on Screen," *Studies in Australasian Cinema* 14, no. 1 (2020): 3–14; Lyndal Ryan, *The Aboriginal Tasmanians* (St. Lucia, Qld.: University of Queensland Press, 1981).

58 Arrow and Findlay, "A Critical Introduction," 7.

59 Larissa Behrendt, "The Nightingale review – ambitious, urgent and necessarily brutal. But who is it for?" *The Guardian*, August 20, 2019, www.theguardian.com/film/2019/aug/20/the-nightingale-review-ambitious-urgent-and-necessarily-brutal-but-who-is-it-for.

60 *Age,* April, 28 2001, 27. Thanks to Val Noone for this reference.

61 Nakari Thorpe, "Irish President acknowledges role of Irish in persecution of Aboriginal people," *NITV News*, October 17, 2017, www.sbs.com.au/nitv/nitv-news/article/2017/10/19/irish-president-acknowledges-role-irish-persecution-aboriginal-people.

62 McGrath, "Shamrock Aborigines," 64.

CHAPTER 11

White Nationalism and Irish America
A Cultural History Told through Works by James T. Farrell and Eugene O'Neill

Peter D. O'Neill

Introduction

This chapter traces Irish America's place in the lineage of the white nationalist movement and helps explain the remarkable prominence of Irish American Catholics in today's increasingly far-right Republican Party. It is, of course, true that Irish American Catholics are prominent in the Democratic Party's progressive left wing. Nevertheless, the presence of Irish American extreme right-wingers merits deeper investigation, not least because of the vilification that Irish Catholic immigrants endured in prior centuries at the hands of militant white nationalist groupings such as the Know-Nothings and the Ku Klux Klan (KKK). In response, Irish American Catholics set about developing an American patriotism that white nationalists found increasingly hard to resist. This contradictory process was chronicled by a number of writers who had been born into, and seldom fully escaped, Irish Catholic America. Two of the most accomplished and prolific among them were Eugene O'Neill (1888–1953) and James T. Farrell (1904–79). Through analysis of their works, this chapter charts the transmutation of the Catholic Irish from an expendable people in the British colonial state in Ireland into valued American citizens, and in many cases, into white nationalists.

Nationalisms and (White) Irish America

As Cedric J. Robinson has noted, notions of racial supremacy fueled modern European nationalism, and for proof, one need look no further than the role that English nationalism played for centuries in Ireland.[1] United States nationalism is not dissimilar. For nativist groups that formed in the nineteenth and twentieth centuries, such as the Know-Nothings and the KKK, American nationalism was synonymous with whiteness, a view that thrives today among neo-Nazi, and alt-right groups, as well as the

Trumpian Republican Party. That said, American nativist objections to the Famine Irish of the mid-1800s were grounded not so much in race but in religion. Nineteenth-century nativists – predominantly Protestants steeped in notions of an American, individualist democracy – saw threats in the Rome-centered authoritarianism of the Catholic Church to which these immigrants adhered, not to mention the perceived communitarianism of the immigrants themselves. These concerns paled, however, in the face of American capitalism's need for labor; that is, its desire for white labor. As early as 1790, the first U.S. naturalization law decreed citizenship open to "free white persons."[2] From the outset, Irish Catholics, as Europeans, were seen to qualify, and when they began to arrive in droves because of the Famine, they were welcomed to fill American capitalism's apparent need for European – that is, white – migrants who would both drive the economy and maintain the unstable equilibrium of the racial state.[3]

But as I note elsewhere, citizenship, a legal term, is one thing, and nationality, a cultural one, is something different.[4] The Famine Irish, though admitted to U.S. citizenship, were not seen to qualify as American nationals. They had to earn that status. As citizens, Irish people inserted themselves into U.S. state apparatuses, both ideological and repressive, in order to become American nationals, and secure a place in white nationalist America at the expense of non-white peoples.[5]

In importance to Irish America, the first three decades of the twentieth century rank second only to the Famine era, Ron Ebest maintains.[6] The significance of this period cannot be doubted, for it encompasses Russia's revolution and Ireland's struggle for independence, the onset of Britain's imperial decline, and the first global war. The United States saw a Market Crash and Great Depression, a Great Migration, and racist brutalities labeled Jim Crow in the South yet present to varying degrees throughout the country. In my view, however, the period needs to be extended, because Irish Americans' attainment of their cultural status as American nationals as well as the legal status of U.S. citizens, is intimately tied to U.S. imperial ambitions. The scope of this chapter thus reaches ahead of Ebest's cutoff point, to the post-World War II consolidation of U.S. global hegemony. It also reaches back, to 1898, the year that the United States won a short-lived war against Spain, and with it, colonial holdings as near as Cuba and Puerto Rico and as far-flung as Guam and the Philippines.

This period was marked by upward mobility for many Irish. "Of the nearly five million Irish Americans in 1900," writes Kirby Miller, "about two thirds had been born in the United States, and by World War I, the Famine immigrants' grandchildren were coming to maturity."[7] The lack of finances that had barred the Famine migrants of the 1800s from home-steading turned to benefit them by the early 1900s, for as American cities prospered, "the Irish were poised to take advantage of the rise of trade unions and the tremendous growth of urban government, public services, and managerial and white-collar occupations."[8] With Irish entry into the middle class came a lessening of anti-Irish discriminatory practices. Kevin Kenny states that "the Catholicism of Irish Americans excluded them from full respectability in the United States for decades to come, until the election of John F. Kennedy in 1960 finally settled that question."[9] This may be true, but even in the early twentieth century, nativists came to see the Irish as preferable to a newer supposed threat of Jewish, Italian, and Slavic immigrants.[10]

As for the Irish emigrants, over time many came to lose connection to events in Ireland. Interest peaked with the 1916 Easter Rising executions in Dublin, which, as David Brundage records, "paved the way for the greatest outpouring of support for Irish republicanism that the United States had ever seen."[11] It rekindled somewhat with the Irish War of Independence and Terence MacSwiney's death on hunger strike in 1920. But the ensuing Irish Civil War spurred a disillusionment which, coupled with U.S. patriotism, unleashed when America entered World War I, dampened enthusiasm for Irish nationalist causes. As Miller puts it: "By 1923 ... the long dark winter of Irish exile in America was over. The golden summer of Irish-America tourism was about to begin."[12]

A Golden Era of Writing: O'Farrell and O'Neill

This Irish American golden summer also involved a golden era of Irish American writing. Kate Chopin wrote *The Awakening* (1899), the same year America extended its influence to the Pacific, and the years following saw works by authors as varied as F. Scott Fitzgerald, John O'Hara, and Raymond Chandler. Two others, Eugene O'Neill and James T. Farrell, stand out in this group, and not only because of their prodigious output. Their lives, works, and times offer insights into processes of class mobility and of racialization – of the paths by which Catholic Irish America moved from their marginality in the Famine era to their standing in the racial-state politics of today. An examination of the searing accounts of the Irish white nationalist worldview found in Farrell's novels, in tandem with the white blindness visible in O'Neill's so-called Negro Plays, exposes the early twentieth century as a crucial moment of Catholic Irish acceptance as American nationals and, with it, of entry into a white racial state.

A brief consideration of these authors' biographies will set the stage for the study and comparison of their works. Born in 1888 in a New York hotel, O'Neill was, by sixteen years, the elder author. The second of his parents' three sons, he had an affluent east coast childhood, with his father paying for his curtailed Princeton education. After an "unwieldy" start with *Bread and Butter* (1914), O'Neill quickly hit stride, writing at least thirty full-length and nearly two dozen one-act plays. In the process, he won the 1936 Nobel Prize as well as the 1920, 1922, 1928, and 1957 Pulitzers.[13] Recently, one of his last works, *Long Day's Journey into Night* (1957), was named the second-best play of all time, losing out to *Hamlet*.[14] Farrell, meanwhile, was born in 1904 on the South Side of Chicago and grew up poor, in a household with many siblings, five of whom lived till adulthood. He paid his own way at the University of Chicago. Like O'Neill, Farrell was prolific, producing twenty-two novels, over 200 short stories, one book of literary criticism and another that was part memoir and part paean to baseball, a poetry collection, a play, and numerous other essays and stories. Although he would claim no world-renowned prizes, his first books, forming a trilogy known as *Studs Lonigan* (1935), have been ranked among the twentieth century's top thirty novels.[15]

In some respects, the two authors have much in common. All their grandparents, as well as O'Neill's father, were Irish-born Famine immigrants. Both sons of a Knight of Columbus, they were raised Catholic and attended Catholic schools, yet drifted from the faith. Both attended, and dropped out of, prestigious universities. Both grew up in dysfunctional families. O'Neill's childhood was ruined by his father's alcoholism and his mother's morphine addiction, while Farrell's was burdened by poverty, with relatives taking him in when his parents could not afford to support him. As adults, both battled substance abuse and suffered bad marriages. While such commonalities tied the two writers together and were reflected in their intense examinations of the Irish Catholic experience in America, differences in class background and political exposure led O'Neill and Farrell to diverge in political philosophies. This divergence is reflected in their writing.

Farrell's Chronicles of Irish American White Nationalism

Farrell's most celebrated work is his first, the novel *Young Lonigan* (1932), published when the author was in his late twenties. *The Young Manhood of Studs Lonigan* (1934) and *Judgment Day* (1935) followed and were quickly published in a trilogy volume, *Studs Lonigan* (1935).[16] Biographer Edgar M.

Branch considers Farrell's trilogy "truly a single body of work because it expresses his 'psychological life-cycle' through the development of a unified subject."[17] Adding to this cycle were other works, each incorporating autobiographical elements and together affording formidable insights into urban Irish-American Catholic life.[18]

Young Lonigan opens on the day in 1916 that the Democratic Party nominated President Woodrow Wilson for reelection. At the 1914 dedication of a statue of an Ireland-born Revolutionary War hero, Wilson had intoned: "Some Americans need hyphens in their names, because only part of them has come over; but when the whole man has come over, heart and thought and all, the hyphen drops of its own weight out of his name." The hero "was not an Irish American," Wilson said, but "an Irishman who became an American," thus making clear the road that all Irish must travel.[19] Farrell hoped to trace in *Lonigan* the rise of the Famine outcasts and their offspring, or as he put it in an essay on the trilogy, "the process in which many were assimilated into the American petit bourgeoisie and the American labor aristocracy."[20] The influence of Friedrich Engels's work on the family and capitalism is evident when Farrell notes that the "important institutions in the education of Studs Lonigan were the home and family, the church, and the playground."[21] But by starting *Lonigan* with news of a president who insisted on assimilation – and who was known as a racist and segregationist – Farrell underscored U.S. institutions' spiritual impoverishment. The phrase is his own: in a 1949 essay, Farrell wrote that Lonigan's Chicago neighborhood "was several steps removed from the slums and dire economic want"; the poverty he wished to portray was "spiritual."[22] Thus, Studs is an alcoholic, imprisoned in the bondage of an inflated ego and surrounded by persons in similar psychic straitjackets. Thoughts stunted, his words and actions must propel the story forward. As Branch describes it, Farrell's style is "more phonographic than photographic."[23] Farrell expresses spiritual poverty through the bravado of hating the other, through stomach-churning racist speech and acts – but also through words of doubt, of cracks in the veneer of contentment projected by those Irish who reached the middle class. These cracks widen as the trilogy ends, at that moment of deflated American might, known as the Great Depression.

Emblems of this spiritual poverty are the episodes bookending the trilogy. Both feature Studs's father – Pat, or Paddy. The first occurs near the start of *Young Lonigan*. Paddy sits on his porch, sucking on a cigar, recalling his hazy past in a smoke of smug satisfaction. His father was "a pauperized greenhorn," a Famine-era immigrant unable to seize what

America had to offer. A brother, Jack, did answer America's call, only to die in Cuba in the war against Spain. Farrell's pointed reference to the first U.S. foray into overseas colonialism appears lost on Paddy, who proceeds to list the misfortunes of other siblings. Bill ran away at seventeen. Mike languishes back east, and Joe works as a lowly motorman. Catherine, a "scarlet woman," turned to prostitution when the family abandoned her for getting pregnant out of wedlock. Paddy pinpoints the source of their failures: "They hadn't had, none of them, the persistence that he had. He had stuck to his job and nearly killed himself working. But now he was reaping his rewards."[24] His successful painting business and portfolio of properties prove he "pulled himself up by his own bootstraps ... and pretty soon he would be worth a cool hundred thousand berries." An ideal of rugged individuality, Paddy remains "a good Catholic, and a good American, a good father, and a good husband."[25] James Byrne sees in this passage a key to understanding Irish American racial politics and ideology. Paddy embraces the "American dream (mythologically available to all immigrants)," succeeding "through the application of Emersonian individualism, the true tenet of American identity." Like others of his generation, Paddy attains the middle class "through the disavowal of the communal nature of working class or 'shanty' Irish" life.[26]

Paddy further disavows newcomers in words one would rather not reprint. Migration has brought Black Americans from the South and Jewish immigrants from Europe to the city. "But now, well," he says, "the n*****s and the k***s were getting in, and they were dirty, and you didn't know but what, even in broad daylight, some n***** moron might be attacking his girls."[27] Paddy shifts quickly and often from complaint to concern. "Such oscillation between security and fear, pivoting around the relative status of African Americans," writes Lauren Onkey, "characterizes Farrell's depiction of Irish Americans in the *Studs Lonigan* trilogy. His Irish characters in Chicago measure their status and potential for success according to how close they are, literally, to African Americans."[28]

As one might expect from a novel titled *Judgment Day*, the final pages of the final book of the trilogy hold no candle for the so-called land of opportunity. The Depression has decimated Paddy's fortune, while his favorite son lies on his deathbed. In search of answers to barely articulated questions, Paddy returns to where his Emersonian journey began. Kneeling at his old parish church in the neighborhood he had abandoned in an act of white flight, he curses Jews for America's financial problems and then asks God to spare Studs. God's silence deafens. Walking his old streets, Paddy is startled by a "Red parade," men and women, young and old, of all races, marching to upbeat music behind a trade union banner. "What a shame! What a crime!," Paddy says when his companion, Officer Jim Doyle, sees two neighborhood kids, the O'Neills, marching; "And they were taught by the sisters at St. Patrick's. Once, they must have been decent kids like my own."[29] An Irish Workers Club banner comes into view: "Say, they must be left-handed turkeys and Orangemen to be with this outfit," Paddy continues; "You'd never find a good Irishman who was true to the church and the memory of his good old Irish mother in this outfit." And yet, unlike himself, "they seemed happy."[30] He repeats this observation twice more in quick succession.

Paddy had pursued happiness, one of the "inalienable rights" mentioned in the U.S. Declaration of Independence, but happiness, it seems, had not returned the favor. His work ethic, in the end, counted for little. He had "staked everything on the American capitalist ethos of individual effort," Ann Douglas observes, "pulling himself up, as he often boasts, by his own bootstraps."[31] He is at a loss when, on *Judgment Day*, the bootstraps snap.

Where he might turn – where other Catholic Irish in America did and do now turn – is to institutions and individuals that claim to protect their American freedom often by disparaging others. Evidence of both options is present in the *Lonigan*. At one point, Paddy insists Studs join the Knights of Saint Christopher, alongside him and "nearly every leading Catholic of importance in this country.'"[32] The son reluctantly accedes, and after a bizarre ritual, is sworn in as a member. He "raised his right hand, and in a mood of solemnity, repeated a simple oath pledging secrecy and the defense of the faith and his country."[33] Farrell's model is the Knights of Columbus, a Catholic men's organization founded in 1881 by a son of Famine escapees, Father Michael McGivney. "Columbus" was chosen to appeal beyond the Irish community and to evoke the idea of American loyalty.[34] Today, the Knights claim two million members worldwide.[35] Self-described as a charitable organization, the Knights, and especially those designated knights of the "Fourth Degree," have aligned Catholicism with American patriotism, and in the process, veered ever more to the political right. An official 2001 publication stresses the group's American patriotic achievements, taking particular pride in what it calls the "campaign to protect the flag from desecration symbolized by the Fourth Degree's commitment to compete with those groups that perceived the flag as a sign of capitalism's oppression and of U.S. exploitation of the global markets."[36] The passage indicates the extent to which the culture wars of recent decades have lurched the Knights, among other Catholic organizations, toward today's hard-right Republican Party, an alliance surely unimaginable during the presidency

of John F. Kennedy. *Studs* helps us see how this shift away from the liberalism of the Democratic Party that began in the 1960s, had its roots in a
much earlier period.

It also shows how the appeal of today's Trumpian-style demagoguery for a
considerable number of Irish American Catholics has, in fact, had a long history too. Farrell's portrayal of Paddy, as his world turns upside down, shows
us this. We see how someone like him might turn to individuals offering
easy answers to complex problems. Toward the end of the *Lonigan* trilogy
Paddy, parroting anti-Semitism spewed on the radio by a priest called Father
Moylan, hopes "a man like Mussolini" might emerge "to take things out
of the hands of the Jew International bankers and the gangsters."[37] Farrell
modeled Moylan on Irish American Catholicism's own real-life demagogue,
Father Charles Coughlin, another descendant of Famine escapees. For much
of the 1920s and 1930s, millions of people, Catholics and Protestants alike,
listened as the charismatic priest aimed populist attacks at Bolsheviks, bankers, and Jews. Only Pearl Harbor managed to curtail his efforts, for with the
deployment of U.S. troops to fight World War II abroad came an urgent
need to silence fascist sympathizers at home.[38]

Studs Lonigan, a classic work of American realism, exposes Irish-
American racism of the early twentieth century like no other work of fiction. Its success lies in the linkage Farrell makes between Irish American
class mobility (and immobility) and the racialization processes at work in
the United States. The trilogy's brutal realism is informed both by Farrell's
precarious upbringing, and early political education. Drawn to Marxism
as a young man, he had read Leon Trotsky's *Literature and the Revolution*,
a work that stresses the inextricable links between revolutionary politics,
social history, and art, and was deeply influenced by it.[39] Though he never
closely affiliated with any group, he considered himself a socialist, engaging frequently with the politics of the left. For example, he spoke at the
American Writers' Congress organized by the Communist Party USA in
1935, the day after his third novel appeared. He was far from a CP hack,
though. He broke early with the Stalinism that dominated the American
communist movement of the pre- and post-Second World War years and
set about exposing what he considered to be its distorted socialist thinking. He even promoted American democracy over Russian totalitarianism
at a 1949 gathering in Paris, stating that the United States was "one of the
freest countries in the world."[40] While Farrell made that particular utter-
ance to counteract the Stalinist propagandists active at the conference,
he knew full well that this was a far from accurate statement. As a friend
of *Native Son* (1940) author Richard Wright, and as one who frequently

decried anti-Black violence and who joined in A. Philip Randolph's campaign against segregation in the armed forces, he knew that notions of American "freedom" did not extend to Black American citizens. As we shall see, when it came to race, although both flawed, Farrell differed from O'Neill significantly.[41]

O'Neill's White Liberal Blindness

The Second World War also silenced Eugene O'Neill, though in a quite different way from the demagogue Fr. Coughlin. In 1939, just as the conflict consumed Europe and menaced the United States, O'Neill completed *The Iceman Cometh*, one of his most acclaimed plays, in which patrons of Harry Hope's bar slowly kill themselves with drink while dreaming of greatness and success.[42] The play shows "that mankind requires life-sustaining pipe-dreams to endure the terrifying realities of modern life," writes Robert Dowling.[43] But in 1939, that message seemed untimely. "No, *The Iceman Cometh* would be wrong now," O'Neill told a journalist, and "a New York audience could neither see nor hear its meaning. The pity and the tragedy of defensive pipe dreams would be deemed unpatriotic."[44] No less a figure than J. Edgar Hoover labeled O'Neill's earlier work an assault on "the American way" and wrote, in an FBI memo, that the playwright was under investigation for treason.[45] O'Neill postponed *Iceman*'s premiere until after the war.

"Pipe dreams," of course, mirrors "American Dream," the myth that O'Neill's plays frequently eviscerate, often in tribute to America's dispossessed.[46] I have written elsewhere about the American Dream in relation to the Famine Irish, finding the roots of this coinage in the 1776 Declaration of Independence and in the U.S. cultural imaginary's fetishization of the words "liberty" and freedom" – terms that the Founding Era reserved for persons, males, of European descent.[47] America's contemporary white nationalists claim direct inheritance of that tradition.

The playwright himself laid the hypocrisy bare: "Telling the world about our American Dream!… If it exists, as we tell the world, why don't we make it work in one small hamlet in the United States?" O'Neill scoffed at a journalist, and then took aim at American exceptionalism. "If we taught history and told the truth," he insisted, "we'd teach school children that the United States has followed the same greedy rut of every other country. We would tell who is guilty. The list of guilty ones responsible would include some of our greatest heroes. Their portraits should be taken down and burned."[48] Similar views, of sympathy toward indigenous peoples and antipathy toward false patriotism, recur throughout O'Neill's oeuvre, with his biographer Dowling describing one work as "a frontal assault on the excesses of American cultural imperialism."[49]

Yet even while nodding approval at views that code as "liberal," we must not ignore a glaring anomaly in the playwright's work. African Americanist Sterling A. Brown had observed in 1933 that to white writers "searching for 'life in the raw,' Negro life and character seemed to be for exploitation. There was the Negro's savage inheritance, as they conceived it: hot jungle nights, the tom-tom calling to esoteric orgies."[50] O'Neill was in this camp. Though sensitive to some dispossessed, he seemed blind to the racism of his so-called Negro Plays. Perhaps for that reason, few African Americanists engage with his work.

A notable exception is Cedric Robinson. While acknowledging the debt theater owes O'Neill, Robinson criticizes five of his plays that center on or contain Black characters, as being rife with "threadbare clichés."[51] Their timing is crucial to Robinson's argument. He observes that O'Neill "inserted them into American dramatic theater at a transformative moment in the country's racial regime. Lynching, segregation, and peonage were constants on the domestic front, while imperialism and colonialism profoundly altered the nation's cultural infrastructure."[52] O'Neill's depictions only served to further the already rampant racist stereotyping of the day. One does not have to look hard to find such clichés in the plays. For example, *All God's Chillun Got Wings* (1924) concerns a tormented Black man trapped in a marriage to a crazed Irish American woman; *Thirst* (1914) involves the tragic mulatto; *Moon of the Caribbees* (1917) features Black prostitutes; *The Dreamy Kid* (1918) centers on the young Black murderer, and *The Emperor Jones* (1920) is about a corrupt (and murderous) Black politician.

The politician in that last-named play is a one-time Pullman porter, Brutus Jones – a role for which O'Neill, against considerable resistance from the white theater establishment, cast Charles Gilpin, the first Black lead in a Broadway play. Jones escapes prison after murdering a white guard, then lands on an island where he overthrows the Black ruler and declares himself Emperor. (Stage directions situate the play on an unnamed West Indian island "as yet not self-determined by White Marines," a reference to the U.S. Marines' invasion of Haiti a few years before.[53]) Jones's meteoric rise spirals into insanity, his trappings of modernity stripped away so that, by the time of his death, he is reduced to a primitive state – a state O'Neill used, Kurt Eisen writes, "as a kind of mask of the modern alienated self."[54] The play thus "offered its predominantly white audiences a bracing contrast to the formulaic, escapist fare of most American theater and invited them into the heart of their own darkness."[55]

Others have been less impressed. During production, Gilpin and O'Neill had frequent and often vicious fights over the playwright's profligate use of the "N" word and other racist epithets in the script.[56] Nearly a century later, echoing Brown, Robinson would provide his own critique of O'Neill's turn to the primitive. "*The Emperor Jones* became the real," writes Robinson, "and the real was drowned out by O'Neill's tom-toms."[57] The play may well be an examination of the savagery that resides in the human heart, but, as Carme Manuel maintains, "it shows it is confined to the heart of black America."[58] O'Neill, like Farrell, resisted the American urge to repress blackness, yet his artistic primitivism, like that of his contemporaries who gathered under its umbrella, was a racist form of art. O'Neill, as Aoife Monks notes, "like many other primitivists, nonetheless reaffirmed many of the stereotypes of blackness by confining black identity to the authentic and primitive 'black body,' a body that was both radical *and* reductive in performance in the 1920s."[59] She wonders whether white artists staging representations of Black identity were really representing blackness or were more concerned with their own white identity.[60] The heart of their own darkness, then, is their whiteness.

The interplay between whiteness and darkness is a trope familiar to theater. Its long history encompasses earlier Irish-American performances of blackness in nineteenth-century blackface minstrelsy. Undoubtedly, English colonialism's designation of less-than-white status to the Irish contributed to Irish American insecurity in the face of American white nationalist policies, and this in turn fueled their participation in blackface as a means to denigrate Black Americans and bolster their place in the American white nationalist fold. O'Neill himself rejected the minstrelsy tradition, and yet unconsciously maintained it in *Emperor Jones*. Despite his successes, he was well aware that his Irish Catholic background barred access to the upper echelons of U.S. society. He was exposed to anti-Irish bigotry growing up in Connecticut, and the experience never left him. Thus, when regarded from the perspective of his Irish American ethnicity, the play may be viewed as grounded in the Irish American minstrelsy tradition after all. Indeed, O'Neill had adorned "brownface" in one of his earliest plays. Thus, Monks argues, "O'Neill, like Brutus Jones, was liminally and precariously 'coloured.'"[61]

Notwithstanding the racist tropes recounted in this chapter, some of O'Neill's plays, not to mention the casting of a Black lead, irked white supremacists as well as whites who considered themselves more moderate. Klan threats precluded *Emperor Jones*'s national troupe from touring farther south than Richmond.[62] Four years later, at a time when nearly a third of all U.S. states outlawed miscegenation, white America confronted O'Neill's depiction in *All God's Chillun Got Wings* of a Black husband and an Irish American wife.[63] (Remarkably, at no point in the controversy was the whiteness of the intermarried woman cast into doubt.) An outraged Klan leader threatened to disappear O'Neill's son if the play continued, and O'Neill scrawled in the return post, "Go Fuck Yourself!"[64]

For well over a decade, O'Neill did not again represent a Black person on stage. Then the cast of characters in *The Iceman Cometh*, finished in 1939 and first mounted in 1946, included Joe Mott. Described as a "one-time proprietor of a Negro gambling house," Mott constituted another of O'Neill's "threadbare clichés" no less than many of his earlier Black characters.[65] Mott's characterization, however, displayed more nuance. Mott withstood a barrage of racist abuse unbowed and achieved equality of sorts with his white fellow habitués of Hope's bar. Like them, he clung to a doomed belief in future success, a pipe dream as fanciful as that of other Americans.

Conclusion

Even as it demystifies the American Dream of success, *The Iceman Cometh* fails to elucidate the structures upon which that dream has been constructed. Society's racial underpinning peeks out when Joe Mott is labeled a "Negro" fitting a stock stage type. Mott's eventual acceptance by other patrons appears to push racism back. But this resolution depends on Mott's having sustained and survived racial invective. The racial state remains, hidden by a curtain yet nonetheless ever-present. Whether the playwright, Eugene O'Neill, saw this is debatable. Indeed, it is doubtful, given that his prior cycle of so-called Negro Plays turned on, indeed celebrated, the stereotypes of racism. His Black characters were raw, primitive, derisible, and even, as with the brutal self-appointed Emperor, Brutus Jones, hateable.

Shortcomings in O'Neill's work may be traced in part to his embrace of individualism, a tradition rooted in America's puritanism and flourishing in the libertarian movement that today buttresses the hard-right Republican Party. Asked about his politics during rehearsals for *Iceman*, O'Neill replied: "I am a philosophical anarchist … which means, 'Go to it, but leave me out of it.'"[66] Clearly, telling the KKK to "fuck off" fell far short of any activist approach to the dismantling of white American nationalism. He had embraced philosophical anarchism as a young man when came under the influence of a publisher named Benjamin R. Tucker. Tucker was a leading light of a branch of "an American individualist-anarchist movement that," as the Gelbs put it, "advocated attacking the establishment with words."[67] Descended from New Englanders, Tucker favored individualists like Ralph Waldo Emerson and Henry David Thoreau, as well as German anarchist Max Stirner.[68] His so-called philosophical anarchy – prizing the individual above all, using words and not actions to express opposition to social or political issues – appealed to the self-indulgent O'Neill. This belief in philosophical anarchism, which stressed the primacy of the individual over external forces like the state, remained with him throughout his life. It blinded him not only to the systemic racialization processes at work in the U.S. but also to his own racist representations of Black people.

Standing in stark contrast was O'Neill's contemporary of Irish ancestry, James T. Farrell. Through his semi-autobiographical accounts of Catholic Irish life in urban America, Farrell, a realist in writing and socialist in politics, forced readers to see the racial structures that, in his own phrasing, left U.S. society spiritually impoverished. Even as characters in the *Studs Lonigan* trilogy repeat shameful epithets, even as they mimic the actions of hate, the reader is made at once to see them as hateful. So too is the emptiness of the American dream, revealed by Farrell's work in a manner more intimate, more indeterminate, than that of O'Neill.

Together, the lives and works of these two men help to explain the pulls felt by others like them, other Americans descended from Irish Famine emigrants and trying to attain status in the U.S. Assimilation for many vacillated between a struggle to navigate generational memories of subjection in Ireland and the demand they embrace, accept, or at least tolerate, the structures of white American nationalism. The pulls are evident today in the prominence of Irish Americans, both in the extremist white nationalist ranks of the U.S. right and in the liberal or progressive ranks of the U.S. left.

Despite other shortcomings, O'Neill deeply understood the force of history. Words uttered by Mary Tyrone in his masterwork *Long Day's Journey into Night* thus may serve as a call to think upon unthinkable histories to avoid their repetition: "The past is the present, isn't it," she remarks. "It's the future too."[69]

Yes, it is, if we ignore it.

Notes

1 Cedric J. Robinson, *Black Marxism: The Making of the Black Radical Tradition* (Chapel Hill: University of North Carolina Press, 1983). The work is breathtaking in its scope and ambition – the rewriting of the rise of Western civilization and includes a critique of the Eurocentric assumptions of Marxism.

2 See Peter D. O'Neill, *Famine Irish and the American Racial State* (New York: Routledge, 2017).

3 O'Neill, *Famine Irish*, 14.

4 O'Neill, *Famine Irish*, 4–7.

5 See Louis Althusser, *Lenin and Philosophy & Other Essays*, trans. Ben Brewster (New York: Monthly Review Press, 1971), 95–100.

6 Ron Ebest, *Private Histories: The Writing of Irish America, 1900–1935* (Notre Dame: University of Notre Dame Press, 2005), 11.

7 Kirby Miller, *Emigrants and Exiles: Ireland and the Irish Exodus to North America* (Oxford: Oxford University Press, 1985), 493.

8 Miller, *Emigrants and Exiles*, 493.

9 Kevin Kenny, *The American Irish: A History* (New York: Pearson Educational, 2000), 181.

10 A drastic decline in Irish immigration likely also contributed to this dynamic. See Kenny, *The American Irish*, 182.

11 David Brundage, *Irish Nationalists in America: The Politics of Exile, 1978–1998* (Oxford: Oxford University Press, 2016), 147.

12 Miller, *Emigrants and Exiles*, 555.

13 Robert L. Daniels, "Bread and Butter," *Variety*, September 7, 1998, https://variety.com/1998/film/reviews/bread-and-butter-1200455313/.

14 Andy Propst, "The best plays of all time," *Time Out*, July 17, 2021, accessed July 31, 2021, www.timeout.com/newyork/theater/best-plays-of-all-time.

15 "100 Best American Novels," *Modern Library*, accessed July 31, 2021, www.modernlibrary.com/top-100/100-best-novels/. *Studs Lonigan* is ranked twenty-ninth on a list in which the first three positions are occupied by the Irish writer James Joyce and the Irish American writer F. Scott Fitzgerald.

16 James P. Farrell, *Studs Lonigan* (New York: Penguin, [1935] 2001).

17 Edgar M. Branch, *James T. Farrell*, Pamphlets on American Writers Number 29 (Minneapolis: University of Minnesota Press, 1963), 10.

18 After the *Studs* trilogy, Farrell's most important work is the Danny O'Neill pentalogy, composed of *A World I Never Made* (1936), *No Star is Lost* (1938), *Father and Son* (1940), *My Days of Anger* (1943), and *The Face of Time* (1953). Also worth noting is his Bernard Carr trilogy, comprising *Bernard Carr* (1946), *The Road Between* (1949), and *Yet Other Waters* (1952).

19 Quoted in James P. Byrne, "Seeking Agency, Finding Nothing: Irish American Identity as a His-Story of Absence in James T. Farrell's *Studs Lonigan*," *Foilsiú: An Interdisciplinary Journal of Irish Studies* 3, no. 1 (Spring 2003): 7.

20 James T. Farrell, *The League of Frightened Philistines and Other Papers* (New York: Vanguard, 1949), 87.

21 Farrell, *The League*, 87–88. This statement also anticipated the work of French Marxist Louis Althusser who argued that such things operated as ideological state apparatuses. See Althusser, *Lenin and Philosophy*.

22 Farrell, *The League*, 86–87.

23 Edgar M. Branch, *James T. Farrell* (New York: Twayne Publishers, 1971), 38.

24 Farrell, *Studs Lonigan*, 15.

25 Farrell, *Studs Lonigan*, 16.

26 Byrne, "Seeking Agency," 11.

27 Farrell, *Studs Lonigan*, 18.

28 Lauren Onkey, "James Farrell's *Studs Lonigan* Trilogy and the Anxieties of Race," *Éire-Ireland* 40, no. 3–4, (2005): 105.

29 Farrell, *Studs Lonigan*, 838.

30 Farrell, *Studs Lonigan*, 839.

31 Ann Douglas, "Introduction," in *Studs Lonigan*, James T. Farrell (New York: Penguin, 2001), xiii.

32 Farrell, *Studs Lonigan*, 587

33 Farrell, *Studs Lonigan*, 615.

34 Douglas Brinkley and Julie Fenster, *Parish Priest: Father Michael McGivney and American Catholicism* (New York: Harper Collins, 2006), 119.

35 Susan Klemond, "Supreme Knight Carl Anderson highlights Knights' efforts worldwide," *National Catholic Reporter*, August 13, 2019, www.ncronline .org/news/people/supreme-knight-carl-anderson-highlights-knights-efforts-worldwide.

36 Christopher J. Kauffman, *Patriotism and Fraternalism in the Knights of Columbus* (New York: Crossroad Publishing Company, 2001), 114.

37 Farrell, *Studs Lonigan*, 734.

38 See Sheldon Marcus, *Father Coughlin: The Tumultuous Life of the Priest of the Little Flower* (Boston: Little Brown, 1973). Bizarrely, in places Coughlin's charisma seems to have ensnared this biographer. Coughlin is an obvious forerunner of other extreme right demagogues, such as Senator Joseph McCarthy, himself a grandson of Famine migrants. Farrell returned to the subject of Coughlin and Irish American fascism in his 1939 novella, *Tommy Gallagher's Crusade*.

39 Alan Wald, "Farrell and Trotsky," *Twentieth Century Literature* 22, no. 1 (1976): 93.

40 Robert K Landers, *An Honest Writer: The Life and Times of James T. Farrell* (San Francisco: Encounter Books, 2004), 308; see also Wald, "Farrell and Trotsky," 98–102.

41 See Landers, *An Honest Writer*, 135; see also Mary Hricko, *The Genesis of the Chicago Renaissance: Theodore Dreiser, Langston Hughes, Richard Wright, and James T. Farrell* (New York: Routledge, 2009), 128. Indeed, Mary Hricko claims that *Studs Lonigan* served as inspiration for Wright's American literary classic, *Native Son* (1940).

42 All quotations from O'Neill's plays are from: Eugene O'Neill, *Complete Plays*, 3 vols. (New York: Library of America, 1988).

43 Dowling, *Eugene O'Neill*, 429.

44 Quoted in Dowling, *Eugene O'Neill*, 429.

45 Dowling, *Eugene O'Neill*, 256.

46 In this group, in addition to *The Iceman Cometh*, are *The Hairy Ape* (1922) and *Anna Christie* (1921).

47 Peter D. O'Neill, "The Famine Irish, the Catholic Church and the Cultural Dynamics of the American Middle Class," in *The Great Irish Famine and Social*

Class: Conflicts, Responsibilities, Representations, eds. Marguérite Corporaal and Peter Gray (Oxford: Peter Lang, 2019), 257–75.

48 Quoted in Robert Dowling, *Eugene O'Neill: A Life in Four Acts* (New Haven: Yale University Press, 2014), 453.

49 Dowling, *Eugene O'Neill*, 339, referring to *Marco Millions* (1925). Sympathy toward the indigenous is apparent in *The Fountain* (1922), while questions about patriotism occur in *Ah Wilderness* (1932). There, Richard complains to his father: "I don't believe in this silly celebrating the Fourth of July – all this lying talk about liberty – when there is no liberty. The land of the free and the home of the brave! Home of the slave is what they ought to call it – the wage slave ground under the heel of the capitalist class, starving, crying for bread for his children, and all he gets is stone! The Fourth of July is a stupid farce!" O'Neill, *Complete Plays*, 3:13.

50 Quoted in Carme Manuel, "A Ghost in the Expressionist Jungle of O'Neill's 'The Emperor Jones,'" *African American Review* 39, no. 1–2 (2005): 80.

51 Cedric J. Robinson, "Ventriloquizing Blackness: Eugene O'Neill and Irish-American Racial Performance," in *The Black and Green Atlantic: Crosscurrents of the African and Irish Diasporas*, eds. Peter D. O'Neill and David Lloyd (Basingstoke: Palgrave, 2009), 50.

52 Robinson, "Ventriloquizing Blackness," 50.

53 O'Neill, *Complete Plays*, 1:1030. The "as yet self-determined" remark is a clear dig at President Woodrow Wilson and his notion of on the right of small nations to self-determination. It was Wilson who had sent had US troops into Haiti, as well as Cuba, and the Dominican Republic, among other places.

54 Kurt Eisen, "Theatrical Ethnography and Modernist Primitivism in Eugene O'Neill and Zora Neale Hurston," *South Central Review* 25, no. 1 (Spring 2008): 57.

55 Eisen, "Theatrical Ethnography," 56.

56 All O'Neill scholars that I have read on this subject label Gilpin a drunk, which is indeed rich. For a perhaps more balanced view on Gilpin, see David Krasner, "Whose Role is it Anyway?: Charles Gilpin and the Harlem Renaissance," *The African American Review* 29, no. 3 (1995): 483–96.

57 Robinson, "Ventriloquizing Blackness," 62.

58 Manuel, "A Ghost," 80.

59 Aoife Monks, "'Genuine Negroes and Real Bloodhounds': Cross-Dressing Eugene O'Neill, the Wooster Group, and The Emperor Jones," *Modern Drama* 48, no. 3 (2005): 544.

60 Monks, "'Genuine,'" 541, original emphasis.

61 Monks, "'Genuine,'" 545.

62 Dowling, *Eugene O'Neill*, 214.

63 See William D. Zabel, "Interracial Marriage and the Law," in *Interracialism: Black-White Intermarriage in American History, Literature, and Law*, ed. Werner Sollers (Oxford: Oxford University Press, 2000).

64 Dowling, *Eugene O'Neill*, 281.

65 Robinson, "Ventriloquizing Blackness," 50.

66 Quoted in Mark W. Estrin, ed., *Conversations with Eugene O'Neill* (Jackson: University Press of Mississippi, 1990), 220–21.
67 Arthur and Barbara Gelb, *O'Neill: Life with Monte Cristo* (New York: Applause, 2000) 216.
68 Gelb and Gelb, *O'Neill*, 217; Dowling, *Eugene O'Neill*, 436–37.
69 O'Neill, *Complete Plays*, 3:765.

CHAPTER 12

Diasporic Afterlives
An Irish–Jewish Archive for Ruth Gilligan's
Nine Folds Make a Paper Swan

Stephen Watt

My title references two provocative discourses in contemporary critical parlance, both of which inform my reading of Ruth Gilligan's extraordinary novel, *Nine Folds Make a Paper Swan* (2016). The latter term "Afterlives" alludes to Paige Reynolds's *Modernist Afterlives in Irish Literature and Culture* (2016), which begins with a definition I will extend here: "*Modernist Afterlives in Irish Literature and Culture* explores how the themes, forms, and practices of high modernism are manifest in Irish literature and culture produced subsequent to that cultural movement." More specifically, contributors to this volume consider "how Irish writers and artists from the mid-twentieth century forward engage with modernism as they endeavor to forge new modes of expression."[1] One motive for this project is inherently subversive: namely, to undermine "pat narratives" by recovering modernism's "global influences" and to challenge notions of Irish culture's insularity or "strictly national" ambition.[2] Following Reynolds's lead, I hope to expand the very useful idea of "afterlives" here and revise such terms as "diaspora" and "race" while constructing an archive for Gilligan's novel.

That is to say, at present, other forms of afterlife are thriving, as exceptional writers – most of them Irish or Northern Irish – have returned to transformative episodes in modern and recent Irish history to create "new modes of expression" and representation. Paramount among these are the 1916 Easter Rising, the Troubles, formally concluded by the Good Friday Agreement of 1998, and the fall of the Celtic Tiger in the later 2000s. One distinguished novel in the library of Troubles' texts, for example, is Anna Burns's *Milkman* (2018), with its innovative form and insight into the everyday lives of women in the North. In the novel, gendered maxims such as "Marriage, after territorial boundaries, is the foundation of the state" provide an ideological force to the narrative; the narrator observes that just as guns and bombs destroy lives, the unrelenting buzz of rumor victimizes women with similar efficiency because even "at the outer limits of absurdity and contradiction, people will make up anything."[3] Like Burns, playwrights David Ireland and Jez Butterworth have also contributed to this afterlife with, respectively, *Cyprus Avenue* (2015) and *The Ferryman* (2017), both of which employ graphic violence to prompt awareness of the brutality of this period. Similarly, novels like Dermot Bolger's *Tanglewood* (2015) reveal the deeply psychical impact of the Celtic Tiger's implosion, a crisis responsible for one of the three narrative lines of *Nine Folds Make a Paper Swan*.

In its other two narrative strands, Gilligan's novel portrays the complexities of Jews' lives in Ireland at the beginning and middle of the twentieth century, thus making it an unusually rich afterlife text that not only provides a unique purchase on the economic crisis of the early 2000s, but also revisits the arrival of Jews in Ireland, a topic in Irish and Anglo-Irish fiction from Maria Edgeworth's *Castle Rackrent* (1800) to James Joyce's *Ulysses* (1922) and beyond.[4] For this reason, the genealogy of Gilligan's novel is both more various and more global than that of most diasporic texts. This is hardly surprising; after all, as Gilligan's irreverent Alf Huff observes, Irish stories and Jewish stories are often "variations ... on the same fecking theme."[5] My sympathy with this view is not intended as a rebuttal of the "blurb" displayed in the novel's front matter that, in *Nine Folds Make a Paper Swan*, Gilligan relates the "fascinating untold story" of Jews in twentieth-century Ireland. Still, her portraits of emigrant subjectivity – her engagement with Jewishness and racism in Ireland – are not created *ex nihilo*. On the contrary, *Nine Folds Make a Paper Swan* emerges from both Irish history and an archive of literary texts, including several from the canon of Jewish American fiction: Anzia Yezierska's *Salome of the Tenements* (1923) and *Bread Givers* (1925), Mike Gold's *Jews without Money* (1930), and Henry Roth's *Call It Sleep* (1934), to name just a few. Other texts in the archive include British and Irish titles: Israel Zangwill's *Children of the Ghetto: A Study of a Peculiar People* (1895), his play *The Melting Pot* (1908), Robert Welch's *Groundwork* (1997), and David Marcus's *To Next Year in Jerusalem* (1954), a novel I will at times juxtapose to Gilligan's in what follows. And, because Irish and Jewish stories often *do* resemble each other, Colm Tóibín's *Brooklyn* (2009), in which a young woman from Enniscorthy moves to New York in the 1950s, forms part of this construction as well. The catalog of texts in the *diasporic archive*, in short, is both formidable and multifoliate.

Like "afterlife," the term "diaspora" requires brief unpacking, as do the ways in which race and racism inform Gilligan's novel. For some, "diaspora," particularly when used as a synonym for migration, minimizes or even occludes the diversity of Irish migrants and the ways they and their descendants identified. For this and other reasons, Michelle Granshaw endorses "mobility studies" and its privileging of such phenomena as "social and economic mobility."[6] Wariness about the homogenization of racial or ethnic groups, however, is hardly new, as Granshaw realizes. In *Censoring Racial Ridicule: Irish, Jewish, and African American Struggles over Race and Representation* (2015), M. Alison Kibler cautions against casting Irish Americans, Jews, and Black Americans in monolithic terms by ignoring such factors as class and gender.[7] In this regard, students of the emigration of some two million Ashkenazi Jews to North America between 1880 and the start of World War I are well aware of their diversity. New arrivals to America, or "greenhorns," for instance, embodied difference as they also became objects of derision and even apprehension that they might impede the project of assimilation. The opening pages of Roth's *Call It Sleep* demonstrate how easily a greenhorn's clothing, speech, or overall "crudity and ignorance" could be decoded by Jews who had preceded them to America.[8] Waiting on a Saturday afternoon in 1907 for the docking of the *Peter Stuyvesant* – her decks "thronged by hundreds upon hundreds of foreigners" that included his wife and child – Albert Schearl was outraged by his son's "distinctly foreign" outfit and hat, which would almost certainly become a source of embarrassment.[9] A similar semiosis obtains in *Brooklyn* when, as Eilis Lacey nears Ellis Island, a more experienced traveler warns that her suitcase looks "too Irish" and, as a result, immigration officials might detain her.[10] In late-nineteenth-century Vienna, a teenaged Sigmund Freud most likely learned anti-Semitic slurs from Western European Jews "anxious to differentiate themselves" from *Ostjuden*, or East European Jews.[11] Diasporas invite generalization, in other words, but the impulse to generalize should be queried if not resisted.

But because my goal here is neither sociological nor demographical, but literary – and because my reading of Gilligan's novel foregrounds the subjectivities of migrant characters – more conventional understandings of diaspora, suitably revised, will serve. To begin, when scholars theorize diasporas, they invariably turn to two matters: the anxious sense of home that afflicts many migrant peoples and, in turn, their divided or riven identities. In fact, James Clifford's seminal essay "Diasporas" begins with the question, "How do diaspora discourses represent experiences of displacement, of constructing homes away from home?"[12] This problem of creating a home – and *feeling* at home – resides at the core of Gilligan's representation of emigrant subjectivity. Yet, insofar as *Nine Folds Make a Paper Swan* or, for that matter, Marcus's *To Next Year in Jerusalem* is concerned, one factor Clifford underscores is more or less moot: namely, a new arrival's painful memories of fleeing a country in what Kerby Miller, describing Famine-era Irish emigrants, terms "panicked desperation."[13] Nor is collective memory or a racial unconscious, both frequently represented in diaspora texts, much in evidence. Such hypothetical constructs actually work *against* the thrust of my argument, as neither Gilligan's Ruth Greenberg nor Marcus's Jonathan Lippman suffers such traumatic displacement: Ruth arrived in Cork as a child (as did Jacob Sless, who refers to himself as the "Cork Jew," in Welch's *Groundwork*), and Jonathan was born in Ireland. Anxieties about "home" in both novels are far more varied than these largely backward-looking definitions of the diasporic subject admit. To take one example, *To Next Year in Jerusalem*, set in a small Irish town in 1947–48, depicts Irish Jews' interest in an ever-changing Palestine, adding Zionism and the notion of "homeland" to an already plural sense of home. So, even though nostalgia and traumatic memory are "shared by a broad spectrum of minority and migrant populations," this aspect of "geopathology" is subordinated in *Nine Folds Make a Paper Swan* and *To Next Year in Jerusalem*.[14] Instead, Gilligan and Marcus create *individuals* whose emotions, while at times inflected by race, are not blanched into homogeneity by collective memory or a racial unconscious.

This quality of *Nine Folds Make a Paper Swan*, this braiding of race with individual subjectivity, partially accounts for its unique location in the diasporic archive. Here, I want to acknowledge the influence of Sander Gilman's "Freud, Race, and Gender," which reviews debates at the *fin de siècle* of the nineteenth century over the "mental unity" of crowds as a prelude to defining Freud's views of race.[15] Quoting from Gustave Le Bon's *The Crowd: A Study of the Popular Mind* (1895), a polemic Freud interrogates in *Group Psychology and the Analysis of the Ego* (1921), Gilman argues that "one of the definitions of the Jew which [Freud] would have internalized was a racial one."[16] But not in the way Le Bon theorizes race:

> Our conscious acts are the outcome of an unconscious substratum created in the Mind…. This substratum consists of the innumerable common characteristics handed down from generation to generation, which constitutes the genius of race…. It is more especially with respect to these unconscious elements which constitute the genius of race that all the individuals belonging to it resemble each other.[17]

As he outlines in *Group Psychology*, Freud objected to this formulation for at least two reasons: first, it erases difference by attributing an individual's action to racial inheritance; second, and more important, Le Bon's unconscious "contains the most deeply buried features of the racial mind, which as a matter of fact lies outside the scope of psycho-analysis."[18] In addition, Freud contends, "other manifestations" of group action "operate in a precisely opposite sense" from the rebarbative excesses of the crowd.[19] One such manifestation is the capacity for ironic self-deprecation, a critical faculty that Le Bon's masses lack and Jewish "tendentious jokes" exhibit, as Freud notes in *Jokes and Their Relation to the Unconscious* (1905): "I do not know whether there are many other instances of a people making fun to such a degree of its own character."[20] Years later, Freud also revealed that "'Jewishness is still very important to me emotionally,'" providing him a sense of "belonging together."[21] Given the terms with which writers depict emigrant feeling and desire – "longing" (Gilligan), "racial craving" (Marcus), "intensity of spirit" (Yezierska) – race is similarly generative of emotion in the archive. And if, like racism, race is at times also represented as intrinsic to the collective mind of the crowd or the unconscious of the ethnic other, as it is in Yezierska's *Salome of the Tenements*, for instance, Gilligan conceives of the matter in a very different way.

Homes and Divided Subjects

After a brief preface, *Nine Folds Make a Paper Swan* begins in 1901 with a battered ship transporting 120 Jews from Riga, Latvia to America. Its passengers include Moshe Greenberg, his wife Mame, and their two daughters, ten-year-old Esther and eight-year-old Ruth. But within a paragraph, the creaking vessel that once took cattle to slaughter crashes into an iceberg, or perhaps a whale. The Greenbergs' ten days of seasickness and of overhearing others' retching – or, perhaps, spasms of homesickness, which "spews just the same" – had concluded.[22] Fortunately, Moshe, a dramatist whose one finished play had moved successfully from a shtetl theater to a playhouse in Vilnius and then to a larger venue in Moscow, was laden with "unused ideas" that resembled so many stones in his pockets; and with them he entertained his family with tales of Manhattan skyscrapers and a "giant lady with a crown and a torch who welcomed the weary ships in."[23] Aware of his listeners' hopes, his stories echo the anticipation inherent to so many diaspora narratives, again recalling the opening pages of Roth's *Call It Sleep*. Once on land in New York and shocked by her husband's haggard appearance, Albert's wife Genya realizes the hollowness of such expectations: "And this is the Golden Land ... You must have suffered in this land."[24] The disappointment of Gilligan's migrants is tinctured with even more irony, for no crowded metropolitan subways or "Center Park" await them, only a Cork City that "lay slouched in sleep, snoring off last night's dregs, dreaming of anything other than the unexpected arrival of a Russian slaughterhouse ship."[25] After saving for years – after Uncle Dovid and his sisters had gone ahead to work in America and sent them extra money to pay their fares – Moshe, Mame, Esther, and Ruth would never see New York skyscrapers or Central Park. Their new home was Ireland.

The history of the Greenbergs' years in Ireland, as I have mentioned, is one of three stories that comprise *Nine Folds Make a Paper Swan*. And, at different points in the novel, these intersect in surprising and poignant ways. A second story, set in a Catholic hospital in 1958, concerns Shem Sweeney, institutionalized by his parents because he inexplicably became mute after his bar mitzvah five years earlier, and his roommate, Alf Huff, a gregarious amputee approaching sixty. Alf and Shem are the only two Jews in the institution, which is why administrators placed them together. Given to both ethnic generalization and profanity, Alf is dubious of Shem's Jewishness after learning about his infirmity:

> "Sure, that's unnatural".... "Like a duck who can't swim. A ... a Paddy allergic to spuds. Jaysus, without a voice sure, he's not even really a *Jew* for fuck's—"[26]

Shem's muteness, we discover, was caused by the shock of witnessing his mother's infidelity at about the time of his bar mitzvah. Nevertheless, his mother, Máire Doyle Sweeney, who had converted to Judaism some years earlier, remained the most important figure in Shem's life, his source of hope for a return to the world outside the institution. Because of his condition, writing occupies much of Shem's time, and he soon becomes Alf's scribe, structuring the most important episode in his friend's life into a coherent account that begins, "It had all started on Clanbrassil Street in 1941."[27] What had "started" in 1941 was an all-too-brief affair with Ruth Greenberg violently disrupted by Nazi bombs – an accident, or so the German government later claimed. But the attack on what was once known as the "Jewish quarter" or "New Jerusalem" neighborhood in Dublin, just south of the Liffey River, led many to fear that the bombing was intentional.[28] Accident or not, precious lives were lost. And survivors' lives were devastated, including Ruth's and Alf's.

The conversion of Shem's mother creates another unlikely intersection between the novel's main narratives, as the primer she used to study Judaism resurfaces in the story of Aisling Creedon, an aspiring journalist from Dalkey who moved to London in 2011. Aisling left Ireland in the wake of the country's economic collapse, landed a job at a newspaper writing obituaries, and, not long after, began a two-year relationship with Noah Geller, a successful banker and amateur magician with a unique talent for folding paper into birds, swans, for instance. Their relationship grows serious enough for Noah to invite Aisling to his family's Chanukah dinner and, later, to ask her to convert to Judaism as part of his proposal of marriage. Not surprisingly, some awkwardness attends the early moments of the Chanukah dinner; yet eventually his parents, who at first seemed to stare at her as if "she were speaking in tongues," grew familiar and comforting. Later, Aisling "smiled at the memory," reflecting on how "foreign the discomfort with his parents seems."[29] In time, a welcome feeling enveloped her:

> ...all her nerves finally faded and something else [grew] there instead, a warmth and a welcome she hadn't known in a long time, maybe even since she had first arrived to this godforsaken country, yes, maybe this almost felt a bit like—[30]

"Home," Noah intuited in finishing her sentence – "Home." Later, sitting in his car with Aisling, he presents her with an unexpected gift, a well-worn book with a torn back cover and impressive gold lettering for which his mother had searched assiduously: an Irish edition of *A Voyage of Discovery – Considering a Judaic Conversion*. "I want to marry someone Jewish," he explained, which startled Aisling so thoroughly that Gilligan's narrator alludes to "the self she wouldn't be anymore."[31] She exits the car, retreats to her apartment, and slams the door. Her new emotional home with Noah was now in jeopardy, and we learn in the novel's final pages that *A Voyage of Discovery* once belonged to Shem's mother: Máire Doyle Sweeney.

"Home" evolves into *the* dominant trope in *Nine Folds Make a Paper Swan*, the most psychically resonant of the many thematic afterlives in Gilligan's novel. But there are others. For example, like so many of the more than 3,000 Jewish émigrés in Ireland in 1901,[32] Moshe set aside his personal ambitions to support his family, peddling small items (including pencils, ironically). Working hard, Moshe and his neighbors in Cork's "Jewtown" nevertheless endured such aspersions as "Bloodsuckers," "Murderers," and "Moneylenders," commonly heard in Ireland at a time when an unprecedented number of Jewish emigrants arrived. As Peter Hession notes, such denigrations relied on several stereotypes. After the 1897 publication of *Dracula*, "Blood-suckers" linked emigrants with Bram Stoker's "crypto-Jewish" character, as "images of Jews as 'vampires' and 'bloodsuckers' were part and parcel of a wider biological and racialized rendering of Jewish space." As Hession explains, these same deprecations were hurled at peddlers like Moshe, "money lending vampires" who supposedly hoodwinked gullible housewives into buying items they did not need and could not afford.[33] Like many Jewish wives, the ever-combative Mame Greenberg responded in kind to anti-Semitic slurs, at one point proclaiming bad hygiene to be a quintessential Irish failing, "which in turn was a product of their alcoholism – drunkards one and all!"[34] In American tenements, such disparagements targeted both race and religion. Through the tissue-thin walls of her apartment in *Jews Without Money*, Mike Gold's mother overheard the violent arguments of an Irish couple, leading her to exclaim, "It is worse than the whores ... having Christians in a tenement is worse."[35]

Accusations are similarly leveled against Irish Catholics in post-war Drumcoole, the setting of Marcus's *To Next Year in Jerusalem*. Jonathan Lippman, in love with Aileen MacDonagh, is shocked by the anti-Catholic sentiments of his own family. "Normal" and "level-headed" about most things, his father and aunt were "totally and uncompromisingly prejudiced about the mere thought of any such association with a *shiksah*."[36] Later, his aunt Esther denigrates his friend, the local parish priest: "That's right, Jonathan.... They're feathering their own nest all the time. Not one of them is to be trusted – the priests least of all."[37] Having diagnosed anti-Semitism as a contagious "disease" that insinuates itself "into the blood of a man and into the bloodstream of the whole Christian race before him" – race standing in here, as it frequently does, for religion – Jonathan turns to his aunt in exasperation: "Well, talk about anti-semitism."[38] And, albeit well-liked, the captain of a sports team, and able to converse in Irish, Jonathan is later accused by a jealous acquaintance of being a "Jewboy," putting on the "supercilious airs" so "typical of your kind."[39] This contagion of the blood – what Michael Davitt once referred to as the "barbarous malignity" of anti-Semitism – mutates with apparent ease: anti-Catholicism is thus, in this instance, merely a variant of anti-Semitism.[40]

More potentially destructive than racial prejudice, tensions arising from internal disagreement in the Greenberg family complicate notions of home in *Nine Folds Make a Paper Swan*. For Ruth, the matter is simple: *Ireland is home*. One day in 1911, birds suddenly fell out of the sky "all along the redbrick terrace they had called 'home' for almost ten years now. Or at least, that Ruth had called 'home' whenever her mother wasn't listening."[41] But Cork was never home for Mame or for Ruth's sister, Esther. And, by contrast, Ruth's father resided much of the time in an imaginary "home" – a mythical fifth province. He even completed a play entitled

The Fifth Province and submitted it to Lady Gregory at the Abbey Theatre. After mailing several unanswered inquiries about the manuscript, he finally received an invitation to see Lady Gregory's *The Deliverer* (1911), which features parallels between Moses and Charles Stewart Parnell. As Moshe discovered, however, Lady Gregory's invitation reflected her desire for a Jewish critique of the Irish–Jewish analogies in her play, not an interest in staging his play. And Mame, when she was not arguing with Moshe, could think only of a homeland in Palestine. Similarly, as violence raged there in 1947, residents of Marcus's Drumcoole feared what might happen on May 15, 1948, when British forces were scheduled to leave: "on the day the Jewish race was ... hoping for the re-establishment of their ancient home, the five Arab countries on its borders would ... wipe out that hope for all time."[42] "Ancient home," old home/new home, fifth province as home, America as a Promised Land, lovers forming their own home – Gilligan, and Marcus before her, presents these possibilities and more. For many emigrants, as Jonathan reflects near the end of *To Next Year in Jerusalem*, "so many homes and none of them seemed right."[43] (297). Thus it was with the Greenbergs – except for Ruth.

So, in 1912 and now twenty-one, Esther decided to travel to New York and work either on Broadway or in the nascent film industry, another conventional lure in diasporic texts. Brian Friel adapts this quasi-utopian fantasy about life in America for *Philadelphia, Here I Come!* (1964), as Gar O'Donnell, eager to escape his father's sleepy Ballybeg shop, does not aspire to be an actor but rather fantasizes about enjoying the "dash" of American nightlife with "Great big sexy dames and night clubs and high living and films and dances and –."[44] Without anyone knowing, Esther quietly purchased a one-way ticket from "CORK TO NYC," eventually taking yet another boat that never arrived in America. When Mame learned of her daughter's plan, she tried to persuade Esther to move instead to Palestine, but to no avail; her boat left Queenstown Port for New York only to sink in the North Atlantic a few days later. A distraught Moshe – now laden with real stones in his pockets to weigh him down – waded into the water on his own one-way voyage. Some years later, Mame left for Palestine. But even before then, Ruth began to feel that all was lost: Esther had gone west, Mame would eventually travel east, and Moshe found his home in the land of the dead.

One thing, however, was not lost: Ruth's conviction that Ireland was her home. Unlike Jonathan in Marcus's novel, Ruth never felt rootless; she never asked, as he did, "Which is our real home?" or "Which is the right road home – the road ahead or the road back?" She never compared "the home we have" with the one "we want."[45] As George Bornstein notes,

Jonathan, like David Marcus, is a "hyphenated Jew," an Irish–Jew possessive of a "hybrid identity."[46] By contrast, and although adherent to many
Jewish customs, Ruth was hardly "hyphenated" save for the times during
the years of World War II when prejudice imposed hybridity upon her.
Ireland, she insisted, *is* her home, although she "wondered if she would
ever be described as 'all-Irish' herself."[47] A metaphor for her self- identification as Irish tempering her Jewishness, Ruth in several scenes exca-
vates the land itself to forge Irish roots. Preparing the family cutlery for
Passover, for example, she worked on her hands and knees in the yard,
plunging knives into the soil to ensure they were purified. And, perhaps
most telling, before her mother left for the homeland in the mid-1920s,
she quarreled once again with her daughter over the idea of Ireland as a
"home," but Ruth could not be persuaded:

> *Come on, Ruthie, it is time to go.*
> *But, Mame, this is my home.*
> *Home? Do not be stupid, my girl – you do not*
> *even know the meaning of the word.*[48]

Her family gone, Ruth trained as a midwife and moved to Clanbrassil
Street in 1928, delivering babies at the Dublin Lying-In Hospital and making a modest home in a bed-sit she rented nearby.

A few years later, disturbing headlines began to litter magazines
sold at the canteen she frequented: "IRELAND FOR THE IRISH! A
JEWRIDDEN RACE!" Unfazed, she continued her work and, in 1941,
during the Emergency, handed out flyers to passersby, attempting to
recruit a brigade to dig peat, as fuel was in desperately short supply. This is
how she met Alf. As she had when preparing cutlery for Passover, Ruth was
again penetrating the land, this time at a bog extending west to County
Clare. After a week of hard work, she and Alf returned to Dublin, exhila-
rated by their labor and by each other. At her bed-sit, they exchanged
stories and kisses – and enjoyed one night of passion before Nazi bombs
demolished the neighborhood. Surrounded by rubble, Alf searched franti-
cally for Ruth the next morning, but she was not there; he didn't know
that she had arisen early, ridden her bike to the Forty Foot to bathe, and
then stopped at a Monkstown bakery for poppy seed bagels. After returning home, she surveyed the destruction and searched for Alf to no avail.
Both had survived, yet neither knew it. Blind with rage, Alf joined the
British Army, determined to avenge himself on as many Nazis as he could,
and lost his legs in the attempt. Ruth returned to the maternity ward,
although after the attack, some expectant mothers began to request a

"native midwife.... As if, even after forty years, that half of her just didn't exist."[49] In a reiteration of Ruth's commitment to Ireland, Gilligan's narrator offers a clarification of her motivation for cutting turf – "To rediscover the layers and layers of her country, the ones she had recently come so close to forgetting" – which lends credence to Shem's later assertion of Ruth's Irish identity:

> Because every bit of her now has been immortalized, a legacy of love that will live forever—one of the great Irish tales, never to be forgotten.[50]

As the heroine of the tale, Ruth is Irish at last.

"Home" similarly complicates Aisling's qualms about converting to Judaism. After receiving the book from Noah, she flies to Ireland for Christmas and is greeted at the airport's arrivals hall by the signs routinely displayed there, including one that shouts, "WELCOME HOME!" Taking a taxi to her parents' house in Dalkey, she finally allows herself to collapse, for in this moment she feels at home and fully ready for that reassuring cup of tea. Soon after, however, she remembers Noah's idea of their getting matching tattoos with an intricate design spelling "THIS IS HOME" – they, together, constitute home.[51] Plagued by uncertainty about where she truly belongs, Aisling dreads one possible result of her conversion, as intimated by an admonition in the book she is studying:

> *The sense of alienation and abandonment, that one may "never be able to go home" (both literally and metaphorically), will plague one for many months.*[52]

But, after meeting with a now-decrepit Shem Sweeney and returning his mother's book to him, Aisling feels as if a weight has been lifted from her shoulders. Deciding to call her parents later, she heads directly for the airport and returns to England as Noah's fiancée – and a convert to Judaism. Her negotiation of an Irish–Jewish identity is just beginning, which necessitates a reconsideration of what counts as home. Her decision also confirms a dismal truth: the 110 years separating Aisling's arrival in North London from Ruth Greenberg's in Cork have not mitigated emigrants' challenges of finding a home *and* feeling at home there.

Each woman, it should be noted, experiences a conflict of identity that differs significantly from Jonathan's internal division in *To Next Year in Jerusalem*, caught between a "yearning for modernity" and "restless Hebrew desire for new vistas" on the one hand, and the pressure of an older generation's "racial craving for security and respectability" on the other.[53] Unlike Ruth and Aisling, whose senses of identity seem largely devoid of racial complications, Jonathan negotiates race on both sides of his internal conflict.

The result is that while he had no wish to "eradicate" his Jewishness as he studied Irish, excelled at both Gaelic football and hurley, and initiated a relationship with a Catholic girl, he nevertheless hoped to vanquish the "feeling of otherness" it caused.[54] In these different ways, Irishness and Jewishness, tethered to race throughout the diaspora archive, inflect individual emotions and underlie some characters' riven subjectivities – but not necessarily Ruth's or Aisling's.

Affective Transactions: Race and Feeling

Of all the omissions in my account of *Nine Folds Make a Paper Swan*, the most potentially resonant relates to an unusual fact: Ruth Greenberg has one brown eye and one green eye. When introducing this anomaly, Gilligan's narrator remarks that she "had been born deformed," and as frequently as scenes of her contact with Irish soil recur in the novel, so too do references to her mismatched eyes – but never again couched as a defect or disfigurement.[55] Dazzled by them, Alf describes her eyes as "gorgeous" and "smashing," the most exotic appeal of a woman he found irresistible. On their return to Dublin from cutting turf, Alf sat beside Ruth and, while relating the event to Shem, alluded again to "her two different-colored eyes," conjuring up for Shem "the image afresh – the strange mismatch – one green and one brown."[56] Alf had mentioned earlier that "there was something about her that made me feel I should go," and his young scribe was amazed by the woman's transformative effect on his otherwise callous and at times difficult friend:

> ...I couldn't quite believe what I was hearing; couldn't believe the way this fucker changed when he spoke of her—the wet in his eye, the child in his face—a different man entirely from the one I spent my time inside the house avoiding.[57]

Alf's fascination with Ruth's eyes and their affective impact on him evoke comparisons with similar, more overtly racialized moments of intense feeling in the diaspora archive. And, in my view, Gilligan presents this matter in a productively ambiguous way: Are her eyes really a sign of deformity, of the other as monstrous, as they are first introduced, or are they figures of exoticism and a resulting emotional engagement? As the former, they anticipate slurs of Jews as "bloodsuckers," as vampires and predators; as the latter, Ruth's eyes and Alf's emphasis on how she made him *feel* – and Shem's incredulity about his friend's metamorphosis into "a different man entirely" – intimate a different psychical calculus. In either case, whether a person is enthralled by or terrified of Jewishness, Ruth's mismatched eyes suggest one connotation of race too often overlooked: that is, as a phenomenon capable of exciting the most extreme of emotions.

This assertion, I hope, complements Gilman's thesis about Freud and race, particularly his claim that for Freud after the turn of the century, race "moves from a purely biological category to a purely psychological one."[58] This includes the construction of gender as well, as Gilman argues: "the relationship between race and gender in the fin de siècle [also] frames Freud's answers."[59] Although the complexities of this frame cannot be satisfactorily discussed here, I will note that the coupling of gender and Jewishness is a dominant motif in the diaspora archive, frequently an intensifier of the feminine in modern literature. So, too, is the positing of a kind of Jewish "racial mind" and racialized unconscious – exactly the kind of "unconscious" that Freud ruled "outside the scope of psycho-analysis."[60]

Such an unconscious, albeit largely absent from Gilligan's representation of the Greenbergs in *Nine Folds Make a Paper Swan*, frequently defines the psychologies of Jewish emigrants, those, for example, of the central characters in Yezierska's *Salome of the Tenements* and Irish American poet Lola Ridge's masterwork, "The Ghetto" (1918). Yezierska's émigré Sonya Vrunsky contemplates the "seeds buried in the darkness of me that will never blossom – echoes, longings, suppressed desires of past generations clamoring for expression in me that will never find voice." A beautiful Russian Jew who triggers her male admirer's "primitive fascination" with "the oriental," Sonya burned with the "intensity of spirit of the oppressed races."[61] This fire not only defined her emotions, but also overwhelmed the equipoise of her Gentile socialite lover (and, for a short time, husband) John Manning, melting his icy Puritanism. Sonya's eyes "pierced through the very roots of his being" and, at the same time, a "mysterious resistless force swayed him."[62] Similarly, in Section 1 of "The Ghetto," Ridge traces the struggles of Jewish women in New York's Lower Seat Side back to an ancient maternal experience:

> Flesh of this abiding
> Brood of those ancient mothers who saw the dawn
> Break over Egypt.

In a later stanza, much like Sonya's psychical overwhelming of Manning, a young sweatshop worker "charms and shrews" her "Gentile lover."[63] And in both texts, this bewitching power emanates from a collective or racial unconscious.

But even without this sense of an ancient unconscious underlying conscious ideation or generative of feeling, the archive encompasses numerous texts that associate Jewish women with an overpowering "Oriental" exoticism. Near the end of Joyce's "A Little Cloud" from *Dubliners* (1914), for example, a distraught Little Chandler gazes at a photograph of his wife, finding her eyes cold, repellent, and irritating. There was "no passion in them, no rapture" – the exact opposite of the "dark Oriental eyes" of the Jewesses, "full" of passion and "voluptuous longing" about which he and his friend Gallaher had fantasized earlier.[64] In the opening chapter of Bernard Shaw's *An Unsocial Socialist* (1883), Sidney Trefusis rationalizes his abdication from his recent marriage as caused by the intoxicating, almost debilitating, "spell" of his young Jewish wife, Henrietta. He must abandon this "beautiful and luxurious creature," he claims, if he is ever to advance his politically progressive cause.[65]

This conception of bewitchment or, at times, contagion – the metaphor Le Bon employs to characterize the individual's "sacrifice of personal interest to the collective interest"[66] – thus parallels but does not replicate Jonathan's characterization of race and racism in *To Next Year in Jerusalem* as invasive of the bloodstream (or psyche) of the person it afflicts. This is as true of anti-Semitism and extreme fear as it is of Sonya's exoticism and Little Chandler's desire. Recall Maria Edgeworth's *Harrington* (1817) in which the eponymous protagonist, as a six-year-old child, was terrified by tales of the violence old Jewish men inflicted upon children and was immediately "seized" with his "usual fit of nerves." Years later, whenever he "heard or saw the word JEW," he experienced overwhelming fear (which he fortunately outgrew to become a staunch opponent of anti-Semitic discourse).[67] Here, race implies a transactional process, as it engenders a profound disorder in the person coming into contact with the racial other. By contrast, in Jonathan's case, "race" serves as a reassuring counterbalance to the hazards of complete assimilation, so that in *To Next Year in Jerusalem*, he can applaud the Jewish "racial genius for adaptability, for fitting in while still preserving individuality, for being, in short, two things at the same time."[68] In this formulation, race inflects the internal lives of diasporic peoples, creating a kind of rootedness in another land, other soil, while allowing for an individual, if "hyphenated," identity.

Gilligan's Ruth Greenberg, with one dazzling brown eye and one smashing green eye, only occasionally – when arguing with her mother and after the World War II bombing of her New Jerusalem neighborhood – suffered the pressures of what might be called a hyphenated or hybrid identity. A century later, Aisling Creedon will negotiate this division, most likely with great success. But as I hope to have shown here, other characters are not so fortunate. In other words, sometimes one can find a large measure of comfort in one's new land, can *feel* at home there, and sometimes this is impossible. The Greenbergs beautifully exemplify this individualization, which is conveyed by another metaphor in *Nine Folds Make a Paper Swan*: namely, a family "who had arrived to Ireland once upon a time and then left again in the very same way. *North. South. East. West.*"[69] This family, Gilligan implies, viewed as a collective and therefore undifferentiated by the Cork bigots who deride Moshe as a "Bloodsucker" and "Moneylender," was composed of four individuals with four very different paths to pursue. "Home" and "homeland" for each of them are as complex as they are emotional and transactional. For these and many other reasons, Ruth Gilligan's *Nine Folds Make a Paper Swan* is an exceptional example of the afterlife of the Irish–Jewish novel.

Notes

1 Paige Reynolds, "Introduction," *Modernist Afterlives in Irish Literature and Culture*, ed. Reynolds (London: Anthem, 2016), 1.
2 Reynolds, *Modernist Afterlives*, 4.
3 Anna Burns, *Milkman: A Novel* (London: Faber & Faber, 2018), 42, 306.
4 Fintan O'Toole quips that, in the era of the Celtic Tiger, the "diasporic life was now lived at home"; instead of Irish labor "moving towards American capital, American capital had moved towards Irish labour." See *Ship of Fools: How Stupidity and Corruption Sank the Celtic Tiger* (New York: Public Affairs, 2010), 181–82.
5 Ruth Gilligan, *Nine Folds Make a Paper Swan* (Portland, OR: Tin House Books, 2016), 114.
6 Michelle Granshaw, *Irish on the Move: Performing Mobility in American Variety Theatre* (Iowa City: University of Iowa Press, 2019), 12, 5.
7 See M. Alison Kibler, *Censoring Racial Ridicule: Irish, Jewish, and African American Struggles over Race and Representation* (Chapel Hill: University of North Carolina Press, 2015), 8–20.
8 See my book *"Something Dreadful and Grand": American Literature and the Irish-Jewish Unconscious* (New York: Oxford University Press, 2015), 1–28. The phrase "crudity and ignorance" comes from Henry Roth's *A Star Shines over Mt. Morris Park* (1994). Irish "greenhorns" were also disparaged by Irish Americans, as Mary Tyrone's deprecations in Eugene O'Neill's *Long Day's Journey into Night* suggest.
9 Henry Roth, *Call It Sleep* (New York: Farrar, Straus and Giroux, 1934), 9, 10.
10 Colm Tóibín, *Brooklyn* (New York: Scribner, 2009), 52.
11 Moshe Gresser, *Dual Allegiance: Freud as a Modern Jew* (Albany: State University of New York Press, 1994), 43.

12 James Clifford, "Diasporas," *Cultural Anthropology* 9, no. 3 (August 1994): 302.
13 Kerby A. Miller, *Ireland and Irish America: Culture, Class, and Transatlantic Migration* (Dublin: Field Day, 2008), 74. Here, Miller detects in the letters of Famine-era immigrants the "acute home sickness" of an "unhappy exile." See Miller, 10–12.
14 Clifford, "Diasporas," 304. I am borrowing the term "geopathology" from Una Chaudhuri, *Staging Place: The Geography of Modern Drama* (Ann Arbor: University of Michigan Press, 1995).
15 Gustave Le Bon, *The Crowd: A Study of the Popular Mind* (London: T. Fisher Unwin, [1895] 1903), 26.
16 Sander L. Gilman, "Freud, Race and Gender," *American Imago* 49, no. 2 (1992): 156.
17 Le Bon, *The Crowd*, 31.
18 Sigmund Freud, "Group Psychology and the Analysis of the Ego," in *The Standard Edition of the Complete Psychological Works of Sigmund Freud*, ed. James Strachey, vol 18 (London: The Hogarth Press and the Institute of Psycho-analysis, 1953), 75.
19 Freud, *Group Psychology, SE* 18: 82, 74.
20 Freud, *Group Psychology, SE* 18: 78; *Jokes and Their Relation to the Unconscious, SE* 8: 112.
21 Quoted in Gresser, *Dual Allegiance*, 182.
22 Gilligan, *Nine Folds*, 11.
23 Gilligan, *Nine Folds*, 12.
24 Roth, *Call It Sleep*, 11.
25 Gilligan, *Nine Folds*, 15.
26 Gilligan, *Nine Folds*, 43.
27 Gilligan, *Nine Folds*, 107.
28 See Peter Hession, "'New Jerusalem': Constructing Jewish Space in Ireland, 1880–1914," in *Irish Questions and Jewish Questions: Crossovers in Culture*, eds. Aidan Beatty and Dan O'Brien (Syracuse: Syracuse University Press, 2018), 49–53. Hession parses the differences between "Jewish quarter" and "New Jerusalem," noting that the latter not only connotes an "ethnic enclave" akin to the multicultural spaces of many cities around the world, but also "serves to diminish the physical imprint of the Jewish presence itself" (49).
29 Gilligan, *Nine Folds*, 57.
30 Gilligan, *Nine Folds*, 66.
31 Gilligan, *Nine Folds*, 72–73.
32 In *Jews in Twentieth Century Ireland: Refugees, Anti-Semitism and the Holocaust* (Cork: Cork University Press, 1998), Dermot Keogh sets the number of Jews in Ireland in 1901 at 3006, almost twice as many as in the previous decade. In *Jewish Ireland in the Age of Joyce: A Socioeconomic History* (Princeton: Princeton University Press, 2006), Cormac Ó Gráda places the number of Jewish and Russian-born immigrants in Ireland in 1901 at 3898, growing to over 5000 a decade later.
33 Hession, "New Jerusalem," 55.
34 Gilligan, *Nine Folds*, 84.

35 Michael Gold, *Jews Without Money*, 2nd ed. (New York: Carroll & Graf, [1930] 1996), 169.
36 David Marcus, *To Next Year in Jerusalem* (London: Macmillan, 1854), 123.
37 Marcus, *To Next Year*, 158.
38 Marcus, *To Next Year*, 148, 158.
39 Marcus, *To Next Year*, 274, 273.
40 See George Bornstein, "Irish, Jewish, or Both: Hybrid Identities of David Marcus, Stanley Price, and Myself," in *Irish Questions and Jewish Questions: Crossovers in Culture*, eds. Aidan Beatty and Dan O'Brien (Syracuse: Syracuse University Press, 2018), 133.
41 Gilligan, *Nine Folds*, 80.
42 Marcus, *To Next Year*, 235.
43 Marcus, *To Next Year*, 297.
44 Brian Friel, "Philadelphia, Here I Come!," in *Brian Friel: Plays One* (London: Faber, 1984), 55.
45 Marcus, *To Next Year*, 13.
46 Bornstein, "Irish, Jewish, or Both," 128–29.
47 Gilligan, *Nine Folds*, 151.
48 Gilligan, *Nine Folds*, 228.
49 Gilligan, *Nine Folds*, 281.
50 Gilligan, *Nine Folds*, 282, 334.
51 Gilligan, *Nine Folds*, 203.
52 Gilligan, *Nine Folds*, 261.
53 Marcus, *To Next Year*, 34.
54 Marcus, *To Next Year*, 43.
55 Gilligan, *Nine Folds*, 23.
56 Gilligan, *Nine Folds*, 113.
57 Gilligan, *Nine Folds*, 108, 109.
58 Gilman, "Freud, Race and Gender," 156.
59 Gilman, "Freud, Race and Gender," 174.
60 Freud, *Group Psychology*, SE 18: 75. This distinction between a "personal" or individual unconscious and a collective one distinguishes Freud's thought from that of his one-time colleague Carl Jung. See C. G. Jung, *Dreams*, trans. R. F. C. Hull (Princeton: Princeton University Press, 1974), 77–78.
61 Anzia Yezierska, *Salome of the Tenements* (Urbana: University of Illinois Press, [1923] 1995), 100, 101.
62 Yezieska, *Salome*, 101.
63 Lola Ridge, *The Ghetto and Other Poems* (New York: Huebsch, 1918), 7, 9.
64 James Joyce, "A Little Cloud," in *Dubliners* (New York: Penguin, [1914] 1993), 78.
65 Bernard Shaw, *An Unsocial Socialist* (London: Constable, [1883] 1932), 10–11.
66 Quoted in Freud, *Group Psychology*, SE 18: 75.
67 Maria Edgeworth, *Harrington*, ed. Susan Manly (Toronto: Broadview, [1817] 2004), 79, 80.
68 Marcus, *To Next Year*, 40.
69 Gilligan, *Nine Folds*, 297.

CHAPTER 13

"Dubh"
Poets of Color and New Irish Poetry
Ailbhe McDaid

In its currency as "the *lingua franca* of Irish poetry," the lyric poem dominates the poetic tradition, "but ... its ties to the old communal obligations
of Irish poetry don't help it," according to Eavan Boland.[1] Sandeep Parmar
observes that the "border guards" of the lyric "I" are "literary gatekeepers
of shared assumptions about experience, language and tradition," including "its inherent premise of universality, its coded whiteness."[2] As both
the poet and critic point out, the representative responsibilities associated
with poetry generate an exclusivity that necessarily denies authority to
those occupying minority positions, especially to poets of color. While
some scholars trace the evolution of Irish identity as a model of hospitable
hybridity, others question a congratulatory construct of assimilation that
disregards the lived experiences of racism and discrimination in contemporary Ireland.[3]

The cultural sector reflects the wider societal realities of exclusion – a 2021
survey conducted by Words Ireland found that all ethnic groups aside from
white Irish were underrepresented in the literature sector.[4] Under organi-
zational equality and diversity commitments, a number of high-profile fellowship programs have been established in recent years.[5] These initiatives
certainly go toward meeting Boland's call for a "generous vital conversation about diversity" in Irish poetry, but might also be seen as what Alice
Feldman and Anne Mulhall identify as "the gesture of reception" that functions as a "sign of 'our' inclusivity."[6] In any case, to date, Irish poetry publishing reproduces what it recognizes, remaining an almost-exclusively white
Irish space.[7] Writing about British poetry culture in 2003, Kwame Dawes
notes with regard to Black British poets that "publishers have absolutely no
interest in the kind of work they are doing, viewing it as racially defined and
too dissimilar from the work these publishers do publish."[8] A similar observation pertains to the Irish context: before 2022, no current Irish poetry publisher had published a full-length volume by a poet of color based in Ireland.[9]
While undoubtedly there are differences between Irish and British society

in terms of demographic diversity, the common experience of racial exclusion in poetry publishing is self-evident and quantitatively documented.[10] Within this conservative poetry culture, how can new writers from diverse backgrounds, especially writers of color, find space for their work?

As this chapter outlines, while gatekeepers to publishing implement official policies and public commitments to diversity initiatives, vibrant communities of migrant, transnational, and racially and ethnically diverse poets, including Felispeaks, Nidhi Zak/Aria Eipe and Dagogo Hart, are producing works of critical, social, and artistic significance via alternative channels, including through spoken word poetry, e-publications, multimedia innovations, and collaborative ventures. Their methods of publication exemplify the barriers to entry for poets of color and, at the same time, challenge the mainstream publication industry's authority as the pathway to publicizing and circulating creative work. This chapter offers an overview of the critical and academic discourse on new Irish poetry, followed by a survey of new poets of color currently writing, performing, and publishing in Ireland. The chapter concludes with a brief study of works by Denise Chaila, Felispeaks, and Nidhi Zak/Aria Eipe, demonstrating the diversity of aesthetic, formal, and thematic concerns at play in contemporary Irish poetry.

Resisting Change under the "Banner of Standards": Tracing Exclusion[11]

Irish literature has not been distinguished by diversity to date. Familiar debates about gender representation in poetry publishing and scholarship continue, and those conversations have recently extended to issues relating to race.[12] As editors and publishers disavow "identity politics" and assert their commitment to "selection on merit" and "quality," the facts of exclusion remain.[13] The demographic shifts in the Irish population have critics calling for a reconfiguration of the constructs of national identity in ways that might destabilize the kinds of notions of universality that underpin the lyric tradition. Recognizing in 2008 that "social and political questions of inclusion and exclusion based on race and minority identity [are] fundamental to the articulations of Irishness," scholars such as Borbála Foragó and Moynagh Sullivan, as well as Anne Mulhall, Pilar Villar-Argáiz, Sara Martin Ruis, and others, have drawn attention to the manifestation of issues of race and the racialized other in recent Irish poetry.[14] Such interventions have been crucial in expanding the critical discourse in the academic scholarship around contemporary literature and race, but the inhospitable nature of Irish poetry publishing in relation to minority writers and writers of color remains unchanged. The experimental poet Christodoulos Makris lays out the situation starkly in his found poem "XXXXX," which takes the form of a letter. "Dear Christodoulos," the poem begins, in the voice of an unnamed publisher, "Thank you for your letter and for your interest in being published by xxxxx. Of course I remember our session in xxxxx":

> ... We may have a problem —as you'll see from our notes we can only (at this time at least) consider work by Irish authors.... I need to ask you to clarify/confirm your nationality....
>
> Best wishes,
>
> Sincerely,
>
> xxxxx[15]

Makris's found poem bluntly states what many minority ethnic poets in Ireland encounter when approaching institutions of publishing. In reproducing the letter with the crucial details blanked out, Makris deftly signals the intimacy and the exclusions defining poetry publication in Ireland. As Mulhall notes, "[f]or many migrant writers, the established Irish literary institutions have operated as another kind of border control,"[16] the contours of which are considered in the poem "Territorial," strategically placed on the page facing "XXXXX" in Makris's collection *The Architecture of Chance*. "Territorial" uses contracted line length and enjambment to convey the anxieties of asserting personal and emotional space when continually confronted with one's non-belonging and "entitlement to shrinking / space, control."[17]

The unnamed publisher's demand for Makris to "clarify/confirm" his nationality sounds a familiar refrain in Irish literary culture. In her interview with Jody Allen Randolph in 2010, Pamela Akinjobi, cofacilitator of the *Women Writers in the New Ireland Network*,[18] comments that "there appear to be ethnic boundaries in Irish literature, which set conditions as to who can be included and who cannot."[19] Similarly, Ifedinma Dimbo recalls the reception of her novel in 2012: "When I published [*She was foolish?*] I was told by a reputable bookshop that nobody is interested in what a Nigerian has to say."[20] On the other hand, Chiamaka Enyi-Amadi reflects upon her experience of how Irish literary culture fetishizes blackness and migrant identity, to the disregard of her creative practice.

> There is a difference in Ireland between how the spoken and written words of black and ethnic writers are received. There is this question of: "is the

writing good or is it just black?" They'll invite me to come speak at events, about my experience as a black woman and a migrant in Ireland, but nothing is said about my writing. If you look at all the media coverage around [the edited collection] *Writing Home*, I am asked about what it's like being black and a migrant in Ireland, but not about my writing or my editorial process.[21]

In the recorded panel discussion between cultural practitioners in *Are We Doing Diversity Justice? Challenging Homogeneity in Irish Literary Spaces*, Enyi-Amadi and Nidhi Zak/Aria Eipe agreed on the white cultural expectations of writing by poets of color, that "we only feel pain, we don't feel pleasure," and that this "is something missing in black literature."[22] Mary Jean Chan discusses the similar expectation in British literary and review culture that "continues to perpetuate problematic expectations that the BAME poet either portray herself as 'authentically' traumatized as the suffering Other, or else come across as the perfectly assimilated migrant who is defiant yet empowered."[23] Proscription is as effective a technique as exclusion in controlling diverse perspectives, especially when access to literary spaces is conditional on migrant matriculation to white literary expectations. In this way, gatekeepers "replicate and reinforce the racial power structures that keep UK and Irish poetry and its critical culture white, either by choice or by failing to interrogate their commissioning and editorial practices."[24]

New poetry in Ireland has been served with two high-profile interventions in recent years, both undertaken by Dedalus Press: *Landing Places* (2010) and *Writing Home* (2019).[25] In Pat Boran's introduction to *Writing Home*, he considers the voluntary act of travel for "study, work and simple curiosity" as well as the "outward journey ... undertaken with considerable reluctance" and the experience of those "who never enjoyed safety or understanding in their 'homelands' or 'first homes.'"[26] Boran goes on to outline "three general groups" of poets:

> Here are poets who were born "elsewhere" and now make their life—or part of their life—here in Ireland (poets whose kitchens smell of the herbs and imported ingredients of other lands, one might say). Here too are poets who were born here but who dream in the culture or language of another place, inheritors of their parents' aspirations and memories. And here too are a small number of poets born and perhaps raised in this country, but who have subsequently spent enough times outside of it that, sometimes, it too seems like an "elsewhere" to them now.[27]

The observation of Rosi Braidotti is pertinent here, as she argues that "the point is neither to dismiss nor to glorify the status of marginal, alien others, but to find a more accurate, complex location for a transformation of the very terms of their specification and of our political interaction."[28] Anthologization necessarily smooths out difference and simplifies complex truths about individual and collective experiences as minority citizens and/ or residents of twenty-first-century Ireland.

There is no editorial introduction by Enyi-Amadi, so the extent to which these groupings are a shared editorial observation is unclear in *Writing Home*.[29] However, speaking at the *Irish University Review* Roundtable Discussion, "Displacing the Canon," which took place during the annual conference of the International Association for the Study of Irish Literatures at Trinity College Dublin in 2019, Enyi-Amadi reflected on her experience as coeditor of *Writing Home*.[30] Although she does not explicitly cite the theoretical framework of Braidotti, Enyi-Amadi invokes the concerns around "sameness" and erasure by articulating her discomfort with the central thematic thrust of connection that binds the collection:

> Focusing on the event of migration itself meant that the core focus of the book was on tracing and even celebrating cultural connections between white Irish migration and all other migration. However, this left very little space to explore the experience of institutional racism in the Irish state and everyday interactions with Irish people where racial stereotypes persist. Everyday feelings and sensations of being a minority are political and, in order to actually give space to this experience, it is necessary not to erase difference in pursuit of connection.[31]

Other critics of color have noted the problematic implications of the expectation conferred upon minority writers by white gatekeepers to perform a racialized identity that "portray[s] a narrow and stereotypical version of 'authenticity.'"[32] As Steven G. Yao argues in his work on Chinese American poetry, the dominant literary cultural insistence on "a hermeneutic of authenticity" results in "a *de facto* reification of the categories [of] 'ethnicity,' 'identity,' and 'experience,'" thereby consolidating categorical constructs of exoticization and otherness demanded by the cultural dominant.[33] Enyi-Amadi also alludes to debates between herself and her coeditor on what constituted legitimate "migrant" writing and to her dissatisfaction with the title *"New Irish,"* invoking Sara Ahmed's concept of "complaint as diversity work," a theoretical concept that unpacks the power structures, hierarchies, and prejudices that lie beneath the performative inclusivity of institutional gestures of reception.[34] Romana Huk sums up the white editorial impulse toward writers of color as "meaning that they expect/encourage raced work to be informative about difference, 'other' enough to be worth reading, but then ultimately not comparable with 'native' work."[35] The impact of gathering writers of diverse backgrounds and poetic styles under the blanket of "migrant writing," particularly given the limited access of writers of color to publication in Irish poetry avenues, is simultaneously solicitous and segregative, ostensibly opening up literary space while narrowly proscribing the terms of participation.

The pipeline from emergence through establishment is faulty when it comes to writers of color in Ireland. While new writers of color are identified, heralded, and even funded at the outset of their careers, few have proceeded to amass a body of published work that is available and accessible, or to attain a public profile as a poet in Ireland.[36] This highlights one of the fundamental issues in attempting to trace the emergence of poetry by writers of color in Ireland – the actual poetry itself is scattered, occasional, difficult to locate, and unsupported by any archival or institutional initiative that would act as a bulwark against the erasure of recent writing. While the edited collections by Dedalus Press certainly offer a valuable glimpse, it is revealing to note that *Embers of Words*, the 2012 collection edited by poet and academic Theophilus Ejorh and published by the Migrant Writers and Performing Artists Ireland (MWPAI) and Choice Publishing, is out of print. The "centring of the dominant white 'native' point of view on the 'migrant other'" is the inevitable consequence of a homogenous literary culture, underpinned by commercial expectations of what constitutes "migrant writing" for the reading public.[37] Undertaking "the struggle to break with the hegemonic modes of seeing, thinking, and being," the emerging generation of poets of color operate in new poetic spaces in which they self-represent in the aesthetic, formal, and thematic modes of individual choice.[38] As the remainder of this chapter outlines, new poets of color challenge notions of essential Irishness by inhabiting idiosyncratic identities rather than conforming to collective otherings and by forming creative networks that resist the "hegemonic modes" of white Irish coding.

"Because Nothing Is Like Anything": Emerging Poets of Color

One notable energizing of the literary scene is the development of spoken word and performance poetry among new Irish artists, confirming what Susan B. A. Somers-Willett identifies as one of the crucial elements of slam, that it "opens the door not only to the sociopolitical issue of who has access to poetry but also to the critical question of what poetry is and how it should be evaluated."[39] If Makris's correspondence from the unnamed publisher asked the explicit question of nationality, a decade later, participants in the 2020 *International Literary Festival Dublin* responded resoundingly in the Compass event entitled "Say It Aloud – We're Irish!" This spoken word performance was curated by Beyond Representation, run by Jess Majekodunmi, Ola Majekodunmi, and Zainab Boladale, and it involved writers Lorde Fuhl, Chiamaka Enyi-Amadi, and Kayssie Kandiwa.[40] Reviewing *Landing Places* in 2010, Justin Quinn says of the contributors, "I doubt that these aliens are forming literary communities of their own, as the Americans did in Paris in the 1920s."[41] The opposite is true when it comes to the more recent generation of poets of color. There is a vibrant creative community of poets and performers who, through social media, self-publishing, and alternative platforms, produce a body of fresh and challenging work unconcerned with the traditional markers of literary acceptance. As Dave Lordan observes,

> [T]he revolution of poetry has also been a revolution of autonomy, of proving that twenty-first century poets require neither the support nor the regulation of the state, nor the patronage of vested interests within the literary world to make original and impactful work that reaches a wide audience. Digital and performance mediums have therefore offered a much needed path of independence from the neo-liberal state and state-regulated arts bureaucracy to many poets.[42]

This generation of creative practitioners is assertive in claiming space within the body of the nation while expressing pride in diverse heritage, and they circumvent some of those power dynamics and marketplace proscriptions by curating events and publications via alternative channels. In these multimedia, multidisciplinary interventions in Irish poetry, artists are redefining the contours of Irish literary culture.

Denise Chaila, a spoken word poet and rap artist, exemplifies the new generation of innovative, and assertive creative practitioners. Her spoken word poem, "Duel Citizenship," integrates musical, literary, and sociopolitical influences that comprise her Irish Zambian heritage, repeating in the opening lines the relentless question that stalks non-white people in Ireland: "So where are you from, originally?" The strategic use of the titular homophone is especially neat in its oral subtlety, signaling the steely eyed objective that steers Chaila's aesthetic:

> We are unashamed of our heritage
> We have nothing to prove
> And sometimes there's a pain in these roots
> That our being is anchored to
> But you will see beauty when this forest grows
> You will see us for what we are.[43]

Chaila's work to date is deeply personal and powerfully political – a jux-taposition that is arresting in its openness. Her performance as part of the National Gallery raised her profile as a musician in 2020, but Chaila's work with Rusangano Family and her recent sole-authored EP are essentially interdisciplinary, lying somewhere at the intersection between performance poetry and rap. The speaker in her piece, "Chaila," demands to be seen and heard and is unflinching in her dismissal of inaccurate articulations of her name, with its refrain of "that's not my name. / Say my name." "Chaila" also skewers offensive interpretations of her racial identity in the scathing line that fluently deploys Irish cultural references to devastating effect: "I don't need your concern / if you look at me and see a Trócaire kid."[44]

Other poets are also producing work that resists classification, forming countercultural creative communities outside the literary mainstream. Spoken word Nigerian Irish poet Felispeaks (Felicia Olusanya) is an increasingly prominent figure on the Irish cultural radar, as suggested by the addition of her poem "For Our Mothers" to the 2023 Leaving Certificate curriculum.[45] Felispeaks is also a member, with Dagogo Hart and Samuel Yakura, of WeAreGriot, a Poetry Performance/Production collective of Nigerian Irish poets and storytellers with a stated ambition to "stretch the boundaries of poetry" and to "serve both art and agenda."[46] Lagos-born and Dublin-based, Hart created *The Home Project* (Figure 13.1), a series of three multimedia poetry-films "centred around the migrant experience of 'home.'"[47] *Poetry Ireland* commissioned a debut collection from Nithy Kasa, which was published by Doire Press in 2022 as *Palm Wine Tapper and the Boy at Jericho*. Kasa is originally from the Democratic Republic of Congo and was brought up in Galway. Her poem, "Charcoal Iron," is a sensual, evocative piece featured by the Adrian Brinkerhoff Poetry Foundation.[48] Among the upcoming generation are Lorde Fuhl, Evgeny Shtorn, Tari Takavarasha, Kayssie Kandiwa, Chinedum Muotto, and Jafaris, whose works span performance, spoken word, page, and multimedia poetry.[49] The polyvalent nature of this emerging work challenges the (white) establishment literary space by pursuing a poetics "that experiments with form, genre, and medium in ways that circumvent established literary norms and circuits of exchange."[50] In their review of Felispeaks and Hart's 2018 spoken word theater show "See True," Melissa Ridge and Melanie O'Donovan recognize "the beginning of a cross-category movement, the breakdown of a genre and medium, and the cross-pollination of other genres [that] can be felt seeping into the spoken word style of performance across the community."[51] Poets of color whose work crosses genres are often "left 'without' (or outside) any single, recognizable category and

Figure 13.1   Dagogo Hart's *Uruemu's Home*
Credit: Tobi Manuwa, Manuwa Photography.

criteria for judgment," and therefore find themselves excluded from critical discourse, as *Boundless and Bare* and numerous other small-press journals and magazines attest; a reconsideration of the codes of poetry criticism opens up Irish poetry to new possibilities.[52] As Mulhall suggests, "the literary establishment in Ireland may be learning to listen to the way emergent migrant writers of color in Ireland are writing rather than waiting for them to write the way we are used to reading."[53] As the aesthetic ambition and formal diversity of these artists indicate, there is no shortage of either imagination or talent in the Black Irish poetry community.

"Another Boy Has Eaten the Pavement": Felispeaks's *Dubh*

Felispeaks's *Dubh* is an example of the power and urgency of the performance poem. Performed as part of the Dublin Theatre Festival in 2021, in both its aesthetic and political affect, *Dubh* exemplifies the possibilities realized in the cross-disciplinary space that sits outside of the traditional print poetry publishing structures. As Dawes notes, "if we can accept that the page is as much a performance space as is the stage, we may begin to find ways to speak about poetry without … prejudices."[54] *Dubh* is alternately described as spoken word poetry and collaborative theater, and foregrounds the Black body in order to explore themes of "Repression, Sexuality, Grief and Joy."[55] It is a work in three parts, written and directed by Felispeaks and performed by Felispeaks, Andrea Williams, and Walé Adebusuyi. In inhabiting the stage instead of the page, *Dubh* emphasizes the physicality and intimacy of the work as it moves through issues of sexuality, shame, sorrow, structural racism, parental love, police violence, and mourning. The opening section meditates on female sexuality under repressive, patriarchal regimes that speak to both Irish and Nigerian culture, as the movement of Williams's body on the stage transcends the intergenerational shame narrated by Felispeaks (Figure 13.2). The energy ebbs and flows in this section before accelerating markedly as Part Two, entitled "Eating Concrete," unfolds.

Opening with the arresting image – "Boys' bodies eat the streets in D15" – the poem proceeds to narrate the death of George Nkencho, the twenty-seven-year-old man shot dead by armed Gardaí in west Dublin on December 30, 2020.[56] It is an extremely powerful piece of art, both visually and aurally. During this section, the poet is center stage on a set strewn with spilled soil and scattered red petals while Williams, dressed white, embodies grief and Adebusuyi, in a black hoodie and trousers and holding a basket of white flowers, stands upstage in the shadows, his face hidden. As the story begins, the poem loses its composure, falling into a desperate repetitive recitation.

Figure 13.2   Felispeaks's *DUBH*
Credit: Bobby Zithelo.

> They didn't care that his mind wasn't with him
> That if boy could he'd keep his mind on him like an id
> Like a travel pass
> Like his driver's licence
> Like his walking papers
> Like his life depended on it
> Like his driver's licence
> Like his walking papers
> Like his driver's licence
> Like his walking papers
> Like his life depended on it

The invocation of official documents as an attempt to legitimize the male Black body's presence in public space speaks to global events as well as the specifics of Nkencho's death, while the passage evokes Linton Kwesi Johnson's "It Dread Inna Inglan (for George Lindo)" through its engagement with the ordinary individual. If the demand for documentation sounds a troubling note in Makris's "XXXXX," the implications of biopolitics and racial profiling reach a deadly apotheosis in *Dubh*.

In its intimate depiction of grief and loss, there are also elements of the *caoineadh* in this charged female lament. The poem is commingled with an audio track of Horatio Spafford's "It is well with my soul," a gospel hymn that signals another form of communal mourning, and its lyrics break into the performance at points. These intertwined cultural aesthetics reflect those of the Black Irish community of whom the poem speaks, a community whose position in wider Irish society is understood within the poem as tenuous, as conjured by the casual devastation of the simile: "boy's body chilled like a Guinness glass tipped over in the front yard."

The final section of *Dubh* moves away from the danger of the threshold space of the front yard and back into the domestic, to a sitting room with a couch and chair. As the poem moves toward healing, the shadowy figure of the boy is reanimated and brought back into the light, both physically and poetically. *Hair Joy* opens by winding back through time, the male figure seated on a chair while his mother tends to his hair, as Felispeaks gently narrates him back to life and to innocence.

> When you were small, a brown bundle of beauty
> When your white vest stopped a cartoon underpants
> you used to fall asleep to the aliveness of fingers in your coil.

The fragility of this section is profoundly affective, particularly as the physical intimacy reveals the innate human vulnerability of the previously shadowy figure on stage. Yet the poem moves beyond grief as the connection between mother and son is reestablished, and the lyric gains a quiet momentum in its reassertion of the Black body as legitimate and animate. The imagery of the poem's final lines work to soothe the trauma of the stage set – the spilled compost soil, the scattered red petals like blood, the funeral wreaths – as well as of the poem's narrated violence against the individual and the collective. Directing the eye to the mirror, *Dubh* concludes by turning the focus inward, away from structural racism and intergenerational shame and toward the unassailable strength of self-acceptance.

> And you will learn what way a pencil is with time
> With moisture
> With shea butter
> How it doesn't really matter what layers you use to protect it
> As long as when you meet your garden hair in the mirror
> You love the flower before you.

"wandering / through this folklore": Nidhi Zak/Aria Eipe

Another of the writers injecting Irish poetry culture with new energy and talent is Nidhi Zak/Aria Eipe. Her bifurcated middle name – a division of her given name Zakaria – is a nod to the Czesław Miłosz poem "Ars Poetica?," specifically the penultimate stanza:

> The purpose of poetry is to remind us
> how difficult it is to remain just one person,
> for our house is open, there are no keys in the doors,
> and invisible guests come in and out at will.[57]

While Eipe inhabits Miłosz's truism for her own nomenclature, the Czech poet's reflection might also be considered a reflection on the affect of poetry as a complicating, nuancing, challenging mode that seeks to destabilize essentialist constructs of identity. The oblique stroke (as the punctuation mark is known) functions for Eipe as an enabling tool in her poetic position. Her poem "Be/cause" deploys the stroke sparingly and exquisitely in the title and in the very final lines of the poem, where the punctuation moves syntactical position, thereby changing the affect of the lines from negation ("not/because it was true") to autonomy ("but/because I wanted to"). This fragility of inherited truths in favor of self-assertion is seeded throughout the poem:

> because nothing is like anything
> else, an approximation will always break
>   down when you need it most[58]

There is a deliberateness in her work that does not strain at concepts of identity and belonging; instead, her poetry calmly and carefully winds itself around the nub of the image or the idea, "feeling its likenothingelse." Eipe's poem, "Everything flows," inhabits the characteristic fluidity of her poetic style while keeping focus, in this instance, on the prehistoric elk of Barrie Cooke's *Megaceros Hibernicus*.[59] While elsewhere the oblique slash is Eipe's distinguishing punctuation mark, in "Everything flows" an opening dash establishes a continuum ("– and when we finally fell") with Cooke's elk, with the bog and its offerings, with the processes of nature, and with those preceding poetic voices that have engaged the imaginative potential of Ireland's "wet centre."[60] For Eipe, Cooke's native beast is a unifying image, its insistence a kind of solace that reminds of a shared rather than contested past, albeit now beyond reach.

> now & again you surface
> and again you surface
>
> last of your kind still
> life will remind us how
> we were once this ache
> this generous together

Ending on the collective "together," "Everything flows" models restoration through loss in the elegiac promise that embraces cohesion at its conclusion. Eipe describes her response to Cooke's painting as drawing "on a deep elemental solace embodying the cyclical yet elemental nature of existence."[61]

Born in India, Eipe has lived in Ireland for years, and her work has been featured in the *Irish Times* as part of the *RTÉ Illuminations* series, and, notably, in the UCD Poetry Reading Archive. She has been awarded an array of fellowships and prizes: Poetry Ireland Introductions 2020, the Next Generation Artist Award in Literature from the Arts Council of Ireland, Words Ireland National Mentoring Programme 2020, and the Ireland Chair of Poetry Trust 2019 Student Prize.

Her commissioned poem for Galway2020, entitled "wandersong," is an ode to Bealtaine and demonstrates Eipe's powerful poetic imagination as well as the range of influences her work engages.[62] The poem explicitly sets itself in terms of W. B. Yeats's "The Song of Wandering Aengus" by retaining the form and end-words of each line of the original poem but reworks the original to find a new perspective within the myth. Whereas

Yeats sets the reader with Angus through the use of the personal pronoun "I," Eipe addresses an imagined "you." This shift of position is characteristic of her aesthetic, which embraces the reader, finding space for surprising subject positions. In "wandersong," the reader sees "a goddess rising from the stream / sunkissed by darting silver trout" and joins her to "race now, across the valley floor / footsparks that set a heart a-flame."

Just as "wandersong" demonstrates the poet "wandering / through this folklore," Eipe's expansive range of reference and the ease with which she slips between cultural vocabularies are perhaps the defining characteristics of a twenty-first century poet. Her debut collection, *Auguries of a Minor God* (2021), is blurbed as follows:

> Nidhi Zak/Aria Eipe's spellbinding debut poetry collection explores love and the wounds it makes. Its first half is composed of five sections, corresponding to the five arrows of Kāma, the Hindu God of Love, Desire and Memory. The second is a long narrative poem, "A is for العرب [Arabs]," which follows a different kind of journey: a family of refugees who have fled to the West from conflict in an unspecified Middle Eastern country. With an extraordinary structure, it is a skillful and intimate account of migration and exile, of home and belonging.[63]

An extract from "A is for العرب [Arabs]" is published in *Ko Aotearoa Tātou | We Are New Zealand*, the introduction to which quotes Sandeep Parmar's review of Jay Bernard's *Surge*: "Where, the poet asks, does the body sit across the categorisations of national, local and ethnic identities if the traumas of personal and systemic violence make being at home impossible?"[64] In Eipe's abcedarian, "a" is not, in fact, for "Arabs" – it's for "and." The opening conjunction indicates the poem's sense of itself as a glimpse in the longer, larger, and infinitely more complex lives of the migrant family it depicts. Eipe's motivation is to pare prejudice back to poetry, rooting the poem in "current conversations surrounding human migration, conflict, exile, and xenophobia as well as wider questions concerning identity, belonging, and home."[65] The Fibonacci form in which the poem is written is essentially structured flow, and it infuses the poem with a relentless momentum that is intensified by the reader's knowledge of the fate toward which the poem propels, the Christchurch massacre in March 2019. The "broadboned mare" of the "b" section begins to gallop as the poem accelerates, while Eipe peppers the various sections with alliterative phrases that tilt the poem back and forth, lending a roiling motion to the poem while never sending it out of control. Indeed, as the poem itself approximates a boat on rough seas, the stanzas like waves rising on the page, the specter of refugees on the Mediterranean arising implicitly and then explicitly:

> full, for perhaps he understood what it felt like to be
> foreign, to be flung far from the familiar, to live in
> frequent fear for your life, for those you love, to ferry
> five children across the fiercefoaming sea[66]

Auguries of a Minor God is a collection of great urgency, insight, and craft that speaks out of a global consciousness. Her work is simultaneously political and personal, accomplished in its poise and challenging in its position. Contemporary Irish poetry is greatly enhanced by Eipe's presence and participation on the poetic circuit.

Conclusion: "Diverse and Gently Anarchic"[67]

In the editorial to *Trumpet 9*, Chandrika Narayanan-Mohan declares her purpose as the first guest editor of Poetry Ireland's occasional pamphlet: "My intention is that the voices in this issue will be diverse and gently anarchic, brimming with an energy that embraces the darkness while baring its teeth."[68] The publication achieves its ambition, presenting lively and provocative voices in a range of forms. Narayanan-Mohan's appointment to the post of editor signals some institutional willingness for diversification at the crucial level of decision-making.[69] As discussed earlier, such initiatives suggest a willingness on the part of organizations not only to diversify the writers they support, but also to implement the necessary structural changes in order to support emerging writers, editors, and arts activists from underrepresented backgrounds in Irish poetry and literature. However, as the experience of poets of color in Ireland to date suggests, if these moves are not reflected in broader representation in the poetry publishing landscape, such gestural efforts have little impact.

The overwhelming homogeneity of cultural gatekeepers in the Irish literary scene indicates that there remains much work to be done to support thorough and just diversification. The layers of exclusion in contemporary Irish poetry – from derisive diktats about literary "quality" to tokenistic individual inclusions – require sustained commitment from organizations and funding bodies to address the systemic barriers experienced by creative practitioners and writers of color in Ireland. Effective inclusion of emerging poets' work must be comprised of practical support through mentorship as well as the crucial act of publication, which enables writers to be promoted through publishing houses, reviews, and other public appearances. Furthermore, inclusion initiatives must be responsive to establish a new poetry culture "that takes the politics of intersectionality seriously [and is] actively doing things to facilitate that change."[70] In Felispeaks's contribution to "They," she invokes a line by Greek poet Dinos Christianopoulos: "They tried to bury us but they didn't know we were seeds."[71] The flowering of this generation of poets of color is well underway – it remains to be seen if the Irish poetry establishment will sufficiently nurture its growth.

Notes

1 Eavan Boland, "Where Poetry Begins: Eavan Boland in Conversation," *American Poet*, January 9, 2001, https://poets.org/text/where-poetry-begins-eavan-boland-conversation.

2 Sandeep Parmar with Bhanu Kapil, "Lyric Violence, the Nomadic Subject and the Fourth Space," *Poetry London* (Summer 2017): 29.

3 Declan Kiberd, "Strangers in Their Own Country: Multiculturalism in Ireland," in *The Irish Writer and the World* (Cambridge: Cambridge University Press, 2005), 503; Gerardine Meaney, *Gender, Ireland and Cultural Change: Race, Sex and Nation* (New York: Routledge, 2010), 16.

4 Words Ireland, *Survey*, 2021, https://wordsireland.ie/surveys/.

5 In 2021, these include *Play It Forward* run by *The Stinging Fly* and *Skein Press*, https://skeinpress.com/play-it-forward-fellowship/; Irish Writers' Centre, *Uplift: Young Leaders of Colour in Literature Initiative*, https://irishwriterscentre.ie/opportunities/uplift-young-leaders-of-colour-in-literature-initiative/; and *Diversifying Irish Poetry: Critics of Colour*, led by Dr. Catherine Gander of Maynooth University in collaboration with Poetry Ireland, www.maynoothuniversity.ie/DIPoetryCritics; Smock Alley Theatre's *Baptiste* Program, https://smockalley.com/baptiste-programme/.

6 Eavan Boland, "Editorial," *Poetry Ireland Review* 125 (2017), www.poetryireland.ie/publications/poetry-ireland-review/editorial/issue-125; Alice Feldman and Anne Mulhall, "Towing the Line: Migrant Women Writers and the Space of Irish Writing," *Éire-Ireland* 47, no. 1–2 (2012): 202; citing Sara Ahmed, *Strange Encounters: Embodied Others in Post-Coloniality* (London and New York: Routledge, 2001), 4.

7 In 2021, Gallery Books published Grace Wilentz's *The Limit of Light*. Wilentz was born in New York and currently resides in Dublin. 2020 saw the publication by Dedalus Press of *My Name is Polina* by Polina Cosgrave, a Russian-born, Wicklow-based poet. The now-defunct Wurm Press published *The Architecture of Chance* by Nicosian-born, Dublin-based poet Christodoulos Makris in 2015. It should also be noted that the establishment of publishing house Skein Press in 2017, with its stated objective "to publish writers whose work is fresh and thought-provoking and features outlooks and experiences not often represented in Irish publishing" has provided space for new voices

in fiction and non-fiction. Skein Press has published three books to date: *This Hostel Life* (2017) by Nigerian Irish author Melatu Uche Okorie, *Why the Moon Travels* (2020) by Mincéir writer Oein deBhairduin, and *Settled* (2021) by Rosemary McDonagh, a playwright and feminist disability activist from an Irish Traveller background.

8 Kwame Dawes, "Black British Poetry, Some Considerations," *Wasafiri* 18, no. 38 (2008): 44.

9 In 2022, Doire Press published two new volumes by debut Black Irish writers: *Palm Wine Tapper and the Boy at Jericho* by Nithy Kasa and *Home is Neither Here nor There* by Nandi Jola. Two notable new collections by poets of color based in Ireland were published by UK publishers in 2021: Nidhi Zak/Aria Eipe's *Auguries of a Minor God* (London: Faber & Faber) and Supriya Kaur Dhaliwal's *The Yak Dilemma* (London: Makina Books).

10 Ledbury Poetry Critics's *State of Poetry and Poetry Reviewing 2020* included some Irish publications in its survey: www.liverpool.ac.uk/media/livacuk/schoolofthearts/documents/english/State,of,Poetry,and,Poetry,Reviewing,2020,Ledbury,Critics,Report,-,final.pdf.

11 Boland, "Editorial."

12 *The Cambridge Companion to Contemporary Irish Poetry*, ed. Gerald Dawe (Cambridge: Cambridge University Press, 2017); *FIRED! Irish Women Poets and the Canon: Preamble to the Pledge*, www.rascal.ac.uk/institutions/fired-irish-women-poets-and-canon; See also *MEAS: Measuring Equality in the Arts Sector*, www.measorg.com.

13 Deirdre Falvey, "Two-thirds of published poets are male, so does poetry have a gender problem?" *Irish Times*, August 17, 2019, www.irishtimes.com/culture/books/two-thirds-of-published-poets-are-male-so-does-poetry-have-a-gender-issue-1.3984922. See also Martin Doyle, "A miracle, not a crime: gender balance, race and poetry in *Irish Times*," *Irish Times*, January 31, 2020, www.irishtimes.com/culture/books/a-miracle-not-a-crime-gender-balance-race-and-poetry-in-the-irish-times-1.4156357; also, Dave Coates, "Turning a Page: The State of Poetry Criticism 2011–18," *Brixton Review of Books*, no. 6 (Summer 2019).

14 Borbála Faragó and Moynagh Sullivan, eds., *Facing the Other: Interdisciplinary Studies on Race, Gender and Social Justice in Ireland* (Newcastle: Cambridge Scholars Publishing, 2008): 1; Borbála Faragó, "'I am the Place in Which Things Happen': Invisible Immigrant Women Poets of Ireland," in *Irish Literature: Feminist Perspectives*, eds. Patricia Coughlan and Tina O'Toole (Dublin: Carysfort Press, 2008): 145–66; Sinéad Moynihan, *"Other People's Diasporas": Negotiating Race in Contemporary Irish and Irish-American Culture* (New York: Syracuse Press, 2013); Pilar Villar-Argáiz, ed., *Literary Visions of Multicultural Ireland: The Immigrant in Contemporary Irish Literature* (Manchester: Manchester University Press, 2014); Borbála Faragó, "Migrant Poet(h)ics," in *From Literature to Cultural Literacy*, eds. Naomi Segal and Daniela Koleva (London: Palgrave Macmillan, 2014); Claire Bracken, *Irish Feminist Futures* (London: Routledge, 2016); Claire Bracken and Tara

Harney-Mahajan, "A Continuum of Irish Women's Writing: Reflections on the Post-Celtic Tiger Era," *Lit: Literature Interpretation Theory* 28 no. 1 (2017): 1–12; Anne Mulhall, "Arrivals: Inward Migration and Irish Literature," in *Irish Literature in Transition: 1980–2020*, eds. Eric Falci and Paige Reynolds (Cambridge: Cambridge University Press, 2020): 182–200.

15 Christodoulos Makris, "XXXXX,'" *The Architecture of Chance* (Portarlington: Wurm Press, 2015), 18.

16 Mulhall, "Arrivals," 192.

17 Christodoulos Makris, "Territorial," *The Architecture of Chance* (Portarlington: Wurm Press, 2015), 19.

18 The Women Writers in the New Ireland Network was established in 2007 by Alice Feldman and Anne Mulhall and cofacilitated by Nessa O'Mahony and Pamela Akinjobi. See Feldman and Mulhall "Towing the Line." The network appears to be inactive in recent years: https://wwinc.wordpress.com.

19 Jody Allen Randolph, "Women Writers in the New Ireland Network," in *Close to the Next Moment: Interviews from a Changing Ireland* (Manchester: Carcanet, 2010): 196.

20 Sara Martín-Ruiz, "'The Way the Irish Asylum System Turns People into Un-human is My Problem': An Interview with Ifedinma Dimbo," *Estudios Irlandeses* 10 (2015): 114.

21 Chiamaka Enyi-Amadi and Emma Penney, "Are We Doing Diversity Justice?: A Critical Exchange," *Irish University Review* 50 no. 1 (2020): 113.

22 "Are We Doing Diversity Justice? Challenging Homogeneity in Irish Literary Spaces: An evening of readings, discussions and songs," UCD Library Special Collections YouTube Channel, @ucdlibspecialcoll, www.youtube.com/watch?v=ErLU6lXjSIU.

23 Mary Jean Chan, "'Journeying is Hard': Difficulty, Race and Poetics in Sarah Howe's Loop of Jade," *Journal of British and Irish Innovative Poetry* 12 no. 1 (2020): 25.

24 Dave Coates, "Race and Reviewing: The Ledbury Poetry Critics Programme," 2020, www.liverpool.ac.uk/media/livacuk/schoolofthearts/documents/english/State,of,Poetry,and,Poetry,Reviewing,2020,Ledbury,Critics,Report,-,final.pdf.

25 Eva Bourke and Borbála Faragó, eds., *Landing Places: Immigrant Poets in Ireland* (Dublin: Dedalus Press, 2010); Pat Boran and Chiamaka Enyi-Amadi, eds., *Writing Home: The 'New Irish' Poets* (Dublin: Dedalus Press, 2019).

26 Pat Boran, "Introduction," in *Writing Home: The 'New Irish' Poets* (Dublin: Dedalus Press, 2019), xiv.

27 Boran, "Introduction," xvi.

28 Rosi Braidotti, *Nomadic Subjects* (Columbia: Columbia University Press, 2011), 7.

29 Enyi-Amadi states, "For instance, I recently co-edited *Writing Home: The 'New Irish' Poets*. I was given two weeks to write an introduction. So there is no editor's introduction from me, no words on the page." Enyi-Amadi and Penney, "Are We Doing Diversity Justice?" 113.

30 This conversation was subsequently published: Enyi-Amadi and Penney, "Are We Doing Diversity Justice?" 113–114.

31 Enyi-Amadi and Penney, "Are We Doing Diversity Justice?," 115.

32 Chan, "'Journeying is Hard,'" 4.

33 Steven G. Yao, *Foreign Accents: Chinese American Verse from Exclusion to Postethnicity* (Oxford: Oxford University Press, 2010), 263.

34 Enyi-Amadi's uneasiness echoes the reflections of one of the editors of the earlier anthology of "immigrant" writing, *Landing Places*. In her piece, "Minor Transnational Writing in Ireland," Borbála Faragó intimates tension between the publisher's objective and the editorial authority in the process of editing *Landing Places*, stating that "immigrant" was a term the publisher chose for marketing purposes arguing for ease of recognition for a potential audience; Sara Ahmed, "Closing the Door: Complaint as Diversity," Public Lecture, University College Cork, May 16, 2019. See also www.saranahmed.com.

35 Romana Huk, "In AnOther's Pocket: The Address of the 'Pocket Epic' in Postmodern Black British Poetry," *The Yale Journal of Criticism* 13, no. 1 (2000): 30.

36 Anne Mulhall, Borbála Faragó, and Claire Bracken have identified and analyzed the work of poets Rosemary Ozuto Abu, Christine Aguilera, Oritsegbemi Emmanuel Jakpa, Landa Wo, Nyaradzo Masunda, Nita Mishra, and Jane Beatrice Ovbude in critical interventions that seek to highlight "work that centres migrant of colour consciousness." Some of these poets have built substantial publications via online and print journals but none have published a full-length volume to date. The *Women Writers in the New Ireland Network* (WWINI) is regularly referenced in surveys of emerging voices: established by funding from the IRCHSS in 2007 and the subject of Feldman and Mulhall's "Towing the Line"; however, it appears to be inactive in recent years.

37 Mulhall, "Arrivals," 183.

38 bell hooks, *Black Looks: Race and Representation* (Boston, MA; South End Press, 1992), 2.

39 Susan B. A. Somers-Willett, "Slam Poetry and the Cultural Politics of Performing Identity," *The Journal of the Midwest Modern Language Association* 38, no. 1 (2005): 51.

40 "Say it Aloud – We're Irish!," *International Literature Festival Dublin*, October 25, 2020, www.crowdcast.io/e/beyond-representation/register; The International Literature Festival Dublin introduced a new strand to its programing in 2020, under the "Compass" banner, which was comprised of six events borne out of "an open call for event proposals from Black, Asian and Minority Ethnic artists and writers in February 2020." The events included "a unique sonic journey across the landscape of contemporary Ukrainian poetry" by Olesya Zdorovetska; "Storytelling in eighteenth century China" by Xun Liu; *The Journey*, a one woman play of monologues and dance by poet and writer Nandi Jola; "The Language I Cannot Speak" by Tariro Takavarasha and Kayssie Kandiwa; "Say it Aloud – We're Irish!," "a fresh and vibrant spoken word event, which explores perspectives on what it means to be Irish today"; and "Writing Home – The 'New Irish' Poets," featuring

Chiamaka Enyi-Amadi, Chandrika Narayanan-Mohan, Kayssie Kandiwa, and Evgeny Shtorn.

41 Justin Quinn, "Outsiders on the Inside: Review of *Landing Places*," *Irish Times*, March 20, 2010.

42 Dave Lordan, "The Multimedia Revolution in Poetry," *The Stinging Fly* 33, no. 2 (2016): 223.

43 Denise Chaila, "Duel Citizenship," Narolane Records (YouTube), www .youtube.com/watch?v=gUoKGcNbOKk.

44 Denise Chaila, "Chaila," Narolane Records (YouTube), www.youtube.com/ watch?v=ODTU_FewdHc. Trócaire and Concern are Irish charities involved in fundraising for communities in the developing world. A prominent annual fund-raising campaign run by Trócaire distributed collection boxes featuring an image of a Black baby to Irish schoolchildren. See Robbie McVeigh, "The Specificity of Irish Racism," *Race and Class* 33, no. 4 (1992) and V. Sheridan, David Landy and Vanessa Stout, "The Return of the 'Black Babies': How Development Education Affects Schoolchildren's Attitudes to the Majority World – the Trócaire 2012 Lenten Campaign," *Race, Ethnicity and Education* 22, no. 6 (2019).

45 Among her many recent performances and productions, Felispeaks's piece "Still" was commissioned by RTÉ's *Prime Time* special on *The Next Normal* in 2020: www.youtube.com/watch?v=ChMfddNBoHQ; According to their website, Felispeaks' poetry has been included for Leaving Cert. 2023 and 2025: "'For Our Mothers' is in the English Ordinary Level Leaving Cert. Curriculum for examination year 2023 and 2025, as is [the] poem "Rainbow Blood" for 2025," www.felispeaks.com/label.

46 Dublin Fringe Festival 2020 Installation, www.fringefest.com/festival/whats-on/utopia-or-bust-manifestos-for-a-new-era.

47 "Poetry Ireland announces two new commissions with poets Nithy Kasa and Dagogo Hart," November 9, 2020, www.poetryireland.ie/news/poetry-ireland-announces-two-new-commissions-with-poets-nithy-kasa-and-dago.

48 Nithy Kasa, "Charcoal Iron," www.brinkerhoffpoetry.org/poems/charcoal-iron. Kasa is featured in *Poetic Lives: Poetry, Migration, Ireland*, a series of interviews on NearFm in 2015 and which showcased six poets from diverse backgrounds in feature-length interviews considering their creative practice; also featuring Jennifer Matthews, Nita Misra, Özgecan Kesici, Joseph Horgan, and Theophilus Ejorh.

49 Lorde Fuhl, "Stories on this island," performed at "Say it Loud – We're Irish!," www.youtube.com/watch?v=EzqLGUVMWao; Evgeny Shtorn, "From the Confinement," produced by the Adrian Brinkerhoff Poetry Foundation in association with Druid Theatre, www.brinkerhoffpoetry.org/programs/ coole-park-poetry-series-exhibition; Tari Takavarasha with Kayssie Kandiwa, *Compass: The Language I Cannot Speak*, www.crowdcast.io/e/compass-the-language-i-cannot-speak; see also https://boundlessandbare.com/podcast/ 2019/7/9/tari-takavarasha-on-rhyme-rhythm-amp-race; Christie Kandiwa (Kayssie Kandiwa), Two Poems: "The Seat" and "Nguva Champupuri Chinosumudza Mugwagwa Mudenga," in *Irish University Review* 50,

no. 2 (2020): 261–262; see also "My Sister as a Body," part of the Adrian Brinkerhoff Poetry Foundation's Read By series of poetry films, www .youtube.com/watch?v=Hk4LJpKnGMc; Chinedum Muotto, "IJE-OMA by MR. NoGoFollow," *Irish University Review* 50, no. 2 (2020): 263; Felispeaks and Jafaris, "They," https://districtmagazine.ie/counter-culture/ premiere-they-a-film-about-race/.

50 Mulhall, "Arrivals," 183.
51 Melissa Hart and Melanie O'Donovan, "Spoken word theatre has arrived to light a fire in the Big Smoke: Review of Felispeaks and Dagogo Hart 'See True,'" *Boundless and Bare*, August 20, 2019.
52 Huk, "In AnOther's Pocket," 39.
53 Mulhall, "Arrivals," 197.
54 Dawes, "Black British Poetry," 44.
55 Felispeaks, *Dubh*, Dublin Theatre Festival, October 7, 2021, https://youtu.be/ S91fzqqBos8.
56 Conor Gallagher, "George Nkencho Shooting: Racial Tensions in Dublin's Suburbs," *Irish Times*, January 9, 2021, www.irishtimes.com/news/crime-and-law/george-nkencho-shooting-racial-tensions-in-dublin-s-suburbs-1.4452459\. As outlined in the article, D15 was also the location of the murder of Toyosi Shittabey, a 15-year-old Nigerian Irish boy stabbed to death in 2010.
57 Czesław Miłosz, "Ars Poetica," in *The Collected Poems: 1931–1987* (New York: The Ecco Press, 1988).
58 Nidhi Zak/Aria Eipe, "Be/ cause," *Poetry Ireland Review* 128 (2019): 56.
59 Barrie Cooke, *Megaceros Hibernicus*, IMMA Collection: Gordon Lambert Trust, [1983] 1992.
60 Seamus Heaney, "Bogland," in *Door into the Dark* (London: Faber & Faber, 1969), 55.
61 Nidhi Zak/Aria Eipe, "Everything flows," www.rte.ie/special-reports/illumina tions2020/nidhi-zak-aria-eipe/.
62 Nidhi Zak/Aria Eipe, "wandersong," 2020, www.ariaeipe.com/poetry-1.
63 Book blurb: www.faber.co.uk/blog/faber-announces-two-new-urgent-and-masterly-acquisitions-for-the-2021-poetry-list/.
64 Sandeep Parmar, "Review of Jay Benjamin *Surge*," *The Guardian,* July 6, 2019.
65 Michelle Elvy, Paula Morris, and James Norcliffe, eds., *Ko Aotearoa Tātou | We Are New Zealand* (Dunedin: Otago University Press, 2020).
66 Nidhi Zak/Aria Eipe, "A is for العرب[Arabs]," *Auguries of a Minor God* (London: Faber & Faber, 2021): 42.
67 Chandrika Narayanan-Mohan, "Editorial," *Trumpet* 9, www.poetryireland.ie/ publications/trumpet/back-issues/issue-9.
68 Narayanan-Mohan, "Editorial."
69 In 2020, Poetry Ireland appointed Felispeaks to its Board.
70 Azad Ashim Sharma, "'Race Poetry and Poetics UK 2': Queens College, Cambridge, 26th to 27th October 2018," *Journal of British and Irish Innovative Poetry* 11, no. 1 (2019): 2.
71 Felispeaks and Jafaris "They."

CHAPTER 14

Split Selves and Double Consciousness in Recent Irish Fiction

Oona Frawley

Irish literary fiction of the 2010s enjoyed great success as a new genera-tion of writers gained global attention. Post-Troubles, pre-Brexit Irish fic-tion announced itself through writers such as Sara Baume, Paul Lynch, Danielle McLaughlin, and many others. Such success was not the sole preserve of the novel. Pioneering journals such as *gorse, The Stinging Fly, Banshee*, and *The Tangerine* fostered the short story, creative non-fiction, and auto-fiction forms. In addition, a new crop of literary magazines – most notably *Tolka* and *The Waxed Lemon* – has begun to reflect the non-fiction and auto-fictional successes of Kevin Breathnach, Doireann Ní Ghríofa, Mark O'Connell, and Emilie Pine. The Irish literary world might be forgiven for feeling smug at the production of such a body of writing and the global attention it attracted, confirmed by Anna Burns's Booker Prize in 2018 and Sally Rooney's Costa Award for Best Novel in the same year. However, despite plaudits and prizes, Irish fiction has until recently retained an alarming attachment to conceptualizations of Irishness and Irish identity reminiscent of Revivalist imaginations from a century ago. Such conceptualizations are predictably white and speak of Irishness in terms that are at odds with Ireland's multiracial, multiethnic present. Recent fiction of this kind thus might be said to replicate and repeat the violence that underwrote the notorious Citizenship Referendum of 2004 in the Republic of Ireland. As is well known, the referendum ushered in the Twenty-Seventh Amendment of the Constitution of Ireland, which revoked *jus soli* citizenship and targeted immigration to the country, par-ticularly from African states.[1] In addition to the legal and ethical ques-tions that arose from Ireland's revoking of natal citizenship rights, the Referendum has left an affective legacy that lingers as discrimination and structural racism in Irish society. According to the most recent census of 2016, 17.3 percent of Irish residents were born outside of the Republic of Ireland, placing Ireland third highest in the EU in terms of the percent-age of foreign-born residents.[2] Overall, approximately one in six people residing in the Republic, and one in twenty in Northern Ireland, are born outside of Ireland. However, it is still relatively rare that we encounter this multiethnic and multiracial Ireland in contemporary Irish literature, whether in terms of representative characters or authorship.

There were exceptions within the Irish literary world during the early 2000s and early 2010s that reflected the critical need and growing demand for a diversification in Irish fiction in particular, the genre that I highlight here. Roddy Doyle, though "overprivileged" as a chronicler of "Irish multiculturalism"[3] due to his prominence and popularity as a writer, made what *The Guardian* deemed an "intervention" with the publication of *The Deportees* in 2007.[4] While emphasizing a white Irish perspective, the collection of stories testified to structural racism and prejudice as well as to a culture that believed itself immune to these things, at least in part because of its long-term subjugation under British rule. As sociologist Robbie McVeigh describes it, "the existence of a long and proud internationalist and anti-imperial tradition in Ireland has disguised other contradictory and reactionary strands in Irish politics and identity."[5] Claire Keegan (*Walk the Blue Fields*, 2007), Éilis Ní Dhuibhne (*Fox, Swallow, Scarecrow*, 2007), and Chris Binchy (*Open-handed*, 2009), among others, all published fiction in the same period as Doyle's *The Deportees* that referenced Ireland's changed social landscape through foreign-born characters, most of them minor. Hugo Hamilton's novel *Hand in the Fire* (2010) – noted by Anne Enright as "the first in the Irish tradition … written from an Eastern European point of view" – saw a more intercultural approach, in this case about the friendship between the Serbian Vid and the Irish Kevin.[6] A decade on, however, characters of color remained largely absent in Irish fiction, with Kevin Curran's Kembo Pereira in *Beatsploitation* (2013) and Sandrine in this author's *Flight* (2014) among the exceptions. Anne Fogarty, writing of Ní Dhuibhne's *Fox, Swallow, Scarecrow*, astutely observed the ways in which that novel's characters reveal "the degree to which the Irish literary scene is stirred by the prognostications about the emergence of new immigrant voices but … not sufficiently attuned to take them on board."[7] Unfortunately, this analysis of the fictional Irish literary scene also accurately summarized an ongoing problem of the real one, in which questions of access for writers of color as well as representation of characters of color persist.

Mary Gilmartin and Jenny Lagg, in an important 2018 report, proposed that Ireland adopt new markers for the assessment of successful integration by immigrants into Irish society, advising "participation in voluntary organisations," "membership in trade unions," "membership in political parties," and "political activity" as markers of what they call "active citizenship."[8] What also needs inclusion here, though, is something ineffable and much more difficult to measure. In order to move beyond the othering of "new Irish," and beyond that problematic phrase itself, immigrants to this island and Irish people of color need to be included in crucial cultural frames like literature. While Gilmartin and Lagg do not explicitly acknowledge the importance of including Black and other immigrant narratives in the contemporary literary canon of Ireland, that inclusion is, I argue, a significant part of "active citizenship."

As has been pointed out for decades by Black American scholars and artists, the replication of whiteness as normative Americanness not only alienates citizens by phenotype but also violently emboldens the infrastructure of wider racism.[9] A similar danger presents itself in the Irish context if, while celebrating Irish writing, scholars hegemonically silence or erase Irish writing that is not white. Irish publishers and the literary community are increasingly aware of this danger and are acting to oppose that silence and erasure: key initiatives by Irish arts bodies, publishers, and journals enacted in recent years, but particularly since the Black Lives Matter protests, all attest to a changing landscape, actively working toward inclusion. Only in these last few years and under these particular conditions has a body of creative work begun to challenge the fact that Ireland is no longer distinguished so predictably by its white skin, by the fact of its population being Irish-born or of Irish descent. This new wave of writing includes fiction, poetry, performance poetry, theater, and memoir, as well as mixed genre forms. While at the start of the millennium there were few well-known Irish writers of color – Irish Indian playwright Ursula Rani Sarma is one notable exception – this has changed in a matter of a few short years.[10]

Crucially, writers and publishers have become directly involved in initiatives to diversify Irish writing. Kit de Waal, born in Birmingham to an Irish mother and Caribbean father, has been an inspiring presence on the Irish literary scene following the great success of her debut novel *My Name is Leon* (2014). Her efforts at encouraging a more diverse representation in literature highlight what has been an overt absence of Black and minority ethnic writers and working-class writers from Irish writing. Other notable writers in this new wave include Irish-Nigerian writer, academic, and television presenter Emma Dabiri, whose non-fiction books *Don't Touch My Hair* (2019) and *What White People Can Do Next* (2021) were both bestsellers in several countries. Cauvery Madhavan, born in India and resident in Ireland since the late 1980s, has produced three critically acclaimed novels (*Paddy Indian*, 2001; *The Uncoupling*, 2003; *The Tainted*, 2020). Yan Ge,

the lauded Chinese-born fiction writer and resident in Ireland since 2015,
has recently begun to publish in English, with her first English-language
story collection published in 2023; she also sits on the selection panel for
the Laureate of Irish Fiction.[11] The poet and editor Nidhi Zak/Aria Eipe is
another example of how much the Irish literary landscape has changed in
rapid time. Born in India and brought up across the Middle East, Europe,
and North America, Eipe founded the Play it Forward Fellowships for
writers historically underrepresented in Ireland,[12] serves as poetry editor
for several Irish arts organizations (Fallow Media, Skein Press, *The Stinging
Fly*), and is also an expert advisor to Culture Ireland, a government body.[13]
In addition to these editorial and service roles, her first collection, *Auguries
of a Minor God* (2021), was a finalist for the Dylan Thomas Prize of 2022,
among other awards. Other significant contributions toward diversifying
the Irish literary landscape have been made by Felicia Olusanya, known
as Felispeaks, a Nigerian Irish performance poet and playwright who has
received commissions from the Dublin Theatre Festival (for the extraordinary *Dubh*) and who sits on the board of Poetry Ireland. In a sign of the
profound shift in culture, Felispeaks's poem "For Our Mothers" was put
on the national English Leaving Certificate curriculum in 2021 for the 2023
exam with the result that all final-year students in the Irish school system
study her work.[14] Other up-and-coming writers include Chiamaka Enyi-
Amadi, a Nigerian Irish poet and fiction writer nominated for the Irish
Book Awards Short Story of the Year in 2020,[15] and Christie Kandiwa, a
Zimbabwean Irish poet whose work has been anthologized and performed
at the International Literature Festival Dublin.[16] Chandrika Narayanan-
Mohan, who was born in India and has lived in Sweden, Turkey, and
North America, has published widely in Irish journals and magazines
and is involved in the Breaking Ground Ireland program initiated by
Cúirt International Festival of Literature and the National University of
Ireland Galway in 2022.[17] Narayanan-Mohan, who sits on the board of
the Irish Writers Centre, is also currently working on a book of personal
essays, a genre that is still awaiting diversification in an Irish context. A
highly anticipated intervention on that front was Suad Aldarra's debut
memoir, *I Don't Want to Talk About Home* (2022), which documents the
author's movement from Saudi Arabia to Syria, to Egypt, and eventually,
to Ireland.[18] It is not only in the realm of adult literature that inroads are
being made. Adiba Jaigirdar, a Bangladeshi Irish author, has produced
acclaimed Young Adult novels that provide what she has called a "missing
mirror" for brown LGBTQIA+ Irish teens.[19] These publications and active
interventions into the ways in which Irish literature is curated are not to

be underestimated: they indicate a significant and overdue shift toward representation of multiracial and multiethnic Ireland.

As the Irish population has become more diverse in recent decades, there has also been an increasing body of scholarship on Ireland and issues of race. Drawing on foundational work in critical race studies by theorists like Kimberlé Crenshaw, Richard Delgado, and David Theo Goldberg on the modern state as racialized and also racist, a range of scholars across disciplines in a specifically Irish context have stressed the need for Irish society to work toward a model of inclusion.[20] Ronit Lentin's work has been at the forefront of this scholarship for several decades, as has the work of sociologist Ronan Fanning, but recent scholarship by Black academics such as Ebun Joseph, who set up the first Black Studies course in Ireland at University College Dublin, has been important in extending the critical framework of race studies in an Irish context.[21] There has been a lazy and pervasive belief in Ireland that the country is committedly antiracist because of its own historical oppression. However, just as critical race scholars have argued is the case in other national contexts, the Irish State is "instrumental in generating some of the terms within which racialized categories are made effective within the social sphere, most obviously in conceiving of immigration solely as a social problem, and adopting a rhetoric of crisis and alarm in response to particular groups of immigrants."[22] While the influence of such racialized categories was evidenced in the 2004 vote, the legacy of that vote is apparent not only in concrete policies, but also in the lack of representation of "other voices" in an Irish cultural system that has historically seen itself as being colorblind and thus fair. Critical race theory has increasingly advised against the supposed colorblindness adopted by the modern Irish State as well as others: "Colorblind, or 'formal,' conceptions of equality, expressed in rules that insist only on treatment that is the same across the board," Delgado and Jean Stefancic argue, "can ... remedy only the most blatant forms of discrimination."[23] While the absence of representation in literature is not "blatant" discrimination (in that it is not illegal), it is nonetheless a persistent issue that requires redressal in Ireland as elsewhere.

In what follows, I examine Donal Ryan's *From a Low and Quiet Sea* (2018), Melatu Uche Okorie's *This Hostel Life* (2018), and Stephen Rea's and Jessica Traynor's *Correspondences* (2019), an edited collection calling for an end to Ireland's dehumanizing immigration infrastructure known as Direct Provision. These three publications offer insight into the directions being taken by contemporary Irish literature to address the absence of Black and minority ethnic peoples from Irish literature. I argue that these three texts demonstrate distinct forms of what W.E.B. Du Bois called "double consciousness." Despite the fact that race questions have been central to the settler colonial context of Ireland for centuries, it is only in the last two decades that Irish Studies has engaged a more holistic conceptualization of racialization in Irish culture; it is only now that we are seeing an entwined creative and scholarly response to the profound absence of blackness and minority ethnic representation in contemporary Irish contexts.

Double consciousness is often traced to Du Bois's seminal definition in his 1903 publication *The Souls of Black Folks*: "It is a peculiar sensation, this double-consciousness, this sense of always looking at one's self through the eyes of others..." At this crucial moment in the text, Du Bois points out the collision between blackness and Americanness that defines Black American identity: "One ever feels his two-ness ... two warring ideals in one dark body, whose dogged strength alone keeps it from being torn asunder."[24] Du Bois's articulation of double consciousness in an American context marks an important point in the theorization of otherness – extended by writers from Frantz Fanon (1967) to Edward Said (1978) – which continues to be deliberated in contemporary critical race theory. The context within which Du Bois conceived of double consciousness is specific to Black American experience, of course, and in using the phrase "double consciousness," I do not suggest that the experience of people of color in Ireland is comparable to the extended history of ongoing violent oppression that is Black American history. Rather, I use the term as both an acknowledgement of Du Bois's influence and as a springboard from which to consider the demands placed on people of color in the Irish literary context. I take up Du Bois's idea of "two-ness" and suggest that the trauma these authors attach to migrating into Ireland is observable as a concurrent splitting or fragmentation of the self, and that what Du Bois calls "dogged strength" is not enough to prevent it. Since double consciousness is not simply the result of *internal* longing for fully realized subjectivity but represents the impact of *external* factors on the individual, particularly structural racism and sexism, I suggest that double consciousness and fragmented senses of self are often simultaneously experienced – and, indeed, it is often not only double but a form of triple consciousness that results when gender and other categories are accounted for.

Split Selves in *From a Low and Quiet Sea*

Booker Prize-nominated Donal Ryan's *From a Low and Quiet Sea* was published in 2018, following several successful publications that largely examined rural- and small-town west of Ireland experience. Reviewing the novel, John Boyne begins by noting its difference from that earlier work: "There comes a moment in every novelist's career where they must decide whether to plough the same furrow that has brought them great success or make their way cautiously into another field, uncertain whether the soil on neighbouring land is as rich. In his fourth novel, Donal Ryan has not only bounded over a wall into new territory, but built himself a castle there."[25] It is telling that Boyne's review deploys metaphors of movement, suggesting that the novelist has migrated into "new territory," since ideas of movement and migration are central to the text, though the same freedom of movement is not afforded to all. Like Ryan's first novel *The Spinning Heart* (2012), *From a Low and Quiet Sea* is told from the perspective of several characters in discrete pieces, with the story unifying in a final part, "Lake Islands," which draws three central characters together.

Most relevant for the purposes of this essay is the first section, which follows the thoughts of Farouk, a Syrian medical doctor and refugee who will end up in Ireland. As a member of a privileged class in his home country, Farouk had the resources to attempt escape from the ongoing war for himself and his family, but the trip across the Mediterranean goes tragically wrong, as we know it has done for tens of thousands of refugees. Farouk's wife and child perish. Although Farouk survives, he suffers terrible trauma in memories and flashbacks from a refugee camp, which is located possibly somewhere in Italy or Greece; "Perhaps he had never had a daughter or a wife. They no longer seemed possible: the sea when he looked at it always seemed quiet; the storm that had thrown their boat from trough to crest to trough and splintered it to pieces didn't seem like a thing that could really have happened."[26] Convinced that his wife and daughter survived but have been merely kept separate from him for reasons of either recovery or procedure, Farouk moves through the days in a haze of denial and severe shock until the camp's medical professionals confront him with the truth of his situation, triggering a profound reliving of the trauma. As the text describes, "And so the storm came heaving down around him. The memory of it, as real and as violent as the thing itself."[27]

Ryan's gentle and eminently empathetic narrative tack sees Farouk in no-man's land. He has gotten out of Syria but is in a deliberately unnamed location that is not-yet-Ireland. In this no-man's land, Farouk faces, for the second time, the trauma of his loss. The recurrence of his thoughts and the way in which his experience is "unclaimed" provide a textbook example of trauma.[28] The resulting split sense of self, the division from his previous self in a stark "before" and "after" of the cataclysmic event, is seen most powerfully just as he is overwhelmed by the realities of his loss:

> He went to where the sand dunes were. To where he had thought the women and children would most likely be. …there was no special quarantine or quarter for mothers and daughters separate from their husbands and fathers, and the beach was empty save for a man in corduroy trousers and a white shirt, and he was barefoot, and the man looked up at him, and he shook his head, and Farouk looked back at the man, and Farouk looked up from the water's edge at the man by the fence, and shook his head, and the man on the beach and the man at the fence fell to his knees and screamed, and his scream joined the wind that blew across the water from the east.[29]

It is this moment of confronting his divided self that closes Farouk's narrative, leaving the reader unaware of how Farouk will cope subsequently. The reader knows that he has applied for refugee status in other, also unnamed spaces, but is left uncertain as to whether, in being forced to reexperience and repeat his trauma, he will effectively work through it. As Dominic La Capra argues, "working through trauma does not imply the possibility of attaining total integration of self, including the retrospective feat of putting together seamlessly (for example, through a harmonizing or fetishistic narrative) the riven experience of past trauma…. [W]orking-through does not mean total redemption of the past and its traumatic wounds."[30] Farouk's trauma is defining, and the abrupt, searing ending implies the trauma cannot be harmonized.

If Farouk's experience of the split self is brought about by the overwhelming trauma of his forced migration, that split self arrives in a nation state in which double consciousness will be forced upon him as a man whose ethnic background immediately racializes him. Following Farouk's section, the novel moves on to two white characters "born and bred" in Ireland and whose narratives provide insight into the ways that people like Farouk are read and received. Lampy, whose thoughts occupy the central section of the novel, is a thoughtful and also angry young Irishman recovering – badly – from first heartbreak and trying to come to terms with his lack of a father. In Lampy's section, the narrative notes in passing a nurse in the care home he works in, a "small round foreign lady who always seemed sad." A retiree on the bus that Lampy drives for at the nursing home tells him of his own time as a driver: "A gentler occupation this side of the water by far. Not as many darkies or thugs. We've our fair share all the same, though. And the woman next to Mr Collins shushed him and Mr Collins talked on regardless." Preoccupied with his own sadness, Lampy does not express curiosity about the "foreign lady;" nor, however, does he appear to agree with the kind of casual and endemic racism betrayed by Mr Collins's remark, despite his notable silence at such statements. Like Farouk, he is immediately preoccupied with his sense of personal crisis, which leads him, in a moment that mirrors the crux of Farouk's narrative, to experience his own sense of split self. He thinks, "Would he do this for ever? Drive buses and sit in day rooms and change sheets and talk to people while they wait to die? He felt like he'd stepped outside himself, somehow, replaced himself with this new incarnation, this strange, quiet man, this regretful person he didn't really know."[31]

For a time, in order to escape this new self, Lampy considers emigrating to Canada – highlighting the possibilities of safe migration open to some world citizens – and discusses with his grandfather his desire to see the world. His grandfather's response embodies the racism and exclusionary mindset indicated by the Citizenship Referendum: "World? Isn't half the fuckin world after landing here? You've only to go down the town to see the whole world, these days. More in your line stay here and marry a girl and have proper Irish children before the foreign johnnies breed us out."[32] Lampy, though, wants something more.

> He wanted to have no past, no address, to just be from Ireland. Not this town, or the Villas, or the house at the end of the terrace with the broken gatepost. He wanted to tell a romantic story to explain his father, to say that he was missing somewhere, in action maybe, last seen crossing an Afghan pass or a desert or a flooding river.[33]

In one of the sad, pointed ironies of the novel, Lampy desires precisely what Farouk has in his new Irish life, post-trauma: anonymity, a past that has been utterly swallowed up by the present, and what (with lack of empathy) could be called a "romantic story" that includes the "missing." Lampy's desire for elsewhere and otherwise betrays the same unthinking privilege of his more obviously racist compatriots. While he does not "mean" to diminish the trauma of a stranger like Farouk, his oblivious-ness to the state in which others live amounts to a dismissal of other states of being.

Lampy's lack of awareness informs the shape of the text, for Farouk begins the novel, but remains largely outside of it. It is telling that Farouk has a voice outside of Ireland, even when he is at his most trau-matized and fragmented: even when he is refusing speech, indeed *cannot* speak because of his trauma, we have access to his inner thoughts. Once he reaches Ireland, however, we do not. We can read Ryan's decision to control Farouk's narrative space as indicative of the state of affairs whereby a "foreign national" or one of the "new Irish" does not truly have narrative rights in either, within the North or the Republic. We can also read Ryan's representation as a critique of this fact and a condemnation of it; the condemnation can be found in the slurs that we find in other narrative voices of the novel and in the fact that Ryan's writing of Farouk is enormously sympathetic.[34] The narrative form of *From a Low and Quiet Sea* offers the reader insight into the mind of a traumatized contemporary refugee, while attempting, interestingly, to induce double consciousness in its reading subject. Ryan asks the reader to observe and be disturbed by the absence of Farouk's narrative, the way in which it has been shut down and silenced. However, the fact that the reader is allowed insight only into Farouk's trauma and not into his daily life suggests the problem facing writers who pursue such subjects: on the one hand, it is necessary that such stories are heard, and on the other, there is the danger that they provide space not for the individual but for the individual's trauma. There is the risk of fetishizing and appropriating that trauma, honing in on it at the expense of the human who has experienced it. As Anne Mulhall notes about non-fictional narratives of refugees in an important article entitled "The Ends of Irish Studies? On Whiteness, Academia, and Activism," "In terms of the politics of the asylum regime, foregrounding the traumatic story or the speaking wounds that validate the claims of the asylum seeker to compassion works through 'humanising' the person to those with more power.... The full existence and complexity of the living person is buried, subject to erasure and non-recognition."[35] Through the publication of *I Don't Want to Talk About Home*, the previously mentioned debut memoir of Suad Aldarra, Irish literature has at last seen a first-person perspective of a Syrian refugee in an Irish context that goes beyond the narrative silence with which Ryan's book feels compelled to conclude.

Double-Consciousness in *This Hostel Life*

In contrast to this erasure of narrative possibility in Ireland and the withholding of voice is *This Hostel Life* (2018) by Melatu Uche Okorie. Born in Nigeria, Okorie migrated to Ireland in 2006, two years after the Citizenship Referendum, and was placed in Direct Provision. Established as a stop-gap system for asylum seekers and refugees, Direct Provision has now been in operation for almost twenty-five years. Okorie began writing while in the Direct Provision system, and her work found a home at Skein Press, which, while in business only five years, is at the forefront of action to diversify Irish literature. The press states in its mission statement:

> We are avid readers who noticed a gap in Irish publishing from authors from a Black and minority ethnic background. Cultural diversity in Ireland has grown rapidly in the last 20 years and the Irish publishing landscape can only be enriched by making this writing available. As well as writers from a Black and minority ethnic background, we hope to foster writers whose work is fresh and thought-provoking and features outlooks and experiences not often represented in Irish publishing.[36]

The press's first publication was an important one. As with Roddy Doyle's self-conscious attempts to highlight multiculturalism in an Irish context, Okorie's short collection of stories is an intervention, one that has been deservedly well-received and which opens up the bounds of Irish literature.[37]

The collection's title story, also the longest, focuses on characters who live in a hostel in Ireland's Direct Provision system, in which asylum seekers and refugees – who are not automatically allowed to work in Ireland – receive "provision" and a meager financial contribution in settings which lack cooking facilities and the ability to live autonomously. Envisioned as a system to provide temporary accommodation of up to six months while asylum applications were processed, Direct Provision has become a controversial, long-term institutional set up in which families have lived for years and into which children continue to be born; Okorie herself lived for eight years in the system. While there has been increasing protest against this system, voices of those living in Direct Provision have remained unsettlingly absent from public life in Ireland. There has been discourse *about and around* asylum seekers and those living in the Direct Provision system, but not from them on a wide scale. "This Hostel Life" changed this fact, revealing the hardship of life for those who, like Farouk in the unnamed refugee camp, are in limbo. While waiting with other asylum seekers for provisions on the appointed day, the story's narrator lets the reader observe with her:

> Everybody start to talk for same time about Shakespeare, except for Mummy Dayo. She is busy for look inside Ngozi Lidl bag, and she is count all the provision inside. Me I have to say dat I look small, and me I see two box for Rice Krispies, two box for Cornflakes, one packet for sugar, one packet for Lyons tea. Me I cannot see the things under but me I can see that Mummy Dayo is try to see dat. Maybe she want to know if Ngozi is get more provision than she. Me I know some people come for dining room just to see what provision is dis person or dat person collect, and after that, dey gonna

use it for fight staff. Me I have complain about dis to Ngozi, but she see it
different. She say why staff not give everybody the same because everybody
for equal. She say to give some persons special things is quick way for cause
trouble for a place like dis.[38]

The narrator, a Congolese woman, uses what Okorie describes as a language
she invented, "a mixture of Nigerian pidgin English and some American
slang words which [the narrator] speaks in a strong Kinsala accent. This
idea was born from" Okorie's "observation of how the different nationalities in the direct provision hostel were reconstructing language in order to
communicate with one another."[39] The narration therefore highlights the
fact that the diverse characters populating the story use a variety of pidgin Englishes to communicate with each other; it also references the long
history of the creolization of English. The play with English grammatical
structures as in the passage above also shows how the narrator's self is always
doubly inserted in the text in an example of a literal doubling of consciousness: "Me I have to say"; "Me I cannot see"; "Me I know"; "Me I have
complain." The rhetorical result is to insist on the presence of the self in the
story, in the asylum system, in Ireland and, ultimately, in Irish literature.

Given the inhumane system of Direct Provision under which the characters live, it is not surprising to find that the text functions as a critique
of the asylum system in Ireland and the ways in which the system works:

> "Only two people is serve all dis number of people?" Me I shout for surprise.
> "Dem dey outside dey smoke," Mummy Dayo nod her head like she is
> know many things we don know. "After that, dem go take break. Dat's Irish
> people for you!"[40]

While the tone of "This Hostel Life" remains playful despite inherent critique, "Under the Awning," which takes up residence with an African-
born family who have followed their mother to Ireland and who are
outside of the Direct Provision system, is markedly more serious. Our
narrator this time is an insightful young woman who reads Ireland as she
moves through it: "...you had noticed that their children would abandon
their games and run inside if they saw that any member of your family was
coming outside," she observes, already exhausted by the constant sense of
having to be watchful of herself from others' perspectives, knowing how
she is being read. The burden of double consciousness that the youthful narrator experiences is heart-wrenching, particularly when the racism
and fear of other- and foreign-ness she experiences is contrasted with the
simultaneous claiming of Barack Obama as an Irishman when he visits
Ireland: "Aunty Muna said to your mother that wasn't it interesting that

the same people who were quick to claim this black man from America were the same people who said the black girl from London could not be a Rose of Tralee...."[41] The racialized discourse of migrancy in Ireland is further highlighted when Aunty Muna

> told your mother how once in her daughter's school, all the children's pictures were put up on the wall with their countries of origin written above it and how the children with non-national parents had their parents' countries of origin. She said weren't children of any parentage born in Britain, British or those born in Australia, Australian. You asked her what children born here were called and she said, "migrant children or children of non-nationals, depending on who their parents were". She told your mother that she asked her daughter's teacher to change her daughter's country of origin, but the next day, all the pictures were taken down.[42]

This story in particular seems to spill out of the narrator: the dam bursting on all of the indignities over time, the ways in which the senses of alienation pound down each day. The passage captures the conflict of the image of Ireland embracing President Obama while so many people, including schoolchildren born in Ireland, are somehow not considered Irish – another clear legacy of the 2004 Referendum.

Okorie explains in her introduction that she presented an early draft of "Under the Awning" to a creative writing group, and it was critiqued for being too bleak. The author's reworking of the story provides the frame of a girl going into a creative writing workshop to present her work, which allows for the unusual second-person narrative to remain intact: in a reversal of the insistent, unstoppable "Me I" of the first story, here the reader is drawn in by a character whose sense of self has disappeared so entirely as to have made her a "You," a persona outside of herself. As in Ryan's text, once again it is the experience of trauma resulting from displacement that results in both a doubling and splitting of consciousness:

> You were so excited to join your mother and had imagined she lived in a big house and drove a big car. Your aunt and your cousins had thought so too because of the money your mother sent every month for your upkeep. In the coming months, you would find out that your mother stacked shelves in a supermarket. She had been a manager at a telecommunications company before she left your father.[43]

Forced emigration, in contrast to the kind of optional emigration that Lampy considers in *A Low and Quiet Sea*, results in many cultural and personal losses, and it is these losses that the narrative describes. There is lost social status, indicated here by the fact that the girl's mother was once a

OONA FRAWLEY

manager and now "stacked shelves." There is also the sense of lost anchors and lost community, particularly when the opportunities for successful integration are not consistently available. Our protagonist, for instance, notes disjunctions between herself and her peers:

> In the college your mother enrolled you in to study travel and tourism, the girls wore a lot of make-up and looked so dark from their tanning, they confused you sometimes. They asked you where you learnt to speak English so well and if it were true Africans lived in trees and how they could never live in a hot country because they would melt.[44]

The narrator, while studying "travel and tourism," thus has to answer for all Africans, for misconceptions and racist stereotypes.

She is also forced to deal with perceptions of difference and her skin color as both a threat and an exotic, sexualized lure: "how you hurried with your shopping because the security men followed you around the shops blatantly and ... the man who got on the same bus with you from school, and how he would wave and smile, and you would wave and smile back, until the day he told you that he would give you €100 if you slept with him." The everyday racism experienced by the narrator creates a disturbing distance from the self that indicates the impact of trauma, exacerbated by the sexism, misogyny, and objectification that she additionally encounters as a woman. Finally, it is also made plain that the narrator sees Irish culture clearly, understanding precisely how her presence as an African woman has reordered structures and hierarchies of discrimination in Ireland. The narrator thinks "about the woman at church who told you that a Traveller woman had said that Travellers were no longer the lowest class since the arrival of the Africans."[45] In 2018, the year of *This Hostel Life*'s publication, the Irish Network Against Racism (INAR) recorded the highest ever number of racially motivated assaults, while 2019 saw a worsening situation, with an increase in reports generally, including assaults, racial profiling, discrimination, and hate speech; there has only been an increase since that time.[46] The cultural context in which Okorie's book emerged was thus one of active racism, which has far from disappeared; 2023 has seen active protests against the presence of Direct Provision centers in many places in Ireland.[47]

The use of the writers workshop as a framing device means that readers are also privy to some of the peer feedback on the girl's story. Okorie thus incorporates and foregrounds the way in which her story has already been read. "I think the story should have a bit of light and shade to it, so that it's not all bleak and negative," one member of workshop tells the girl. Another reader tells her that the "only issue with the story was the lack of a narrative thread."[48] This feedback is particularly important, because – despite being incorrect, as the young girl's story has a clear narrative thread centered around her racialized experience of living in Ireland – what is presented in *This Hostel Life*, as a project, are forms of narration that have not often been encountered in Ireland and which readers might think lack a "narrative thread" if they do not present the recognizable signposts of Irish fiction.

Voices in *Correspondences*

While writers cannot be required to write outside of their experience or venture into territory that provokes discomfort – there are issues of cultural appropriation to be conscious of – readers *should* continue to demand that the publishing industry makes ongoing efforts to provide space for a range of narratives.[49] This means that literary Ireland, which Anne Enright claimed as recently as 2015 "did not have a VIP room,"[50] needs to continue to do more to recognize and celebrate difference, following the lead of publishers like Skein Press and other key organizations and outlets. As Susan Tomaselli, founder and editor of *gorse* magazine tweeted, "There may not, as Anne Enright says, be a VIP room in Irish publishing, but there is a top table. We all need to do better, to be less insular, more risky, more inclusive, more diverse."[51]

Just such an attempt to be "more inclusive, more diverse" is seen in the 2019 publication, *Correspondences: An Anthology to Call for an End to Direct Provision*, edited by Stephen Rea and Jessica Traynor. *Correspondences* is distinctive not only for the work it contains – poetry, prose, artwork, and photography – but also in its attempts to work toward the kind of integration outlined by Gilmartin and Lagg's report discussed at the start of this chapter, in this case in the arts. "We wanted," Traynor writes in the introduction, "to pair artists and writers in the [Direct Provision] system with Irish writers for mentorship opportunities, in the hope that these working relationships and friendships would outlast the process of the anthology itself."[52] The result is an eclectic and often profound text that exists as an expression of what Marc Black refers to as "multilateral double consciousness," in which all members of a society "shar[e] the burden of double consciousness,"[53] moving toward a recognition of and empathic understanding of others' experiences. The pairing of writers and artists as a literal doubling of consciousness produces striking and moving "correspondences."

In the foreword to an anonymous narration by an Afghan man that she transcribed, Dr. Natasha Remoundou argues that "in our privilege of freedom of movement we have a duty to act as intermediaries, a sort of modern day scribe [sic] of stories of refugee survivors, many of whom are children collecting institutionalized childhood memories in a perpetual state of waiting in direct provision."[54] Another anonymous narration begins with the blunt admission of a division from self: "I gazed into the mirror, and the reflection I saw grabbed all my attention. Though the image looked everything like me, the eyes had no resemblance to mine."[55] The writer goes on to break a long-kept silence, stating, "Behind my unspoken words is a story, a story of lives trapped behind walls and under ceilings. My story is a hidden one.... To gain a full insight into me as an asylum seeker, why I am here, and how I expect to be supported as I integrate into this new life, all starts from listening." Emilie Pine responds to this anonymous narrative with an impassioned plea that Ireland end Direct Provision. She writes, "As a system it shows that Ireland is not wiser or more careful or more compassionate than it was in the 1950s. Instead, we are still capable of gross structural callousness, still capable of withholding the basic respect due to our fellow humans, and still capable of closing our minds to the abuse happening right in front of us."[56] The challenge, as the work in *Correspondences* attests, is to encourage everyone to see from another's perspective in order to limit the damage and the trauma being continually inflicted, particularly on asylum seekers and refugees, and on those who do not align with stereotypical notions of Irishness. "I'm waiting at the border, the limit – of your imagination," Insaf Yalcinkaya writes.[57]

Conclusions

The power of these three distinctive texts is that they force readers to confront themselves and conceptions of Irishness in a new way. In the post-Brexit, post-Covid pandemic era, amid the closing and extensive policing of national boundaries and an already drawn-out war in Ukraine, there remains a preoccupation on this island with borders, with ongoing questions of what it means to be Irish and who is allowed in. It is vital to remain cognizant of the fact that inhabitants of this island are experiencing other borderlands within the self, living in limbo, trying to find room for their voices. This was explicitly acknowledged in the Arts Council of Ireland's 2019 Report on Equality, Human Rights and Diversity, in which, as part of a three-year plan, the Arts Council sought to "undertake a substantive consultative process with artists from diverse backgrounds to gain a more informed perspective on the issues they face in advancing their careers as artists" (2.3).[58] Its first follow-up report, published in March 2021, noted that artists from "Black," "Black Irish," and "any other Black backgrounds" received support at a "noticeably lower" rate than their "White Irish" counterparts, as did

Asian or Asian Irish applicants.[59] That the Arts Council is strategizing in order to change this pattern is significant. Beyond those already mentioned here, other initiatives also suggest a changing landscape. "Diversifying Irish Poetry," for instance, was an Irish Research Council-funded program that provided mentorship to "reviewers of poetry from underrepresented ethnic groups who identify as non-white, and whose access to critical culture is hindered by structural racism and migration."[60] In other words, it is no longer enough to seek merely representation of Black and ethnic minority voices, but to support the expression of those voices directly. This is a key way in which the idea of Irishness itself will be diversified. "What does 'Irishness' look like?," a 2018 documentary by journalist Ola Majekodunmi, shows that these voices can come from outside of literature and in many forms.[61] The globalization of Black Lives Matter in 2020 following the murder of George Floyd in the U.S. is currently contributing to a long-overdue public acknowledgement of Ireland's structural racism, with stronger calls to end Direct Provision, to repeal the 27th Amendment that resulted from the 2004 referendum, and for more public attention paid to race in general. Ebun Joseph notes that, under these circumstances, "race and racism has for the first time become a central theme in Ireland and worldwide."[62] There is a need for readers and viewers to support publishing endeavors like that of Skein Press, the editors and authors of *Correspondences*, and documentary makers like Majekodunmi, and a need in the publishing industry to not just make space for new voices but to seek out voices that have not yet been heard.[63] If publishers and members of the literary community do not play an active role in doing this, there is the danger of silencing and thus retraumatizing generations of people who have been born in Ireland or who will live their lives in Ireland without any real sense of belonging, without seeing themselves reflected in the culture of which they are a part. Rather than allowing that to continue, all people living in Ireland need to become doubly conscious, and thus help to ensure that unriven subjectivity is a universal privilege.

Notes

1 On the racialized nature of the citizenship debate, see, for instance, two articles by Ronit Lentin, "Racial State and Crisis Racism," *Ethic and Racial Studies* 30, no. 4 (2007): 610–27, and "Illegal in Ireland, Irish Illegals: Diaspora Nation as Racial State," *Irish Political Studies* 22, no. 4 (2007): 433–53. See also Bryan Fanning and Fidele Mutwarasibo, "Nationals/non-nationals: Immigration, Citizenship and Politics in the Republic of Ireland," *Ethic and Racial Studies* 30, no. 3 (2007): 439–60.

2 All data for the Republic of Ireland can be found at the Central Statistics
   Office: www.cso.ie/en/census/. While the 2004 citizens' referendum campaign was fuelled by fearful media reports about planes and boats of imagined,
   often African, others arriving to give birth in Ireland, the CSO reveals that,
   in fact, of the top ten nationalities living in the Republic of Ireland, only one
   group – Brazilians – are from outside the EU. Arriving in greatest numbers
   are Poles and citizens of the UK. These numbers are echoed in a minor way
   in statistics for Northern Ireland from 2011. While non-UK and non-ROI-
   born individuals increased to an overall 4.5 percent of the population, the
   locations from which people are emigrating is relatively similar (with three of
   the top ten nationalities represented from outside of the EU: the USA, India,
   and China). As in the ROI, most people are moving from Poland. See Anna
   Krausova and Dr Carlos Vargas-Silva, "Northern Ireland: Census Profile,"
   June 26, 2014. Report available at: https://migrationobservatory.ox.ac.uk/wp-
   content/uploads/2016/04/CensusProfile-Northern_Ireland.pdf.

3 Amanda Tucker, "Strangers in a Strange Land?: The New Irish Multicultural
   Fiction," in *Literary Visions of Multicultural Ireland*, ed. Pillar Villar-Argáiz
   (Manchester: Manchester University Press, 2013): 124.

4 Ian Samson, "Black Stripes on the Celtic Tiger," *The Guardian*, September 1,
   2007, www.theguardian.com/books/2007/sep/01/society.roddydoyle.

5 Robbie McVeigh, "The Specificity of Irish Racism," *Race and Class* 33, no. 4
   (1992): 31.

6 Anne Enright, "*Hand in the Fire* by Hugo Hamilton," *The Guardian*, April 17, 2010,
   www.theguardian.com/books/2010/apr/17/hand-fire-hugo-hamilton-review.

7 Anne Fogarty, "'Many and Terrible are the Roads to Home': Representations
   of the Immigrant in the Contemporary Irish Short Story," in *Literary Visions
   of Multicultural Ireland*, ed. Pilar Villar-Argáiz (Manchester: Manchester
   University Press, 2013): 235.

8 Mary Gilmartin and Jennifer Dagg, *Immigrant Integration and Settlement
   Services in Ireland*, Project Report, Irish Research Council, 2018, 12, http://
   mural.maynoothuniversity.ie/10114/1/Immigrant%20Integration%20
   Final%20Report%202018%20%28002%29.pdf. See also Gilmartin, *Irish
   Migration in the 21st Century* (Manchester University Press, 2015).

9 This is illustrated, for example, in Toni Morrison's first novel, *The Bluest Eye*
   (1970), in which the sharp-eyed child narrator Claudia resents her erasure
   from culture, resents the lack of brown-skinned dolls and the fetishization of
   white-skinned beauty. Just as Morrison's act of writing Claudia was a move
   toward both recovery and acknowledgment of that unacceptable erasure and
   fetishization, there is a need in Ireland for action-inducing resentment over
   absence, and a need for recovery and acknowledgment.

10 Sarma's work has been performed to acclaim in Ireland, the United States, and
   the UK, and she has been commissioned by the National Theatre in England
   and the Abbey Theatre in Dublin, as well as by ACT in San Francisco.

11 Martin Doyle, "Irish writers in running for big prizes and Yan Ge signs
   two-book deal with Faber," *Irish Times*, June 18, 2021, www.irishtimes.com/

culture/books/irish-writers-in-running-for-big-prizes-and-yan-ge-signs-two-book-deal-with-faber-1.4597018. See also www.artscouncil.ie/Arts-in-Ireland/Literature/Laureate-for-Irish-Fiction/Selection-Panel/Yan-Ge/.

12 Play It Forward fellowships are a joint initiative by Skein Press and *The Stinging Fly*, with the inaugural fellows named for 2021/22. See https://skeinpress.com/play-it-forward-fellowship/ and https://stingingfly.org/news/play-it-forward-pilot-fellowships-programme/.

13 See Eipe's website for further information: www.ariaeipe.com/.

14 Felispeaks, "For Our Mothers," www.felispeaks.com/media.

15 See *Writing Home: The New Irish Poets*, eds. Pat Boran and Chiamaka Enyi-Amadi (Dedalus Press, 2019). Enyi-Amadi was longlisted for her story "Dishonouring the Dead." See www.writing.ie/news/an-post-irish-book-awards-writing-ie-short-story-of-the-year-longlist-2020/.

16 "Compass: The Language I Cannot Speak with Tariro Takavarasha and Christie Kandiwa," https://ilfdublin.com/archive/compass-the-language-i-cannot-speak-with-tariro-takavarasha-and-christie-kandiwa/.

17 Chandrika Narayanan-Mohan, "About Me," www.chandrika.ie/about.html.

18 "Doubleday Ireland wins Aldarra memoir in three-way auction," *The Bookseller*, April 13, 2021, www.thebookseller.com/rights/doubleday-ireland-wins-aldarra-memoir-three-way-auction-1252664. See also Aldarra's website, which highlights not only her writing but her work as a data scientist, particularly in relation to tracking "the spreading issue of misinformation about refugees and migrants in the news…": http://suad.io/.

19 Interview in Filomena Kaguako, "Breaking Ground: Ireland's ethnic minority writers get a new platform," *Irish Independent*, February 19, 2022, www.independent.ie/entertainment/theatre-arts/breaking-ground-irelands-ethnic-minority-writers-get-a-new-platform-41357359.html. See also Adiba Jaigirdar's website: https://adibajaigirdar.com/.

20 Work in an Irish context has come from literary critics, sociologists, geographers, political scientists, and media scholars: see, for instance, see John Brannigan, *Race in Modern Irish Literature and Culture* (Edinburgh: Edinburgh University Press, 2009); Fanning 2011; 2012; 2018; Fanning and Michael 2018; Gilmartin 2015; Kitching 2014; 2015; Lentin 2007; McVeigh 1992; McVeigh and Lentin 2002; 2006; and Titley 2019.

21 Dr Joseph has been a consistent voice for change in an Irish context, holding talks such as "Becoming Relevant: The Career Path of a Black Scholar in Ireland" (December 18, 2018), for example. During Ireland's lockdown at the start of the Covid-19 pandemic, amid increasing Black Lives Matter protests, Dr Joseph hosted several panel discussions and town hall meetings on Zoom to discuss the protests in an Irish context, including one on "The First Black Studies Module in Ireland" (June 12, 2020), www.youtube.com/watch?v=hfX4a6jst-g.

22 Brannigan, *Race in Modern Irish Culture*, 8.

23 Richard Delgado and Jean Stefancic, *Critical Race Theory: An Introduction* (New York: New York University Press, 2001), 7.

24 W. E. B. Du Bois, *The Souls of Black Folk* (London: Penguin Modern Classics, 2000 [1903]), 6.

25 John Boyne, "*From a Low and Quiet Sea* by Donal Ryan – waves of compassion and anger," *The Guardian*, March 30, 2018, www.theguardian.com/books/2018/mar/30/from-a-low-and-quiet-sea-by-donal-ryan-review.

26 Donal Ryan, *From a Low and Quiet Sea* (London: Doubleday, 2018), 32.

27 Ryan, *From a Low and Quiet Sea*, 43.

28 See, for instance, the field-defining Cathy Caruth, *Unclaimed Experience: Trauma, Narrative, History* (New York: Johns Hopkins Press, 1996).

29 Ryan, *From a Low and Quiet Sea*, 47.

30 Dominick La Capra, *History in Transit: Experience, Identity, Critical Theory* (Ithaca, NY: Cornell University Press, 2004), 118–19.

31 Ryan, *From a Low and Quiet Sea*, 80, 81, 87.

32 Ryan, *From a Low and Quiet Sea*, 89.

33 Ryan, *From a Low and Quiet Sea*, 91–92.

34 It is worth noting, as well, that the novel withholds access to women's voices through the text: Farouk's wife and daughter die, and Lampy's mother, who has suffered her own traumatic loss, reaches the reader only at second-hand, in male imaginings.

35 Anne Mulhall, "The Ends of Irish Studies? On Whiteness, Academia, and Activism," *Irish University Review* 50, no 1 (2020): 104.

36 Skein Press, https://skeinpress.com.

37 See, for instance, "*This Hostel Life* by Melatu Uche Okorie," reviewed by Emma Flynn, *The Stinging Fly*, August 14, 2018, https://stingingfly.org/review/this-hostel-life/.

38 Melatu Uche Okorie, *This Hostel Life* (Dublin: Skein Press, 2018), 16–17.

39 Okorie, *This Hostel Life*, 8.

40 Okorie, *This Hostel Life*, 18–19.

41 Okorie, *This Hostel Life*, 28, 29.

42 Okorie, *This Hostel Life*, 29.

43 Okorie, *This Hostel Life*, 31.

44 Okorie, *This Hostel Life*, 32.

45 Okorie, *This Hostel Life*, 34, 36.

46 See INAR annual reports for 2018 (https://inar.ie/inars-2018-ireport-ie-reports-of-racism-in-ireland-published/) and 2019 (https://inar.ie/inars-2019-ireport-ie-reports-of-racism-in-ireland-published/).

47 Incidents are increasingly reported as occurring in online spaces as well as in person. See Conor Lally, "'Irish far right fake news' helps spur record number of racist incidents," March 23, 2021, *Irish Times*, www.irishtimes.com/news/crime-and-law/irish-far-right-fake-news-helps-spur-record-number-of-racist-incidents-1.4517295. See also Eoghan Maloney, "Dublin family fleeing racist attacks now lives in church," January 26, 2022, *Irish Independent*, www.independent.ie/irish-news/crime/my-kids-are-traumatised-dublin-family-fleeing-racist-attacks-now-living-in-church-41281190.html.

48 Okorie, *This Hostel Life*, 37, 38.

49 In contrast to critics who have angrily written against "cultural appropriation" is Zadie Smith, who states that "what insults my soul is the idea – popular in the culture just now, and presented in widely variant degrees of complexity – that we can and should write only about people who are fundamentally 'like' us: racially, sexually, genetically, nationally, politically, personally." Instead, Smith argues for what she calls "profound-other-fascination." See "Fascinated to Presume: In Defense of Fiction," *New York Review of Books*, October 24, 2019, www.nybooks.com/articles/2019/10/24/zadie-smith-in-defense-of-fiction/.

50 In Sarah Davis-Goff, "'Irish publishing has no VIP room:' why Irish writing is a movement having a moment," *Irish Times*, September 29, 2015, www .irishtimes.com/culture/books/irish-publishing-has-no-vip-room-why-irish-writing-is-a-movement-having-a-moment-1.2371147.

51 Susan Tomaselli on Twitter: @STomaselli, October 17, 2018.

52 Jessica Tranyor, "Foreword," in *Correspondences: An Anthology to Call for an End to Direct Provision* (Dublin: SprintPrint, 2019), x.

53 Marc Black, "Fanon and DuBoisian Double Consciousness," *Human Architecture: Journal of the Sociology of Self-Knowledge* 5, no. 3 (2007): 400.

54 Natasha Remoundou, "Foreword," in *Correspondences*, 4.

55 Anon., "Because Justice Matters," in *Correspondences*, 33.

56 Emilie Pine, "Repeating the Mistakes of the Past," in *Correspondences*, 38.

57 Insaf Yalcinkaya, "Borders," in *Correspondences*, 50.

58 *Arts Council Equality, Human Rights & Diversity Policy & Strategy*, 2, www .artscouncil.ie/uploadedFiles/EHRD%20Policy%20English%20version%20 Final.pdf.

59 *Diversity and Arts Council Awards: Report on Gender, Disability and Ethnicity in Individual Awards in 2020*, March 12, 2021, www.artscouncil.ie/uploadedFiles/ wwwartscouncilie/Content/About/Equality,_Human_Rights_and_Diversity/ Diversity%20and%20Arts%20Council%20Awards_March%202021.pdf.

60 "Launch of Diversifying Irish Poetry: Poetry Critics of Colour in Ireland," May 14, 2021, www.poetryireland.ie/news/launch-of-diversifying-irish-poetry-poetry-critics-of-colour-in-ireland.

61 Wuraola Majekodunmi, "What does 'Irishness' look like?," www.youtube .com/watch?v=EqWKR7eq-CQ.

62 Ebun Joseph, "Pulling Together in Uncertainties in Ireland: A Townhall Meeting, 18 June 2020," webinar.

63 Responding to the newly-formed Black Writers' Guild, major UK publishers have promised changes (see www.theguardian.com/books/2020/jun/17/uk-publishers-lack-of-diversity-black-writers-guild); similar promises have yet to be made in Ireland at the time of writing.

CHAPTER 15

Race, Place, and the Grounds of Irish Geopolitics[*]

Shirley Lau Wong

Our Walls, Our Borders

In 2019, Donald Trump visited Ireland for the first time during his presidency. The brief stopover was little more than an opportunity for Trump to stay at his hotel and golf resort in County Clare at the start of his European tour, but it nonetheless sparked a frenzy of media attention and protests across Ireland. At Shannon Airport, Trump held a press conference with a visibly tense Taoiseach Leo Varadkar and quickly stumbled into a major gaffe when the conversation drifted to Ireland and Brexit. "I think [Brexit] will all work out very well, and also for your wall, your border. I mean, we have a border situation in the United States, and you have one over here," Trump stated, "but I hear it's going to work out very well here." A journalist reported that there was a collective gasp in the room at the mention of "your wall, your border," and Varadkar took a steadying pause before gently qualifying the comparison of the U.S.-Mexico border and the border between Northern Ireland and the Republic. With a taut smile, the Taoiseach politely interjected: "The main thing we want to avoid, of course, is a border or a wall between both sides."

Trump's blunder was widely reported in both U.S. and Irish media and seen as further evidence of his cluelessness in foreign affairs. After all, one of the great threats of Brexit is the possible return of a "hard border" between Northern Ireland and the Republic, which is now the only land border between the UK and EU; new customs checkpoints and other border infrastructure could become potential targets for sectarian violence and threaten the hard-earned peace of the Belfast Agreement. Although Trump scratched at old and deep political wounds, his misstep was seen as just an unfortunate faux pas that happened to occur on Irish soil.

But a closer look at the slipup reveals a more complicated story of contemporary Irish geopolitics. Trump's acquisition of the County Clare golf resort was an aftereffect of the Celtic Tiger's collapse: the original golf course closed as a result of the economic downturn, and Trump purchased the property at a steep discount in 2012. Two years later, Trump's company filed a petition to build seawalls to protect the resort from coastal erosion, but environmentalists successfully blocked the construction, which would have destroyed local ecosystems. (The media quickly pointed out the irony that the resort's petition cited rising sea levels and extreme storms as potential environmental threats, as meanwhile Trump dismissed climate change as a hoax and withdrew the U.S. from the Paris Agreement.) During his tour through Europe, Trump frequently brought up the Irish resort dispute, calling it a "classic example of EU bureaucracy," nothing more than "environmental tricks," and an altogether "very bad experience."[1] (Some journalists even credit the dispute for sparking Trump's aversion to the EU and pro-Brexit stance.[2]) Because the controversy unfolded as Trump was campaigning on the promise of constructing a "great, great wall" along the U.S.-Mexico border, the proposed seawalls were jokingly referenced in the media and by protestors as "Trump's Irish wall." What's more, Varadkar's restraint during the press conference was not simply an example of international diplomacy but a calculated decision: at the time, the Irish government had been lobbying for access to the E3 visa program, which is seen as a potential pathway toward legal status for the estimated 50,000 undocumented Irish immigrants living in the U.S. If there had been any doubt before about the racism driving the Trump administration's anti-immigrant policies, it should be extinguished by the President's open support of a bill granting work visas to undocumented Irish immigrants.

What seems an accidental gaffe lays bare the complex web of political, environmental, and race relations that underwrites Irish geopolitics today: the ethnonationalism that deems some people "undocumented" but worthy of citizenship and others "illegal" and always "alien"; the battle between environmentalists and multinational corporations over a small stretch of coastal landscape; a world seemingly linked together by a matrix of borders and walls. What is also revealed is the continued centrality of place in the imagining of Irish political identity, whether in the language of "hard borders" and "Irish walls," or the territorial contentions of who does and does not count as a citizen. While the concept of place is well-trodden, if not overdetermined ground in the Irish political and cultural imaginary, far less attention has focused on how such tropes of space and place are interwoven with discourses of race in the context of contemporary Ireland. In what follows, I trace how the relationships between race and place have been and will continue to be crucial to Ireland's geopolitical identity.

Such an analysis uncovers some of the racial ideologies that have undergirded contemporary Irish literature, which continues to be preoccupied

with place, even in the globalized reality of the "new Ireland." In this essay,
I first track the spatial motifs – particularly the rhetoric of "soil" – that have
underlain discussions around race, nation, and citizenship in Irish history,
from the nineteenth century to the present. Then, as a way of suggesting
new insights afforded by this perspective, I take up as a literary case study
Seamus Heaney's famed bog poems, which were inspired by the archaeological excavations of bog bodies across North Atlantic Europe. Despite
the centrality of soil and kinship in these poems' archaeological and genealogical allusions, Heaney's work is rarely studied in relation to race. In this
essay's final section, I show how an interpretive account that considers the
racial discourse around place draws attention to details of Heaney's poetry
that critics have tended to ignore. As Dorothy Wang argues, in studies of
poetry, questions of race are often subsumed under the umbrellas of the
"cultural" and "political" and thereby are sidelined and remain uninterro-
gated: "Race seems to me the most salient, contested, and painfully charged
social difference in the American context, and one that imbues – and must
be disguised by – the more generic terms 'cultural' and 'political' when they
are raised in opposition to the 'literary.'"[3] While Wang makes her incisive
critique in the context of U.S. literature, her arguments expose what is overlooked in criticism on contemporary Irish poetry (particularly Heaney's
poetry), which has often been read against the backdrop of colonialism,
decolonization, and partition but rarely race.[4] What new insights might be
revealed by situating Irish poetry within a framework that forefronts race?

Moreover, such a perspective helps us recognize the pervasive racist
ideologies that have long percolated Irish cultural and political identity.
Racism in Ireland is often seen as a solely contemporary phenomenon
born during the Celtic Tiger. Certainly, during the boom period, there
was a visible rise in racist violence against immigrant communities from
Africa, China, and Eastern Europe. But it is dangerously misleading to
understand racism in Ireland as the exclusive product of the Celtic Tiger –
to see it, as John Brannigan pithily puts it, as having "arrived in the 1990s,
as if on a flight from Lagos or Vilnius."[5] Instead, the recent attention on
racism and xenophobia in the "new Ireland" must be situated within a
longer genealogy of racial discourse in Irish political and cultural life. It is
tempting to see racism in Ireland today as a mere hiccup in the growing
pains of a rapidly globalizing society, or to write it off as the regrettable
but otherwise unrepresentative behavior of a reactionary minority. But
instead, we should understand how the contemporary moment emerges
from a long lineage of racial ideologies that have underwritten the formation of the Irish State over the course of the nineteenth and twentieth

centuries and that continue to endure in and shape the present. It would be an obvious distortion to draw a straight line between the racial ideologies of nineteenth-century Ireland to those of today; instead, in what follows, I highlight pivotal moments when the constructions of Irish racial identity have been entangled with place, that most Irish of obsessions.

From the Sod to the Sky: A Brief History of Race and Soil in Ireland

The intimacies between race and place in Irish political discourse have a long history, stretching back to the plantation of Ireland in the sixteenth and seventeenth centuries. During the plantation era, the English distinguished the Irish as racially other on the basis of their supposedly innate inability to develop a productive and profitable agricultural economy. Of course, this conveniently rationalized the British conquest of Ireland, and as Steve Garner argues "the drive to make Irish soil more productive lies at the heart of the English initiatives from the mid-sixteenth century."[6] Later, this idea of Irish unproductivity would also be used to link the Irish with other colonial subjects. David Lloyd argues that in the nineteenth century, both Irish cottiers and the recently emancipated enslaved peoples in the West Indies were regarded as "surplus populations of the Empire," who lacked the capacity to cultivate the land. The "solution," proposed by nineteenth-century thinkers like John Stuart Mill, was to forcibly transform these populations into productive wage-laborers: "Security of tenure (a 'permanent interest in the soil') would … provide an inducement to labor discipline among the dispossessed. Thus the possessive individual was to be produced out of the former savage."[7] Central to the early racializations of the Irish was the perception of their unproductive relationship with the land, which in turn justified their dispossession.

But the Young Ireland movement subverted this colonial rhetoric of Irish unproductivity and dispossession and used it as an engine to campaign for Irish nationalism. The Young Irelanders capitalized on the practices of absentee landlordism (such as rack-renting and inefficient land management) to argue that Irish tenants had stronger claims to the land than did their negligent Anglo-Irish landlords. Dispossession – what had marked the Irish as racially inferior to the English – was mobilized by the Young Irelanders as the basis for their nationalist cause. As Sara Maurer argues, the Young Irelanders transformed the stain of Irish dispossession into a point of nationalist pride and even the basis of national identity itself. "[The Young Irelanders] imply that what the Irish do not have is what they are," Maurer explains, and in so doing, they "fused Irish identity, Irish possession of the land, and even Irish dispossession from it into one irreducible bond."[8]

Of course, historians have long traced the centrality of "the land question" to Irish nationalism. But what is less emphasized is how the relationship to land was also integral to the formation of Irish racial identity. There is a common perception that culture and not race forms the basis of Irish national identity in the nineteenth century. There is some truth to this claim as the Young Irelanders did promulgate a cross-sectarian sense of nation that could supersede ethnic, religious, and class differences and include both Protestants and Catholics, Anglo-Irish landlords and tenant farmers. For the Young Irelanders, Irish national character is not inherited but rather forged through a shared culture, be it the Irish language, literature, or nationalist politics. This is readily apparent in the famed motto of the *Nation*, the weekly newspaper and political organ of the Young Ireland movement, which aimed "to create and foster public opinion in Ireland, and make it racy of the soil."[9] The grammatical order is crucial to this formula of nationalism: one must first cultivate the proper "public opinion," which in turn is made "racy of the soil." In other words, culture precedes race. For the Young Irelanders, the nation is based on a reverse form of autochthony, in which a nationalist culture precedes and forges a connection between a people and the soil. This is readily apparent in the use of "foster," which suggests that a people severed from their ancestral forefathers could be "restored" to a new line of parentage.

But the language of fostering also brings up notions of biological kinship by implicitly suggesting that there once existed a coherent Irish racial lineage before it had been ruptured by British imperialism. And while the Young Irelanders were propagating an inclusive form of Irish national identity, they also exploited the Celtic-Saxon racial dichotomy that had been wielded against them, often relying on a narrative of the subjugated Celt struggling for liberation from oppressive Saxon reign.[10] Moreover, the Young Irelander's utopian project to create a national identity outside of all ethno-religious difference is part of a larger racial and imperial regime that idealizes a universal and "unmarked" subject, what David Lloyd calls the "Subject without properties," which is "constitutively unavailable or barred to the racialized subject" and also "the philosophical figure for what becomes, with increasing literalness through the nineteenth century, the global ubiquity of the white European."[11]

To be made "racy of the soil," then, is no clear task. The *Nation*'s motto suggests how racial and cultural constructions of Irish identity cannot be easily separated, as well as how the rhetoric of soil has been central to the racial discourses underpinning Irish nationalism. Seamus

Deane explains that the term "soil" carried specific political valences in nineteenth-century Ireland: whereas "land" connoted the legal realm of property rights and tenancy laws, "soil" implied more romantic notions of place-attachment and an even umbilical connection between the Irish and Ireland. James Fintan Lalor makes clear this distinction when he dismisses the abstraction of land in favor of soil in his celebrated clarion call for "Ireland her own – Ireland her own, and all therein, from the sod to the sky. The soil of Ireland for the people of Ireland, to have and to hold from God alone who gave it – to have and to hold to them and their heirs forever." For Lalor, who was arguing against what he saw as the shortsightedness of the Repeal movement, such inalienable rights to the soil are not to be confused with the "mock freedom" of land rights promised by "constitutions, and charters" whose substance is mere "paper and parchment."[12] While previous systems of communal land ownership had been irrevocably corrupted by British proprietary laws, the connection with soil remained unspoiled and therefore could form a viable basis of Irish national identity. As Deane argues, "[Lalor] appeals to the power of the distinction between soil as a material-metaphysical possession and land as a political-legal entity. The nation is of the soil; the state of the land."[13] In this way, the rhetoric of soil acts as a shorthand for the fusion of national identity and land.

Lalor's vision of "the soil of Ireland for the people of Ireland" would reemerge, albeit in transformed form, in Éamon de Valera's St. Patrick's Day radio speech in 1932. Taking office just weeks after a close general election and in a country still healing from the wounds of civil war and partition, de Valera sought to regain some semblance of stability and unity in his speech. Adding to the challenge was the far-reaching audience of de Valera's radio speech, which was simultaneously broadcasted in the Irish Free State and in the U.S. De Valera acknowledges the geographic breadth of the Irish diaspora, the "vastness of the country in which so many of the children of our race have found a home and the magnitude of the dispersion of our people."[14] Addressing his far-flung audience, de Valera repeats Lalor's aforementioned words as the governing precept of the newly elected Fianna Fáil party, explaining that, "I know no words in which I can express [the aims of government] better than those of Fintan Lalor." In Lalor's original formulation, the language of sod, sky, and soil belonging to the Irish and "their heirs" was used to challenge systems of British property laws and to articulate more radical forms of land reform. But in a radio speech directed toward the Irish diasporic community, or the "children of our race," de Valera projects the image of Ireland as a racially homogenous, if geographically scattered people held together by their divine right to the soil of Ireland. In so doing, de Valera affirms the Irish as a racially cohesive community that can sustain the recent blows to Irish national sovereignty and also bridge the geographic expanse of diaspora. As Brannigan argues, "The touchstones of de Valera's nationalism are in these key words, 'soil,' 'people,' and 'God,' and in the relationship between them in which the convergent soil and people hold their sovereignty forever as the gift of God."[15] While Lalor and the Young Irelanders may have articulated conflicting conceptualizations of Irish national identity, under de Valera's vision, the rhetoric of soil became resolutely synonymous with a racialized Irish identity.

The rhetoric of soil has more recently resurfaced with the 2004 Citizenship Referendum, which rescinded *jus soli* ("rights of the soil") nationality laws that granted automatic citizenship to any person born in Ireland. Replacing birthright citizenship laws was the policy of *jus sanguinis* ("rights of the blood"), which dictates that citizenship is determined by the nationality of one's parents. At first glance, the Citizenship Referendum seems incongruent with conceptions of Irish identity that strongly tie together people and territory; as Bernard Ryan argues, the "emphasis on *jus soli* in Irish law, and its application to both the Irish state and Northern Ireland, reflects an underlying territorial understanding of who the Irish are in the first place."[16] Birthright citizenship had existed in Ireland since the establishment of the Free State in 1922, was codified in the Irish Nationality and Citizenship Act in 1935, and later enshrined in the constitution in 1937 and again in the Belfast Agreement in 1998. (In fact, up until the referendum, Ireland was the last remaining country in Europe with nationality laws based on *jus soli*.[17]) The campaign for the Citizenship Referendum was fueled by racist and xenophobic panics over so-called "birth tourism" and the arrival of refugees and asylum seekers during the Celtic Tiger. (The perceived exploitation of Ireland's citizenship laws was hugely overblown. According to a study, births to non-EU national mothers comprised less than 2.4 percent of total births at Dublin's three major maternity hospitals in 2003.[18]) Passed with a landslide of nearly 80 percent of the electorate, the Citizenship Referendum reflected a startling change in the conception of Irish nationality. In the Dáil Éireann debate on the referendum, then Minister of Justice Michael McDowell argued that Ireland's birthright citizenship laws were exploited by "persons with no tangible link to the nation or the state whether of parentage, upbringing or of long-term residence in the state."[19] In other words, the "tangible link" between the Irish citizen and the nation is no longer the shared soil of Ireland but instead race.[20] (The racialization of

Irish citizenship is further underscored by current nationality laws, which allow up to third-generation emigrants to claim citizenship.)

On the surface, the Citizenship Referendum seems to contradict the historically territorial conceptions of Irish national identity. But the referendum is less surprising and more a logical outcome when examined as part of the shifting relationship between race and place in modern and contemporary Ireland. As de Valera's speech makes clear, the rhetoric of soil has also been used as a means to connect the globally dispersed Irish diaspora. Over the 1990s, the concept of the Irish diaspora gained currency in political spheres, popularized first by Mary Robinson during her 1990–97 presidency. In her oft-quoted 1995 Oireachtas address, Robinson championed the diaspora as the cornerstone of Irish identity, asserting that "Irishness is not simply territorial. In fact Irishness as a concept ... can be strengthened again if we turn with open minds and hearts to the array of people outside Ireland for whom this island is a place of origin."[21] But while Robinson and her successors may have intended to accentuate the diversity of the Irish diaspora, they also unwittingly helped lay the groundwork for the Citizenship Referendum in the following decade. As Ronit Lentin argues, by redefining Irish identity in terms of bloodline rather than territory, the conceptualization of Ireland as a "diaspora nation" facilitated the erosion of *jus soli* in favor of *jus sanguinis*.[22] That is to say, the propagation of the Irish diaspora simultaneously fostered a globalized sense of Irish identity and helped solidify Ireland as a racial state. Such deterritorialized notions of the "global Irish family" (President Mary McAleese's favorite term for the diaspora) may seem to encourage liberal viewpoints that would negate nativism and xenophobia. But far from an antidote to ethnonationalism, the globalizing of Irish identity instead often came hand in hand with its racialization.

Kinship and Race in Seamus Heaney's Bog Poems

As this complicated history shows, the rhetoric of soil has provided not so much a stable ground of Irish identity as a fungible trope yoked to different ends. Given then the looming presence of landscape in the Irish literary and political imagination, how do the complex relations between race and place manifest in Irish literature? I make modest steps toward a response by turning to an unlikely archive: the bog poems of Seamus Heaney, which take as their central figure the excavated bog bodies discovered across Northern Europe. Even though there is ample scholarship on these poems, few critics have mined their racial underpinnings despite the abundant allusions to archaeology and prehistoric geography, fields of study that have been pivotal to contemporary conceptions of Irish racial identity.[23] Such an oversight stems from several reasons. First, Heaney frequently turns to Viking histories and mythologies, which are often coded as white or seen as "pre-racial."[24] But more importantly, there is a presiding presumption that race in Ireland is a recent product, born during the Tiger and "imported" from outside. Such assumptions obscure how a major writer like Heaney, considered the poetic spokesperson of Ireland and writing at an earlier moment of history, was deeply interested in questions of race. If my coda so far has outlined how tropes of place are entrenched in Irish racial formation, I conclude by highlighting how that relation has often been obfuscated in Irish cultural criticism, even when it is explicit. That Heaney's work is not thought of in relation to race – even though he so clearly mobilizes tropes of soil, tribalism, ancestry, and kinship – shows how whiteness remains invisible in (and therefore reproduced by) Irish studies scholarship today.[25] It is nothing new to say that Heaney understands Irish identity as rooted in place. But how might we analyze the discourses of indigeneity and nativism underlying Heaney's infamous bog poems as specifically racial discourses?

While the bog poems crop up throughout the poet's early and mid-career collections, they are most closely associated with *North* (1974), in which the landscape is figured as a natal source of life. Heaney flanks the collection's central section with two poems about Antaeus, the Greek deity who was the son of Gaia and who gathered his strength through contact with the earth. In the opening poem, Antaeus declares that, "I cannot be weaned / Off the earth's long contour, her river-veins ... / I am cradled in the dark that wombed me / And nurtured in every artery / Like a small hillock."[26] But in the closing poem, the autochthonous Antaeus is "weaned at last" and defeated by Hercules, who lifts the god off the earth and

> out of his element
> into a dream of loss
>
> and origins—the cradling dark,
> the river-veins, the secret gullies
> of his strength,
> the hatching grounds
>
> of cave and souterrain,
> he has bequeathed it all
> to elegists. Balor will die
> and Brythnoth and Sitting Bull.[27]

Ripped from the earth's "cradling dark," Antaeus bequeaths his legacy to "elegists," who mourn his death alongside other defeated heroes like Balor (the Irish god-king killed by the Tuatha Dé Danann), Byrthnoth (the Anglo-Saxon earl who died at the hands of Viking raiders), and Sitting Bull (the Hunkpapa Lakota chief murdered by Indian agency police). By evoking these mythic and historic figures, Heaney imagines a tradition of indigenous heroes who were defeated by and lost their lands to "invading forces," and in so doing, portrays the Troubles as part of a similar history of dispossession. Like the Young Irelanders, Heaney implies that Irish identity is defined by both an intimate relationship to the land and dispossession from it.

While many scholars have explored the transhistorical dimensions of these poems' archaeological motifs, few have explored their racial implications despite the frequent references to ancient "origins" and indigeneity. (We should note the previous poem's reference to "souterrain," or the Iron Age underground structure thought to have been brought to Ireland and Scotland by the Gauls. The archaeological allusion further demonstrates how Heaney intentionally looks to the prehistoric European Atlantic as a source of Irish indigeneity, even in his poems of Classical mythology.) This scholarly oversight is conspicuous given the prominent role that archaeological and genealogical projects have played in cultivating a racialized sense of Irish identity. As Catherine Nash argues, the racialization of Irish identity was heavily influenced by the country's subsidization of anthropological and population genetics studies such as the Harvard Irish Survey. Although conversations around "natives" and "non-natives," "settlements" and "invasions," have roots stretching back to eighteenth-century antiquarianism, interpretations of prehistoric geography have continued to inform theoretical perspectives in contemporary Irish historiography. As Nash argues, such geographic imaginations of prehistoric origins have not only lingered in the academy but also "disseminate[d] into the public culture of ethnic identification and the making of ethnic distinction."[28] Heaney himself was not immune to the popularity of anthropological archaeology, and in various interviews, the poet frequently recounts his frequent visits to the Viking exhibitions at the National Museum in Dublin and to excavation sites in Denmark in the 1960s and 1970s.[29]

How, then, might we read the archaeological imagery in Heaney's poems as more than just figurative? We can begin with "Kinship," which opens:

> Kinned by hieroglyphic
> peat on a spreadfield
> to the strangled victim,
> the love-nest in the bracken,

> I step through origins
> like dog turning
> its memories of wilderness
> on the kitchen mat...[30]

The poem animates a motif that recurs throughout the poet's career, depicting the Irish landscape as an infinite repository of history that yields to the archaeologist's (or poet's) touch. The bog is "hieroglyphic peat" that is readily deciphered and acts as a storehouse of Ireland's ancient past ("Earth-pantry, bone-vault, / sun-bank, embalmer / of votive goods / and sabred fugitives"). Moreover, its unique preserving qualities work like a topographic time machine through which the speaker can "step through origins" and retrieve "memories of wilderness." Scholars have usually understood "kinship" in the looser senses of the word, reading the poem as a reflection on the paralleled histories of violence in the Iron Age and the Troubles. For instance, Heather O'Donoghue explains that the poem "recognize[s] our kinship with an otherwise strange and distant past" and "makes explicit the link between Ireland and ... Scandinavia."[31] But we might also read "kinship" as denoting blood relation; seen from this more literal reading, the poem emphasizes instead a "kinned" or racial relation between the speaker and the ancestral "strangled victim" that is forged through a common bond to the "hieroglyphic peat." In other words, the bog operates not so much as the grounds of comparison but instead the grounds of racial ancestry.

Such a rereading brings to light the themes of descent and heritage depicted in Heaney's other bog poems like "Belderg," which is set in the Céide Fields, the largest Neolithic site in Ireland and one of the oldest field systems in the world. The poem is comprised of a conversation with a local turfcutter-turned-archaeologist, who unearthed the ancient farmlands when he "stripped off blanket bog" to reveal a "landscape fossilized." (The poem's interlocutor is modeled after Patrick Caulfield, a schoolteacher who originally discovered the site when cutting turf in the 1930s. Inspired by his visit with Caulfield, Heaney wrote "Belderg" and enclosed the poem along with a thank you note to him.) The poem opens with the initial misidentification of the quernstones and other artifacts at Céide: "'They just kept turning up / And were thought of as foreign.'"[32] While the archaeologist does correct the misclassification of the quernstones, the confusion over their perceived "foreignness" is telling, raising questions about who counts as "native" or "non-native" in Ireland's early history. The speaker (a stand-in for Heaney) and archaeologist articulate two competing interpretations of Ireland's prehistoric geography. The speaker "talk[s] of Mossbawn, / A bogland name" and underscores its dual English and Irish etymologies; for him, heritage is a "forked root" made up of different lineages, and it is up to the poet to decide which to emphasize: "I could derive / A forked root from that ground / Make *bawn* an English fort, / A planter's walled-in mound, / Or else find sanctuary / And think of it as Irish." But the archaeologist pushes against this "mutable" interpretation and asks about the "older strains of Norse" that also make up Mossbawn's etymology; he questions, "'But *moss?*'" and later again, "'But the Norse ring on your tree?'" (The word "moss" comes from the Danish and Icelandic words for "bog."[33]) More than simply insisting on the speaker's Norse heritage, the archaeologist conceives of a different vision of history as tree rings, as a "congruence of lives" and a shared timeline of the "iron, flint, and bronze" ages. The poem therefore proposes the possibility of not an analogous but a genealogical relationship between the Norse and the Irish.

If this analysis seems unfair to Heaney, to read too much into his poetry, I should make clear that this reading is not designed to condemn his work as somehow covertly racist. In fact, Heaney's "Belderg" poem ends in a pluralistic, if macabre vision of Ireland's racial past: the "world-tree" or Yggdrasil (the mythical tree in Norse cosmology), which gruesomely grinds and mixes together the vertebrae of Norse, English, and Irish cultures:

> I passed through the eye of the quern,
>
> Grist to an ancient mill,
> And in my mind's eye saw
> A world-tree of balanced stones,
> Querns piled like vertebrae,
> The marrow crushed to grounds.

As Henry Hart argues, the poem concludes with "the painful, cosmic revelation ... in which Heaney envisions himself as no longer possessing an identity, but ground and mixed up in the warring factions of all history."[34] Rather than posit a racially "pure" conception of Irish identity, the poem concludes with an epiphany about its transnational pluralism. But at the same time, Heaney's poems of the soil nonetheless rely on a racial and territorially bound form of Irish identity. By depicting the bog as soft, yielding, and supple, Heaney not only casts the landscape as an archive of Irish history; he also suggests how it literally swallows all those who step foot on Ireland. (In one poem, Heaney describes the bog as an "Insatiable bride."[35]) Heaney seems to conceptualize another version of *jus soli*: to step foot on Ireland – and, more importantly, to be buried there – is to be Irish.

If my essay's primary purpose has been to show how Irish cultural nationalism is deeply tied together with place and race, then its secondary ambition is to show how that racial formation has been erased within Irish studies – and how that erasure itself conflates Irish culture with whiteness. Again, the purpose of this rereading is not to "reveal" an underlying racism in Heaney's poetry but rather to show how racial ideologies are naturalized and therefore go unexamined in the most canonical works of Irish literature. In her groundbreaking *Playing in the Dark*, Toni Morrison argues that "the readers of virtually all of American fiction have been positioned as white," and the consequence of this assumption is that instances of Black presence are marked as racial while figures of whiteness are "race-free" and therefore remain invisible.[36] I see an analogous situation at work in Irish Studies today, where because race is associated exclusively with the "new Irish," something that has emerged only within the twenty-first century, we remain blind to how major works of Irish literature were already deeply invested in race. As I hope to have shown in this essay, it is not enough to tease out the submerged presences of race – which, as I argue, were never that hidden to begin with. Instead, in order to understand race in Irish culture and history, we must examine the instances where it is made explicit and where it is rendered invisible.

Notes

* I would like to thank Mary Mullen for her insightful, eagle-eyed feedback on an earlier draft of this essay.
1 See Caelainn Hogan, "Trump's other wall: is his Irish resort a sign he believes in climate change?" *The Guardian*, November 17, 2016, www.theguardian.com/us-news/2016/nov/17/donald-trump-ireland-golf-resort-wall-climate-change.
2 See Griff Witte, "A wall denied may have made Trump dislike E.U.," *The Washington Post*, February 7, 2017, www.washingtonpost.com/world/europe/trump-tried-and-failed-to-build-a-wall-in-ireland-that-could-mean-big-trouble-for-europe/2017/02/05/4629d02e-e5a0-11e6-a419-eefe8eff0835_story.html.
3 Dorothy Wang, *Thinking Its Presence: Form, Race, and Subjectivity in Contemporary Asian American Poetry* (Stanford: Stanford University Press, 2013), 19.
4 This is not to overlook the work of Irish studies scholars who have paved the way in examining race in modern and contemporary Irish literature, most notably Catherine Eagan, Catherine McIvor, Gerardine Meaney, and Sinéad Moynihan. But these scholars focus on the genres of the novel and drama, and none concentrate on poetry.
5 John Brannigan, *Race in Modern Irish Literature and Culture* (Edinburgh: Edinburgh University Press, 2009), 21.

6   Garner's use of the term "soil" here is borrowed from Edmund Spenser's *View of the Present State of Ireland*: "though Ireland is by nature counted a great soil of pasture, yet had I rather few cows kept and men better mannered than to have such huge increase of cattle and no increase of good conditions." See Steve Garner, "Reflections on Race in Contemporary Ireland," in *Race and Immigration in the New Ireland*, eds. Julieann Veronica Ulin and Heather Edwards (South Bend: Notre Dame University Press, 2013), 178.

7   David Lloyd, "Black Irish, Irish Witness and Atlantic State Formation," in *The Black and Green Atlantic: Cross-Currents of the African and Irish Diasporas*, eds. Peter D. O'Neill and David Lloyd (London: Palgrave, 2009), 10–11.

8   Sara Maurer, *The Dispossessed State: Narratives of Ownership in Nineteenth-century Britain and Ireland* (Baltimore: Johns Hopkins University Press, 2012), 118, 120. As Mary Mullen points out, this rhetoric of fusing together property and identity took on dangerous forms when it crossed the Atlantic. The Young Irelanders' arguments that the Irish were naturally predisposed to "love of land and love of arms" helped legitimize the Irish as settler colonialists and therefore justified the dispossession of Indigenous peoples' land in the U.S. See Mullen, "How the Irish Became Settlers: Metaphors of Indigeneity and the Erasure of Indigenous Peoples," *New Hibernia Review* 20, no. 3 (2016): 81–96.

9   Charles Gavan Duffy, *Young Ireland: A Fragment of Irish History 1840–1845* (Dublin: M. H. Gill and Son, 1884), 23.

10 For more, see Julie M. Dugger, "Black Ireland's Race: Thomas Carlyle and the Young Ireland Movement," *Victorian Studies* 48, no. 3 (Spring 2006): 461–85.

11 David Lloyd, *Under Representation: The Racial Regime of Aesthetics* (New York: Fordham University Press, 2018), 15, 77.

12 James Fintan Lalor, *The Writing of James Fintan Lalor: With an Introduction Embodying Personal Recollections*, eds. John O'Leary and T. O'Donoghue (Dublin: T. G. O'Donoghue, 1895), 64, 68.

13 Seamus Deane, *Strange Country: Modernity and Nationhood Since 1790* (Oxford: Oxford University Press, 1999), 76.

14 Éamon de Valera, "Aims of Fianna Fáil in Office, 17 March 1932," in *Speeches and Statements by Eamon de Valera, 1917–73*, ed. Maurice Moynihan (New York: St. Martin's Press, 1980), 194.

15 Brannigan, *Race in Modern Irish Literature and Culture*, 150.

16 Bernard Ryan, "The Celtic Cubs: The Controversy over Birthright Citizenship in Ireland," *European Journal of Migration and Law* 6, no. 3 (2004): 176.

17 Ireland's policy of *jus soli* was in keeping with many other former British colonies, including the United States, Canada, India, Pakistan, Australia, and New Zealand, which had based their original nationality laws on those of the UK. (The UK had unqualified *jus soli* until the British Nationality Act in 1981.)

18 Dervla King, "Immigration and Citizenship in Ireland," March 31, 2004, www.childrensrights.ie/resources/immigration-and-citizenship-ireland.

19 *Dáil Éireann Debates*, April 21, 2004, www.oireachtas.ie/en/debates/debate/dail/2004-04-21/3.

20 While outside the scope of this essay, another important component to this conversation is the history of discrimination against Irish Travellers in Ireland. The racialization of Travellers often revolves around their nomadism, and their nomadic cultural practices became increasingly criminalized (usually in the form of trespassing laws) during the Celtic Tiger, when large tracts of land were rapidly developed as real estate. For more, see Sindy Joyce, "Divided Spaces: An examination of everyday racism and its impact on young Travellers' spatial mobility," *Irish Journal of Anthropology* 18, no. 1 (2015): 15–23.

21 Mary Robinson, "Cherishing the Irish Diaspora: On a Matter of Public Importance," Address to the House of the Oireachtas, February 1995.

22 Ronit Lentin, "Illegal in Ireland, Irish Illegals: Diaspora Nation as Racial State," *Irish Political Studies* 22, no. 4 (2007): 433–53.

23 No other works of Irish poetry have generated as much simultaneous praise and ire. Depending on which critic, Heaney's poetry is either the defining work of the Troubles or a sacrilegious aestheticization of the sectarian conflict. For the major voices in the critical reception of Heaney's bog poems, see: David Lloyd, *Anomalous States: Irish Writing and the Post-Colonial Moments* (Durham: Duke University Press, 1993); Helen Vendler, *Seamus Heaney* (Cambridge: Harvard University Press, 2000); Ciaran Carson, "Escaped from the Massacre?," *Honest Ulsterman* 50 (1975): 183–86.

24 Such misunderstandings of Vikings as homogeneously white belie the multicultural and multiracial realities of this period of history. More disturbingly, the fantasia of Viking history – and the medieval period more largely – as a "preracial" white space has been a large part of white supremacist culture. For more, see Dorothy Kim, "White Supremacists Have Weaponized an Imaginary Viking Past," *Time*, April 15, 2019.

25 Scholars such as Alison Garden and Richard Rankin Russell have examined race in Heaney's poetry, but their analyses emphasize the cross-racial affinities in Heaney's work, highlighting the poet's comparisons between the experiences of Northern Irish Catholics and those of other oppressed peoples. While it is worthwhile to situate Heaney's poetry in broader comparative frameworks, such approaches necessarily situate the Irish as the racialized other, obscuring how these poems also participate in the construction of whiteness as fundamental to Irish identity.

26 Seamus Heaney, *North* (London: Faber & Faber, 1975), 3.

27 Heaney, *North*, 46.

28 Catherine Nash, "Irish Origins, Celtic Origins: Population Genetics, Cultural Politics," *Irish Studies Review* 14, no. 1 (2006): 11–37.

29 See Heaney, *Preoccupations*, 54; Heaney, *Stepping Stones*, 163.

30 Heaney, *North*, 33.

31 Heather O'Donoghue, "Heaney, Beowulf and the Medieval Literature of the North," in *The Cambridge Companion to Seamus Heaney*, ed. Bernard O'Donoghue (Cambridge: Cambridge University Press, 2009), 196. I acknowledge that it would be an overreach to take at face value any claims about Irish racial ancestry made in Heaney's poetry. As O'Donoghue points

out, the main inspiration for *North* was P. V. Glob's archaeological study *The Bog People* (1965), whose interpretations were drawn from literary (rather than historical) sources and have since been challenged by many scholars. Rather, my essay analyzes the imagination of racial ancestry and lineage in Heaney's poetry. For a more nuanced historical overview of the Viking raids of Ireland, see: Donnchadh Ó Corráin, "Ireland, Wales, Man, and the Hebrides," in *The Oxford Illustrated History of the Vikings*, ed. Peter Sawyer (Oxford: Oxford University Press, 1997), 83–109.

32 Heaney, *North*, 4–5.

33 See O'Donoghue, "Heaney, *Beowulf* and Medieval Literature," 193.

34 Henry Hart, *Seamus Heaney: Poet of Contrary Progressions* (Syracuse: Syracuse University Press, 1992), 82.

35 Heaney, *North*, 34.

36 Toni Morrison, *Playing in the Dark: Whiteness and the Literary Imagination* (Cambridge: Harvard University Press, 1992), xii.

Select Bibliography

Adams, R. M., *Surface and Symbol: The Consistency of James Joyce's* Ulysses (Oxford: Oxford University Press, 1962).

Ahmed, S., "Closing the Door: Complaint as Diversity," Public Lecture, University College Cork, May 16, 2019, www.saranahmed.com.

Ahmed, S., *Strange Encounters: Embodied Others in Post-Coloniality* (London and New York: Routledge, 2001).

Ahmed, S., *The Cultural Politics of Emotion* (Edinburgh: Edinburgh University Press, 2004).

Allen, K., "Neo-liberalism and Immigration." In *Immigration and Social Change in the Republic of Ireland*, edited by Bryan Fanning, 84–98 (Manchester: Manchester University Press, 2007).

Althusser, L., *Lenin and Philosophy & Other Essays*, trans. Ben Brewster (New York: Monthly Review Press, 1971).

Anon. [James Hunt], "Knox on the Celtic Race." *The Anthropological Review* 6, no. 21 (1868): 175–91.

Anon., *Lebor Gabála Érenn: The Book of the Taking of Ireland*, edited by Robert Alexander Stewart Macalister, 5 vols. (Dublin: Irish Text Society, 1938–56).

Anon. [Thomas Carlyle], "Occasional Discourse on the Negro Question." *Fraser's Magazine for Town and Country* 40, no. 240 (December 1849): 670–79.

Aristotle, *The Basic Works of Aristotle*, trans. Richard McKeon (New York: Random House, 1941).

Arnold, M., *On the Study of Celtic Literature* (London: Smith, Elder and Co., 1867).

Arnold, T., *Introductory Lectures on Modern History*, 2nd ed. (London: B. Fellowes, 1843).

Arrow, M., and Findlay, J., "A Critical Introduction to *The Nightingale*: Gender, Race and Troubled Histories on Screen." *Studies in Australasian Cinema* 14, no. 1 (2020): 3–14.

Arts Council of Ireland., Equality, Human Rights and Diversity Policy and Strategy. 2019, www.artscouncil.ie/uploadedFiles/EHRD%20Policy%20English%20version%20Final.pdf.

Backus, M. G., "'Not Quite Philadelphia, Is It?': An Interview with Eamonn McCann." *Éire-Ireland* 36, no. 3–4 (Fall/Winter 2001): 174–69.

Baer, W., ed., *Conversations with Derek Walcott* (Jackson: University of Mississippi Press, 1996).

Bagnall, K., and Couchman, S., eds., *Chinese Australians: Politics, Engagement and Resistance* (Leiden: Brill, 2015).

Baldwin, J., *The Fire Next Time* (New York: Random-Vintage, 1962).

Barnett, A., "People's Democracy: A Discussion on Strategy." *New Left Review* 1, no. 55 (May–June 1969): 1–27.

Baucom, I., *Specters of the Atlantic: Finance Capital, Slavery, and the Philosophy of History* (Durham, NC: Duke University Press, 2005).

Baum, B., *The Rise and Fall of the Caucasian Race: A Political History of Racial Identity* (New York: New York University Press, 2006).

Beasley, E., *The Victorian Reinvention of Race: New Racisms and the Problem of Grouping in the Human Sciences* (London: Routledge, 2010).

Beckett, S., "Censorship in the Saorstat." In *Disjecta: Miscellaneous Writings and a Dramatic Fragment*, edited by Ruby Cohn, 84–88 (New York: Gove Press, 1984).

Beddoe, J., *The Races of Britain: A Contribution to the Anthropology of Western Europe* (Bristol and London: J. W. Arrowsmith and Trubner, 1885).

Behrendt, L., "The Nightingale Review – Ambitious, Urgent and Necessarily Brutal. But Who Is It For?" *The Guardian*, August 20, 2019, www .theguardian.com/film/2019/aug/20/the-nightingale-review-ambitious-urgent-and-necessarily-brutal-but-who-is-it-for.

Bellanta, M., "The Larrikin's Hop: Larrikinism and Late Colonial Popular Theatre." *Australasian Drama Studies* 52 (2008): 131–47.

Bender, A., "British Israelites, Irish Israelites, and the End of an Analogy." In *Irish Questions and Jewish Questions: Crossovers in Culture*, edited by Aidan Beatty and Dan O'Brien, 17–30 (Syracuse: Syracuse University Press, 2018).

Bénéjam, V., "The Reprocessing of Trash in *Ulysses*: Recycling and (Post) Creation." *Hypermedia Joyce Studies* 5:1, n.p. (2004). http://hjs.ff.cuni.cz/archives/v3/benejam.html.

Bertaux, S., "Demographic Knowledge, 'Race Suicide' and the Making of Racial Jews in Interwar Europe." *European Journal of Turkish Studies* 16 (December 2013): 1–14, https://journals.openedition.org/ejts/4848.

Bhreathnach, E., MacMahon, J., and McCafferty, J., eds., *The Irish Franciscans, 1534–1990* (Dublin: Four Courts Press, 2009).

Black, M., "Fanon and DuBoisian Double Consciousness." *Human Architecture: Journal of the Sociology of Self-Knowledge* 5, no. 3 (2007): 393–404.

Boeninger, S. P., *Literary Drowning: Postcolonial Memory in Irish and Caribbean Writing* (Syracuse: Syracuse University Press, 2020).

Boittin, J. A., "Black in France: The Language and Politics of Race in the Late Third Republic." *French Politics, Culture & Society* 27, no. 2 (2009): 23–46.

Boland, E., "Editorial." *Poetry Ireland Review* 125 (2017): 5–6, www.poetryireland .ie/publications/poetry-ireland-review/editorial/issue-125.

Boland, E., "Where Poetry Begins: Eavan Boland in Conversation." *American Poet*, January 9, 2001, https://poets.org/text/where-poetry-begins-eavan-boland-conversation.

Bolt, C., *Victorian Attitudes to Race* (London: Routledge and K. Paul, 1971).

Boltwood, S., "'The Ineffaceable Curse of Cain': Race, Miscegenation, and the Victorian Staging of Irishness." *Victorian Literature and Culture* 29, no. 2 (2001): 383–96.

Bond, C. J., "Causes of Racial Decay Distribution of Natural Capacity: The Need for a National Stocktaking." *Eugenics Review* 20 (April 1928): 5–19.

Boran, P. and Enyi-Amadi, C., eds., *Writing Home: The 'New Irish' Poets* (Dublin: Dedalus Press, 2019).

Bornstein, G., "Irish, Jewish, or Both: Hybrid Identities of David Marcus, Stanley Price, and Myself." In *Irish Questions and Jewish Questions: Crossovers in Culture*, edited by Aidan Beatty and Dan O'Brien, 127–39 (Syracuse: Syracuse University Press, 2018).

Bourke, E. and Faragó, B., eds., *Landing Places: Immigrant Poets in Ireland* (Dublin: Dedalus Press, 2010).

Boyne, J., "*From a Low and Quiet Sea* by Donal Ryan – Waves of Compassion and Anger." *The Guardian*, March 30, 2018, www.theguardian.com/books/2018/mar/30/from-a-low-and-quiet-sea-by-donal-ryan-review.

Bracken, C., *Irish Feminist Futures* (London: Routledge, 2016).

Bradshaw, B., Hadfield, A., and Maley, W., eds., *Representing Ireland: Literature and the Origins of the Conflict, 1534–60* (Cambridge: Cambridge University Press, 1993).

Bradshaw, D., "Eugenics: 'They Should Certainly Be Killed.'" In *A Concise Companion to Modernism*, edited by David Bradshaw, 34–55 (Malden, MA: Blackwell, 2003).

Bradshaw, D., "The Eugenics Movement in the 1930s and the Emergence of *On the Boiler*." *Yeats Annual* 9 (1992): 189–215.

Brady, C., *James Anthony Froude: An Intellectual Biography of a Victorian Prophet* (Oxford: Oxford University Press, 2013).

Braidotti, R., *Nomadic Subjects* (Columbia: Columbia University Press, 2011).

Braithwaite, K., *The Arrivants: A New World Trilogy* (Oxford: Oxford University Press, 1981).

Branch, E. M., *James T. Farrell* (New York: Twayne Publishers, 1971).

Branch, E. M., *James T. Farrell. Pamphlets on American Writers Number 29* (Minneapolis: University of Minnesota Press, 1963).

Brannigan, J., "'Ireland, and Black!': Minstrelsy, Racism, and Black Cultural Production In 1970s Ireland." *Textual Practice* 22, no. 2 (2008): 229–48.

Brannigan, J., *Race in Modern Irish Literature and Culture* (Edinburgh: Edinburgh University Press, 2009).

Brantlinger, P., *Dark Vanishings: Discourse on the Extinction of Primitive Races, 1800–1930* (Ithaca: Cornell University Press, 2003).

Brantlinger, P., *Taming Cannibals: Race and the Victorians* (Ithaca: Cornell University Press, 2011).

Braxton, J. M., and Diedrich, M. I., eds., *Monuments of the Black Atlantic: Slavery and Memory* (Münster: Transaction Publishers, 2004).

Breitman, G., "How a Minority Can Change Society." *International Socialist Review* 25, no. 2 (Spring 1964): 34–41.

Brennan, M., *The Young Man from Rathmines* (Dublin: Talbot Press, n.d.).

Brinkley, D., and Fenster, J., *Parish Priest: Father Michael McGivney and American Catholicism* (New York: Harper Collins, 2006).

Brodsky, J., Heaney, S., Murray, L., and Walcott, D., "Poet's Roundtable: 'A Common Language,'" interview by Michael Schmidt, *PN Review* 15, no. 4 (1989): 39.

Brooke, C., *Reliques of Irish Poetry (1789)*, edited by Lesa Ní Mhunghaile (Dublin: Irish Manuscripts Commission, 2009).

Broome, R., *Aboriginal Australians: A History since 1788*, 4th ed. (Sydney: Allen and Unwin, 2010).

Brown, T., *Ireland: A Social and Cultural History 1922–2002* (London: Harper Perennial, 2004).

Brundage, D., *Irish Nationalists in America: The Politics of Exile, 1978–1998* (Oxford: Oxford University Press, 2016).

Buncombe, A., "Inside the Data that Debunks the 'Great Replacement' Theory," *Independent*, May 16, 2022, www.independent.co.uk/news/world/americas/buffalo-shooting-great-replacement-theory-b2080389.html.

Burke, M., "Irish Travellers, the Environment, and Literature." In *History of Irish Literature and the Environment*, edited by Malcolm Sen, 206–26 (Cambridge, Cambridge University Press, 2022).

Burke, M., *Race, Politics, and Irish America: A Gothic History* (Oxford: Oxford University Press, 2023).

Burkett, J., *Constructing Post-Imperial Britain: Britishness, "Race" and the Radical Left in the 1960s* (Basingstoke: Palgrave, 2013).

Burns, A., *Milkman: A Novel* (London: Faber & Faber, 2018).

Butt, I., *Land Tenure in Ireland: A Plea for the Celtic Race*, 3rd ed. (Dublin and London: John Falconer & Longmans, Green, Reader, and Dyer, 1866).

Byrd, J. A., *The Transit of Empire: Indigenous Critiques of Colonialism* (Minneapolis: University of Minnesota Press, 2011).

Byrne, A., and O'Sullivan, E., "Arensberg, Kimball and de Valera: A Story of Sex and Censorship." *Irish Journal of Sociology* 27, no. 3 (2019): 227–50.

Byrne, J. J., *Dáil Éireann Debates*. October 19, 1928, www.oireachtas.ie/en/debates/debate/dail/1928-10-19/2/.

Byrne, J. P., "Seeking Agency, Finding Nothing: Irish American Identity as a His-Story of Absence in James T. Farrell's *Studs Lonigan*." *Foilsiú: An Interdisciplinary Journal of Irish Studies* 3, no. 1 (Spring 2003): 7–20.

Byrne, K., "Simple Devices are Always Best': An Examination of the Amateur Play Publishing Industry in the United States." *The Papers of the Bibliographical Society of America* 108, no. 2 (2014): 217–37.

Camiscioli, E., "Producing Citizens, Reproducing the 'French Race': Immigration, Demography, and Pronatalism in Early Twentieth-Century France." *Gender & History* 13, no. 3 (November 2001): 593–621.

Campbell, G. L., *Strange Creatures: Anthropology in Antiquity* (London: Duckworth, 2006).

Canny, N. P., *Making Ireland British, 1580–1650* (Oxford: Oxford University Press, 2001).

Carden, M., "The Few and the Many: An Examination of W. B. Yeats's Politics." *Studies: An Irish Quarterly Review* 58, no. 229 (1969): 51–62.

Carew, M., *The Quest for the Irish Celt: The Harvard Archaeological Mission to Ireland, 1932–1936* (Newbridge: Irish Academic Press, 2018).

Carey, J., *The Irish National Origin-Legend: Synthetic Pseudohistory* (Cambridge: Dept of A-SNAC, University of Cambridge, 1994).

Carlyle, T., *On the Repeal of the Union* (London: Leadenhall Press, 1889).

Carmichael, S., *Stokely Speaks: Black Power Back to Pan-Africanis* (New York: Vintage Books, 1971).

Carson, C., "Escaped from the Massacre?" *Honest Ulsterman* 50 (1975): 183–86.

Carter, G. T., "'A Shplit Ticket, Half Irish, Half Chinay': Representations of Mixed-Race and Hybridity in Turn-of-the-Century Theater." *Ethnic Studies Review* 31, no. 1 (2008): 32–54.

Cathcart, R., *The Most Contrary Region: The BBC in Northern Ireland, 1924–84* (Belfast: Blackstaff, 1984).

Chaila, D., "Chaila." Narolane Records (YouTube), www.youtube.com/watch?v=ODTU_FewdHc.

Chaila, D., "Duel Citizenship." Narolane Records (YouTube), www.youtube.com/watch?v=gUoKGcNbOKk.

Chakrabarty, D., *Provincializing Europe: Postcolonial Thought and Historical Difference* (Princeton, NJ: Princeton University Press, 2000).

Chan, M. J., "'Journeying is Hard': Difficulty, Race and Poetics in Sarah Howe's Loop of Jade." *Journal of British and Irish Innovative Poetry* 12, no. 1 (2020): 1–29.

Chaudhuri, U., *Staging Place: The Geography of Modern Drama* (Ann Arbor: University of Michigan Press, 1995).

Cheng, V. J., *Joyce, Race, and Empire* (Cambridge: Cambridge University Press, 1995).

Cheng, V. J., "White Horse, Dark Horse: Joyce's Allhorse of Another Color." *Joyce Studies Annual* 2 (Summer 1991): 101–28.

Childs, D., "Class and Eugenics." In *W. B. Yeats in Context*, edited by David Holdeman and Ben Levitas, 169–78 (Cambridge: Cambridge University Press, 2010).

Childs, D., *Modernism and Eugenics: Woolf, Eliot, Yeats and the Culture of Degeneration* (Cambridge, Cambridge University Press, 2001).

Christodoulos M., *The Architecture of Chance* (Dublin: Wurm Press, 2015).

Clifford, J., "Diasporas." *Cultural Anthropology* 9, no. 3 (1994): 302–38.

Coates, D., "Race and Reviewing: The Ledbury Poetry Critics Programme." 2020, www.liverpool.ac.uk/media/livacuk/schoolofthearts/documents/english/State, of,Poetry,and,Poetry,Reviewing,2020,Ledbury,Critics,Report,-,final.pdf.

Coates, T., *Between the World and Me* (Melbourne, Australia: Text Publishing, 2015).

Cockrell, D., *Demons of Disorder: Early Blackface Minstrels and their World* (Cambridge: Cambridge University Press, 1997).

Cohen, A. L., *The Global Indies: British Imperial Culture and the Reshaping of the World, 1756–1815* (New Haven: Yale University Press, 2020).

Cohen, W., and Johnson, R., eds., *Filth: Dirt, Disgust, and Modern Life* (Minneapolis: University of Minnesota Press, 2005).

Collini, S., Whatmore, R., and Young, B. W., eds., *History, Religion, and Culture: British Intellectual History, 1750–1950* (Cambridge: Cambridge University Press, 2000).

Comyn, M., *Seanad Éireann Debates*. April 11, 1929, www.oireachtas.ie/en/debates/debate/seanad/1929-04-11/3/.

Conor, L., *Skin Deep: Settler Impressions of Aboriginal Women* (Perth: University of Western Australia Press, 2016).

Cooke, B., *Megaceros Hibernicus*. IMMA Collection: Gordon Lambert Trust, [1983] 1992.

Cottom, T. M., *Thick and Other Essays* (New York: The New Press, 2019).

Crenshaw, K. W., Harris, L. C., HoSang, D. M., and Lipsitz, G., eds., *Seeing Race Again: Countering Colorblindness across the Disciplines* (Oakland: University of California Press, 2019).

Cullingford, E. B., *Ireland's Others: Ethnicity and Gender in Irish Literature and Popular Culture* (Cork: Cork University Press, 2001).

Cullingford, E. B., *Yeats, Ireland and Fascism* (London: Macmillan, 1981).

Cunningham, B., *The World of Geoffrey Keating: History, Myth and Religion in Seventeenth-century Ireland* (Dublin: Four Courts Press, 2000).

Curley, T. M., *Samuel Johnson, the Ossian Fraud and the Celtic Revival in Great Britain and Ireland* (Cambridge: Cambridge University Press, 2009).

Curtis, E., *A History of Ireland: From Earliest Times to 1922* (London and New York: Routledge, [1936] 2002).

Curtis, L. P., Jr., *Anglo-Saxons and Celts: A Study of Anti-Irish Prejudice in Victorian England* (Bridgeport, Conn.: Conference on British Studies at the University of Bridgeport, 1968).

Curtis, L. P., Jr., *Apes and Angels: The Irishman in Victorian Caricature* (Washington, D.C.: Smithsonian Institution Press, [1971] 1997).

Cusack, F. M., *The Illustrated History of Ireland from the Earliest Period* (London: Longmans and Co., 1868).

Dabiri, E., *What White People Can Do Next: From Allyship to Coalition* (Harper Perennial: London and New York, 2021).

Dáil Éireann Debates. April 21, 2004, www.oireachtas.ie/en/debates/debate/dail/2004-04-21/3.

Davis, D. B., *The Problem of Slavery in the Age of Revolution, 1770–1823* (New York: Oxford University Press, 1999).

Davis, T., *Literary and Historical Essays by Thomas Davis* (Dublin: James Duffy, 1846).

Dawe, G., *The Cambridge Companion to Irish Poets* (Cambridge: Cambridge University Press, 2017).

Dawes, K., "Black British Poetry, Some Considerations." *Wasafiri* 18, no. 38 (2008): 44–48.

de Bhaldraithe, E., "Mixed Marriages and Irish Politics: The Effect of 'Ne Temere.'" *Studies: An Irish Quarterly Review* 77, no. 307 (1988): 284–99.

de Nie, M., *The Eternal Paddy: Irish Identity and the British Press, 1798–1882* (Madison: University of Wisconsin Press, 2004).

de Valera, E., "Aims of Fianna Fáil in Office, 17 March 1932." In *Speeches and Statements by Eamon de Valera, 1917–73*, edited by Maurice Moynihan (New York: St. Martin's Press, 1980).

Deane, S., *Strange Country: Modernity and Nationhood since 1790* (Oxford: Oxford University Press, 1999).

Deane, S., "Heroic Styles: The Tradition of an Idea," in *Ireland's Field Day* edited by Seamus Deane, Seamus Heaney, Richard Kearney, Declan Kiberd, and Tom Paulin, 45–58 (Notre Dame: Notre Dame University Press, 1986).

Deane, S., Andrew, C., and Williams, J., eds., *The Field Day Anthology of Irish Writing* (Derry, Northern Ireland: Field Day Publications, 1991).

DeBhairduin, O., *Why the Moon Travels* (Dublin: Skein Press, 2020).

Delgado, R., and Stefancic, J., *Critical Race Theory: An Introduction* (New York: New York University Press, 2001).

Dent, R.W., *Colloquial Language in* Ulysses: *A Reference Tool* (Cranbury, NJ: Associated University Presses, 1994).

Dhaliwal, S. K., *The Yak Dilemma* (London: Makina Books, 2021).

Dinsman, M., "Politics, Eugenics, and Yeats's Radio Broadcasts." *International Yeats Studies* 3, no. 1 (2018): 65–80.

Djubal, C. R., "What Oh Tonight: The Methodology Factor and Pre-1930s Variety Theatre." PhD diss., University of Queensland, 2005. https://espace .library.uq.edu.au/view/UQ:107238.

Dolan, T. P., *A Dictionary of Hiberno-English* (Dublin: Gill and Macmillan, 2004).

Dominique, L. J., *Imoinda's Shade: Marriage and the African Woman in Eighteenth-century British Literature, 159–1808* (Columbus: The Ohio State University Press, 2012).

Douglas, A., "Introduction," *Studs Lonigan: A Trilogy Comprising Young Lonigan, The Young Manhood of Studs Lonigan, and Judgment Day*, written by James T. Farrell (New York: Penguin, [1935] 2001).

Dowling, R., *Eugene O'Neill: A Life in Four Acts* (New Haven: Yale University Press, 2014).

Doyle, L., *Freedom's Empire: Race and the Rise of the Novel in Atlantic Modernity, 1640–1940* (Durham, NC: Duke University Press, 2008).

Du Bois, W. E. B., *The Souls of Black Folk* (London: Penguin Modern Classics, 2000).

Duffy, C. G., *The Ballad Poetry of Ireland* (Dublin: James Duffy, 1845).

Dugger, J. M., "Black Ireland's Race: Thomas Carlyle and the Young Ireland Movement." *Victorian Studies* 48, no. 3 (2006): 461–85.

Dyer, R., *White: Essays on Race and Culture* (London: Routledge, 1997).

Ebest, R., *Private Histories: The Writing of Irish America, 1900–1935* (Notre Dame: University of Notre Dame Press, 2005).

Edgeworth, M., *Harrington*, edited by Susan Manly (Toronto: Broadview, [1817] 2004).

Eipe, N., (Zak/Aria), *Auguries of a Minor God* (London: Faber & Faber, 2021).

Eipe, N., (Zak/Aria), "Be/cause." *Poetry Ireland Review* 128 (2019): 56.

Eipe, N., (Zak/Aria), "wandersong." 2020, www.ariaeipe.com/poetry-1.

Eise, K., "Theatrical Ethnography and Modernist Primitivism in Eugene O'Neill and Zora Neale Hurston." *South Central Review* 25, no. 1 (2008): 56–73.

Eisen, K., *The Theatre of Eugene O'Neill: American Modernism on the World Stage* (London: Bloomsbury, 2018).

Ejorh, T., *Embers of Words: An Irish Anthology of Migrant Poetry* (Drogheda, Co. Louth: MWPAI, 2012).

Ellingson, T. J., *The Myth of the Noble Savage* (Berkeley: University of California Press, 2001).

Elliot, M., *When God Took Sides: Religion and Identity in Ireland: Unfinished History* (Oxford: Oxford University Press, 2009).

Ellis, G., *Irish Ethnology Socially and Politically Considered: Embracing a General Outline of the Celtic and Saxon Races, with Practical Inferences* (Dublin: Hodges and Smith, 1852).

Ellmann, R., *Yeats: The Man and the Masks* (New York: Norton, 1948).

Elvy, M., Morris, P., and Norcliffe, J., eds., *Ko Aotearoa Tātou | We Are New Zealand* (Dunedin: Otago University Press, 2020).

Emmet, T. A., *Ireland under English Rule; or, a Plea for the Plaintiff* (New York and London: G. P. Putnam's Sons, 1903).

Enenkel, K. A. E., and Ottenheym, K. A., eds., *The Quest for an Appropriate Past in Literature, Art and Architecture* (Leiden: Brill, 2018).

Engels E., and Glick, T. F., eds., *The Reception of Charles Darwin in Europe* (London and New York: Continuum, 2008).

Enright, A., *"Hand in the Fire* by Hugo Hamilton." *The Guardian,* April 17, 2010, www.theguardian.com/books/2010/apr/17/hand-fire-hugo-hamilton-review.

Enyi-Amadi, C., and Penney, E., "Are We Doing Diversity Justice?: A Critical Exchange." *Irish University Review* 50 no. 1 (2020): 112–19.

Essed, P., *Understanding Everyday Racism: An Interdisciplinary Theory* (London: Sage, 1991).

Evans, D., "'These Off-beat "Crazy Kids and Gals": Jazz in Ireland, 1918–1960." *Journal of the Society for Musicology in Ireland* 14 (2018–19): 3–30.

Fanning, B., *Immigration and Social Cohesion in the Republic of Ireland* (Manchester: Manchester University Press, 2011).

Fanning, B., *Migration and the Making of Ireland* (Dublin: University College Dublin Press, 2018).

Fanning, B., *Racism and Social Change in the Republic of Ireland* (Manchester: Manchester University Press, 2002).

Fanning, B., and Michael, L., "Racism and Anti-racism in the Two Irelands." *Ethnic and Racial Studies* 41, no. 15 (2018): 2656–72.

Fanning, B., and Mutwarasibo, F., "Nationals/non-nationals: Immigration, Citizenship and Politics in the Republic of Ireland." *Ethic and Racial Studies* 30, no. 3 (2007): 439–60.

Fanon, F., *Black Skin White Masks* (London: Penguin, [1967] 2020).

Fanon, F., *The Wretched of the Earth*, trans. Constance Farrington (New York: Grove Press, 1968).

Faragó, B., "'I am the Place in Which Things Happen': Invisible Immigrant Women Poets of Ireland." In *Irish Literature: Feminist Perspectives*, edited by Patricia Coughlan and Tina O'Toole, 145–66 (Dublin: Carysfort Press, 2008).

Faragó, B., "Migrant Poet(h)ics." In *From Literature to Cultural Literacy*, edited by Naomi Segal and Daniela Koleva, 86–105 (London: Palgrave Macmillan, 2014).

Faragó, B., "Minor Transnational Writing in Ireland." *CLCWeb: Comparative Literature and Culture* 18, no. 4 (2015): http://docs.lib.purdue.edu/clcweb/vol18/iss4/5.

Faragó, B., and Sullivan, M., eds., *Facing the Other: Interdisciplinary Studies on Race, Gender and Social Justice in Ireland* (Newcastle: Cambridge Scholars Publishing, 2008).

Farrell, J. P., *Studs Lonigan* (New York: Penguin, [1935] 2001).

Farrell, J. P., *The League of Frightened Philistines and Other Papers* (New York: Vanguard, 1949).

Farrell, L. A., *The Origins and Growth of the English Eugenics Movement 1865–1925* (New York: Garland, 1985).

Farrell, M., *Northern Ireland: The Orange State* (London: Pluto Press, 1975).

Fawkes, R., *Dion Boucicault* (London: Quartet, 2011).

Fay, W. G. and Carswell, C., *The Fays of the Abbey Theatre: An Autobiographical Record* (London: Rich and Cowan, 1935).

Feldman, A. and Mulhall, A., "Towing the Line: Migrant Women Writers and the Space of Irish Writing." *Éire-Ireland* 47, no. 1–2 (2012): 201–20.

Felispeaks, "For Our Mothers," www.felispeaks.com/latest-news.

Felispeaks, "Still." RTÉ *Prime Time: The Next Normal* (2020), www.youtube.com/watch?v=ChMfddNBoHQ.

Felispeaks, *Dubh*. Dublin Theatre Festival, October 7, 2021, https://youtu.be/S9ifzqqBos8.

Felispeaks and Jafaris, "They." https://districtmagazine.ie/counter-culture/premiere-they-a-film-about-race/.

Fitzgerald, J., *Big White Lie: Chinese Australians in White Australia* (Sydney: University of New South Wales Press, 2007).

Fitzgerald-Kenney, J., *Seanad Éireann Debates*. April 11, 1929, www.oireachtas.ie/en/debates/debate/seanad/1929-04-11/3/.

Fogarty, A., "'Many and Terrible are the Roads to Home': Representations of the Immigrant in the Contemporary Irish Short Story." In *Literary Visions of Multicultural Ireland*, edited by Pilar Villar-Argáiz, 234–55 (Manchester: Manchester University Press, 2013).

Foster, K., "Irish Minstrels – Why Not?," Irish Independent, February 10, 1928, 6.

Foster, R. F., *Modern Ireland, 1600–1972* (London: Penguin Books, 1989).

French, D., "Nasty Not Nice: British Counter-insurgency Doctrine and Practice, 1945–1967." *Small Wars & Insurgencies* 23, no. 4–5 (October-December 2012): 744–61.

Freud, S., *The Standard Edition of the Complete Psychological Works of Sigmund Freud*, edited by James Strachey, 24 vols. Vol. 18, 18–78 (London: The Hogarth Press and the Institute of Psychoanalysis, 1953).

Friel, B., *Philadelphia, Here I Come!*. In *Brian Friel: Plays One*, 23–99 (London: Faber and Faber, 1984).

Froude, J. A., *The English in Ireland in the Eighteenth Century* (New York: Scribner, Armstrong, and Co., 1873).

Fuhl, L., "Stories on this island," performed at *Say It Aloud – We're Irish!* October 25, 2020, www.youtube.com/watch?v=EzqLGUVMWao.

Gailey, A., *Irish Folk Drama* (Cork: Mercier Press, 1969).

Gallagher, C., "George Nkencho Shooting: Racial Tensions in Dublin's Suburbs." *Irish Times*, January 9, 2021.

Galton, F., "Africa for the Chinese," *Times*, June 5, 1873.

Galton, F., *Hereditary Genius: An Inquiry into its Laws and Consequences* (London: Macmillan, 1869).

Galton, F., *Inquiries into Human Faculty and its Development* (London: Macmillan, 1883).

Gandhi, L., *Affective Communities: Anticolonial Thought, Fin-de-Siècle Radicalism, and the Politics of Friendship* (Durham, NC: Duke University Press, 2006).

Garamvolgyi, F., and Borger, J., "Orbán and US Right to Bond at Cpac in Hungary over 'Great Replacement' Ideology," *The Guardian*, May 18, 2022, www.theguardian.com/world/2022/may/18/cpac-conference-budapest-hungary-viktor-orban-speaker.

Garner, S., *Racism in the Irish Experience* (London: Pluto, 2004).

Garner, S., "Reflections on Race in Contemporary Ireland." In *Race and Immigration in the New Ireland*, edited by Julieann Veronica Ulin and Heather Edwards, 175–204 (South Bend: Notre Dame University Press, 2013).

Gaskill, H., ed., *The Reception of Ossian in Europe* (London: Thoemmes Continuum, 2004).

Gaunson, S., "Ned Kelly and the Movies 1906–2003: Representation, Social Banditry and History." PhD, diss., RMIT University, 2010.

Gelb, A., and Gelb, B., *O'Neill: Life with Monte Cristo* (New York: Applause, 2000).

Gerald of Wales, *The History and Topography of Ireland (1185)*, trans. John O'Meara (London: Penguin, 1982).

Gessen, M., "Ireland's Strange, Cruel System for Asylum Seekers." *The New Yorker*, June 4, 2019, www.newyorker.com/news/dispatch/irelands-strange-cruel-system-for-asylum-seekers.

Gibbons, L., *Gaelic Gothic: Race, Colonization, and Irish Culture* (Galway: Arlen House, 2004).

Gibbons, L., "Race against Time: Racial Discourse and Irish History," *Oxford Literary Review* 13, no. 1 (1991): 95–117.

Gifford, D., Ulysses *Annotated: Notes for James Joyce's* Ulysses (Berkeley: University of California Press, 1989).

Gildea, R., *Empires of the Mind: The Colonial Past and the Politics of the Present* (Cambridge: Cambridge University Press, 2019).

Gillen, U., "Theobald Wolfe Tone and the Common Name of Irishman in 1960s Ireland." In *Uncertain Futures: Essays about the Irish Past for Roy Foster*, edited by Senia Pašeta, 212–2 (Oxford: Oxford University Press, 2016).

Gillespie, M. P., and David W., "'After the Race' and the Problem of Belonging." In *Collaborative Dubliners*, edited by Vicki Mahaffey, 108–24 (Syracuse: Syracuse University Press, 2012).

Gilligan, R., *Nine Folds make a Paper Swan* (Portland, OR: Tin House Books, 2016).

Gillingham, J., *The English in the Twelfth Century: Imperialism, National Identity, and Political Values* (Woodbridge and Rochester: Boydell Press, 2000).

Gilman, S. L., "Freud, Race and Gender." *American Imago* 49, no. 2 (Summer 1992): 155–83.

Gilmartin, M., *Irish Migration in the 21st Century* (Manchester: Manchester University Press, 2015).

Gilmartin, M. and Lagg, J., *Immigrant Integration and Settlement Services in Ireland.* Dublin: Irish Research Council, 2018. http://mural .maynoothuniversity.ie/10114/1/Immigrant%20Integration%20Final%20Report% 202018%20%28002%29.pdf.

Gilmore, J., "Showing Character." *Portrait Magazine* 54: n.p. (2016).

Gogarty, O. St. J., *Seanad Éireann Debates.* April 11, 1929, www.oireachtas.ie/en/ debates/debate/seanad/1929-04-11/3/.

Gold, M., *Jews without Money*, 2nd ed. (New York: Carroll & Graf, [1930] 1996).

Goldberg, D. T., *The Racial State* (Malden: Blackwell, 2002).

Gordon, P. E., and Breckman, W., eds., *The Cambridge History of Modern European Thought*, (Cambridge: Cambridge University Press, 2019).

Gough, K., *Kinship and Performance in the Black and Green Atlantic* (New York: Routledge, 2014).

Government of Northern Ireland, Census of Population 1961: General Report (Belfast: HMSO, 1965).

Government of Northern Ireland, Disturbances in Northern Ireland (Cameron Report) (Belfast: HMSO, 1969).

Graham, C., and Kirkland, R., eds., *Ireland and Cultural Theory: The Mechanics of Authenticity* (Houndmills and New York: Macmillan and St. Martin's Press, 1999).

Granshaw, M., *Irish on the Move: Performing Mobility in American Variety Theatre* (Iowa City: University of Iowa Press, 2019).

Grant, M., *The Passing of the Great Race: or The Racial Basis of European History* (New York: Charles Scribner's Sons, 1916).

Green, A. S., *Irish Nationality* (New York and London: Henry Holt and William & Norgate, 1911).

Green, J. P., "'In Dahomey' in London in 1903." *The Black Perspective in Music* 11, no. 1 (1983): 23–40.

Greenblatt, S., ed., *Cultural Mobility: A Manifesto* (Cambridge: Cambridge University Press, 2009).

Gregory, A., *Our Irish Theatre* (Buckinghamshire: Colin Smythe, 1972).

Gresser, M., *Dual Allegiance: Freud as a Modern Jew* (Albany: State University of New York Press, 1994).

Grimshaw, A., *The C. L. R. James Reader* (Oxford: Wiley-Blackwell, 1992).

Grose, F. and Ledwich, E., *The Antiquities of Ireland by Francis Grose Esqr. F.A.S.*, 2 vols. (London, 1791–94).

Guinnane, T., *The Vanishing Irish: Households, Migration, and the Rural Economy in Ireland, 1850–1914* (Princeton: Princeton University Press, 1997).

Hale, D. S., *Races on Display: French Representations of Colonized Peoples, 1886–1940* (Bloomington: Indiana University Press, 2008).

Hall, D., "'Now Him White Man': Images of the Irish in Colonial Australia." *History Australia* 11, no. 2 (2014): 167–95.

Hanley, B., and Scott, M., *The Lost Revolution: The Story of the Official IRA and the Workers' Party* (Dublin: Penguin, 2009).

Hannaford, I., *Race: The History of an Idea in the West* (Washington, D.C. and Baltimore, MD: Woodrow Wilson Center Press and Johns Hopkins University Press, 1996).

Harris, J. W., "Etiquette, Lynching, and Racial Boundaries in Southern History: A Mississippi Example." *American Historical Review* 100, no. 2 (1995): 387–410.

Hart, H., *Seamus Heaney: Poet of Contrary Progressions* (Syracuse: Syracuse University Press, 1992).

Hart, M. and O'Donovan, M., "Spoken word theatre has arrived to light a fire in the Big Smoke: Review of Felispeaks and Dagogo Hart 'See True,'" *Boundless and Bare*, August 20, 2019. https://podcasts.apple.com/us/podcast/boundless-bare/id1378110282.

Hartman, S. V., *Scenes of Subjection: Terror, Slavery, and Self-making in Nineteenth-century America* (New York: Oxford University Press, 1997).

Hayton, D., "From Barbarian to Burlesque: English Images of the Irish, c. 1660–1750." *Irish Economic and Social History* 15 (1998): 5–31.

Heaney, S., "An Authentic Poetic Voice that Bridges Time, Cultures." Review of *Collected Poems: 1948–1984*, by Derek Walcott, *Boston Globe*, February 9, 1986: A28.

Heaney, S., "Belfast," *Preoccupations: Selected Prose 1968–1978* (London: Faber and Faber, 1980).

Heaney, S., *Door into the Dark* (London: Faber & Faber, 1969).

Heaney, S., *Field Work* (London: Faber and Faber, 1979).

Heaney, S., *North* (London: Faber & Faber, 1975).

Heaney, S., *Stepping Stones: Interview with Seamus Heaney*, interview by Dennis O'Driscoll (New York: Farrar, Straus, Giroux, 2008).

Heaney, S., *The Cure at Troy: A Version of Sophocles' Philoctetes* (New York: Noonday Press, 1990).

Heaney, S., *Wintering Out* (London: Faber and Faber, 1972).

Herlihy, C. J., *The Celt above the Saxon; or, a Comparative Sketch of the Irish and English People in War*, 2nd ed. (Boston: Angel Guardian Press, 1904).

Hession, P., "'New Jerusalem': Constructing Jewish Space in Ireland, 1880–1914." In *Irish Questions and Jewish Questions: Crossovers in Culture*, edited by Aidan Beatty and Dan O'Brien, 47–60 (Syracuse: Syracuse University Press, 2018).

Higgins, M. D., "Ireland And Australia – A Deep, Historic And Valuable Contemporary Relationship." Speech to Parliament of Western Australia, October 10, 2017, www.president.ie/en/media-library/speeches/speech-at-the-parliament-of-western-australia.

Hildreth, R., *The White Slave*. Electronic Edition. https://docsouth.unc.edu/neh/hildreth/hildreth.html.

Hogan, C., "Trump's other wall: is his Irish resort a sign he believes in climate change?" *The Guardian,* November 17, 2016, www.theguardian.com/us-news/2016/nov/17/donald-trump-ireland-golf-resort-wall-climate-change.

Hogan, R. and Burnham, R., *The Years of O'Casey, 1921–1926: A Documentary History* (Newark: University of Delaware Press, 1992).

Holt, T., *The Problem of Freedom: Race, Labor, and Politics in Jamaica and Britain, 1832–1938* (Baltimore: Johns Hopkins University Press, 1992).

hooks, b., *Black Looks: Race and Representation* (Boston: South End Press, 1992).

Hooper, G., and Graham, C., eds., *Irish and Postcolonial Writing: History, Theory, Practice* (London: Palgrave, 2002).

Horsman, R., "Origins of Racial Anglo-Saxonism in Great Britain Before 1850." *Journal of the History of Ideas* 37, no. 3 (1976): 401–2.

Howe, S., *Ireland and Empire: Colonial Legacies in Irish History and Culture* (Cambridge: Cambridge University Press, 2000).

Howes, M., *Yeats's Nations: Gender, Class, and Irishness* (New York: Cambridge University Press, 1996).

Hricko, M., *The Genesis of the Chicago Renaissance: Theodore Dreiser, Langston Hughes, Richard Wright, and James T. Farrell* (New York: Routledge, 2009).

Huberman, L. and Sweezy, P., *Cuba: Anatomy of a Revolution* (New York: Monthly Review Press, 1960).

Hudson, N., "'Hottentots' and the Evolution of European Racism." *Journal of European Studies* 34, no. 4 (2004): 308–32.

Hudson, T., "From 'Nation' to 'Race': The Origin of Racial Classification in Eighteenth-century Thought." *Eighteenth Century Studies* 29, no. 3 (1996): 247–64.

Hughes, G., *An Encyclopedia of Swearing: The Social History of Oaths, Profanity, Foul Language, and Ethnic Slurs in the English-Speaking World* (London: M. E. Sharpe, 2006).

Huk, R., "In AnOther's Pocket: The Address of the 'Pocket Epic' in Postmodern Black British Poetry." *The Yale Journal of Criticism* 13, no. 1 (2000): 23–47.

Hutchinson, F., *A Defence of the Antient Historians, with a Particular Application of it to the History of Ireland and Great Britain, and other Northern Nations* (Dublin: John Smith and William Bruce, 1734).

Hyde, D., "The Necessity for De-Anglicising Ireland," In *The Revival of Irish Literature: Addresses by Sir Charles Gavin Duffy, George Sigerson, and Dr. Douglas Hyde*, edited by Charles Gavan Duffy (London: T. Fisher Unwin, 1894).

Ignatiev, N., *How the Irish Became White* (London: Routledge, 1995).

Igoe, V., "'Spot the Winner': Some of the Horses in *Ulysses.*" *Dublin James Joyce Journal* 4 (2011): 72–86.

Imtheachta Aonaighe na n-Gaedheal ib-Páris, Eanair, 1922: Proceedings of the Irish Race Congress in Paris, January, 1922 (London: Cahill, 1922).

International Literature Festival Dublin, "Say it Aloud – We're Irish!" October 25, 2020, www.crowdcast.io/e/beyond-representation/register.

Irish Folklore Commission, "St Stephen's Day Questionnaire," 1947, UCD National Folklore Collection, MSS 1088, 1089, 1090.

Irish Race Congress, *Imtheachta Aonaighe na n-Gaedheal ib-Páris, Eanair, 1922* (London: Cahill & Co., 1922).

Jackson, J. W., "The Race Question in Ireland." *The Anthropological Review* 7, no. 24 (1869): 54–76.

Jacobs-Jenkins, B., *An Octoroon* (New York: Dramatists Play Service, 2015).

Jafaris and Felispeaks, *They.* https://districtmagazine.ie/counter-culture/premiere-they-a-film-about-race/.

JanMohamed, A. R., "The Economy of Manichean Allegory: The Function of Racial Difference in Colonialist Literature." *Critical Inquiry* 12, no. 1 (1985): 59–87.

Johnston, R., *Century of Endeavour: A Biographical and Autobiographical View of the 20th Century in Ireland* (Dublin: Lilliput Press, 2002).

Jola, N., *Home is Neither Here nor There* (Galway: Doire Press, 2022)

Jones, G., "Eugenics in Ireland: The Belfast Eugenics Society, 1911–15." *Irish Historical Studies* 28, no. 109 (1992): 81–95.

Jones, G., "Nation and Religion: The Debate about Darwinism in Ireland." In *The Reception of Charles Darwin in Europe*, edited by Eve-Marie Engels and Thomas F. Glick, 66–78 (London: Continuum, 2008).

Jones, I., *Ned Kelly: A Short Life* (Melbourne: Lothian Books, 1995).

Jones, W., *Works*, 6 vols. (London: n.p., 1799).

Joseph, E., "Whiteness and Racism: Examining the Racial Order in Ireland." *Irish Journal of Sociology* 26, no. 1 (2018): 46–70.

Joyce, J., *Dubliners* (London: Penguin, 1992).

Joyce, J., *Dubliners* (New York: Penguin, 1993).

Joyce, J., *Finnegans Wake* (London: Penguin, 1992).

Joyce, J., *Letters, I.* Ed. Stuart Gilbert (New York: Viking, 1957).

Joyce, J., *Letters, II.* Ed. Richard Ellmann (New York: Viking, 1966).

Joyce, J., *Occasional, Critical, and Political Writing*, edited by Kevin Barry (Oxford: Oxford University Press, 2000): 77–79, 305.

Joyce, J., *Ulysses* (New York: Vintage, 1986).

Joyce, S., "Divided Spaces: An Examination of Everyday Racism and Its Impact on Young Travellers' Spatial Mobility." *Irish Journal of Anthropology* 18, no. 1 (2015): 15–23.

Jung, C. G., *Dreams*, trans. R. F. C. Hull (Princeton: Princeton University Press, 1974).

Kalter, C., *The Discovery of the Third World: Decolonization and the Rise of the New Left in France, c.1950–1976* (Cambridge: Cambridge University Press, 2016).

Kandiwa, C., (Kayssie Kandiwa), "Two Poems: 'The Seat' and 'Nguva Champupuri Chinosumudza Mugwagwa Mudenga.'" *Irish University Review* 50, no. 2 (2020): 261–62.

Kandiwa, C., "My Sister as a Body," Adrian Brinkerhoff Poetry Foundation, www.youtube.com/watch?v=Hk4LJpKnGMc.

Kasa, N., "Charcoal Iron," Adrian Brinkerhoff Poetry Foundation, www .brinkerhoffpoetry.org/poems/charcoal-iron.

Kasa, N., *Palm Wine Tapper and the Boy at Jericho* (Galway: Doire Press, 2022).

Kauffman, C. J., *Patriotism and Fraternalism in the Knights of Columbus* (New York: Crossroad Publishing Company, 2001).

Kavanagh, P., *The Irish Theatre* (Tralee: The Kerryman, 1946).

Keane, J., *Seanad Éireann Debates*. April 11, 1929, www.oireachtas.ie/en/debates/debate/seanad/1929-04-11/3/.

Keating, G., *Foras Feasa ar Éirinn: The History of Ireland*, edited and translated by David Comyn and Patrick Stephen Dineen, 4 vols. (London: The Irish Texts Society, 1902–14), 1: 35–36.

Keating, K., and McDaid, A., "Poetry Reviewing in the Irish Times." MEAS: *Measuring Equality in the Arts Sector*, http://measorg.com/images/irishtimesreport.pdf.

Keating, S., "Ireland's Wildest Playwright," *Irish Times*, July 20, 2010. www .irishtimes.com/culture/stage/ireland-s-wildest-playwright-1.624084.

Kelly, J., ed., *The Cambridge History of Ireland* (Cambridge: Cambridge University Press, 2018).

Kendi, I. X., *How to Be an Antiracist* (New York: One World, 2019).

Kennedy, D., *The Widening Gulf: Northern Attitudes to the Independent Irish State, 1919–49* (Belfast: The Blackstaff Press, 1988).

Kennedy, S., "FIRST LOVE: Abortion and Infanticide in Beckett and Yeats." *Samuel Beckett Today/Aujourd'hui* 22 (2010): 79–91.

Kenny, K., *The American Irish: A History* (New York: Pearson Educational, 2000).

Kenyon Davies, J., "Genos." In *The Oxford Classical Dictionary*, edited by Simon Hornblower and Antony Spawforth (Oxford: Oxford University Press, 2012).

Keogh, D., *Jews in Twentieth Century Ireland: Refugees,* Anti-Semitism *and the Holocaust* (Cork: Cork University Press, 1998).

Kiberd, D., "Losing Ireland, Inventing America: O'Neill and After." *Eugene O'Neill Review* 39, no. 1 (2018): 1–16.

Kiberd, D., *The Irish Writer and the World* (Cambridge: Cambridge University Press, 2005).

Kibler, A. M., *Censoring Racial Ridicule: Irish, Jewish, and African American Struggles over Race and Representation* (Chapel Hill: University of North Carolina Press, 2015).

Kidd, C., *British Identities before Nationalism: Ethnicity and Nationhood in the Atlantic World 1600–1800* (Cambridge: Cambridge University Press, 1999).

Kidd, C., "Gaelic Antiquity and National Identity in Enlightenment Ireland and Scotland." *English Historical Review* 109, no. 434 (1994): 1197–214.

Kidd, C., *The Forging of Races: Race and Scripture in the Protestant Atlantic World* (Cambridge: Cambridge University Press, 2006).

Kim, D., "White Supremacists Have Weaponized an Imaginary Viking Past." *Time.* April 15, 2019, https://time.com/5569399/viking-history-white-nationalists/.

Kinealy, C., ed., *Frederick Douglass and Ireland* (London: Routledge, 2018).

King, D., "Immigration and Citizenship in Ireland." March 31, 2004. www.childrensrights.ie/resources/immigration-and-citizenship-ireland.

King, M. T., *Between Birth and Death: Female Infanticide in Nineteenth-century China* (Stanford: Stanford University Press, 2014).

Kirkpatrick, K., ed., *Border Crossings: Irish Women Writers and National Identities* (Tuscaloosa: University of Alabama Press, 2000).

Kirkpatrick, K., "'Gentlemen Have Horrors Upon this Subject': West Indian Suitors in Maria Edgeworth's *Belinda.*" *Eighteenth-Century Fiction* 5, no. 4 (1993): 331–48.

Kitching, K., "How the Irish became CRT'd? 'Greening' Critical Race Theory, and the pitfalls of a normative Atlantic state view." *Race Ethnicity and Education* 18 (2015): 163–82.

Kitching, K., *The Politics of Compulsive Education: Racism and Learner-Citizenship* (London: Routledge, 2014).

Klimke, M., *The Other Alliance: Student Protest in West Germany and the United States in the Global Sixties* (Princeton: Princeton University Press, 2011).

Knox, R., *The Races of Men: A Philosophical Enquiry into the Influence of Race over the Destinies of Nations* (London: H. Renshaw, 1862).

Koch, J. T., and Carey, J., *The Celtic Heroic Age: Literary Sources for Ancient Celtic Europe and Early Ireland & Wales* (Aberystwyth: Celtic Studies Publications, 2005).

Krasner, D., "Whose Role is it Anyway?: Charles Gilpin and the Harlem Renaissance." *The African American Review* 29, no. 3 (1995): 483–96.

Kuch, P., "Kilkenny, Melbourne, New York: George Tallis and the Irish Theatrical Diaspora." In *Irish Theatre in America: Essays on Irish Theatrical Diaspora*, edited by John Harrington, 78–92 (Syracuse: Syracuse University Press, 2009).

Kühl, S., *Nazi Connection: Eugenics, American Racism, and German National Socialism* (Oxford: Oxford University Press, 1994).

La Capra, D., *History in Transit: Experience, Identity, Critical Theory* (Ithaca, New York: Cornell University Press, 2004).

Lake, M., and Reynolds, H., *Drawing the Global Colour Line: White Men's Countries and the International Challenge of Racial Equality* (Melbourne: Melbourne University Press, 2008).

Lalor, J. F., *The Writing of James Fintan Lalor: With an Introduction Embodying Personal Recollections*, edited by John O'Leary and T. O'Donoghue (Dublin: T. G. O'Donoghue, 1895).

Landers, L., and Robert, K., *An Honest Writer: The Life and Times of James T. Farrell* (San Francisco: Encounter Books, 2004).

Larsen, N., *Passing* (New York: Penguin, [1929] 2018).

Laurence, P., *Elizabeth Bowen: A Literary Life* (Cham, Switzerland: Palgrave, 2019).

Le Bon, G., *The Crowd: A Study of the Popular Mind.* (London: T. Fisher Unwin, [1895] 1903).

Ledwich, E., *Antiquities of Ireland* (Dublin, n.p., 1790).

Ledwich, E., *Antiquities of Ireland*, 2nd ed. (Dublin: John Jones, 1804).

Ledwich, E., to Walker, J.C., 17 April 1787, March 1787. Correspondence of Joseph Cooper Walker. Ms. 1461(2), fols. 225, 202. Manuscripts and Archives, Trinity College Dublin.

Leerssen, J., "Englishness, Ethnicity and Matthew Arnold." *European Journal of English Studies* 10, no. 1 (2006): 63–79.

Leerssen, J., *Mere Irish and Fíor-Ghael: Studies in the Idea of Irish Nationality, Its Development and Literary Expression prior to the Nineteenth Century*, rev. ed. (Cork: Cork University Press, 1996).

Leerssen, J., *Remembrance and Imagination: Patterns in the Historical and Literary Representation of Ireland in the Nineteenth Century* (Cork: Cork University Press, 1996).

Lentin, R., "Black Bodies and Headless Hookers: Alternative Global Narratives for Twenty-First Century Ireland." *Irish Review* 33 (Spring 2005): 1–12.

Lentin, R., "Illegal in Ireland, Irish Illegals: Diaspora Nation as Racial State." *Irish Political Studies* 22, no. 4 (2007): 433–53.

Lentin, R., "(M)other Ireland: Migrant Women Subverting the Racial State?" In *Race and Immigration in the New Ireland*, edited by Julieann V. Ulin, 51–74. (Notre Dame: University of Notre Dame Press, 2016).

Lentin, R., "Racial State and Crisis Racism." *Ethic and Racial Studies* 30, no. 4 (2007): 610–27.

Lentin, R., and McVeigh, R., *After Optimism?: Ireland, Racism and Globalisation* (Dublin: Metro Éireann, 2006).

Lentin, R., and McVeigh, R., eds., *Racism and Anti-racism in Ireland* (Dublin: Beyond the Pale Publications, 2002).

Lhamon Jr., W. T., *Raising Cain: Blackface Performance from Jim Crow to Hip Hop* (Cambridge: Harvard University Press, 1998).

Lindfors, B., *Ira Aldridge: The Vagabond Years, 1833–1852* (Rochester: University of Rochester Press, 2011).

Lipset, S. M., *Rebellion in the University: A History of Student Activism in America* (London: Routledge, 1972).

Little, P. J., *Dáil Éireann Debates.* October 18, 1928, www.oireachtas.ie/en/debates/debate/dail/1928-10-18/19/.

Litvack, L., and Hooper, G., eds., *Ireland in the Nineteenth Century: Regional Identity* (Dublin: Four Courts Press, 2000).

Lloyd, D., *Anomalous States: Irish Writing and the Post-Colonial Moments* (Durham, NC: Duke University Press, 1993).

Lloyd, D., "Black Irish, Irish Whiteness and Atlantic State Formation," in *The Black and Green Atlantic: Cross-Currents of the African and Irish Diasporas*, edited by Peter D. O'Neill and David Lloyd, 3–19 (Basingstoke: Palgrave, 2009).

Lloyd, D., *Under Representation: The Racial Regime of Aesthetics* (New York: Fordham University Press, 2018).

Loftis, J., "Whig Oratory on Stage: Sheridan's *Pizarro*." *Eighteenth-Century Studies* 8, no. 4 (1975): 454–72.

Lordan, D., "The Multimedia Revolution in Poetry." *The Stinging Fly* 33, no. 2 (2016): 222–23.

Lott, E., *Love & Theft: Blackface Minstrelsy and the American Working Class* (Oxford: Oxford University Press, 2013).

Lovett, L. L., *Conceiving the Future: Pronatalism, Reproduction, and the Family in the United States, 1890–1938* (Chapel Hill: University of North Carolina Press, 2007).

Lowe, L., *The Intimacies of Four Continents* (Durham, NC: Duke University Press, 2015).

Lydon, J., *The Flash of Recognition: Photography and the Emergence of Indigenous Rights* (Sydney: University of New South Wales Press, 2013).

M'Elheran, J., *The Condition of Women and Children Among the Celtic, Gothic, and Other Nations* (Boston: Patrick Donahoe, 1858).

Mac Laughlin, J., "'Pestilence on Their Backs, Famine in Their Stomachs': The Racial Construction of Irishness and the Irish in Victorian Britain," in *Ireland and Cultural Theory: The Mechanics of Authenticity*, edited by Colin Graham and Richard Kirkland, 50–76 (Houndmills and New York: Macmillan and St. Martin's Press, 1999).

MacDonagh, O., *States of Mind: A Study of Anglo-Irish Conflict 1780–1980* (London: George Allen & Unwin, 1983).

MacDougall, H. A., *Racial Myth in English History: Trojans, Teutons, and Anglo-Saxons* (Hanover, NH: University Press of New England, 1982).

MacManus, S., *The Story of the Irish Race: A Popular History of Ireland* (New York: Devin-Adair, [1921] 1977).

Macready, W., *The Irishman in London – or the Happy African: A Farce* (London: Longman, 1799).

Mahaffey, V., "Fantastic Histories: Nomadology and Female Piracy in *Finnegans Wake*." In *Joyce and the Subject of History*, edited by Mark Wollaeger, Victor Luftig, and Robert Spoo, 157–76 (Ann Arbor: University of Michigan Press, 2006).

Mahaffey, V., "Love, Race, and *Exiles*: The Bleak Side of *Ulysses*." In Moshe Gold and Philip Sicker, Eds., *Joyce Studies Annual*, 92–108 (New York; Fordham University Press, 2007).

Mahaffey, V., *Reauthorizing Joyce* (Cambridge: Cambridge University Press, 1988).

Mahaffey, V., "Wunderlich on Joyce: The Case Against Art." *Critical Inquiry* 17 (Summer 1991): 171–91.

Mahaffey, V. and Truran, W., "Feeling *Ulysses*: An Address to the Cyclopean Reader." In Ulysses: *Philosophical Perspectives*, edited by Philip Kitcher, 100–31 (Oxford: Oxford University Press, 2020).

Majekodunmi, W., *What Does Irishness Look Like?* (Documentary, 2018). www .youtube.com/watch?v=EqWKR7eq-CQ.

Makris, C., *The Architecture of Chance* (Portarlington: Wurm Press, 2015).

Malcolm, E., and Hall, D., *A New History of the Irish in Australia* (Sydney: NewSouth, 2018 and Cork: Cork University Press, 2019).

Maney, G., "White Negroes and the Pink IRA: External Mainstream Media Coverage and Civil Rights Contention in Northern Ireland." In *The Troubles in Northern Ireland and Theories of Social Movements*, edited by Lorenzo Bosi and Gianluca De Fazio, 71–90 (Amsterdam: Amsterdam University Press, 2017).

Mannion, E., "The Dublin Tenement Plays of the Early Abbey Theatre." *New Hibernia Review* 14, no. 2 (Summer 2010): 69–83.

Manuel, C., "A Ghost in the Expressionist Jungle of O'Neill's 'The Emperor Jones.'" *African American Review* 39, no. 1–2 (2005): 67–85.

Marcus, D., *To Next Year in Jerusalem* (London: Macmillan, 1954).

Marcus, S., *Father Coughlin: The Tumultuous Life of the Priest of the Little Flower* (Boston: Little Brown, 1973).

Marinetti, F. T., "War, the only Hygiene of the World." In *Futurism: An Anthology*, edited by Lawrence Rainey, Christine Poggi, and Laura Wittman, 84–85 (New Haven: Yale University Press, 2009).

Martín-Ruiz, S., "'The way the Irish Asylum System Turns People into Un-human is My Problem': An Interview with Ifedinma Dimbo." *Estudios Irlandeses* 10 (2015): 109–14.

Martin, F. X., "Gerald of Wales, Norman Reporter on Ireland." *Studies* 58, no. 231 (1969): 279–92.

Maurer, S., *The Dispossessed State: Narratives of Ownership in Nineteenth-century Britain and Ireland* (Baltimore: Johns Hopkins University Press, 2012).

McAuley, J., ed., *Sydney Owenson, Florence Macarthy: An Irish Tale* (London: Pickering & Chatto, [1818] 2012).

McBride, J., *The Color of Water: A Black Man's Tribute to His White Mother* (New York: Riverhead Books, 1996).

McCann, E., *War and an Irish Town* (London: Penguin, 1974).

McCann, E., *War and an Irish Town* (London: Pluto Press, 1993).

McCarron, B., "'Make it too hot for them to stop in the colony': The Irish Stance on the Chinese Question in Australia, 1851–1901." *Australasian Journal of Irish Studies* 20 (2020): 99–124.

McCormack, W. J., *Blood Kindred: W.B. Yeats: The Life, the Death, the Politics* (London: Pimlico, 2005).

McDermott, A., "Who Said the Kelly Letters? The Question of Authorship and the Nature of Wild Language in the Cameron and Jerilderie Letters." *Australian Historical Studies* 33, no. 118 (2002): 255–72.

McDermott, E., "Law and Disorder." In *Twenty Years On*, edited by Michael Farrell, 147–60 (Brandon: Dingle, 1988).

McDonagh, R., *Settled* (Dublin: Skein Press, 2021).

McFeely, D., *Dion Boucicault: Irish Identity on Stage* (Cambridge: Cambridge University Press, 2012).

McGillycuddy, R., *Seanad Éireann Debates*. April 11, 1929, www.oireachtas.ie/en/debates/debate/seanad/1929-04-11/3/.

McGrath, A., "Shamrock Aborigines: The Irish, the Aboriginal Australians and Their Children." *Aboriginal History* 34 (2010): 55–84.

McHugh, R., *Annotations to Finnegans Wake* (Baltimore: Johns Hopkins University Press, 2016).

McIvor, C., *Performing Intercultural Ireland* (Basingstoke: Palgrave, 2016).

McKenna, B., "Yeats, *On the Boiler*, the Aesthetics of Cultural Disintegration and the Program for Renewal 'of our own rich experience.'" *Journal of Modern Literature* 35, no. 4 (2012): 73–90.

McLaren, A., *Our Own Master Race: Eugenics in Canada, 1885–1945* (Toronto: University of Toronto Press, 2014).

McLoughlin, C., "Artistic Director's Note," *An Octoroon Show Program* (Dublin: Abbey Theatre, 2022).

McMahon, C. T., *The Global Dimensions of Irish Identity: Race, Nation, and the Popular Press, 1840–1880* (Chapel Hill: University of North Carolina Press, 2015).

McMahon, R., *The Races of Europe: Construction of National Identities in the Social Sciences, 1839–1939* (Basingstoke: Palgrave Macmillan, 2016).

McPherson, H., "Caricature, Cultural Politics, and the Stage: The Case of *Pizarro*." *Huntington Library Quarterly* 70, no. 4 (2007): 607–63.

McVeigh, R., "Racism in the Six Counties." In *Race and Immigration in the New Ireland*, edited by Julieann V. Ulin, 75–106 (Notre Dame: University of Notre Dame Press, 2016).

McVeigh, R., "The Specificity of Irish Racism." *Race and Class* 33, no. 4 (1992): 31–45.

Meagher, M., "Jenny Saville and a Feminist Aesthetics of Disgust." *Hypatia* 18, no. 4 (2003): 23–41.

Meaney, G., *Gender, Ireland and Cultural Change: Race, Sex and Nation* (New York: Routledge, 2010).

Mendelssohn, M., *Making Oscar Wilde* (Oxford: Oxford University Press, 2019).

Mentxaka, A. L., *Kate O'Brien and the Fiction of Identity: Sex, Art and Politics in Mary Lavelle and Other Writings* (Jefferson: McFarland & Co., 2011).

Merrill, L and Saxon, T., "Replaying and Rediscovering *The Octoroon*." *Theatre Journal* 69, no. 2 (2017): 127–52.

Michael, L., "Reports of Racism in Ireland." *Irish Network Against Racism*, 2020. https://inar.ie/wp-content/uploads/2021/03/2020_iReport-Reports-of-Racism-in-Ireland.pdf.

Miller, A. K., *Ireland and Irish America: Culture, Class, and Transatlantic Migration* (Dublin: Field Day, 2008).

Miller, K., *Emigrants and Exiles: Ireland and the Irish Exodus to North America* (Oxford: Oxford University Press, 1985).

Miłosz, C., *The Collected Poems: 1931–1987* (New York: Ecco Press, 1988).

Miso-Dolos [Sylvester O'Halloran], "*The Poems of Ossine, the Son of Fionne Mac Comhal, Reclaimed by a Milesian*." *Dublin Magazine* (January 1763): 21–23.

Mitchel, J., *The History of Ireland, from the Treaty of Limerick to the Present Time* (New York: D. J. Sadlier & Co., 1868).

Mitchel, J., *The Last Conquest of Ireland (Perhaps)* (Glasgow: R. & T. Washbourne, 1876).

Mitchell, C., and Rentschler, C., eds., *Girlhood and the Politics of Place* (New York: Berghahn Books, 2016).

Monks, A., "'Genuine Negroes and Real Bloodhounds': Cross-Dressing Eugene O'Neill, the Wooster Group, and *The Emperor Jones.*" *Modern Drama* 48, no. 3 (2005): 540–64.

Mooney, J., *Irish Stereotypes in Vaudeville, 1865–1905* (London: Springer, 2015).

Morrison, B., *Seamus Heaney* (London: Methuen, 1982).

Morrison, S. S., *The Literature of Waste: Material Ecopoetics and Ethical Matter* (New York: Palgrave Macmillan, 2015).

Morrison, T., *Playing in the Dark: Whiteness and the Literary Imagination* (Cambridge: Harvard University Press, 1992).

Morrow, J., "Thomas Carlyle, 'Young Ireland' and the 'Condition of Ireland Question?'" *The Historical Journal* 51, no. 3 (2008): 643–67.

Mosse, G. L., *Toward the Final Solution: A History of European Racism* (Madison: University of Wisconsin Press, [1978] 1985).

Moynihan, S., *"Other People's Diasporas": Negotiating Race in Contemporary Irish and Irish-American Culture* (New York: Syracuse Press, 2013).

Mulgrew, J., "Paddy Jackson Dressed as Slave," *Belfast Telegraph*, July 11, 2014. www.belfasttelegraph.co.uk/news/northern-ireland/ulster-rugby-players-wear-black-make-up-in-ethiopian-photo-paddy-jackson-dressed-as-slave-30424197.html.

Mulhall, A., "Arrivals: Inward Migration and Irish Literature." In *Irish Literature in Transition: 1980–2020*, edited by Eric Falci and Paige Reynolds, 182–200 (Cambridge: Cambridge University Press, 2020).

Mullen, M., "How the Irish Became Settlers: Metaphors of Indigeneity and the Erasure of Indigenous Peoples." *New Hibernia Review* 20, no. 3 (2016): 81–96.

Mulhall, A., "The Ends of Irish Studies? On Whiteness, Academia, and Activism." *Irish University Review* 50, no. 1 (2020): 94–111.

Muotto, C., "IJE-OMA by MR. NoGoFollow." *Irish University Review* 50, no. 2 (2020): 263.

Nadel, I. B., *Joyce and the Jews: Culture and Text* (Iowa City: University of Iowa Press, 1989).

Nally, C. V., "The Political Occult: Revisiting Fascism, Yeats and *A Vision.*" In *W. B. Yeats's "A Vision": Explications and Contexts*, edited by Neil Mann, Matthew Gibson, and Claire V. Nally, 329–43 (Clemson: Clemson University Digital Press, 2012).

Nash, C., "Irish Origins, Celtic Origins: Population Genetics, Cultural Politics." *Irish Studies Review* 14, no. 1 (2006): 11–37.

Nelson, B., *Irish Nationalists and the Making of the Irish Race* (Princeton: Princeton University Press, 2012).

Nixon, C., "Statement of Evidence Given before the Royal Commission on the Feebleminded." *Dublin Journal of Medical Science* cxxiv (1912): 192–215.

Nixon, R., "The Less Selfish Gene: Forest Altruism, Neoliberalism, and the Tree of Life." *Environmental Humanities* 13, no. 2 (2021): 348–71.

Nussbaum, F. A., *The Limits of the Human: Fictions of Anomaly, Race, and Gender in the Long Eighteenth Century* (Cambridge: Cambridge University Press, 2003).

Ó Buachalla, B., *Aisling Ghéar: Na Stíobhartaigh agus an tAos Léinn, 1603–788* (Dublin: An Clóchomhar Tta, 1996).

Ó Gallchoir C., and Ingman, H., eds., *A History of Modern Irish Women's Literature* (New York: Cambridge University Press, 2018).

Ó Gráda, C., *Jewish Ireland in the Age of Joyce: A Socioeconomic History* (Princeton: Princeton University Press, 2006).

O'Brien, J. A., ed., *The Vanishing Irish: The Enigma of the Modern World* (New York: McGraw, 1953).

O'Brien, J., *Irish Celts: A Cyclopedia of Race History* (Detroit: L.F. Kilroy & Company, 1884).

O'Brien, K., *Mary Lavelle* (London: Virago, [1936] 2000).

O'Brien, K., *The Land of Spices* (London: Virago, [1942] 2006).

O'Brien, K., *Without My Cloak* (London: Virago, [1936] 2001).

O'Casey, S., *Autobiographies Volume 1* (London: Macmillan, 1963).

O'Casey, S., *Autobiographies Volume 2* (London: Macmillan, 1968).

O'Conor, C., *Dissertations on the Antient History of Ireland* (Dublin: n.p., 1753).

O'Donnell, W. H., ed., *The Collected Works of W.B. Yeats, Vol. V: Later Essays* (New York: Charles Scribner's Sons, 1994).

O'Donoghue, H., "Heaney, *Beowulf* and the Medieval Literature of the North." In *The Cambridge Companion to Seamus Heaney*, edited by Bernard O'Donoghue, 192–205 (Cambridge: Cambridge University Press, 2009).

O'Farrell, P., *The Irish in Australia*, 3rd ed. (Sydney: University of New South Wales Press, 2000).

O'Halloran, C., *Golden Ages and Barbarous Nations: Antiquarian Debate and Cultural Politics in Ireland, c.1750–1800* (Cork: Cork University Press, 2004).

O'Halloran, C., "Irish Re-creations of the Gaelic Past: The Challenge of Macpherson's Ossian." *Past and Present* 124 (1989): 69–95.

O'Hanlon, J. F., *Dáil Éireann Debates*. October 19, 1928, www.oireachtas.ie/en/debates/debate/dail/1928-10-19/2/.

O'Neill, C., "'Harvard Scientist Seeks Typical Irishman': Measuring the Irish Race, 1888–1936." *Radical History Review* 143 (2022): 89–108.

O'Neill, E., *Complete Plays*, 3 vols. (New York: Library of America, 1988).

O'Neill, E., *Conversations with Eugene O'Neill*, edited by Mark W. Estrin (Jackson: University Press of Mississippi, 1990).

O'Neill, P. D., "The Famine Irish, the Catholic Church and the Cultural Dynamics of the American Middle Class." In *The Great Irish Famine and Social Class: Conflicts, Responsibilities, Representations*, edited by Marguérite Corporaal and Peter Gray, 257–75 (Oxford: Peter Lang, 2019).

O'Neill, P. D., "U.S. Nation Building and the Irish American Novel, 1830–1880." In *Irish Literature in Transition. 1830–1880*, edited by Matthew Campbell, 179–96 (Cambridge: Cambridge University Press, 2020).

O'Neill, P. D., *Famine Irish and the American Racial State* (New York: Routledge, 2017).

O'Shea, H., *Ireland and the End of the British Empire: The Republic and its Role in the Cyprus Emergency* (London: Bloomsbury, 2015).

O'Sullivan, D., *The Spice of Life and Other Essays* (Dublin: Browne and Nolan, 1948).

O'Toole, F., *Ship of Fools: How Stupidity and Corruption Sank the Celtic Tiger* (New York: Public Affairs, 2010).

O'Toole, T., *The Irish New Woman* (Basingstoke: Palgrave, 2013).

Okorie, M. U., *This Hostel Life* (Dublin: Skein Press, 2017).

Onkey, L., "James Farrell's *Studs Lonigan* Trilogy and the Anxieties of Race." *Éire-Ireland*, 40, no 3–4 (2005): 104–18.

Owenson, S., *The Missionary: An Indian Tale*, edited by Julia M. Wright (Orchard Park: Broadview Press, [1811] 2002).

Owenson, S., *The Wild Irish Girl: A National Tale*, edited by Kathryn Kirkpatrick (New York: Oxford University Press, [1806] 2008).

Painter, N. I., *The History of White People* (New York and London: W. W. Norton and Company, 2010).

Palmer, P., *Language and Conquest in Early Modern Ireland: English Renaissance Literature and Elizabethan Imperial Expansion* (Cambridge: Cambridge University Press, 2004).

Park, J., "Interrogating the 'Population Problem' of the Non-Western Empire: Japanese Colonialism, the Korean Peninsula, and the Global Geopolitics of Race." *Interventions: The International Journal of Postcolonial Studies* 19, no. 8 (November 2017): 1112–31.

Parkin, A., ed., *Selected Plays of Dion Boucicault* (Gerrards Cross: Colin Smythe, 1987).

Parmar, S., "Review of Jay Benjamin Surge." *The Guardian*, July 6, 2019.

Parmar, S. with Kapil, B., "Lyric Violence, the Nomadic Subject and the Fourth Space." *Poetry London* (Summer 2017): 29–32.

Pašeta, S., "Censorship and Its Critics in the Irish Free State 1922–1932." *Past & Present no.* 181 (2003): 193–18.

Patterson, A. J. (Banjo), "A Bush Christening." *Bulletin*, December 16, 1893.

Paul, D. B., *Controlling Human Heredity: 1865 to the Present* (Atlantic Highlands: Humanities Press, 1995).

Paul, D. B., Stenhouse, J. and Spencer, H. G., *Eugenics at the Edges of Empire: New Zealand, Australia, Canada and South Africa* (Cham: Palgrave, 2018).

Paz, D. G., "Anti-Catholicism, Anti-Irish Stereotyping, and Anti-Celtic Racism in Mid-Victorian Working-Class Periodicals." *Albion* 18, no. 4 (1986): 601–16.

Percy, T., *Northern Antiquities: Or a Description of the Manners, Customs, Religion and Laws of the Ancient Danes, and other Northern Nations*, 2 vols. (London: n.p., 1770).

Perry, K. H., "'Little Rock' in Britain: Jim Crow's Transatlantic Topographies." *Journal of British Studies* 51, no. 1 (January 2012): 155–77.

Pettitt, L., *Screening Ireland* (Manchester: Manchester University Press, 2000).

Petty, W., *Tracts Chiefly Relating to Ireland* (Dublin: Boulter Grierson, 1769).

Pickering, M., *Blackface Minstrelsy in Britain* (Aldershot: Ashgate, 2008).

Pinkerton, J., *A Dissertation on the Origin and Progress of the Scythians or Goths: Being an Introduction to the Ancient and Modern History of Europe* (London: John Nichols, 1787).

Pinkerton, J., *An Enquiry into the History of Scotland Preceding the Reign of Malcolm III, or the Year 1056, including the Authentic History of That Period* (London: John Nichols, 1789).

Pinkerton, J., *Ancient Scottish Poems, Never Before in Print*, 2 vols. (London and Edinburgh, n.p., 1786).

Pinter, H., "Mac." In *Various Voices – Prose, Poetry, Politics, 1978–2005* (London: Faber, 2005).

Pius XI. *Casti connubii*. December 31, 1930, www.vatican.va/content/pius-xi/en/encyclicals/documents/hf_p-xi_enc_19301231_casti-connubii.html.

Platt, L., *Joyce, Race and Finnegans Wake* (Cambridge: Cambridge University Press, 2007).

The Pledge, "FIRED!": Preamble to the Pledge, www.rascal.ac.uk/institutions/fired-irish-women-poets-and-canon.

Powell, A., ed., "Racist Lyrics in Song Sources and Early Versions of the Song 'I've been Working on the Railroad.'" http://pancocojams.blogspot.com/2018/06/racist-lyrics-in-song-sources-of-and.html.

Powell, K., and Raby, P., eds., *Oscar Wilde in Context* (Cambridge: Cambridge University Press, 2013).

Price, C. A., *The Great White Walls are Built: Restrictive Immigration to North America and Australasian, 1836–1888* (Canberra: Australian National University Press, 1974).

Purdie, B., *Politics in the Streets: The Origins of the Civil Rights Movement in Northern Ireland* (Belfast: Blackstaff, 1990).

Quinn, J., "Outsiders on the Inside: Review of Landing Places." *Irish Times*, March 20, 2010.

Quinn, J., *Young Ireland and the Writing of Irish History* (Dublin: University College Dublin Press, 2015).

Ramazani, J., ed., *The Cambridge Companion to Postcolonial Poetry* (Cambridge: Cambridge University Press, 2017).

Ramazani, J., *The Hybrid Muse: Postcolonial Poetry in English* (Chicago: University of Chicago Press, 2001).

Rainger, R., "Race, Politics, and Science: The Anthropological Society of London in the 1860s." *Victorian Studies* 22, no. 1 (1978): 51–70.

Randolph, J. A., *Close to the Next Moment: Interviews from a Changing Ireland* (Manchester: Carcanet Press, 2010).

Raymond, A., *A Short Preliminary Discourse to the History of Ireland, To be published by Anthony Raymond, D.D. and sometime Fellow of Trinity College near Dublin* (London, 1725).

Rea, S., and Traynor, J., eds., *Correspondences: An Anthology to Call for an End to Direct Provision* (Dublin: SprintPrint, 2019).

Reece, B., *Daisy Bates: Grand Dame of the Desert* (Canberra: National Library of Australia, 2007).

Reeder, J., *The Forms of Informal Empire: Britain, Latin America, and Nineteenth-century Literature* (Baltimore: Johns Hopkins University Press, 2020).

Reizbaum, M., *Joyce's Judaic Other* (Stanford: Stanford University Press, 1999).

Renan, E., *Qu'est-ce qu'une nation? Conférence faite en Sorbonne, le March 11, 1882* (Paris: Calmann Lévy, 1882).

Renan, E., *The Poetry of the Celtic Races, and Other Essays*, trans. William G. Hutchison (London: Walter Scott Publishing Co., 1896).

Rentoul, R. R., *Race Culture; or, Race Suicide: (A Plea for the Unborn)* (London: Walter Scott Publishing Company Limited, 1906).

Reynolds, P., "Introduction." In *The New Irish Studies*, edited by Paige Reynolds, 1–22 (Cambridge: Cambridge University Press, 2020).

Reynolds, P., ed., *Modernist Afterlives in Irish Literature and Culture* (London: Anthem, 2016).

Riach, D. C., "Blacks and Blackface on the Irish Stage, 1830–1860." *Journal of American Studies* 7, no. 3 (1973): 231–41.

Rich, P. B., "Social Darwinism, Anthropology and English Perspectives of the Irish, 1867–1900." *History of European Ideas* 19, no. 4–6 (July 1994): 777–85.

Richards, E., "The 'Moral Anatomy' of Robert Knox: The Interplay between Biological and Social Thought in Victorian Scientific Naturalism." *Journal of the History of Biology* 22, no. 3 (1989): 373–436.

Ridge, L., *The Ghetto and Other Poems* (New York: Huebsch, 1918).

Rix, R., "Thomas Percy's Antiquarian Alternative to Ossian." *Journal of Folklore Research* 46, no. 2 (May-August 2009): 197–229.

Roach, J., *Cities of the Dead Circum-Atlantic Performance* (New York: Columbia University Press, 1996).

Robinson, C. J., *Black Marxism: The Making of the Black Radical Tradition* (Chapel Hill: University of North Carolina Press, 1983).

Robinson, C. J., *Forgeries of Memory and Meaning: Blacks and the Regimes of Race in American Theater and Film Before World War II* (Chapel Hill: University of North Carolina Press, 2007).

Robinson, C. J., "Ventriloquizing Blackness: Eugene O'Neill and Irish-American Racial Performance." In *The Black and Green Atlantic: Crosscurrents of the African and Irish Diasporas*, edited by Peter D. O'Neill and David Lloyd, 49–63 (Basingstoke: Palgrave Macmillan, 2009).

Robinson, M., "Cherishing the Irish Diaspora: On a Matter of Public Importance," Address to the House of the Oireachtas, February 1995.

Rockett, K., "Dion Boucicault, Staging, and Early Cinema." *Princeton University Library Chronicle* 68, no. 1–2 (2007): 33–59.

Roediger, D. R., *The Wages of Whiteness: Race and the Making of the American Working Class.* (London: Verso, [1991] 1999).

Roosevelt, T., "On American Motherhood." Speech, March 13, 1905. National Center for Public Policy Research. https://nationalcenter.org/ncppr/2001/11/03/theodore-roosevelt-on-motherhood-1905/.

Roosevelt, T., "Prefatory Letter." In *The Woman Who Toils: Being the Experiences of Two Gentlewomen as Factory Girls*, written by Mrs. John Van Vorst and Marie Van Vorst, vii–ix (New York: Doubleday, 1903).

Rose, S., "A Deadly Ideology: How the 'Great Replacement Theory' Went Mainstream," *The Guardian*, June 8, 2022, www.theguardian.com/world/2022/jun/08/a-deadly-ideology-how-the-great-replacement-theory-went-mainstream.

Ross, E. A., "The Causes of Race Superiority." *The Annals of the American Academy of Political and Social Science* 18 (July 1901): 67–89.

Ross, E. A., *The Changing Chinese* (New York: The Century Co., 1920).

Ross, E. A., *The Old World in the New: The Significance of Past and Present Immigration to the American People* (New York: The Century Co., 1914).

Roth, H., *Call It Sleep* (New York: Farrar, Straus and Giroux, 1934).

Rule, P., "Challenging Conventions: Irish-Chinese Marriages in Colonial Victoria," in *Irish-Australian Studies: Papers Delivered at the Ninth Irish-Australian Conference, Galway, April 1997*, edited by Fiona Bateman, 205–16 (Sydney: Crossing Press, 2000).

Russell, R. R., *Seamus Heaney's Regions* (Notre Dame: University of Notre Dame Press, 2014).

Ryan, B., "The Celtic Cubs: The Controversy over Birthright Citizenship in Ireland." *European Journal of Migration and Law* 6, no. 3 (2004): 173–93.

Said, E., *Orientalism* (New York: Pantheon Books, 1978).

Salesa, D. I., *Racial Crossings: Race, Intermarriage, and the Victorian British Empire* (Oxford: Oxford University Press, 2011).

Samson, I., "Black Stripes on the Celtic Tiger," *The Guardian*, September 1, 2007, www.theguardian.com/books/2007/sep/01/society.roddydoyle.

Schaffer, G., "Till Death Us Do Part and the BBC: Racial Politics and the British Working Classes 1965–75." *Journal of Contemporary History* 45, no. 2 (April 2010): 454–77.

Schofield, C., *Enoch Powell and the Making of Postcolonial Britain* (Cambridge: Cambridge University Press, 2013).

Scully, R., and Quartly, M., "Using Cartoons as Historical Evidence." In *Drawing the Line: Using Cartoons as Historical Evidence*, edited by Richard Scully and Marion Quartly, 11–26 (Melbourne: Monash University Press, 2009).

Sebastiani, S., *The Scottish Enlightenment: Race, Gender, and the Limits of Progress* (New York: Palgrave Macmillan, 2013).

Sen, M., "An Ordinary Crisis: SARS-CoV-2 and Irish Studies." In *Routledge International Handbook of Irish Studies*, edited by Renée Fox, Mike Cronin, and Brian Ó Conchubhair, 471–84 (London: Routledge, 2021).

Sen, M., "Joyce and Race in the Twenty-first Century." In *The New Joyce Studies*, edited by Catherine Flynn, 35–49 (Cambridge: Cambridge University Press, 2022).

Sharma, A. A., "'Race Poetry and Poetics UK 2': Queens College, Cambridge, 26th to 27th October 2018." *Journal of British and Irish Innovative Poetry* 11, no. 1 (2019), n.p.

Shaw, B., *An Unsocial Socialist* (London: Constable, [1883] 1932).

Sheaffer, L., *O'Neill, Son and Playwright* (Boston: Little, Brown and Company, 1968).

Sheridan, V., Landy, D., and Stout, V., "The Return of the 'Black Babies': How Development Education Affects Schoolchildren's Attitudes to the Majority World – the Trócaire 2012 Lenten Campaign." *Race, Ethnicity and Education* 22, no. 6 (2019): 858–74.

Shtorn, E., "From the Confinement." Produced by the Adrian Brinkerhoff Poetry Foundation in association with Druid Theatre, www.brinkerhoffpoetry.org/programs/coole-park-poetry-series-exhibition.

Silvestri, M., "'The Sinn Fein of India': Irish Nationalism and the Policing of Revolutionary Terrorism in Bengal." *Journal of British Studies* 39, no. 4 (October 2000): 454–86.

Simon C., "Irish played part in atrocities against Aboriginal people – Australian MP." *Irish Times* October 18, 2017.

Slobodian, Q., *Foreign Front: Third World Politics in Sixties West Germany* (Durham, NC: Duke University Press, 2012).

Slosson, E. E., "Leland Stanford Junior University." *The Independent* 66, no. 3148–3160 (January–June 1909): 661–81.

Smedley, C., "Shem's 'strabismal apologia': The Split Vision of the Famine in I.7." In *Joyce's Allmaziful Plurabilities: Polyvocal Explorations of Finnegans Wake*, edited by Kimberly J. Devlin and Christine Smedley, 114–32 (Gainesville: University Press of Florida, 2015).

Smith, M. J., *Empire in British Girls' Literature and Culture* (Basingstoke: Palgrave, 2011).

Smith, P. J., *Between Two Stools: Scatology and its Representations in English Literature, from Chaucer to Swift* (Manchester: Manchester University Press, 2012).

Smith, Z., "Fascinated to Presume: In Defense of Fiction." *New York Review of Books*, October 29, 2019, www.nybooks.com/articles/2019/10/24/zadie-smith-in-defense-of-fiction/.

Sneddon, A., "Hutchinson, Francis," *Dictionary of Irish Biography*. Accessed February 5, 2021.

Soloway, R. A., *Demography and Degeneration: Eugenics and the Declining Birthrate in Twentieth-century Britain* (Chapel Hill: University of North Carolina Press, 1995).

Somers-Willett, S. B. A., "Slam Poetry and the Cultural Politics of Performing Identity," *The Journal of the Midwest Modern Language Association* 38, no. 1 (2005): 51–73.

Spenser, E., *A View of the State of Ireland*, edited by Andrew Hadfield and Willy Maley (Oxford: Blackwell, 1997).

Spencer, H., *Principles of Biology* (London: Williams and Norgate, 1864).

Stanfield, P. S., *Yeats and Politics in the 1930s* (Houndmills: Macmillan, 1988).

Stanley, A. P., ed., *The Miscellaneous Works of Thomas Arnold* (London: B. Fellowes, 1845).

Steinberg, O. Y., *Race, Nation, History: Anglo-German Thought in the Victorian Era* (Philadelphia: University of Pennsylvania Press, 2019).

Stepan, N., *The Idea of Race in Science: Great Britain: 1800–1960* (Houndmills: Macmillan, 1982).

Stewart, Ian B., "The Mother Tongue: Historical Study of the Celts and Their Languages(s) in Eighteenth-century Britain and Ireland." *Past and Present* 243 (May 2019): 85–86.

Stocking, G. W., Jr., *Victorian Anthropology* (New York: Free Press, 1987).

Sullivan, A. M., *The Story of Ireland; A Narrative of Irish History, from the Earliest Ages to the Insurrection of 1867* (Providence: H. McElroy, 1883).

Takavarasha, T. and Kandiwa, K., *Compass: The Language I Cannot Speak*. www .crowdcast.io/e/compass-the-language-i-cannot-speak.

Terada, R., *Derek Walcott's Poetry: American Mimicry* (Boston: Northeastern University Press, 1992).

Thomas, A., *The Hate U Give* (London: Walker Books, 2017).

Thompson, S., "Yeats and Eugenicism: The Garrison Mentality in a Decolonizing Ireland." In *W. B. Yeats and Postcolonialism*, edited by Deborah Fleming, 27–49 (West Cornwall: Locust Hill Press, 2001).

Thurston, K. C., *Max* (London: Harper & Brothers, 1910).

Titley, G., *Racism and Media* (London: Sage Publications, 2019).

Tóibín, C., *Brooklyn* (New York: Scribner, 2009).

Tomlinson, B.R., "What was the Third World?" *Journal of Contemporary History* 38, no. 2 (April 2003): 307–21.

Tone, T. W., *Memoirs of Theobald Wolfe Tone*, (London: Henry Colburn, 1827).

Townsend, Sarah L., "Direct Provision, Immigrant Detention, and the Wonderful World of Avoca." *Éire-Ireland* 57, no. 3–4 (Fall/Winter 2022): 64–91.

Trumpener, K., *Bardic Nationalism: The Romantic Novel and the British Empire* (Princeton: Princeton University Press, 1997).

Tucker, A., "Strangers in a Strange Land?: The New Irish Multicultural Fiction." In *Literary Visions of Multicultural Ireland*, edited by Pillar Villar-Argáiz, 118–40 (Manchester: Manchester University Press, 2013).

Tucker, W. H., *The Cattell Controversy: Race, Science, and Ideology* (Urbana: University of Illinois Press, 2009).

Tyler, I., *Revolting Subjects: Social Abjection and Resistance in Neoliberal Britain* (London: Zed Books, 2013).

Ulin, J. V., "Introduction: Ireland's New Strangers." In *Race and Immigration in the New Ireland*, edited by Julieann V. Ulin, 1–19 (Notre Dame: University of Notre Dame Press, 2016).

Valente, J., "Ageing Yeats: From Fascism to Disability." In *Irish Literature in Transition, 1880–1940*, edited by Marjorie Elizabeth Howes, 173–95 (Cambridge: Cambridge University Press, 2020).

Vallancey, C., *A Vindication of the Ancient History of Ireland* (Dublin: Luke White, 1786).

Vallancey, C., *An Essay on the Antiquity of the Irish Language. Being a Collation of the Irish with the Punic Language* (Dublin: S. Powell, 1772).

Van Voris, W., *Violence in Ulster: An Oral Documentary* (Amherst: University of Massachusetts Press, 1975).

Vendler, H., *Seamus Heaney* (Cambridge: Harvard University Press, 2000).

Villar-Argáiz, P., ed., *Literary Visions of Multicultural Ireland: The Immigrant in Contemporary Irish Literature* (Manchester: Manchester University Press, 2014).

Villar-Argáiz, P., "Introduction to Discourses of Inclusion and Exclusion: Artistic Renderings of Marginal Identities in Ireland." *Nordic Irish Studies* 15, no. 1 (2016): 1–8.

Villar- Argáiz, P., ed., *Irishness on the Margins: Minority and Dissident Identities* (Basingstoke: Palgrave Macmillan, 2018).

Walcott, D., *Conversations with Walcott*, edited by William Baer (Jackson: University of Mississippi Press, 1996): 119.

Walcott, D., "Heaney in Ireland." *AGENDA* 47, no. 3–4 (2013): 14.

Walcott, D., *In a Green Night: Poems, 1948–60* (London: Cape, 1969).

Walcott, D., *The Arkansas Testament* (New York: Farrar, Straus, Giroux, 1987).

Walcott, D., *The Poetry of Derek Walcott: 1948–2013*, selected by Glyn Maxwell (New York: Farrar, Straus, Giroux, 2014).

Walcott, D., *The Star-Apple Kingdom* (New York: Farrar, Straus, Giroux, 1979).

Walcott, D., *What the Twilight Says: Essays* (New York: Farrar, Straus, Giroux, 1998).

Wald, A., "Farrell and Trotsky." *Twentieth Century Literature* 22, no. 1 (1976): 90–104.

Walsh, E., *The Walworth Farce* (London: Nick Hern, 2006).

Wang, D. J., *Thinking Its Presence: Form, Race, and Subjectivity in Contemporary Asian American Poetry* (Stanford: Stanford University Press, 2013).

Waterhouse, R., *From Minstrel Show to Vaudeville: The Australian Popular Stage, 1788–1914* (Sydney: New South Wales University Press, 1990).

Watt, S., *"Something Dreadful and Grand." American Literature and the Irish-Jewish Unconscious* (New York: Oxford University Press, 2015).

Weiss, T., "The 'Black Beast' Headline: The Key to an Allusion in 'Ulysses.'" *James Joyce Quarterly* 19, no. 2 (1982): 183–6.

Weng, J. M., "'Decorticated' Brains and 'Steriliz[ed]' Minds: Samuel Beckett and Irish Censorship." *Éire-Ireland* 51, no. 3–4 (2016): 188–215.

West, C., "A Genealogy of Modern Racism." In *Race Critical Theories*, edited by Philomena Essed and David Theo Goldberg, 90–112 (Oxford: Blackwell, 2002).

Wheeler, R., *The Complexion of Race: Categories of Difference in Eighteenth-century British Culture* (Philadelphia: University of Pennsylvania Press, 2000).

White, C., *An Account of the Regular Gradation in Man and in Different Animals and Vegetables* (London: Printed for C. Dilly, 1799).

White, T., *China's Longest Campaign: Birth Planning in the People's Republic, 1949–2005* (Ithaca: Cornell University Press, 2006).

Williams, D. G., *Ethnicity and Cultural Authority: From Arnold to Du Bois* (Edinburgh: Edinburgh University Press, 2006).

Williams, S., "The Magical Whiteness of Being Irish: Language and Song in American White Nationalism." *New Hibernia Review* 25, no. 4 (Winter 2021): 134–48.

Wills, C., *Lovers & Strangers: An Immigrant History of Post-war Britain* (London: Penguin, 2017).

Witte, G., "A wall denied may have made Trump dislike E.U.," *The Washington Post*, February 7, 2017, www.washingtonpost.com/world/europe/trump-tried-and-failed-to-build-a-wall-in-ireland-that-could-mean-big-trouble-for-europe/2017/02/05/4629d02e-e5a0-11e6-a419-eefe8eff0835_story.html.

Woolf, V., *A Room of One's Own* (New York: Penguin, [1929] 1945).

Words Ireland, Survey. 2021. https://wordsireland.ie/surveys/.

Yao, S. G., *Foreign Accents: Chinese American Verse from Exclusion to Postethnicity* (Oxford: Oxford University Press, 2010).

Yeats, J. B., *Sligo* (London: Wishart, 1930).

Yeats, W. B., "A Race Philosophy." Appendix. In *W. B. Yeats: Man and Poet*, edited by A. Norman Jeffares, 326 (New York: Palgrave, 1996).

Yeats, W. B., "Censorship in Ireland: The Free State Bill: Senator W. B. Yeats's Views." Interview by Irish Correspondent. *Manchester Guardian*, August 22, 1928.

Yeats, W. B., "Easter 1916." In *The Collected Poems of W. B. Yeats*, edited by Richard J. Finneran, 180–82 (New York: Scribner, 1983).

Yeats, W. B., "Genealogical Tree of Revolution." Appendix. In *W. B. Yeats: Man and Poet*, edited by A. Norman Jeffares, 325 (New York: Palgrave, 1996).

Yeats, W. B., "Mr. Yeats on Irish Censorship: Driving Intellect into Exile: New Bill 'Full of Danger.'" Interview by Special Correspondent. *Sunday Times*, October 21, 1928.

Yeats, W. B., *On the Boiler*. In *The Collected Works of W.B. Yeats, Vol. V: Later Essays*, edited by William H. O'Donnell, 220–51 (New York: Charles Scribner's Sons, 1994).

Yeats, W. B., *Seanad Éireann Debates*. June 11, 1925, www.oireachtas.ie/en/debates/debate/seanad/1925-06-11/12/.

Yeats, W. B., "The Irish Censorship." Appendix V. In *The Senate Speeches of W. B. Yeats*, edited by Donald R. Pearce, 175–80 (Bloomington: Indiana University Press, 1960).

Yezierska, A., *Salome of the Tenements* (Urbana: University of Illinois Press, [1923] 1995).

Young, H., "Thomas Percy's Racialisation of the European Middle Ages." *Literature Compass* 16, no. 9–10 (September-October 2019): 1–11.

Young, K., *Performing the Unstageable: Success, Imagination, Failure* (London: Bloomsbury, 2020).

Young, R. J. C., *The Idea of English Ethnicity* (Malden: Blackwell, 2008).

Zabel, W. D., "Interracial Marriage and the Law." In *Interracialism: Black-White Intermarriage in American History, Literature, and Law*, edited by Werner Sollers, 54–60 (Oxford: Oxford University Press, 2000).

Index

Abbey Theatre, 73, 108, 250, *See also* Boucicault,
    Dion; O'Neill, Eugene
abolition movement, 63–64, 68, 106
Act of Union, 44, 84
Adigun, Bisi, 73
Akinjobi, Pamela, 261
Aldarra, Suad, 284, 290
Aldridge, Ira, 64
Allingham, William, 117
Alvarez, A., 193
American Writers' Congress, 232
Anglo-Saxonism, 35, 45, 50–51, 99,
    196, 311
antiquarianism, 3, 43–44, 46, 311, *See also*
    Ledwich, Edward; Macpherson, James;
    O'Conor, Charles; Percy, Thomas;
    Vallancey, Charles
    focus on origins, 26, 30
anti-Semitism, 11, 110, 125–29, 131, 194, 208, 210,
    230, 232, 244, 247–49, 251–55
Appointments, 213
Aristotle, 131
Arnold, Matthew, 51
Arnold, Thomas, 45, 51
Arts Council of Ireland, 272, 296–97
Asmal, Kadar, 182
Astaire, Fred, 72
Astor, John Jacob, 97
Australia
    Asian migration to, 212–13
    gold rush, 207, 213, *See also New Gold*
    Mountain
    indigenous people of, 206, 215,
    217–20
    Irish migration to, 207
    White Australia Policy in, 213, 215
Avoca, 4

Baldwin, James, 127–29, 131
Beckett, Samuel, 134, 152
Behn, Aphra, 64
Belfast Agreement. *See* Good Friday Agreement

Belfast Eugenics Society, 148
birth control, 144, 149–53, 160
Black Lives Matter movement, 74, 76, 283, 297
Black Panther movement, 179–80
Black Power movement, 173–76, 178
Blacker, Carlos, 155–56
blackface. *See also Octoroon, The;* Stratton,
    Eugene
    Australia and, 210–11, 220
    contemporary Ireland and, 73
    Irish folk culture and, 114–17
    Irish performers in, 69–73
    Joyce, James and, 110–112, 133
    link with Stage Irishman, 65, 68, 70, 106, 133
    in nineteenth-century Ireland, 62–64,
    106, 108
    O'Neill, Eugene and, 235
    as origin of golliwog, 183
    in twentieth-century Ireland, 106–7
    wren boys in, 115, 116
    Yeats, Jack B. and, 113–14
blackness, 2, 104, 107–8, 110, 113, 131, 133, 235,
    261, 286
blood, 45, 248–49
    as conferrer of Irishness, 42, 308–9
Boladale, Zainab, 265
Boland, Eavan, 259
Bolger, Dermot, 243
Book of Invasions, The. See Leabhar Gabhála
    Érinn
Booker Prize, 281, 286
Boran, Pat, 262
Boucicault, Dion, 209, 210, *See also*
    Octoroon, The
    Abbey Theatre and, 69, 76–77
    cast as Stage Irishman, 74–75
    Colleen Bawn, The, 59, 61, 68, 75, 110
    early acting career of, 68
    performing in redface, 61, 75
    Poor of New York, The, 61
    Shaughraun, The, 59, 75
Bowery Theatre, 65

348

Brathwaite, Edward Kamau, 193, 203
Breitman, George, 176
Brennan, Matthew. *See Young Man from Rathmines, The*
Brexit, 296, 302
British Army, 173, 179, 182, 183, 205, 219, *See also* Roach, Everton
  Irish in the, 173, 184, 207, 251
British empire, 1, 10, 44, 193, 305
  decline of, 82–83, 181, 184, 226
  feminist fiction and, 90
  Latin America and, 86, 87
British navy, 111–12
Broadway theatre, 60, 69, 72, 234, 250
Brooke, Charlotte, 35, 36, 82
Brown, James, 2
Buffalo mass shooting, 143
Burns, Anna, 242, 281
Butterworth, Jez, 243

Camus, Renaud, 164
Caribbean, the, 2, 97, 173, 190–93, 197, 199, 201
Carlson, Tucker, 143
Carlyle, Thomas, 2, 46–47
Carmichael, Stokely, 175–76, 181
Caulfield, Patrick, 312
Celtic race, 46–51, *See also* Irish race
Celtic Tiger, 8, 10–11, 243, 304, 308
censorship. *See* Irish Free State
Chaila, Denise, 265–66
Chopin, Kate, 227
Christchurch mosque shootings, 273
Christianopoulos, Dinos, 275
Churchill, Winston, 183
citizenship, birthright, 8, 308, 313
Congo, Democratic Republic of, 266, 292
Connolly, James, 177, 182
contraception. *See* birth control
Cooke, Barrie, 272
Coppola, Francis Ford, 72
Corkery, Daniel, 193
Correspondences, 295–96
Cosgrave, Polina, 275
COVID-19 pandemic, 9–10, 296
Craig, May, 70
critical race theory, 12, 103, 285, 286
Crowe Street Theatre, 63
Cuala Press, 162
Cuba, 180, 183, 226, 230
Curran, Kevin, 282
Curtis, Edmund, 53

Dabiri, Emma, 283
Darwin, Charles, 49, 145
Davis, Jack, 217

Davis, Thomas, 46, 155
de Valera, Éamon, 52, 148, 307–8
de Waal, Kit, 283
Deane, Seamus, 159
  Strange Country, 306–7
DeBhairduin, Oein, 276
Democratic Party, 179, 225, 229, 232
Derry Citizens' Action Committee, 172
Devlin, Bernadette, 179–80, 183, 185
Dimbo, Ifedinma, 261
Direct Provision, 4, 7, 10, 77, 103, 290–91, *See also* Okorie, Melatu Uche
  calls to end, 295–96
Doone, Allen, 210–12
Douglass, Frederick, 65, 73, 191
Doyle, Roddy, 73, 291
  The Commitments, 2
  The Deportees, 282
Dublin Drama League, 70
Dublin Theatre Festival, 73, 268, 284
Du Bois, W. E. B., 136, 285–86
Durkin, Tom, 205, 208–9, 213–15

East India Company, 31
Easter Rising, 177, 227, 242
Edgeworth, Maria, 63, 95, 243, 255
Eipe, Nidhi Zak/Aria, 260, 262, 271–74, 284
Ejorh, Theophilus, 264
Embers of Words, 264
Engels, Friedrich, 229
Enright, Anne, 282, 295
Enyi-Amadi, Chiamaka, 261–263, 265, 284
eugenics movement, 148, 150–51, 159–60, *See also* Galton, Francis; race suicide theory
  Yeats's interest in, 145, 154, 156, 162–63
European Union, 10, 94, 281, 303

Falconer, Edmund, 209
Fallon, Gabriel, 109
Fanon, Frantz, 178, 181, 286
Farquhar, George, 70
Farrell, James T.
  biography of, 228, 232–33
  Studs Lonigan, 228–32, 237
Farrell, Michael, 176, 178–79, 182
Fay, William, 108
Felispeaks, 260, 266, 275, 284
  Dubh, 268–71
Finian's Rainbow, 72–73
Fitzsimons, Edward, 63
Foucault, Michel, 118
Fournier, Henri. *See* Joyce, James
Freud, Sigmund, 244–46, 254
Friel, Brian, 250

Fuhl, Lorde, 265, 266
Fun on the Bristol, 110–112

Gaelic race, 168, *See also* Irish race
Gaiety Theatre, 105
Galton, Francis, 49, 145–46, 150, 156–57
Gaugin, Paul, 72
Ge, Yan, 283
Gerald of Wales, 25, 38, 42, 196
Gilpin, Charles, 234
Giraldus Cambrensis. *See* Gerald of Wales
Glitch, 218
Gogarty, Oliver St. John, 149
Gold, Mike, 243, 249
Goldsmith, Oliver, 44
Gonne, Maud, 162
Good Friday Agreement, 10, 242, 302, 308
Goulding, Cathal. *See* Irish Republican Army
Grant, Madison, 163
Great Depression, 229
Great Famine, 47, 50, 226–229, 237, 245
Great Migration (African American), 96, 226
Gregory, Lady Augusta, 250

Hairspray, 74
Hamilton, Hugo, 282
Hart, Dagogo, 260, 266, 267
Harvard University, 5
Heaney, Marie, 197–98
Heaney, Seamus
    "Belfast", 196
    bog poems, 304, 309–14
    caricatures of, 195
    Cure at Troy, The, 201, 202
    Death of a Naturalist, 193
    friendship with Derek Walcott, 190,
        193, 197
    North, 196, 310
    Station Island, 200
    Wintering Out, 195
Hearn, Lafcadio, 194
Higgins, Michael D., 205, 219–20
Hitler, Adolf, 164
Holliday, Billie, 196
Hooton, Earnest Albert, 52, 148, 166
Hutchinson, Francis, 30
Hyde, Douglas, 1–2
    "The Necessity for de-Anglicising Ireland", 51
Hyde-Lees, Georgie, 156, 162

In Dahomey, 69
India, 6, 31, 33, 83, 161, 181, *See also* East
    India Company; Eipe, Nidhi Zak/Aria;
    Madhaven, Cauvery; Narayanan-Mohan,

Chandrika; Owenson, Sydney; Sarma,
    Ursula Rani
    colonies in, 88–89
International Literature Festival Dublin,
    278, 284
Ireland
    Asian migration to, 11
    Civil War, 227, 307
    Jewish migration to, 243, 246–49
    plantation of, 305
Ireland, David, 243
Irish Ambassador, The, 65
Irish Citizenship Referendum, 7, 11, 155,
    281, 285, 289, 290, 297, 308–9, *See also*
    citizenship, birthright
Irish diaspora, 8, 307, 309, *See also* America;
    Australia
Irish Folklore Commission, 114, 116
Irish Free State, 52, 94, 106, 144–45, 307, 308
    censorship debates in, 144, 148, 151–53
Irish Independent, 3, 106
Irish language, 1, 168, 253, 313
    cooption by white nationalism, 4
    origins of, 26, 32–34
Irish Network Against Racism, 10, 12, 294
Irish 1926 census, 150, 152
Irish race, 42, 50–52, *See also* Celtic race; Gaelic
    race; race suicide theory
Irish Race Congress (1922), 52, 166
Irish Republican Army, 173, 180–83, 196, 217
Irish Research Council, 297
Irish Revival, 1, 3, 51, 68, 77, 281
Irish Times, 68, 105, 116, 125, 206, 272
Irish 2016 census, 281
Irish Travellers, 11, 276, 294, 316
Irish Volunteers, 86
Irish War of Independence, 3, 52, 181, 227
Irishman in London, The, 62–63, 68

Jackson, Paddy, 73
Jackson, Samuel L., 73
Jafaris, 266
James, C. L. R., 175–76
Jazz, 67
Jim Crow laws, 75, 226
Johnson, Linton Kwesi, 270
Johnston, Roy, 180–82
Jola, Nandi, 276, 278
Joseph, Ebun, 103, 285, 297
Joyce, James, 200
    Dubliners, 122–24, 255
    Finnegans Wake, 113, 121, 129, 131–136
    Fournier, Henri interview by, 122–23
    Ulysses, 110–13, 121, 125–28, 131
Joyce, Stanislaus, 124, 132

jus sanguinis. See blood
jus soli. See citizenship, birthright

Kandiwa, Kayssie, 265, 266, 284
Kasa, Nithy, 266
Keating, Geoffrey
   Foras Feasa ar Éirinn, 28–30
Kelly, Ned, 217
Kennedy, John F., 227, 232
Knights of Columbus, 231–32
Knox, Robert, 47–48
Ku Klux Klan, 133, 225, 235–36

Lalor, James Fintan, 307–8
Larsen, Nella, 130
Lavin, Mary, 134
Leabhar Gabhála Érinn, 27–28, 30–32, 37, 38
Leah the Forsaken, 110
Leaving Certificate, 266, 284
Ledwich, Edward, 36–38
Lenton, Lance, 212
Lewis, Wyndham, 132
Lhuyd, Edward, 32–33
Lily of Killarney, The, 110
Little Rock school integration crisis, 199–200
Locke, John, 6
Lordan, Dave, 265

Mac Liammóir, Micheál, 70
Macaulay, Lord Thomas, 196
MacManus, Seumas, 52
Macpherson, James, 34–35, 43
MacSwiney, Terence, 227
Madhaven, Cauvery, 283
Majekodunmi, Jess, 265
Majekodunmi, Ola, 265, 297
Makris, Christodoulos, 261, 264, 270, 275
Marcus, David, 244–45, 249–252, 255
Marinetti, Filippo Tommaso, 162
Maturin, Charles, 84
Mayne, Rutherford, 70
McAleese, Mary, 309
McCann, Colum, 191
McCann, Eamonn, 175–80, 182
McCarthy, Joseph, 239
McDermott, Eilis, 179
McDonagh, Martin, 75
McDonagh, Rosemary, 276
McDowell, Michael, 308
McLaughlin, Caitriona, 76
McMaster, Anew, 70
Mikado, The, 74
Milesians, 27, 33, 42, 49
Mill, John Stuart, 87, 305
Miłosz, Czesław, 271

minstrelsy. *See* blackface
Mitchel, John, 49
Morrison, Toni, 314
Muldoon's Picnic, 210
Muotto, Chinedum, 266
music hall, 105–7, 113, 211
mythology, classical, 310

Narayanan-Mohan, Chandrika, 274, 284
Nazism and neo-Nazism, 53, 129, 225, 251
Negro Ensemble Company, 73
New Gold Mountain, 218
new Irish, 8–9, 159, 259–62, 274–75, 282–85,
   289, 296–97, 304, 314, *See also* spoken word
   poetry
   creative career of, 264
   limitations of term, 263
New Woman, 147
   fiction, 90
Ní Dhuibhne, Éilis, 282
Nightingale, The, 205, 218–19
Nkencho, George, 268
Nobel Prize in Literature, 17, 194, 228
Northern Irish Troubles, 191, 192, 195–199,
   217, 242–43, 312, *See also* Good Friday
   Agreement

Ó Cléirigh, Micheál, 28
Ó Dochartaigh, Fionbarra, 172, 174
Ó Ríordáin, Aodhán, 6
Obama, Barack, 292, 293
O'Brien, John, 217
O'Brien, Kate, 84
   Mary Lavelle, 81, 94–95
   As Music and Splendour, 95
   Without My Cloak, 95–97
O'Brien, Mark, 76
O'Casey, Sean, 69, 70
O'Connell, Daniel, 45, 48
O'Conor, Charles, 32–35, 43
Octoroon, The
   Abbey production of, 76–77
   BBC adaptation of, 60
   film adaptation of, 60
   Irish reception of, 59–60, 68–69, 74
   Jacobs-Jenkins production of, 61,
     74–76
   rewritten for London audience, 62
   Sean O'Casey acts in, 69
O'Dea, Jimmy, 73
O'Halloran, Sylvester, 34–35
O'Kelly, Donal, 73
Okorie, Melatu Uche, 276, 290
   This Hostel Life, 291–95
Olusanya, Felicia. *See* Felispeaks

O'Neill, Eugene
  Abbey Theatre and, 70–72
  biography of, 228
  Iceman Cometh, The, 233, 236
  Long Day's Journey into Night, 228, 237
  Negro Plays of, 227, 234–36
Orbán, Viktor, 143
Oroonoko, 64
O'Shea, Milo, 73
Ossianism. *See* Macpherson, James
O'Sullivan, Donal, 105, 107, 113, 116–17
Outis (pseudonym). *See* O'Sullivan, Donal
Owenson, Sydney, 82, 84
  Florence Macarthy, 86–88
  Missionary, The, 83, 88–89
  Wild Irish Girl, The, 83–86

Palestine, 183, 245, 250
Palmer, Mrs. Bandmann, 110
papacy, 28, 153
  Ne Temere decree, 152
Parmar, Sandeep, 259, 273
Parnell, Charles Stewart, 51, 250
Patterson, A. J., 209, 215
Percy, Thomas, 35–36
performance poetry. *See* spoken word poetry
Petty, William, 25, 38
Phillips, Nat, 212
Pike, Anthony Simpson, 76
Pine, Emilie, 296
Pinkerton, John, 37, 44
Pinter, Harold, 70
Pius XI, pope, 153
Poetry Ireland, 266, 272, 274, 284
Potter, Maureen, 73
Powell, Enoch, 184
Protestant Ascendancy, 82, 144–45, 156, 160
Punch, 38, 47

Queen's University Belfast, 176, 178, 194
Quinn, Gavin, 74

race suicide theory, 148–51
  origin of, 143–46
  replacement theory and, 143, 162–63
racialization, 5–7, 10, 94, 99, 190, 195–96, 227,
    237, 288, 305, 311, 316, *See also* Irish race
radio, 60, 70, 106, 232, 307
Randolph, A. Philip, 233
Rea, Stephen. *See Correspondences*
Remoundou, Natasha, 295
Renan, Ernest, 51, 52
Rene, Roy, 212
Repeal movement, 45, 47, 307, *See also*
    O'Connell, Daniel

Republican Party (GOP), 21, 225–26, 231, 236
Ridge, Lola, 254
Roach, Everton, 195–96
Robinson, Mary, 309
Rockefeller, John D., 97
Rooney, Sally, 281
Roosevelt, Theodore, 147–48
Ross, Edward Alsworth, 146–47, 149, 156,
    161, 165
Roth, Henry, 243, 244, 246
Royal Ulster Constabulary, 172, 177–179, 182
Ryan, Donal, 286–90

Said, Edward, 286
Sarma, Ursula Rani, 283
Sartre, Jean-Paul, 180, 181
Sauvy, Alfred. *See* Third World, the
scientific racism, 49, 53, 137, 163, *See also*
    eugenics; Galton, Francis
Senegal, 90
Shakespeare, William, 64, 67, 193
  Hamlet, 110, 228
  Othello, 64, 70, 95
Shakur, Tupac, 130
Shankill Defence Association, 183–85
Shaw, George Bernard, 151, 255
Sheridan, Elizabeth, 82
Sheridan, Richard Brinsley, 63–64
Sheridan, Thomas, 70
Shipp, Thomas, 76
Show Boat, 105
Shtorn, Evgeny, 266
simianization of the Irish, 6, 22, 38, 47, 93, 205,
    208–9, 211, 220
Slave, The, 63
Smith, Abram, 76
Smock Alley Theatre, 70
soil, 305–309, *See also* citizenship, birthright
  Felispeaks's use of, 268, 271
  Heaney, Seamus and, 304, 309–13
  racy of the, 306
Southerne, Thomas, 64
Spafford, Horatio, 270
Spanish-American War, 97
Spenser, Edmund, 25, 42, 315
spoken word poetry, 260, 264–71
Stage Irishman, 62, 65, 213, *See also*
    Boucicault, Dion
  link with blackface, 65, 68, 70, 106, 133
Stewart Denison, Thomas, 213
Stoker, Bram, 248
Stopford Green, Alice, 52
Stratton, Eugene, 105, 110, 112
Sullivan, A. M., 51
Synge, J. M., 73, 191, 202

Takavarasha, Tari, 266
Third World, the, 173–75, 181, 190
    coinage of, 180
Thomas, Angie, 130
Thurston, Katherine Cecil, 83, 89–93
Tóibín, Colm, 243
Tower of Babel, 32
Travatore, Il, 111
Traynor, Jessica. *See Correspondences*
Trotsky, Leon, 176, 232
    Trotskyism and, 175, 176
Trump, Donald, 4–6, 124, 143, 302–3, *See also*
    Republican Party (GOP)
Tuatha Dé Danann, 27, 28, 49, 311

Uncle Tom's Cabin, 62, 68–69, 77, 108
United Irish Rebellion, 44, 83
United Irishmen, 43, 46, 86
United States of America
    Civil War, 59, 104
    Declaration of Independence, 231, 233
    Irish migration to, 96, 149, 303
    Jewish migration to, 244, 246, 254
    lynching in, 76, 111, 196, 234
University of California, 1

Vallancey, Charles, 30–31, 33–35
Vanderbilt, Cornelius, 97
Varadkar, Leo, 5, 302, 303
Vikings, 43
    cooption by white supremacists, 316
    Heaney, Seamus and, 310–12, 317

Walcott, Derek
    Arkansas Testament, The, 198
    "Far Cry from Africa, A", 194, 197
    friendship with Seamus Heaney, 190, 193, 197
    In a Green Night, 192
    Omeros, 201
    Star-Apple Kingdom, The, 191, 193, 194,
        198–200

Trinidad Theatre Workshop and, 199
    "What the Twilight Says", 199–200
Walsh, Enda, 70
Welch, Robert, 243, 245
Welles, Orson, 70
West, Cornel, 103
white nationalism, 4
    Irish assimilation into, 103, 225, 226,
        230–32
    Irish targeted by, 225–26, 235
white privilege, 7, 104
White Slave, The, 68–69
Wilde, Oscar, 65
Wilde, William, 46, 48
Wilentz, Grace, 275
William of Orange, 43, 205
Willmot, Eric, 217
Wilson, Woodrow, 229
Wolfe Tone, Theobald, 43
Women Writers in the New Ireland Network,
    261, 277
Woolf, Virginia, 97
wren boys. *See* blackface
Wright, Richard, 232

Yeats, Jack B., 105, 113–14
Yeats, W. B., 114, *See also* eugenics
    movement
    as exemplar for Derek Walcott, 191
    On the Boiler, 144–45, 156–61
    opposition to Censorship Bill, 144, 151–53
    "Race Philosophy, A", 154–55, 160
    "Song of Wandering Aengus, The", 272
    Vision, A, 154, 155, 162
Yezierska, Anzia, 243, 254
Young Ireland, 46–47, 49, 305–6, 308
    The Nation, 46, 306
Young Man from Rathmines, The, 108–10, 115
Young Socialist Alliance, 176

Zangwill, Israel, 243

Milton Keynes UK
Ingram Content Group UK Ltd.
UKHW012150070124
435615UK00004B/9

9 781316 513118